36?5

SYSTEMIC
FAMILY THERAPY
An Integrative Approach

WILLIAM C. NICHOLS AND CRAIG A. EVERETT

THE GUILFORD PRESS
New York   *London*

Printed in the United States of America
Last digit is print number 9 8 7 6 5 4

Library of Congress Cataloging in Publication Data
Nichols, William C.
    Systemic family therapy.

    (The Guilford family therapy series)
    Bibliography: p.
    Includes index.
    1. Family psychotherapy.   I. Everett, Craig A.
II. Title.   III. Series.   [DNLM: 1. Family.
2. Family therapy.   3. Marital Therapy.
WM 430.5.F2 N623s]
RC488.5.N535   1986   616.89′156   85–17235
ISBN 0-89862-066-X

Acknowledgment is made to the following for permission to reprint excerpts from: C. M.
Bittermann, in *Social Casework* (1966), by permission of *Social Casework*; E. M. Duvall,
in *Family Development*, 4th ed. (1971), by permission of Harper & Row, Publishers; T. F.
Fogarty, in *The Family, Emptiness and Closeness* (1975), by permission of The Center for
Family Learning; J. L. Framo, in *Techniques of Family Therapy* (1973), by permission of
Grune & Stratton and J. L. Framo; E. R. Groves, in *Annals of the American Academy of
Political and Social Science* (1940), by permission of the American Academy of Political
and Social Science; A. Gurman, in *Marriage and Marital Therapy* (1978), by permission of
Brunner/Mazel, Publishers; R. W. Laidlaw, in *The American Journal of Psychoanalysis*
(1967), by permission of Agathon Press, Inc.; H. I. Lief, in *The Family* (1980), by permis-
sion of Brunner/Mazel Publishers; M. Nimkoff, in *Sociology and Social Research* (1934),
by permission of *Sociology and Social Research*; P. Steinglass, in *Marriage and Marital
Therapy* (1978), by permission of Brunner/Mazel, Publishers; E. N. White, in *Social
Forces* (1933), by permission of the University of North Carolina Press.

To Alice, Camille, Bill, and Dave Nichols
                                    —W. C. N.

To Andrew and Jennifer Everett
                                    —C. A. E.

Systemic Family Therapy

Preface

This book, which was nearly 7 years in the making, represents our attempt to provide a statement of our own integrative approach to teaching and practicing family therapy. While we recognize and pay tribute to the contributions of the pioneers in the field, we consider it important for all family therapists to evolve their own orientation and style. Ours took many years to develop as we taught and practiced in a variety of educational and clinical settings. Our hope is that we can help others to shorten the time required to achieve a satisfactory integration of theory and practice for themselves.

Briefly, we move here from historical context and theoretical propositions to an integration of systemic assessment and treatment. We close with an explication of issues in professional development. As we do so, we recognize that the field is in a process of evolution and that integration needs to continue. We invite others to join us in the ongoing struggle to learn and to build on the historical foundations and contemporary integrations of the field.

For a more personal word, we wish to acknowledge the myriad and unsung contributions of students, clients/patients, and colleagues who have challenged us to think more clearly and work more effectively over the years. We also acknowledge with gratitude the general support and explicit helpful suggestions of Alan S. Gurman, Editor of the Guilford Family Therapy Series, and Seymour Weingarten, Editor-in-Chief of The Guilford Press.

William C. Nichols
Craig A. Everett

Contents

Systemic Family Therapy

CHAPTER ONE

The Field of Family Therapy

Family therapy is an approach to dealing with human difficulties and adaptation that is new and different from traditional psychotherapeutic orientations and modalities. Rather than focusing solely on the individual, family therapy is concerned with the person in his or her more significant contexts of living and coping. The family in both current and historical senses is the focus of family therapy in our particular orientation to family therapy.

Family therapists do not see people existing in isolation from other human beings, or apart from networks of social relationships. The difficulties manifested by an individual, therefore, are viewed by family therapists as stemming from sources larger than the person. Symptoms, if we retain that medically oriented and somewhat inappropriate term, have a transactional character and nature. They are neither formed nor maintained solely by an individual in isolation. Created and sustained by the interactions and emotional and intellectual attachments between and among people in significant relationships, symptoms are changed through alteration of the patterns of relationships in which people are involved.

Family therapists focus on family process, rather than simply on intrapsychic process in the individual. As many family therapists have pointed out, the goal is to change family process, to alter the family system, and, thereby, to affect in a positive direction the functioning of the person or persons manifesting symptomatology. What has been defined traditionally as psychotherapy, therefore, must be redefined. Rather than viewing issues in terms of individual dynamics and functioning, the family therapist looks at family functioning and dynamics even though only one member of the family displays pain and stress and presents himself or herself for help. The difficulties manifested by that person, again, are understood as being affected by the family and the processes operating in that system.

Changing the family system is the general goal of family therapists, although there are many techniques used in the pursuit of that goal. The unifying theme of the techniques employed is the identification of the family system and family process as the targets for intervention and alteration. Also unifying the work of most family therapists is a concern with direct intervention and change. Rather than merely talking about symptoms and the systems and settings that produce them, family therapy involves dealing directly with family process and the systems that result in dysfunctional behavior in the identified patient or client. The family therapist generally gains leverage for change not through interpretation, as do many traditionally oriented therapists, but through direct action and direct interference with the functioning of family systems.

Family therapy is characterized by its orientation and not by the number of persons seen by the therapist. One can perform family therapy with a single person present for the interview. One can, in other words, intervene in a family system with only part of the family present. Again, family therapy deals with persons in the context of family. Conversely, some therapists can interview an entire family and still deal with the system as if it were merely a collection of individuals, never identifying or recognizing the interactional processes present in the family.

"Family" as used here refers not only to the nuclear family into which one is born or adopted but also to the extended family of which the nuclear family is a part. In family therapy, "thinking family" typically means conceptualizing things in terms of at least three generations. The therapist also deals conceptually not only with parents and their children but also with the parent's family of origin. Just as family therapy involves thinking of persons in terms of systems and context, so it also implies thinking of families in transgenerational terms. The statement "Any time you find a parent–child problem, you have a three-generational problem" represents one way of approaching the transgenerational nature of family process.

Family therapy represents far more than a set of treatment techniques or a "way of doing therapy." Rather, it both consists of and embodies a different way of looking at human beings and human problems than is found in traditional individual and even group psychotherapy. Evidence abounds that a therapist simply cannot add family therapy to a repertoire of treatment skills previously acquired within an individual orientation because family therapy does represent a radically different way of looking at things. The early history of family therapy had its share of conflict as family therapists attempted to introduce their new way of conceptualizing and dealing with human difficulties into clinical settings that were accustomed to functioning on the individual model (Framo, 1975; Haley, 1975). More than a little cognitive and other dissonance is likely to be created when those with training in individual development and individual psychopathology must work with others who have education in family development and behavior pathology stemming from family systems and family process orientations.

UNDERSTANDING THE DEVELOPMENT OF FAMILY THERAPY

It seems obvious that practitioners in any field that approaches or claims professional status should be acquainted with the historical development of that field and with the antecedents of that development. Unfortunately, there is widespread ignorance of the history of marital and family therapy not only among beginners and students but also among experienced practitioners and well-known leaders in the field.

Although a number of individuals have written accounts of the development of the field from their own perspectives and as a result of their own participation in some of the important occurrences, the majority of these accounts have been limited in scope. Predictably, most have tended to emphasize the developments with which the writers have been familiar and to omit presentations of other events and processes about which they have limited knowledge. The contributions of professional marriage counseling to the development of the field of family therapy have not been known or recognized by many family therapists because they occurred outside the mainstream of psychiatry (M. Nichols, 1984).

A careful study of the development of the field of family therapy conducted over a period of 20 years shows that it emerged primarily from concerns with three different types of problems: marriage relationships, child behavior problems, and schizophrenia. Family therapy is not something brought about solely by clinicians. Particularly with regard to marriage problems, a major part of the initial concern for help came from the public itself, as couples demanded assistance with their troubled marriages. On the other hand, when families have considered a single member to be the problem, clinicians and others have had to persuade such families that working with the family unit is more effective than dealing only with that individual (Lief, 1980).

The development of family therapy did not go forward smoothly or easily. Rather, as with the emergence of any major historical phenomenon, it moved by spurts and lags, unevenly, and without coordination or even awareness of the existence of other parts. Portions of it evolved within the medical world and other parts grew up outside of that framework. Frequently the two worlds, medical and nonmedical, separately went about working on the same issues and finding the same solutions without either being aware of what was occurring outside of their own sphere. To a significant degree, that pattern continues in the present.

Perhaps the most significant barrier to progress faced by both medical and nonmedical psychotherapists in the first half of the 20th century in the United States was the influence of psychoanalytic thought and power. The idea that psychoanalytic treatment and reconstructive work with individuals was necessary in order to deal with most problems combined with strictures against a psychotherapist seeing more than one member of a family to produce a powerful hindrance to the emergence of a family perspective. Those coming into the psychotherapy field in the 1960s and later probably have little basis for appreciating the powerful position of hegemony that psychiatry occupied in psychotherapy and the mental health field in general until well after World War II. Jackson and Satir (1961) concluded that psychoanalysts had acted in both a negative and a positive fashion to encourage the family movement in psychiatry. Their efforts to emphasize the positive aspects, however, seem somewhat strained.

Family therapists made much of the fact that early researchers and practitioners in family psychiatry kept their work underground until the middle and late 1950s. Similar things were happening with nonmedical clinicians for both related and slightly different reasons. For a long time, nonmedical psychotherapists had been careful not to oppose psychoanalytic positions and medicine publicly or to admit that what they were doing constituted psychotherapy. Freeing psychotherapy from the control of the field of medicine and establishing the right of other professionals to work directly with the public was an arduous struggle, the significance of which is difficult to comprehend today when "freedom of choice" legislation prohibits discrimination against specified nonmedical practitioners by third-party payors. Historically, the general devaluation by members of the medical community of psychotherapy and other endeavors performed by nonmedical personnel has maintained barriers to interprofessional cooperation and slowed general progress in the field (Gurman & Kniskern, 1978a; Lief, 1980).

Family therapy is the product of the work of many different individuals and groups. Its origins can best be understood through comprehension and use of the sociologists' and anthropologists' concept of the "culture base" and the related idea of "independent invention." It has long been demonstrated that when the culture base (meaning the knowledge level and the desire or need for a particular item) is sufficiently established, the same discovery or invention may be made separately but essentially simultaneously by different individuals and groups. The result is an "independent invention." This helps to explain why researchers and practitioners in Wisconsin, California, Kansas, New York, England, and on the European continent, for example, can be credited with similar "inventions," "discoveries," or "breakthroughs" in family therapy without being aware of the work of the others.

The 1950s are generally acknowledged as the time during which family therapy was born in the United States. It did not, however, spring forth full-blown from the head of any midcentury American Zeus. Rather, it had its roots in several developments that occurred during the 20th century, particularly following World War I. The "revolution" of the 1950s had a long and complex background. A major point to keep in mind regarding the development of the field of family therapy in the United States is that the picture is much more complicated than is generally depicted. Many developments arose from multiple sources, making it impossible to describe simple streams of events and linear progress. Several major figures in the field are difficult, often impossible, to characterize and classify neatly and without ambiguity. Similarly, streams of influence cannot be charted easily and their outcomes clearly marked out and related to beginnings in a one-to-one fashion. Even the attempt here to describe origins and developments in terms of concerns with marital relationships, child behavior problems, and schizophrenia has some inevitable distortions. However, it does involve an effort to be as comprehensive and accurate as possible in accounting for significant factors in the evolution of family therapy.

One of the most complete and accurate historical discussions available is the sketch by Broderick and Schrader (1981). Except for the fact that it implies a closer relationship between early developments in Europe and the United States than seems to have existed and that it places sex therapy within the framework of family therapy, it is a most useful historical introduction. (Sex therapists and counselors have been credentialed by a specialized organization in the United States—the American Association of Sex Educators, Counselors, and Therapists—and their knowledge and skills have been considered to be different and separate from those of family therapists, although ancilliary in some respects. The American Association for Marriage and Family Therapy adopted a policy statement in the 1970s indicating that sex therapy is a different field of practice from marital and family therapy. Our agreement with that conclusion is the major reason why the development of sex education and sex therapy is omitted from this chapter.)

With regard to the other shortcoming of the Broderick–Schrader presentation, there are a number of publications from the 1930s indicating that what had transpired in Europe generally was not known to Americans. The major thrust of some journal articles in that period was to inform Americans about what had happened in Europe. Ernest R. Groves, probably the most influential and best-informed participant in the family life education and marriage counseling traditions in the United States, called the development of marital counseling here "a movement indigenous to American culture, and not an importation." He did note that it was influenced by European events in terms of the forms that its clinics assumed (Groves, 1940). His reference to the clinical expression probably was to the fact that Abraham and Hannah Stone, who opened one of the early marital consultation clinics in New York City in the late 1920s, had migrated there from Europe. Essentially, the indications are that independent invention brought forth somewhat similar efforts to provide professional assistance to those undergoing marital difficulty in Europe and North America with a minimum of cross-pollenization in the early days.

During the decade of the 1960s, the influences from Europe were stronger. The work of Henry V. Dicks, W. R. D. Fairbairn, and Melanie Klein influenced some American clinicians, as did the thought of R. D. Laing.

Such materials as Ellis's (1964) article on "unconscious collusion in marital interaction" were rare, but those that did appear were influenced by a growing acquaintance by Americans with the work of Dicks and the "English object relations school." Dicks authored a chapter in a widely read volume, *Marriage Counseling in Medical Practice* (Nash, Jessner, &

Abse, 1964), and his own seminal volume, *Marital Tensions* (1967), was published in the United States as well as in England. Some of the influence of Klein's object relations ideas appeared in casework materials and social work practice in the United States by the early 1960s (e.g., Huneeus, 1963). David R. Mace, director of England's Marriage Guidance Council, and later, 1960–1967, executive director of the then American Association of Marriage Counselors, described some of the differences between developments in the two countries in terms of greater professional development in the United States (Mace, 1945, 1958).

One additional point to keep in mind as we sketch the development of family therapy from its beginnings in the essentially separate streams of what we call classical marriage counseling and marital therapy, the widespread child-guidance movement, and the research into schizophrenia and families beginning in the 1940s, is that the exciting explosions of the 1950s not only had a long and complex incubation period preceding them, but that even now the field of family therapy is still very much in the process of knitting together diverse strains of development. Integration is the key theme not only in terms of theory and practice but also with regard to different and sometimes previously unacquainted groups of practitioners, educators, and trainers who are discovering that others are laboring in the same general field of family therapy and in many cases have been doing so for a long time. In fact, integration, rather than dramatic discoveries and breakthroughs, is the hallmark of family therapy in North America today. Understanding the background makes possible a more intelligent and informed comprehension of the current field.

DEMANDS FOR MARITAL ASSISTANCE

Marriage counseling and, later, marital therapy came into being in the United States because of the public demand for help in coping with the problems of contemporary marriage; it did not arise from the development of theory and strategy by professionals. That demand began asserting itself in the period following World War I and has increased through the decades. The finding by a small Canadian family service agency during the 1960s that "more than half of those who applied for service requested marriage counseling" (Brandreth & Pike, 1967), would not be atypical.

Sociologist Meyer Nimkoff, later the guiding force in the founding of an interdivisional doctoral program in marriage and family living at the

Florida State University, headed one of the early U.S. social work clinics that dealt with such difficulties. Although the primary concern of the Institute for Marriage and Family Guidance (Los Angeles) was "the prevention of advanced family difficulties," the facility also attempted to deal with "the treatment of marital discord" (Nimkoff, 1931).

Groves (1940) located the origin of the demand for counseling services in the nature of modern life and the environmental pressures on marriage and family living. By 1928 the American Social Hygiene Association had organized a division of family relations to study the aids that were being made available in response to family demand (White, 1933).

Although as Groves (1940) noted, the impact on the United States of Europe's efforts to establish sex and marital consultation clinics was rather indirect, some American observers did note what was happening on the European scene and report it in American journals. Concord (1924), for example, reported on "the matrimonial advice bureau" opened in Vienna in 1922, calling it "the first municipal bureau to furnish advice to those desirous of founding new families" (p. 61). Several years later, Durand-Weaver (1930) wrote about the first 6 months of operation of an advice bureau that was opened in Berlin in 1928 "to give pre-marital advice to engaged couples and advice on questions of marital adjustment to married couples" (p. 85). White (1933) underlined the fact that Western society considered understanding of and assistance with marital and sexual problems and adjustment something that called for organized efforts. Clinics and bureaus were operating in Austria and Germany, Zurich had established a marriage consultation bureau in 1929 and Basel had founded one in 1933, and the Soviet Union had a government institute for the care of motherhood and childhood in its department of health (White, 1933).

There were difficulties with the kinds of clinics that had opened in Europe.

The experience of the German marriage advice bureaus showed from the start that the purpose of the government in establishing them—that is, race improvement through enlightening applicants concerning their responsibilities to the next generation, and certifying them as to their fitness for marriage and parenthood was much too limited to meet the demand. Husbands and wives who found difficulty and wanted help in family adjustment were the most frequent visitors. (White, 1933, p. 559)

The picture was similar in the United States in that early public health approaches did not meet public needs and demands. As noted by Nelson

(1952), "four of the oldest marriage counseling services in the country were inaugurated under Social Hygiene auspices. However, as specialization developed with its concomitants of different training requirements, the organization withdrew its emphasis" (p. 255).

It is not difficult to understand why the public health and social hygiene constituency dropped out of the marriage counseling picture as it developed in the United States. The question of whether marriage counseling should become an American public health function was considered in an editorial in the *American Journal of Public Health* in 1935. The definition of marriage counseling considered there was much too limited to encompass what was characteristic of the field even at that time.

By marriage counseling we understand such advice by medically trained persons, and others with legal and social or psychological competence as is sought by men and women, unmarried or married, who believe that their lives together will be happier and wiser if they learn, before rather than after they have met in conflict and suffering in marital sex relations, what medical and social experience has gathered and can legally impart to them. (*American Journal of Public Health*, 1935, p. 354)

The editorial included in the definition of such advice and guidance the teaching of safe and effective methods of contraception in order to preserve the family's physical and mental health.

The early attempts to take a public health approach were bucking the tide of human interest and need in the United States as they had in Europe. As Kopp (1938) reported, Europe's clinics—of which there were more than 200 by the early 1930s (Nimkoff, 1934)—had undergone radical change. The original eugenics aim of the European services—the prevention of reproduction by persons presumed to be carriers of hereditary defects—had been only moderately successful. Those most in need of advice had not sought guidance (Kopp, 1938). In Austria, in particular, the earlier approach had been largely abandoned by the mid-1930s, and had been replaced by services closer to American-style family welfare services. By the middle of that decade it was becoming evident on both continents that social hygiene emphases were not consonant with the interests of the public. The concerns of professionals from the social hygiene field in the United States—for example, as manifested in articles on premarital examinations and laws relating to venereal disease and marriage (Johnson, 1938; Talbot, 1937)—did not reflect the interests of most persons seeking marital and family help.

Whether there was clinical work with marital and family problems by professionals in the United States prior to the 1920s is uncertain, but it is clear that during that decade, such work was conducted in a number of settings and under a variety of auspices. White (1933) noted that in the United States "the organized family consultation center developed from a number of different directions. Many urgent family problems, for instance, came to the birth control clinics, which in the ten years since the first center was established in 1921 increased until there are now over one hundred twenty" (pp. 559–560).

By the mid-1930s, there were in operation in the United States "157 marriage advice stations, of which 18 are controlled and served by the local public health authority" (*American Journal of Public Health*, 1935, p. 354). Known by various names in addition to "marriage advice stations," the "marriage and family consultation bureau in the United States" had, according to one writer, "emerged since 1928 out of programs in eugenics, social hygiene, birth control, child development, religion and social welfare. It is the natural outgrowth and extension of experiments in counseling services carried on by different specialists under the auspices of typical programs already existing in the fields mentioned" (Fisher, 1936, p. 8).

The rising divorce rate in the United States in the 20th century served as a specific stimulus to efforts to provide help for marriages. During the early decades, a variety of institutional services were introduced in an effort to stem divorce, but without marked success. Marital conciliation work made its debut early in the 1900s, for example, having as its goal the reconciliation of couples contemplating divorce. Nimkoff (1934) observed that the 26 domestic-relations courts in operation in 1932—the first 2 having been established in Buffalo and New York City in 1910—and the family service agencies were not proving helpful. He cited Mowrer as finding the success rate for cases treated in connection with the conciliation courts in Chicago to be 4%. Referring to the domestic-relations courts and the 376 family welfare agencies that maintained standards entitling them to membership in the Family Welfare Association of America, Nimkoff (1934) concluded, "But as far as being able to effect adjustments in family life is concerned, they have proved to be a dismal failure. Their successes are even fewer than those of the family welfare agencies" (p. 231).

From out of such varied beginnings, marital and family counseling services and clinics began to emerge and to focus much more directly on the needs and expectations of the public. Gradually, from diverse sources, a clinical profession began to develop.

What we call classical marriage counseling did not evolve directly from psychiatry, clinical psychology, or social work but, according to Leslie (1964b), from developments in education and social science. As we shall note, certain of its spokespersons were careful to claim that they were not doing psychotherapy. The marital therapy branch of development was concerned with psychotherapy and not merely with working with "essentially normal persons." It developed from the work of traditional clinicians, such as some psychoanalysts and clinical psychologists, as well as from that of individuals who came from other backgrounds and were evolving approaches to dealing with serious marital and personal difficulties.

The background of classical marriage counseling included events in social hygiene and sex education beginning in the 1920s, home economics and child development (beginning, for example at the Merrill–Palmer School, later Institute, in Detroit, around 1920), and the marriage education movement that was started by Groves in 1924. The first generation of practitioners was self-taught, and even into the 1950s, most individuals entering the field had to secure training after they had completed their formal academic education (Leslie, 1964b).

Groves (1940), writing about the 1930s, the decade in which the foundations for classical marriage counseling were laid, said:

There has been some increase in the number of persons who carry on counseling as their chief professional service or as an important by-product. The greatest hazard in the field of counseling comes from the growing exploitation of the growing desire for it. The only possible protection must come from a more general education of the public, that they may realize the responsibilities that belong to the counselor. This will lead to a demand for a standard of ethics which alone can safeguard counseling. (p. 79)

Clinics concerned directly and solely with marital and family counseling began to open in the United States around 1930. In 1929, the Stones, who were physicians, opened a marriage consultation center at the Labor Temple in New York City to provide guidance for young persons who were about to be married and for those already married. They moved it to the Community Church of New York in 1932 (Stone, 1949). Paul Popenoe opened a clinic at the American Institute of Family Relations in Los Angeles in 1930. The Marriage Council of Philadelphia, which long had a casework emphasis under the leadership of Emily H. Mudd, began to offer services in 1932. Other clinics and centers included the Consultation Service of the Maternal Health Service of Cleveland, which established a marriage counseling service in 1931; and the Counseling Service in Boston, opened in 1925, which eventually began to offer assistance for marital problems (Mudd, 1951).

The year 1932 was especially important. Not only was the Marriage Council of Philadelphia established, but the Family Consultation Center of the Child Development Institute at Teachers College of Columbia University and the Advisory Service of College Women at the Merrill–Palmer School also opened that year. As described by White (1933):

The Family Consultation Service at Columbia University . . . was founded as a result of the Institute's experience in child development and parent education, which showed that they needed a broader basis for their work with children.

The Merrill–Palmer Advisory Service for College Women . . . undertakes to give help on any matter brought to it by a woman, single or married, who has attended or is attending college. (pp. 560–561)

The founding of the Advisory Service was one of the developments that led in subsequent decades to the Merrill–Palmer Institute's program in training and clinical service.

From several perspectives, the most important development in 1932 was probably the opening of the Marriage Council of Philadelphia. Under the energetic leadership of Mudd, it combined marriage counseling and marriage and family life education and communicated with the medical profession in ways that influenced the medical community's perceptions of nonmedical practitioners for decades to come.

The work and focus of the Marriage Council of Philadelphia were delineated in a large number of publications by Mudd (e.g., Mudd, 1937; Mudd & Lundien, 1940; Mudd & Rose, 1940). In the 1950s, the pioneering service and training institution was officially affiliated with the School of Medicine, University of Pennsylvania and became an operational unit of the Division of Family Study of the Department of Psychiatry. As described by its director, Mudd (1955), the Marriage Council "has always employed professional trained staff as counselors, primarily social workers with a psychiatrist part time. Its work with clients has been under the supervision of a medical and a legal supervisory committee" (p. 111).

The theoretical framework under which the Marriage Council operated during the Mudd years included the following hypothesis: "That, if an individual can experience during the counseling process, new understanding of himself and his marriage partner and more satisfying ways of using himself in his daily relationships in marriage and with his family he should be able to apply these acquired abilities to other problem situations as these may arise in his daily living" (Mudd, 1955, pp. 111–112). Most of the treatment was of very brief duration. Although there was a wide range of interviews, the average marital counseling term was six to ten sessions (Mudd, 1955).

The Marriage Council began to give "advanced supervised training in marriage counseling," initially under grants from the W. T. Grant Foundation of New York City. Trainees had to have a "graduate degree, an M.S.W. in social work, a Ph.D. in clinical psychology or a closely related field, or an M.D." One significant aspect of the program was the proviso that training was open only to applicants "whose experience, aptitudes and intentions for future contributions to marriage counseling [included working] *where medical consultation is available*" (italics in original). The program also was used as a field placement for certain doctoral students at the University of Pennsylvania and Columbia University Teachers College (Marriage Council of Philadelphia, 1959). The program continues in operation today and has recently added a much more specific family therapy and systems approach to its traditional marriage counseling/marital therapy focus.

The Merrill–Palmer program for postdoctoral training was put together in the early 1950s from previously disparate offerings and services within the institution, and soon developed into an intensive training effort in individual and marital psychotherapy. Addition of a therapeutic preschool project involving treatment of severely emotionally disturbed preschool children and their families added a distinct family therapy component originally modeled largely along child-guidance lines. For more than a decade, until most of the staff departed in 1969 during a period of financial retrenchment and institutional reorganization, Merrill–Palmer's program offered intensive training in marital therapy for postdoctoral fellows.

The Menninger Foundation established a postdoctoral marriage counseling program in 1950 and subsequently converted it to a program in pastoral counseling.

As marriage counseling continued its development, there was involvement in the field by agencies and practitioners from established helping professions. The movement of social work into the area of individual concerns and relationship problems seems to have come about in a gradual and somewhat indirect fashion and to have included a considerable amount of ambivalence on the part of the profession. According to Ware (1940), "seasoned case workers had been giving thoughtful service in marriage and family problems for many years before counseling and consultation reached its present stage of more conscious development" (p. 231). During the 1930s, that author's agency had begun to accept for marriage and family counseling numbers of individuals and families who had come in specifically for assistance with relationship problems, rather than for help with traditional casework and welfare concerns.

As the social work agencies began to deal with cases on a counseling or therapeutic basis instead of through a welfare approach, they began to reach outside for consultation. Much of the consultation received was from psychiatrists who were psychoanalytically oriented and who focused on the intrapsychic concerns of the person being treated.

Social work's relationship with marital and family counseling and therapy was a source of internal debate and consideration for several decades. Reimers (1941) claimed, for example, at the 1940 Groves Conference, that "the effective caseworker does not deal with problems of family life, but she does deal with individual persons, some of whom are having trouble in this area of life experience!" (p. 66). It is to be presumed that this was a stance consistent with the view that in order to work with marital and family problems, one dealt only with an individual or at least primarily with an individual and his or her personal problems and adjustments.

By contrast, two other social workers at the Groves Conference claimed that "family counseling is not new to the family caseworker, who has been accustomed always to deal not only with the practical problems which arose in families, but also with the more intimate problems of family inter-relationships" (Ware & Goodwin, 1941, p. 10). They went on to contend that counseling services should *not* be separated from financial and other practical services offered by social work agencies.

Psychology's incursions into the field of marriage counseling/marital therapy have been rather infrequent and have tended to be of short duration. Typically in the early years and even into later decades, an occasional program would be presented on a topic of interest but there would be no sustained follow-through or in-depth pursuit of the issues. A well-planned and interesting symposium on neurotic interaction, jointly presented by the divisions of clinical psychology and counseling psychology of the American Psychological Association in 1957, provides an example (Ellis, 1958; Harper, 1958; Lawton, 1958).

Throughout the 1960s, in a series of papers that was actually begun in 1959, Kimber decried psychology's lack of involvement in the field of marriage counseling (Kimber, 1959, 1963, 1967). In a 1961 article, Kimber gave a brief explanation of why referral to a marriage counselor should be made by a physician, minister, educator, or attorney and decribed marriage counseling clearly as a form of psychotherapy. The rapid growth of marriage counseling services was reflected in his studies of advertising in telephone yellow pages. (Kimber, 1963, 1967).

Even now, psychologists receive little formal education or training in marital and family therapy in their doctoral programs. Psychology's continued absence from the current field of family therapy has been noted by Stanton (1975): "Psychology's lack of representation within family therapy probably stems in part from the post–World War II struggle that psychologists faced in being recognized as competent to practice *any* kind of therapy, much less a kind that was new and radically different" (p. 47).

Psychiatry in general began to involve itself with marital and family problems at a very late date, although the efforts of pioneering psychoanalysts who began to treat marital partners in the 1930s and the subsequent involvement of those who ran against the psychoanalytic tide to work with families in the 1950s were of major significance. Even today, family therapy is not a major concern of psychiatry, although it is a growing one (Sugarman, 1981, 1984).

Historically, professionals have approached the treatment of marital discord in three different ways. These have been referred to as the "individual-only," the "relationship-only," and the marital therapy or "triangular" approaches (Nichols, 1973).

The "individual-only" approach holds that marital discord stems from disturbances in the individuals who marry. Bergler's *Divorce Won't Help* (1948) is an extreme expression of the view that marital problems arise from individual neurosis and that only the psychotherapeutic treatment of individuals will change them so that they can deal more maturely with marriage. A more sophisticated version of this theory is found in the ego psychology approach of Blanck and Blanck (1968). The basic source of the individual-only orientation to marital discord evidently is the hold that psychoanalysis has had on the American psychotherapeutic scene, particularly until after World War II. Its emphasis on intrapsychic process, treatment through interpretation of transference in a dyadic therapist–

patient relationship, and strictures against seeing more than one member of a family or marital dyad at a time, lest such contact contaminate the transference relationship between the client and therapist, all mitigated against the development of marital therapy (Gottlieb & Pattison, 1966; Lorand, 1968).

Our attention here will be devoted to the classical marriage counseling approach, which is roughly synonymous with the relationship-only orientation, and subsequently to the marital therapy mode of treatment.

Classical Marriage Counseling

In the early days, classical marriage counseling practitioners often did not have the preparation to do psychotherapy and did not have the legal right to do so. Many, therefore, were quite careful to make it known that they were not doing psychotherapy. Those early practitioners who worked in and near medical facilities considered it essential to refer anyone who manifested individual problems and concerns to a psychiatrist, keeping their own work focused basically on the relationship between the marital partners and on here-and-now issues. Some considered marriage education and marriage guidance to be essentially synonymous and attempted to deal with marital problems through a form of guidance and advisement. By the time the movement was well under way in the 1930s, many practitioners clearly saw themselves doing some form of relationship counseling and not education or advice giving. Still others moved out of the classical mode into performing psychotherapy and labeling what they were doing as psychotherapy.

A more sophisticated variant of the relationship-only approach was described in the first volume of *Family Process* (Gehrke & Moxom, 1962). The social casework approach described by Gehrke and Moxom involved short-term treatment focused on the relationship and aimed at establishing a marital balance. It was an orientation that had moved a considerable distance in the direction of a systems model for dealing with marital discord.

It was within the classical marriage counseling contribution to the field that most of the questions that occupied the growing field and emerging profession arose and were debated. One of these questions was whether marriage counseling was counseling (meaning primarily conscious-level, interaction-in-the-present work) or psychotherapy. Implicit in much of the debate was the question of whether the marriage counselor dealt with intrapsychic factors in a conscious way, although it was sometimes posed as a dichotomy between dealing with the relationship or with personality reorganization.

Different and opposing points of view as to the nature of marital counseling/therapy prevailed during the 1930s and well into the 1950s among practitioners in the field. One stance held that marriage counseling was not a form of psychotherapy. The other maintained that it was a specialized and extremely complex form of psychotherapy. The arguments need to be understood in terms of historical context, particularly in view of the then prevalent idea that medicine owned psychotherapy.

Wortis (1945), a physician identified with the marriage counseling movement, wrote, "it is my belief that marriage counseling clinics are best outside of psychiatric institutions under close supervision of psychiatrically trained physicians" (p. 86).

Mudd (1967), speaking at the Silver Anniversary meeting of the American Association of Marriage Counselors, said:

Marriage counseling was considered a specialized form of family counseling, primarily concerned with the interpersonal relations of husband and wife, wherein the clients are aided to reach a self-determined resolution of their problems. [Quoting herself from a 1955 article, she added:] . . . the focus of the counselor's approach is the relationship between the two people in marriage rather than, as in psychiatric therapy, the reorganization of the personality structure of the individual.

Without attempting to resolve the complicated area of the relationship between psychotherapy and counseling, the Association made it clear at that time [i.e., at the time of its founding in 1942] that psychotherapy and counseling were not considered synonymous. Members of the A.A.M.C. might do psychotherapy—many of them did—but this was not essential to their work in marriage counseling. This activity derived from their own individual basic training and qualifications. The marriage counselor *per se* was not considered to be a psychotherapist. The issue was of special importance in relation to the question of the private practice of non-medical counselors (p. 11).

Mudd expressed similar views in other publications (Mudd, 1951; Mudd, Stone, Karpf, & Nelson, 1958).

Others were less likely to feel the need for medical control and psychiatric supervision or to view marriage counseling/marital therapy as being radically different from psychotherapy. There are other forms of psychotherapy besides those aimed at personality reconstruction. Leslie

(1964b) provided a succinct statement of an opposite view to the "marriage counseling is not psychotherapy" opinion. Others also argued for a frank recognition that marital therapy was a complex and specialized form of psychotherapy in the 1950s. For example, Earle Marsh, a physician associated with the marriage counseling field, was quoted as saying, "Psychotherapy and marriage counseling, to me, are one and the same. Psychotherapy attempts total personality reorganization; marriage counseling only partial reorganization, i.e., enough to make either divorce or continuation of a marriage easier" (Mudd et al., 1958, p. 38).

Stokes (1951a), a psychiatrist and attorney, described marriage counseling as a "specially adapted form of psychotherapy." Elsewhere (1951b), he indicated that physicians did not object to the work of marriage counselors if diagnostic and other work done by the nonmedical persons were done under medical supervison or in a teamwork relationship.

Karpf (1951a, 1951b, 1951c) was one of those who did not regard marriage counseling as a form of psychiatry, psychoanalysis, or psychology. In a series of articles, he contended that the marriage counselor deals mainly with normal people and, like the social worker, can "handle most situations on a conscious level" (1951c, p. 169). Others who discussed Karpf's articles disagreed with the "conscious level" and "normal people only" contentions.

Laidlaw (1950) described marriage counseling as short-term psychotherapy dealing with interpersonal relationships and focusing primarily on the psychosexual components of marriage. Because he perceived that relatively simple techniques were involved, Laidlaw, a psychiatrist, felt that properly trained and qualified nonmedical persons could function as marriage counselors. He also noted that psychiatric training did not provide adequate preparation for either premarital or postmarital counseling. Nevertheless, he felt that all marriage counseling properly fell within the province of psychiatry.

The American Association of Marriage Counselors sponsored a special section in *Marriage and Family Living* (now the *Journal of Marriage and the Family*) from 1951 through 1953. An evaluation of the materials published there showed solid agreement among the clinicians regarding the nature of their work, according to Ellis (1956), who wrote, "The only serious disagreement among the marriage counselors who have published cases here seems to be not whether marriage counseling involves psychotherapy but whether it necessitates psychotherapy of an intensive, prolonged, and unconscious-probing nature" (p. 68). He went on to say that "the best kind of marriage counseling that is now being done usually involves short-term psychotherapy in a face-to-face situation" (p. 70).

Harper (1953) flatly defined marriage counseling as a form of psychotherapy and called for training equivalent to, but not identical with, that of the fully trained psychoanalyst.

The term "marriage counseling" has caused difficulty for many years. Among those who expressed dissatisfaction were some social workers. Brangwin (1955) felt that the term was a misnomer because caseworkers do not do "advising" or "admonishing," which, she thought, the term "counseling" implied. The term "marriage counseling" was retained, however, long after it had been widely recognized that the services provided were psychotherapeutic in nature. Among the reasons for retention of an inappropriate label was the recognition that "many members of the public are willing to go to someone who is called a 'marriage counselor' rather than to someone who is called a 'psychotherapist' " (Ellis, 1956, pp. 70–71). Another factor in the retention was the continuing struggle between medical and nonmedical therapists. Many members of the psychoanalytic community in particular and psychiatrists in general were not willing during the 1950s and in some instances even later to call short-term treatment by the name "therapy" or "psychotherapy." Marriage counseling was viewed as something ancilliary to the work of psychiatry (Mudd, 1955).

Although many within the family therapy field are troubled by the use of the term "counseling," and stringent efforts are sometimes made to distinguish between "therapy" and "counseling," the terms often have been used interchangeably. Examples of the mixed usage of "family counseling" and "family therapy" can be found in the writings of Mowrer (1940), Gomberg and Levinson (1951), Harper (1953, 1958, 1960), Ballard and Mudd (1957), Ellis (1958), Lawton (1958), Lederer and Jackson (1968), Ard and Ard (1969), Greene (1970), Richter (1967), Paul and Paul (1975), Fogarty (1976a), Olson (1976), Hardcastle (1977), Headley (1977), and Lantz (1978).

A distinction was made by Framo (1973):

Although *marriage counseling* has a long and respectable tradition, it should be distinguished from marriage *therapy*, a form of depth treatment, which not only deals with the intrapsychic dynamics of each spouse but also examines the interlocking nature of the marital bond. The motivational feedback system between husband and wife, moreover, occurs in the context of the whole family, including the children, as well as the extended family. It is not surprising, therefore, that many marriage therapists are basically family therapists who view human relationships in systems terms. (p. 88)

It seems highly likely that the perceptions of marriage counseling and marital therapy by those outside the field, particularly by psychiatrists and other physicians, were strongly influenced by terminology and by exposure to those practitioners and spokepersons whom they encountered within medically dominated settings. Mudd, a prolific writer whose professional career has spanned more than a half-century, and who worked with generations of physicians at the Marriage Council of Philadelphia and the Department of Psychiatry at the University of Pennsylvania's Medical School, strongly held that marriage counseling was not psychotherapy and that it was different from the work of medical professionals.

Similarly, Robert G. Foster influenced the views of the psychiatric community through his position at the Menninger Foundation. An outspoken advocate of marriage counseling as an educational endeavor, he emphasized preparation of couples for marriage in his early work (Foster 1935, 1936b). Throughout his career, Foster insisted that there were differences between the work of the marriage counselor and that of the psychiatrist, the psychiatric social worker, and the clinical psychologist. He viewed the latter's work as primarily dealing with problems of pathology, whereas he viewed the marriage counselor's role as that of educating young persons and adults and referring individuals with need for psychotherapeutic help to other professionals (Foster, 1950). Despite the fact that he stood virtually alone in holding that marriage counseling was an educational endeavor, Foster seems to have had a significant impact on perceptions at the Kansas institution. Under the guidance of Foster and his colleague Johnson (1957), marriage counseling at the Menninger Foundation did have a largely educational slant (Crist, 1955, 1956). Interestingly, that was the scene of the early work of Murray Bowen, who not only was dealing with schizophrenia and the family but also was attempting to make psychiatry a respectable part of science.

The program at the Menninger Foundation eventually took another turn, as noted by Leslie (1964b). A postdoctoral marriage counseling training program that was established in 1950 gradually became confined to clergy and eventually was altered to become a program in pastoral care and counseling. An interesting pattern still prevailed in the summer of 1979. The Menninger Foundation advertised workshops and training in both marital and family therapy and marital and family counseling. A query brought the response that the marital and family counseling workshop and training experiences were intended for clergy, the marital and family therapy training and experiences for others.

It seems unquestionably true that those early attempts to demonstrate that marriage counselors or marital and family counselors were doing something different from the work of medical professionals and psychotherapists were have left lasting impressions and continue to play a role in dividing the field.

Complicating the picture even more with regard to the classical marriage counseling approach was the kinship between marriage counseling in its nascent state and family life education. They were related, but not synonymous, although those outside of the related fields frequently did not appreciate the distinctions. Nor, in truth, did all of those associated with the two fields always distinguish between them.

Marriage and family counseling/therapy and family life education in the United States followed related, and at times intertwined but essentially separate, courses of development. Some of the early figures were involved deeply in both fields, as continues to be true to a lesser degree today. In recent decades, family life education has moved more in the direction of an attachment with family studies and research.

Among those early figures who left an impression in both the clinical and the academic areas was Groves. By 1946 he saw the end of the pioneering period in education for marriage, but he still viewed marriage counseling as being in its pioneering era. He distinguished between the two areas as follows:

Whereas instruction in marriage was something distinctly new as a systematic course of study, counseling, on the contrary, has been going on for a long time as an occasional service of the physician, the minister and the lawyer, and more recently the professional social worker. The difference is that the modern marriage counselor is developing special techniques for his role in the field of marriage and is attracting clients chiefly from the middle class and in less degree from the wealthy who through education are in a position to appreciate the new type of professional counseling. It is this change in the type of person seeking help and the definiteness of the problems presented that is giving counseling its professional distinctiveness.

Marriage counseling is an exacting professional service. It is not something that can be carried on in a reputable manner by persons having thin or superficial preparation. (Groves, 1946, pp. 25–26)

The same developments were described by another pioneer in the marriage counseling movement (Stone, 1949):

In the United States, marriage education and counseling developed in close interrelationship, yet have proceeded along several distinct lines: the establishment of courses in marriage and the family by colleges and universities followed by some progress in this direction in the secondary and even in the elementary schools; the organization of marriage consultation centers; the formation of national and regional conferences on marriage and the family; and the carrying on of research in the field. (p. 38)

Another view was expressed by Nelson (1952), who viewed marriage and family counseling as a new profession within the larger field of marriage and family living. Nelson thus saw marriage and family counseling and education for marriage and family living as being bound together. Recently that view has also been espoused by some professionals (e.g., Bloch, 1973) who, in their understanding of what transpired, have lumped together family life education and certain clinical developments that occurred prior to the 1950s.

A more accurate reflection was set forth by Luckey (1963) in a discussion of developments on college campuses. Although they were related to similar constituencies among college students, marriage counseling and marriage education were seen as having separate functions. "Departments concerned with marriage education and counseling services offering marriage counseling need to *work together* to maintain their *separate functions*. If counseling is to be done, well-trained counselors must do it; and the evidence is that family-life educators generally are not adequately trained counselors" (Luckey, 1963, p. 423).

Luckey, in some ways, was following the lead taken by Cuber (1948) more than a decade earlier. A sociologist/marriage counselor who wrote one of the first books on marriage counseling and marriage counselor training, Cuber's thesis was that teaching and counseling are separate and distinct professional roles because they have different traditions and have different administrative statuses. To improve the situation of the teacher–counselor, he called for the establishment of curricula with high professional standards, psychiatric screening of all persons before permitting them to counsel, therapy for the counselor, and possible licensure (Cuber, 1951).

Much of the confusion of professionals viewing the development of marriage counseling from outside arose from a loose use of terms and a general lack of clarity in writing by some of those persons who discussed marriage counseling and family life education. Bowman (1947), for example, in writing on "the teacher as counselor in marriage education" essentially referred to premarital educational work with some emphasis on marital guidance. Others (e.g., Levine, 1953; Marion, 1951) who wrote on the teacher–counselor were not concerned with marital counseling but with individual counseling of students in marriage courses.

A complicating factor in any attempt to simplify the history of the marriage counseling branch of the field was the early emphasis on marriage *and family* counseling that prevailed through the 1930s, 1940s and into the 1950s. While it is not always possible to demonstrate strong connections between certain developments and the later emergence of family therapy, it is possible and accurate to note that several of the emphases in the family life education field, as well as in the child-guidance movement, and in other developments were part of the evolving culture base out of which the emphasis on family intervention and treatment coalesced as a revolution in the 1950s.

Part of the rising culture base out of which family therapy emerged in the 1950s was a growing recognition that working either with individuals or with groups of individuals would not adequately solve problems coming out of a family context. This recognition was occurring in conjunction with a family research focus that was moving beyond considering the individual in the family toward emphasizing the family as a unit (Sperry, 1952). Morgan, Johannis, and Fowler (1953), for example, addressed some of these matters in a 1952 panel presentation at the Fifteenth Annual Groves Conference. Stripped of some of their values, the conclusions of the panelists sound remarkably similar to some of the things that mainline family therapists were saying both a few years and a few decades later:

Family counseling is a re-emphasis on the family as the primary group in which people have a sense of worth, of belonging, of being needed. It is an attempt to get at all the factors involved in the contribution of the family to the individual and the individual to the family. It is an adaptive problem-solving process which focuses on *the total family with its strengths and weaknesses, its interaction and communication patterns, and its impact on various family members as the patterns of living shift and change throughout the family life cycle.* (italics added)

Family counseling moves the focus of the marriage counselor to the relationship of the married pair with all family members. (p. 120)

Although somewhat unsophisticated in terms of current clinical understanding, such ideas were in the mainstream of the emerging concern with the total family unit as the focus of therapy.

Marital Therapy

The marital therapy approach, or what may be called a "triangular" emphasis or orientation, developed later than both the "individual-only" or the "relationship-only" orientations. "Triangular" is an accurate term because it involves an emphasis on the individual personality of the husband and the individual personality of the wife as well as on their interaction and relationship. Some clinicians have referred to three "patients": husband, wife, and relationship/interaction. Some forms of marital therapy, in which there was a strong emphasis on the relationship/ interaction, contained at least the beginnings of a systems approach and some contained more than merely the rudiments of a systems approach.

Marital therapy developed out of two major streams in the general psychotherapy movement. The one that has been the most widely chronicled was the branch stemming originally from psychoanalysis and involving principally the modification of psychoanalytic concepts and techniques that could be applied to married persons and eventually to their relationships. Sager (1966a, 1966b) has described this part of the marital therapy history from its beginnings in the early 1930s onward. Among the more important figures in the development of this branch were C. P. Oberndorf (1934, 1938), a psychoanalyst who analyzed spouses in succession and subsequently discussed their modes of relating in his articles; Bela Mittleman (1944, 1948), another analyst, who treated both spouses during the same general time period but saw them separately; Peter A. Martin and H. Waldo Bird (Bird & Martin, 1956; Martin & Bird, 1953), who treated the spouses separately, one of them seeing the husband and the other the wife, and conferred periodically in what they called the "stereoscopic technique"; and Bernard Greene and associates (Greene, 1960; Greene, Broadhurst, & Lustig, 1965; Greene & Soloman, 1963), who saw couples together in what came to be called "conjoint marital sessions." As with other branches and streams of development, there were other important figures who contributed to the growing practice of treating the extraindividual unit.

The work of such figures within the psychoanalytic field marked a distinct departure from tradition. A study of developments discloses that there was a gradual movement away from the practice of seeing only one member of a family among those therapists. In general, the progression was from the consecutive treatment of spouses, in which one therapist worked with first one of the partners and then the other in psychoanalysis, to other forms of therapy. The serial or consecutive treatment approach generally involved the idea that marital discord stemmed from neurosis in individuals. It was an even greater departure from psychoanalysis in the United States when an analyst worked with the spouses concurrently. Collaborative treatment in which two different therapists worked with the spouses and conferred periodically was a logical further development.

Eventually, conjoint interviewing, in which the husband and wife met together with one therapist, began to be employed by psychodynamically oriented therapists, as it had been by practitioners in the classical marriage counseling movement for decades. Another version of conjoint therapy was the four-person pattern established by Tavistock Clinic therapists in England in which at least part of the therapy consisted of meetings in which the husband and his therapist met with the wife and her therapist. This pattern had a limited and short-lived usage in the United States, partly because of the expense involved and partly because of the growing popularity of three-way conjoint interviewing involving one therapist and a married couple. Demonstration that significant therapeutic work could be done with members of the family, the marital unit in this instance, being seen together contributed markedly to diminishing the hold that conservative psychoanalytic thinking had on the general field of psychotherapy, thus helping to pave the way for the early acceptance that family therapy gained among some professionals.

The other branch of psychotherapy contributing significantly to the swelling stream of marital therapy resulted from a combination of classic marriage counseling and psychodynamic individual psychotherapy. Among the major pioneers in this part of the marital therapy field was Aaron Rutledge, a synthesizer and innovator who developed the "triangular" approach referred to above and led a major training program for a decade and a half at the Merrill–Palmer Institute. Rutledge and others, including Gerald Leslie at Purdue University, brought a strong marital therapy emphasis to the field, primarily through practice, training, and teaching, as well as through their work within the American Association of Marriage Counselors (currently the American Association for Marriage and Family Therapy). In several papers and presentations in the 1950s and 1960s, Rutledge strongly emphasized the necessity of a threefold diagnosis: individual assessments of the man, of the woman, and of their relationship. The individual diagnoses were based on an assessment of the strengths and pathology of each individual as an individual. The relationship diagnosis was based on the marital partners' level of development and on the difficulties between them, as such difficulties were believed to be rooted also in one of several individual developmental levels (Rutledge, 1960).

Similar but broader conceptualizations were offered by the psychiatrist Laidlaw (1960a, 1960b, 1967):

To begin with, I think it is important to consider the individual who first comes seeking help as the "patient." The marriage itself is considered the central problem, but individuals closely related may be asked to participate in the therapeutic effort. This approach I have termed the "constellation approach" to marital problems, and in this constellation may be found the spouse, grown children, relatives, friends, business associates, "the other woman" or "the other man," and in some cases individuals even more peripherally connected. (1967, p. 132)

In some ways Laidlaw's approach was moving very close to a systems approach to marital problems, although there does not appear to be any transgenerational element in his conceptualizing.

Nathan Ackerman was one of the pioneers not only of family therapy as the overarching framework for the field but also for marital therapy as part of the larger field of marital and family therapy. Some of his statements in a 1954 article, for example, were essentially the same in content as those being made by Rutledge and Greene and were squarely in the middle of the marital therapy stream of development. Ackerman (1954) wrote:

A relationship represents more than the sum of the personalities that make it up.

. . . the psychological principles that govern the behavior of an individual and those that govern the behavior of a relationship are not the same, . . . we cannot extrapolate from our knowledge of individual personality to behavior of a relationship.

In marital disorders conflict may be overt or covert, real or unreal, conscious or unconscious, in varying mixtures. (p. 141)

Later, Framo (1973) expressed similar ideas.

At the same time, other developments were taking place within the stream of psychodynamically oriented marital therapy. Eisenstein's (1956) edited work, *Neurotic Interaction in Marriage*, was a highly influential contribution to changing analytic approaches to marital discord. The items covered were not only such matters as neurotic choice of mate, interaction between severely disturbed spouses, and changes in family equilibrium through psychoanalytic treatment, but also problems of family diagnosis, collaborative treatment, and cultural factors. A little more than a decade later, Rosenbaum and Alger (1968) produced another volume that reflected further changes in the views of the psychoanalytic community concerning diagnosis and treatment of marital and family discord.

From a very different perspective, Jay Haley disclosed his version of systems approach to marital therapy in two publications in 1963. In one (1963a), he gave five indications for marital therapy and discussed marital conflict as centering in disagreements about rules for living together, about who is to set those rules, and about attempts to enforce rules that are incompatible with each other. This approach obviously is quite different from the psychoanalytic view that difficulties arise from individual neurosis (unconscious conflicts) and neurotic interaction. Changing the marital system is a major goal in Haley's approach. In the other article (1963b), Haley suggested that marital conflict occurs when spouses define their relationship in conflicting ways and thus impose paradoxical situations. According to Haley, marital therapists can resolve the difficulties when the couple face paradoxical situations that the therapist provides. He later defined marital therapy in terms of a triangle, indicating that the married "couple" actually is a triad, because it is defined by the inclusion or exclusion of someone else, for example, early in the marriage, the parents, subsequently, children, or, in therapy, a therapist (Haley, 1976).

By the mid-1960s, Greene (1965) could note that with regard to the treatment of marital difficulty there was a "six C" classification of techniques. With some adaptation, they included at that time:

- Counseling—a form of supportive therapy emphasizing the "here and now" (the classic relationship-only marriage counseling approach would fit here).
- Classical psychoanalysis (this would be the classic individual-only approach).
- Collaborative therapy—treatment by two different therapists who share information concerning the marriage and marital interaction.
- Concurrent therapy—treatment of both partners separately but simultaneously by the same therapist (this would be a variant of the individual-only approach).
- Conjoint therapy—treatment of both partners in the same session by one therapist.
- Combined therapy—a combination of various methods of interviewing.

Today, collaborative and concurrent therapy are seldom used, and conjoint marital therapy probably is the most widely employed technique for the treatment of marital discord.

The development of conjoint interviewing of marital partners as a significant and major form of therapeutic method was a lengthy and involved process. One of the debated questions during the 1940s and 1950s was whether the marriage counselor or therapist could and should work with both partners. The responses and opinions were as varied as the backgrounds and conceptual orientations of the clinicians. A prevalent social casework approach held that nothing new in technique was needed, that the caseworker could use general casework techniques in doing marriage counseling, but that the caseworker could not do intensive treatment with both partners and should establish a sound relationship with one partner before seeing the second (Schmidl, 1949). The strictures against seeing more than one partner that had been assumed from psychoanalysis were gradually beginning to fade. For example, a group containing several adherents of individual-only as well as relationship-only approaches came down on the side of viewing marriage as an entity in itself that could be treated advantageously by working with both partners, provided the spouses did not have deep emotional hostilities to each other (Saul *et al.*, 1953).

By 1955, Skidmore and Garrett (1955) were writing on the advantages of using joint interviews and necessary safeguards for such therapy. They described three cases handled in that fashion and listed eight values and ten safeguards for use in the joint interview. At the same time, some social workers indicated that attention needed to be given to involving both marital partners in a treatment plan, and noted that an appraisal of the marital interaction was important (Fibush, 1957).

By 1960, several writers were calling for selective use of joint sessions with marital partners. Geist and Gerber (1960) discussed six indications for use of such interviews and four treatment techniques especially useful with joint interviews, along with some contraindications. Various uses of the method were being advocated, including selective or intermittent usage (Lehrman, 1963), as an aid to ongoing marital treatment in which the partners are otherwise being seen by separate therapists (Green, 1964; Gullerud & Harlan, 1962; Huneeus, 1963), and other uses. Typical of the way in which conjoint interviews were used in conjunction with ongoing marital treatment of individuals by a single caseworker was the case described by Jolesch (1962), who worked from a typical, although modified, psychoanalytic orientation. Jolesch used the combination approach for the purpose of "identifying individual reactive patterns basic to the conflict in marital interaction" and attempted to time the conjoint interviews so that they were held "only after each partner had made a positive transference to the caseworker and had become engaged in an examination of his own role performance" (p. 246). The focus of treatment was on the interaction.

The conjoint interview was considered a significant treatment method by the early 1960s. Smith and Anderson (1963) discussed the advantages and disadvantages. Watson (1963) published a widely cited paper on the "conjoint psychotherapy of marital partners" in which he described the use of that approach, its technical problems and advantages, and its indications and contraindications. He noted that the main bar to its use might stem from the therapist's countertransference problems rather than from difficulties experienced with it by the marital partners.

It is interesting to note that Smith and Hepworth (1967) defined marital counseling/therapy in terms of the focus of the sessions, not on the basis of the number of persons interviewed. They concluded that it was possible to diagnose and treat without the second partner being present and also identified some of the dangers and difficulties that working with only one partner entailed. Some of the rudiments of a system approach can be found in the Fibush and Smith articles, although they had not arrived at an explicit systems orientation.

The term "conjoint" evidently first appeared in the literature in connection with family therapy in 1959 (Jackson, 1959). At the same time that conjoint interviewing was becoming widely accepted, there were those who continued to point out difficulties that they perceived in using the method. Psychoanalysts continued to express their familiar concerns that castration fears, oedipal relations, and other issues would be confused by such interviewing (Perelman, 1960).

There were also important and influential practitioners who saw the beginning of marital counseling/therapy as a treatment no different from the launching of individual psychotherapy. Laidlaw (1960a), for example, wrote that "it is the therapist's first task to obtain a thorough understanding of his patient and of the presenting situation. . . . It is, however, only after the patient's entire situation has been clearly delineated that the time arrives for putting into practice the constellation approach" (p. 142). By this he meant that only after one had thoroughly established clinical issues with the individual who had come for help with a marriage did the therapist move to interviewing other members of the family or other significant figures in the presenting client's life. Laidlaw also discussed the potentially disastrous therapeutic results as he saw them of beginning the joint interviews prematurely.

Despite some differences, some professionals were confident by the middle of the 1960s that successful marital therapy could be carried out under a variety of conditions provided that limited objectives were held, adequate assessment was done, and appropriate attention was given to the need to terminate or refer a small number of cases. Vesper and Spearman (1966) stated: "Couples can be successfully treated in marriage counseling even when both partners are severely disturbed and serious acting out is present. Productive treatment can also result when only one partner is available to the worker. Couples who can be responsive to treatment can be detected early in contact by certain prognostic clues" (p. 589).

There were still dissenters. The confidence of Vesper stood in strong contrast to Rivesman's (1957) conclusion that "in very seriously disturbed situations, the effects of treatment on the marital relationship usually cannot be prognosticated early in treatment" (p. 241).

Similarly, a Family Service Association of America project on casework with marital problems concluded that marital clients with compulsive character disorders could be treated but required a particular, limited kind of treatment (Bittermann, 1966):

In such cases, a casework treatment process that is geared toward the current interaction between the partners, with no effort at developing self-awareness for either partner, is indicated. We believe that the primary emphasis should be on stimulating the dependent partner to find some satisfaction in areas outside the marriage to dilute the intensity of emotional yearnings directed toward the spouse. The relaxation of emotional demands then permits the compulsive partner to loosen some of his control. Advice, guidance, and delineation of appropriate roles are the most helpful techniques. (p. 582)

Changes were uneven in social work. Reports on the use of joint interviewing in casework treatment of marital disorders indicated that social caseworkers were failing to use several techniques and procedures emphasized in the literature as useful in conjoint interviewing, were not using the interaction of husband and wife for therapeutic purposes, and were causing the effectiveness of conjoint interviewing to be questioned (Ehrenkranz, 1967a, 1967b).

The 1960s also witnessed a significant use of group therapy for married couples. Use of the technique was not new—Wolf had grouped five couples together for analysis in 1940 (Wolf, 1950)—but as the 1960s began, group therapy for married couples was becoming a popular way of dealing with marital discord. The technique was being tried with a variety of difficulties and client populations, including those with psychophysiological and anxiety reactions (Boyer, 1960) and those with alcoholic problems (Burton, 1962; Burton & Young, 1961).

A review of the literature indicates that most of the early objections to treatment of married couples, either in conjoint therapy or in a group setting, resulted essentially from a priori considerations such as a narrow and rigid commitment to a particular view of psychoanalysis (Gottlieb & Pattison, 1966).

The questions being raised by the middle of the 1960s did not deal with whether or not couples should be treated but with how they should be diagnosed and treated. Typical of some of the attempts to grapple with the diagnostic and treatment questions presented was the stance taken by Grunebaum, Christ, and Neiberg (1969):

It has been suggested that the couple be seen separately when the partners are uncommitted to work on their marriage or when marital problems appear to be secondary to immaturity or severe pathology. When the couple is committed to the marriage, able to communicate with each other, and problems are experienced both within and outside the marriage, they should be seen concurrently. When the couple is committed to the marriage and the symptoms relate almost entirely to the marriage, they should be treated together. If the problems are acute and ego-alien, then conjoint treatment is indicated, whereas if problems are chronic and ego-dystonic, then couple's group psychotherapy is recommended. (p. 202)

Not all therapists, of course, would have agreed with that particular set of indications and contraindications.

Behavioral Marital Therapy

Behavioral approaches to dealing with marital problems became an important part of the therapeutic scene in the late 1960s. One can date the advent of behavioral marital therapy with the appearance of Goldiamond's (1965) report on how the stimuli provided a wife by her husband control her behavior, or with the publications a little later of Stuart (1969), Liberman (1970), and others. Tharp (1965) and Tharp and Otis (1966) had added to the evolving behavioral literature. The behavioral approach reached a high level of productivity and development in the 1970s with the work of Gerald Patterson and his associates at the Oregon Research Institute located at the University of Oregon. Patterson not only played a significant role in creating behavioral marital therapy but also in laying theoretical foundations for applying a social learning approach to family interaction (Jacobson & Margolin, 1979). The extension of learning principles and techniques to marital, and later family, problems was a logical development from behaviorism's beginnings in individual psychotherapy.

Behaviorism has been described as the second major paradigm to emerge in psychology, joining psychoanalysis, which had preceded it (Weeks & L'Abate, 1982). Based on learning theory and emerging from the experimental laboratory rather than from the clinic, behaviorism brought quite different emphases from those of the dominating psychoanalytic model. The emphasis in behaviorism is placed on behaviors and not on the internal processes of the individual (Weiss, 1978). Symptoms, for example, are seen as learned responses that are not adaptive. They are not seen as symbolic or as meaning something else or as indicative of unconscious conflict, as in psychoanalytic theory. The core assumptions in behaviorism are the ideas that behavior is learned, that social reinforcement is the most important source of human motivation, and that intermittent reinforcement produces very durable, continuing behavior (Liberman, 1970).

Therapeutic applications of learning theory began to receive attention with the work of Skinner (1953) and his operant conditioning theory and research. Another contribution to behaviorism came from the classical conditioning approach advanced by Wolpe (1958), whose work on systematic desensitization was applied to a number of individual human difficulties. At the risk of oversimplifying the two approaches, they may be described as follows: Classical (also called "respondent") conditioning basically is concerned with behaviors that are elicited by preceding stimuli. Operant or "instrumental" conditioning and learning focus primarily on the conditions that follow the behavior, that is, the consequences and the absence or presence of rewards. There is a considerable amount of overlap between the two approaches. Both were used in devising treatment methods for individual problems.

Applications of learning theory to marital interaction came from two major sources, operant conditioning and social exchange theory (Thibaut & Kelley, 1959). Operant conditioning theory contributed the idea that the external environment provides significant determinants of behavior. Social exchange theory offered a perspective in which a marriage is viewed in quasi-economic terms. It holds that a relationship is satisfying if the benefits that are derived from being in the relationship exceed the costs; that is, it is concerned with costs and benefits (Weiss, 1978). The degree of satisfaction gained by a marital partner thus stems from the reward–cost ratio. Clinicians using a behavioral approach, therefore, would be concerned with the variables that maintain positive and negative behaviors.

The central emphasis of a behavioral approach to marital therapy has been described (O'Leary & Turkewitz, 1978) as helping spouses to learn more productive and positive ways of causing behavioral changes in one another through such techniques as contingency contracting, problem solving, and communication skills training. Useful definitions as well as a helpful sketch of its history may be found in a review of the literature by Jacobson and Martin (1976).

The concept of reciprocity (Thibaut & Kelley, 1959) came to be applied by some persons in a *quid pro quo* (literally "something for something") manner (Lederer & Jackson, 1968, and others). That is, one partner agrees to do something in exchange for a different behavior of equal weight from his or her partner. For example, a wife may agree to be pleasant and enter into sexual relations once a week, provided the husband manifests certain kinds of attention and offers affection in certain ways. Reciprocity in a general sense refers to the tendency for couples to reward each other at approximately equal rates (Jacobson & Margolin, 1979; Patterson & Reid, 1970). The *quid pro quo* approach, which has not proven to be as effective as early behavioral marital therapists supposed it would be, is only one of two kinds of contracts used. Another is the "good faith" contract introduced by Weiss and colleagues (Weiss, Hops, & Patterson, 1973).

Patterson's group at the University of Oregon (Wills, Weiss, & Patterson, 1974) not only has researched the concept of reciprocity and found evidence supporting it but also has made several other contributions to behavioral marital therapy. These have included the development of several ways of assessing marital relationships, such as the Willingness to Change Scale, the Marital Activities Inventory, the Spouse Observation Checklist, the Oregon Marital Studies Program, and others (L'Abate & McHenry, 1983). In addition, the Oregon group has applied social learning principles to the treatment of disturbed children giving particular attention to training parents to work with their aggressive youngsters (Patterson, 1974).

The social learning approach applied to the treatment of disturbed children by Patterson's group places emphasis on altering the social environment in which the children live. Skills training work is conducted with parents in a effort to teach them to diminish the rates of deviant and undesired behavior by the child and to increase the rates of adaptive and more desirable behaviors and social interaction. Typically, observation procedures are used and the parent's efforts are supervised by the therapist. In one study with families in which at least one male child was aggressive, a 60% reduction in observed target behaviors was noted at the time of termination (Patterson, 1974).

Behavioral marital therapy continues to be a complex matter, involving several different approaches to dealing with marital discord. As a treatment model, it is in a state of transition and change (Gurman, 1980). According to assessments found in existing literature, behavioral marital therapy is no more effective than nonbehavioral approaches to marital difficulty, both types being effective approximately two-thirds of the time (Vincent, 1980). One of the major strengths of behavioral marital therapy has been its concern with the outcome of therapy. Some of its limitations include a lack of emphasis on therapist–client relationships, the assumption that changing behaviors will result in increased marital satisfaction, and a lack of application to severe marital disorders such as those involving alcoholic and psychotic spouses (Gurman & Kniskern, 1978a; L'Abate & McHenry, 1983).

By the early 1980s, much of the early animosity between practitioners of behavioral marital therapy and nonbehavioral approaches appeared to have diminished. Efforts were being made to integrate social learning perspectives with those from other points of view. Behavioral marital therapy had won its place as a significant approach to dealing with marital (and family) difficulties. Paolino and McCrady (1978), for example, attempted to deal with marriage and marital therapy from psychoanalytic, behavioral, and systems perspectives. Seagraves (1982) tried to combine psychodynamic and behavioral approaches into a general approach to marital problems and marital therapy.

Gurman (1980) has described the major challenge of behavioral marital therapy in the 1980s as being that of integration with alternative models of marital treatment. In order to do this successfully, the treatment must pay attention to the fact that family members require reintegration as individuals in order for the family as a system to function effectively

(p. 88). This means, as we interpret Gurman, that individual, intrapsychic elements give significance to interpersonal events and must be taken into consideration in the integration.

With regard to marital therapy in general, by the end of the 1970s, Gurman (1978) could note:

In the last decade, marital therapy has evolved into one of the most significant psychotherapeutic interventions in the mental health field. In addition to its obvious relevance for marital conflicts, marital therapy increasingly has been involved as a potentially powerful general mode of intervention for a wide variety of clinical problems traditionally treated by individual psychotherapy. (p. 445)

In addition, a coalescence of the marital counseling/marital therapy and the family therapy wings of the field of family therapy is reflected in many ways in many places (e.g., Gurman & Kniskern, 1978a; McDonald, 1975). Today, in spite of its earlier and essentially separate development, marital therapy is part of the larger field of marital and family therapy or, more simply, family therapy.

THE CHILD-GUIDANCE MOVEMENT

The child-guidance movement constituted another important forerunner to the emergence of family therapy in the United States. Concerned originally with the behavioral problems of children and adolescents, child-guidance supporters developed clinics that focused on research, clinical service, and the training of workers to provide services. The orthopsychiatric approach in which a psychiatrist, psychiatric social worker, and clinical psychologist worked with disturbed children and their families and environment is generally considered to be one of the major developments and outcomes in the mainstream child-guidance movement in the United States.

Child guidance in its European origins was somewhat different from the North American version. Pioneering child-guidance clinics were organized in Europe early in the 20th century. Alfred Adler, one of the early disciples of Sigmund Freud who broke away to found his own approach to human personality termed Individual Psychology, developed clinics in Vienna. Adler worked with children, their families, and teachers in attempts to alleviate children's feelings of inferiority so that they could form a healthy and functional lifestyle. This was in many respects a preventive approach, in which working with children and parts of their environment was expected to forestall the formation of adult problems and neuroses.

The major disciple of Adler in the United States was Rudolph Dreikurs, one of his students who worked in child-guidance clinics in Chicago. In the early 1950s, Dreikurs advocated working with the whole family (Dreikurs, 1951), but was not able to gain a significant hearing for his ideas. In some ways he was ahead of his time. Dreikurs is more noted for his influence in Adlerian family counseling, in which therapy is used with children and counseling and guidance with the parents, than for any impact on mainstream family therapy developments.

The child-guidance movement in the United States can be regarded as beginning in 1909 with the opening of the Juvenile Psychopathic Institute, a privately supported clinic associated with the Chicago Juvenile Court. The name of the clinic derived from a prevalent idea of the time, namely, that behavior problems were caused by individual pathology. Neurologist William Healy, a towering figure in the movement, founded the institute with a 5-year grant that he had obtained in order to establish a definitive program of research among delinquent youngsters. The purpose was to secure knowledge that could be used to stem delinquent behavior tendencies in adolescents. Since Healy's task was to study individual delinquents and to treat their behavior problems, the institute included both a research project and a clinic. It soon demonstrated its value to the court and attracted judges from juvenile courts around the United States who traveled to Chicago to observe and study the work being done at the institute. When the grant expired, the institute's support was assumed by Cook County and the name changed to the Psychopathic Clinic of the Juvenile Court. Subsequently, it became the Institute for Juvenile Research and is supported by the State of Illinois.

Healy moved on to Boston and founded a clinic with the Judge Baker Foundation in 1917. The name of the clinic was changed in 1933 to the Judge Baker Guidance Center. Healy was also instrumental in founding other clinics and in 1929 began a 5-year intensive study with Yale University's new Institute of Human Relations. The focus of the Yale project was investigating ways to deal with seriously delinquent youngsters and their families by means of total situation treatment methods. Healy's early approach had been to work psychotherapeutically with individual children, to reeducate families, and to modify the child's environment with the help of social agencies, schools, and churches (Healy & Bronner, 1948; Levine & Levine, 1970).

Two additional major centers—at the Boston Psychopathic Hospital and the Henry Phipps Psychiatric Clinic at Johns Hopkins Medical School and Hospital in Baltimore—and several smaller programs were in operation by the time the child-guidance movement took full shape in the United States in 1920. Healy's original idea that delinquent behavior came from pathology in the individual had proven to be incorrect. His studies of individual delinquents had demonstrated that an array of forces and not merely individual psychopathology draw the child into antisocial behaviors. By 1920, the problem was seen to be largely a clinical one, and both direct and indirect treatment approaches were being used.

Child guidance got its big boost with the launching of a broad 5-year program for the prevention of delinquency under the auspices of the Commonwealth Fund in 1921. During the years of the Commonwealth Fund's project, demonstration child-guidance clinics were established in several cities, including St. Louis, Los Angeles, Norfolk, Dallas, Minneapolis–St. Paul, Cleveland, and Philadelphia. Some of the agencies have lasted until the present, while others, such as the St. Louis clinic, did not survive. With the termination of the demonstration project in 1926, the Commonwealth Fund arranged for the National Committee for Mental Hygiene to continue providing assistance to cities wishing to establish such clinics. The field consultation work of the project spawned clinics in Richmond, Milwaukee, Cincinnati, Louisville, New Orleans, Houston, and elsewhere (Stevenson, 1948).

Originally the child-guidance clinics served a low-income population and were designed to modify parts of the community and to provide a therapeutic service. In some respects, they came to resemble today's community mental health clinics as they evolved into treatment facilities that worked with persons from various income levels (Levine & Levine, 1970).

Training of professionals to work in child-guidance programs was one of the major objectives of the Commonwealth Fund project. For a 5-year period, the Fund financed the Bureau of Child Guidance established at the New York School of Social Work in 1921. Not only was the bureau founded to study and treat children with behavior problems but also to train psychiatric social workers to work with youngsters. At the end of the 5-year period, the bureau was replaced with a more elaborately organized and equipped Institute for Child Guidance that also aided in training by providing fellowships for psychiatrists, psychologists, and psychiatric social workers to learn child-guidance methods and techniques (Groves & Blanchard, 1930).

The Philadelphia Child Guidance Clinic, which is today perhaps the best-known such facility to family therapists, was founded in 1925 as the last such clinic established under the Commonwealth Fund project. Many of the important refinements of the concept of professional teamwork and professional interaction within the child-guidance model were manifested in the operation of the Philadelphia clinic. Gradually, the early emphasis on what the staff needed from parents in order to do their job with the children shifted to a focus on what parents and children needed from the clinic in order to secure the help they required. The basic function of the clinic came to be regarded as providing a service for a parent and an emotionally disturbed child. By the time that such a shift had occurred, the work of the clinic was seen to be essentially clinical, although research and training were considered parts of its work from the beginning and have continued to be part of its mission (Allen, 1948).

During the period from 1922 through 1933, the child-guidance movement literally swept the United States. As Lowery (1948b) has pointed out, clinics for children and their problems were founded under many sponsorships and names. Nevertheless, the majority of the emerging clinics followed the prevalent pattern, in which the treatment was conducted by a clinical team composed of a psychiatrist, a clinical psychologist, and a psychiatric social worker (today the term "clinical social worker" would be used). Direct and indirect treatment approaches were used in the early Commonwealth Fund period. In direct treatment, the psychiatrist worked directly with the child, using any pertinent medical measures; the psychologist worked directly with the child using remedial tutoring; and the social worker provided recreational activities. Indirect treatment was primarily under the leadership of the social worker, who worked with the parents to allay ignorance and change attitudes, mobilized community resources to meet the casework needs of the child and family, worked with schools along with the psychologist, and made special placements when necessary (Lowery, 1948b). It was probably 1930 before the direct treatment of the child rather than environmental manipulation by nonclinical agencies was the major focus of treatment (Stevenson, 1948). The essential point in the child-guidance plan of organization was not the introduction of any new treatment technique but the formation of the clinical team of psychiatrist, psychologist, and social worker.

An important outgrowth or concomitant of the concern with the kinds of issues that were involved in the child-guidance work was the formation of the American Orthopsychiatric Association (AOA). Psychiatrist Karl A. Menninger contacted 26 psychiatrists in late 1923 and organized a meeting at the Institute for Juvenile Research in Chicago in January 1924. The group decided to publish the journal that is now the *American Journal of Orthopsychiatry* and, 6 months later, held a second meeting at which William Healy was elected the first president (Lowery, 1948a).

By 1984, the AOA membership directory classified its members under 25 primary discipline codes ranging from anthropology and art therapy to music therapy and nursing and on through speech pathology and vocational rehabilitation and others, in addition to the original trio of psychiatry, psychology, and social work. The directory also listed 27 major practice codes, including early childhood and women, marriage counseling, addiction, abuse/violence, and cross-cultural issues. The AOA has been an important organization in the promotion of child and family therapy through its journal and annual conferences in particular.

Since the 1920s were the period in which the psychoanalytic movement took root in the United State, it is understandable that psychoanalytic procedures came to dominate the work of many clinics (Lurie, 1948). By the 1940s, the criteria used to determine whether direct treatment—usually of a psychoanalytic nature or some adaptation—was to be used with the child included such factors as the treatability of the parents, the age of the identified patient (i.e., the older the child, the more likely direct treatment was to be perceived as necessary), and an assessment of whether manipulation of the environment alone could be used to alleviate symptoms (Gerard, 1948). The 1930s and 1940s witnessed a continuous evolution of treatment methods as direct treatment of the child came to occupy a larger role and then settled into more of a balance with environmental emphases. Among the techniques mentioned in the literature were psychoanalysis, play therapy, release therapy, group therapy, relationship therapy, supportive therapy, and attitude therapy (Lowery, 1948b). Psychoanalysis originally offered little help in understanding crime because psychoanalysts had not been working with criminals (Karpman, 1948), but understanding crime became much more a part of the treatment picture as the child-guidance movement evolved and changed emphases.

One of the early treatment points of view was that because some children came from unsatisfactory home situations and had lost the security of parental acceptance, they were left particularly vulnerable to noxious community influences. Therefore, a primary treatment effort was directed toward improvement of parent–child relationships. Other early views were that as parents were able to work out their own problems with the assistance of social workers and to become better adjusted personally, they would be able to meet the personal and emotional needs of their children and that outside supports could help. To support this approach, therefore, recreational, camp and related experiences were provided to the child (Groves & Blanchard, 1930).

Several developments occurred fairly quickly as the child-guidance clinical movement expanded. It became apparent that educational work with parents, primarily mothers, was not especially helpful to them in dealing with their children. Parents themselves were discovered to be in need of help. Child guidance in many clinics thus gave way to direct treatment for the mother. Although it evidently did not occur in any simple one-to-one fashion, the discovery that mothers could have difficulties of their own soon became linked to holding them responsible for their children's problems. This represented quite a swing away from the early individual pathology orientation and the accompanying strong emphasis on environmental factors. Mothers were soon being blamed in many quarters for the problems of their children and for being noxious influences in their offspring's life. Maternal overprotection, in which mothers either indulged or dominated their children, was blamed for creating psychological problems in the youngsters (Levy, 1943). The concept of the schizophrenogenic mother (Fromm-Reichmann, 1948) was another example of blaming the mother.

At the very same time that the mother was being seen as responsible for the child's problems and in need of help for herself, the father of the child generally was being ignored. Using statistics from a child-guidance clinic, Burgum (1942) showed not only that fathers were being left out of treatment but also that this omission might be related to the high dropout rate that was being encountered with other family members. Jackson and Satir (1961) later pointed out that child analysis had not been able to deal as effectively as originally hoped with neurotic and psychotic children and used the Burgum data as part of an argument for a family therapy approach to dealing with the problems of disturbed children.

Family therapy did not, however, make an early debut at child-guidance clinics. During the period immediately following publication of Burgum's paper, group therapy was used with parents in some settings, although often as an adjunct to individual therapy with them. In the middle 1940s, on an experimental basis, the Council Child Development Center in New York City offered group therapy for parents. One reason was that the available professional resources could not provide individual therapy for each mother and each father in the program. As part of the approach, the staff made a careful psychosocial appraisal of the family as a group (Ackerman, 1956).

Sessions that included the whole family were used occasionally in child-guidance work at London's Tavistock Clinic by John Bowlby, an English psychiatrist and psychoanalyst, on an experimental basis. As described by Bowlby (1949), such "joint" interviews were preceded and followed by individual interviews, and the individual interview continued to be the treatment method used. Bowlby did not follow through to adopt the family as the focus for treatment, although his use of the occasional family session played an interesting role in the adoption of family sessions as the sole method of interviewing by John Elderkin Bell, as we shall describe later in this section.

Certain long-term developments in child-guidance work prepared the way for the emergence of family therapy in both direct and indirect ways. Experience began to demonstrate that treatment of a child alone was not sufficient to produce the needed changes. It also was necessary to alter the family in which the child lived and participated. Originally, the child-guidance workers began to move beyond the child to the mother–child relationship and, eventually, to recognize, at some places and clinics at least, that fathers also needed to be involved in the treatment.

Still other developments occurred, as noted by Nimkoff (1934):

The success of the child guidance clinics, of which there are now about 700 in the United States, has furthered the establishment of clinics devoted primarily to the treatment of marital discord. The child guidance clinic treats the behavior problems of children; thus indirectly it deals with parent–child problems and even husband–wife difficulties.

Still, there is need for more direct attacks upon marriage problems. . . . The kind of family experience a child has depends more than anything else upon the kind of experience his parents have together. (pp. 231–232)

Further developments were recognized a few years later by Groves (1940):

Thus the marriage counselor is making his contribution to the present tendency in services for children by interpreting each problem as the expression of a complexity of environmental and personality influences. The work carried on by the child specialist in like fashion is influencing the counselor as he tries to handle what on the surface seem to be a difficulty of a husband or a wife, but which, when given sufficient analysis, is often found to have ever widening implications. No progress during the past decade is more promising than the realization of the sizableness of marital problems and the significance of the parental element, either potentially or actually present. (p. 80)

The salience of the marital relationship for the children in the family was recognized at the service level in a few places around the country in subsequent years, for example, in a "tax supported marriage counseling service in behalf of children" offered by the Juvenile Welfare Board in St. Petersburg, Florida, beginning in 1949 (Finck, 1962).

By the 1950s, parents were being seen together for work on the parental relationship in some child-guidance clinics. Staff from the Guidance Center of Buffalo reported at a 1956 meeting that they had been doing this kind of work for the past 5 years (Hallowitz, Clement, & Cutter, 1957). At the same time, Nathan Ackerman (1937), a child psychoanalyst in the child-guidance movement, had published a paper on the family as a social and emotional unit and was asking questions about whether the entire family could be treated. Establishment of the Council Child Development Center, as noted, in 1946, with Ackerman as director, provided him with the opportunity to begin experimenting and trying to answer his questions about whether such an approach could be devised. Ackerman's interests at the time appear to have been primarily to gain an opportunity to put psychoanalytic principles to work in a mental health clinic for preschool children and their families (Ackerman, 1956). In doing so he was following in the footsteps of Sigmund Freud whose handling of the "Little Hans" case has been referred to as the first instance of both child analysis and family therapy (Bloch, 1973).

Ackerman moved explicitly into family therapy during the 1950s, wrote *The Psychodynamics of Family Life* (1958), which has been called the first textbook on family therapy, and founded the Family Institute in 1961. In 1961 he cofounded the journal *Family Process*. The depth and breadth of Ackerman's contributions to family therapy can be seen at least partially in *The Strength of Family Therapy: Selected Papers of Nathan W. Ackerman* (Bloch & Simon, 1982). Ackerman remained staunchly psychodynamic in outlook and his death in 1971 removed one of the major proponents of that orientation from the family therapy field. After his death, the Family Institute was renamed the Ackerman Institute for Family Therapy and Donald A. Bloch succeeded him as director.

Another major pioneering figure from the child-guidance movement has been psychologist John Elderkin Bell. Though some speakers have indicated that Ackerman deserved the title "founding father of family therapy," if it were appropriate and accurate to name individual inventors for family therapy, Bell would have as strong a claim as anyone. While visiting London in 1951, he misinterpreted a casual remark of a colleague and concluded that Bowlby was experimenting with group therapy with families. As noted previously, in reality what Bowlby had done was to use an occasional meeting with the entire family as an adjunct to individual psychoanalytic therapy. Nevertheless, on the basis of his misunderstanding, Bell determined to try to treat behavior problems in children with family group therapy as the sole method of treatment, and began doing so later that year.

Family group therapy is regarded by Bell (1975) as an application of small-group psychology to the natural group of the family. Following presentation of a paper at the annual meeting of the Eastern Psychological Association in 1953, Bell became perhaps the single most influential figure in the early days of the family therapy movement (Erickson & Hogan, 1972). His public health monograph, *Family Group Therapy: A New Method of Treatment for Older Children, Adolescents, and Their Parents* (Bell, 1961), was the first handbook of family therapy (Beels & Ferber, 1972). In it he declared that all children 9 years or older and all other adult family members living in the home should be included in family therapy and should be present for all sessions. The material in the book had been developed much earlier. Bell also taught what was probably the first graduate level course on family therapy at the University of California, Berkeley, in 1963 (Stanton, 1975). From 1968 until 1973, Bell was director of the Mental Research Institute in Palo Alto, California, one of the major centers in the branch of the family therapy movement that was conducting research into schizophrenia. Recently, he constructed a new paradigm for family therapy, which he named "family context therapy." The basic aim of that approach is to modify the family environment, rather than to treat the family directly (Bell, 1978).

Another major family therapy figure who emerged from the child-guidance field was Salvador Minuchin, who worked at the Wiltwyck School for Boys in New York during the 1960s and later was director of the Philadelphia Child Guidance Clinic. His first book, *Families of the Slums* (Minuchin, Montalvo, Guerney, Rosman, & Schumer, 1967), developed out of work with delinquent black and Puerto Rican boys from the slums of New York and out of concern also for their families. Structural family therapy, foreshadowed in that book, was more fully developed after 1967, when Minuchin went to Philadelphia, where Jay Haley from California and Braulio Montalvo joined him. One of the more influential approaches to family therapy in the United States, structural family therapy focuses on the here and now and on altering the power structure, functioning, and communication of the family. Minuchin and associates have also made contributions in other areas, including the understanding and treatment of eating disorders. During the decade that Minuchin was director, the Philadelphia Child Guidance Clinic increased in size from 12 to nearly 300 staff members (M. Nichols, 1984).

Social learning theory has also contributed to the treatment of children and adolescents. Perhaps the most important work in the area of childhood disorders and family intervention from the social learning perspective has been done in the research program conducted by Patterson and associates at Oregon over approximately 2 decades (Gurman, Kniskern, & Pinsof, 1985). Parent management training, which involves teaching parents such social learning principles as pinpointing problem behavior, contingency contracting, reinforcement, punishment, and extinction, has been demonstrated to be particularly effective by the Oregon group. Gurman and colleagues (1985) have summarized five major trends that have emerged in the findings of the group:

1. Parent management training has been demonstrated to be superior to no treatment and the effects have been maintained at follow-ups of up to 18 months.
2. The home interventions have been accompanied by changes in the child's school behavior.
3. There have also been significant alterations in nontargeted behaviors in some reports.
4. Parent management training focused on one child has also reduced the deviant behavior of siblings who were at risk for conduct disorders.
5. Increases in mothers' self-esteem and reduction of maternal psychopathology also have been found.

Although there are remaining questions about other factors that influence outcome of interventions beyond the use of parent management training— for example, severe marital disorder, father absence, low socio-economic status, and others—Gurman and associates (1985) have concluded that no other form of intervention has been so thoroughly investigated or has shown such favorable results.

Related research on family therapy with delinquent juveniles and their families has been done by Alexander and colleagues in Utah. The treatment used was functional family therapy, an approach using such behavioral techniques as contingency contracting and modeling and cognitively oriented paradoxical reframing methods. Although the work was largely done with Mormon families that can be assumed to have stronger emotional ties and a more definitive hierarchical organization than many other types of families, and the results have not been replicated elsewhere, the findings are nevertheless impressive (Gurman, *et al.*, 1985).

Child-guidance work and thinking affected clinical work in a wide number and variety of settings throughout the United States and elsewhere. Many approaches to treatment today still use essentially a child-guidance orientation, rather than an explicit family therapy model, in mental health centers and social work agencies.

SCHIZOPHRENIA AND THE FAMILY

Efforts to understand and treat the schizophrenic constituted the third major development leading to the emergence of family therapy. Regarded by some, although not all, family therapists as *the* root of family therapy, this area has received extensive attention in the literature. As there are a number of accounts of historical developments in this area available for the student (e.g., Guerin, 1976; M. Nichols, 1984; Schultz, 1984), our account of the development of family therapy will focus on research about and treatment of schizophrenic persons and their families as part of the background out of which family therapy evolved.

In describing part of the base out of which family therapy arose, Jackson and Satir (1961) referred to important developments in the 1920s and 1930s in the work of Marino, Sullivan, and Beaglehole. J. L. Moreno and others made important contributions in group therapy that certainly had some impact on the subsequent emergence of family therapy. They began to use group therapy with hospitalized patients in 1920, analyzing interaction between individuals in the group and interpreting the interaction in terms of motivation.

Sullivan (1927) published a report on his outstanding work with hospitalized schizophrenics that had definite family implications. Observing the transactions between hospital personnel (physicians, nurses, and aides) and the patient, Sullivan noted that the patients improved when staff members responded to them in ways that were different from those they had come to expect as a result of experience in their family of origin. Patients, according to Sullivan, perceived the staff as an extension of their family and reacted to and dealt with staff in the same way that they did with their family. The "hospital family" therefore was seen by Sullivan as possessing important potential for aiding in the patient's improvement.

As a result of the publication of Beaglehole's research in 1939, family and culture began to be viewed in terms of their possible contributory roles in the occurrence of schizophrenia. Beaglehole (1958) had completed a 10-year study in New Zealand in which he compared the incidence of schizophrenia in two very diverse groups, the native Maoris and whites. The differences were large enough to highlight the possibility of family and cultural factors being etiological agents in the difficult and complex phenomenon of schizophrenia.

Efforts to understand and treat the stubborn and severe mental and emotional disturbances grouped under the general heading of schizophrenia, along with earlier developments in the marriage counseling/marital therapy and child-guidance branches, demonstrate the phenomenon of independent invention and discovery. Clinicians and researchers around the United States were working on similar problems during the early 1950s, generally without knowing that others were doing similar work.

Carl A. Whitaker, noted for his pioneering work with schizophrenic patients and their families, also had a background in working with children in a child-guidance format and with delinquent adolescents in a residential setting. Following such work with children and adolescents in Louisville, Kentucky, he moved in the early 1940s to Oak Ridge, Tennessee, where, in conjunction with John Warkentin, he began introducing family members into therapeutic sessions and doing cotherapy. Both moved to Emory University in Atlanta, Georgia, in 1946, and Thomas Malone joined them in 1948. From 1945 to 1965 Whitaker treated schizophrenics with aggressive play therapy. He and his group experimented with a variety of ways to treat such patients and their families.

Whitaker, originally trained in obstetrics and gynecology, did not have a background in psychoanalysis. Exposed to Rankian influences during his Louisville years, he developed an approach known both as existential psychotherapy and symbolic–experiential family therapy. His approach has been widely demonstrated in workshops and conferences around the United States and elsewhere. Whitaker's contributions are reflected in part in the edited work entitled *From Psyche to System* (Neill & Kniskern, 1982).

Whitaker and associates, together with professionals from Philadelphia, including John Rosen and others, conducted a series of 4-day weekend conferences on the treatment of schizophrenia. The tenth conference (1955), held at Sea Island, Georgia, included Gregory Bateson and Don D. Jackson. Whitaker also published one of the first significant papers on conjoint marital therapy (1958), in addition to being one of the first who brought together other individuals working with family issues for the purpose of sharing their techniques and discoveries (Guerin, 1976). The Whitaker group left Emory in 1955 and went into private practice in Atlanta. Whitaker moved to the University of Wisconsin in 1965 and stayed there until his retirement.

Another pioneering clinician in the family treatment of severe disturbances was Christian Midelfort, who by 1981, in more than 30 years of practice, had seen more than 300 families with a psychotic member (McFarlane, 1983). At the Lutheran Hospital in LaCrosse, Wisconsin, Midelfort worked with and used relatives of psychiatric patients in much the same way that Albert Schweitzer did in Lambarene as early as 1946. Although Midelfort gave a paper on his family therapy techniques and experiences at the 1952 American Psychiatric Association meeting (Midelfort, 1982) and published *The Family in Psychotherapy* in 1957, he has remained largely unrecognized, except by a few, for his groundbreaking therapeutic work.

Much more attention has been given to the work of researchers and clinicians located in the more populous and visible parts of the United States and in the mainstream of professional activity. Among the more highly visible contributors were Theodore Lidz and associates, Lyman C. Wynne and associates, Murray Bowen, the Palo Alto group, and Ivan Boszormenyi-Nagy and associates. Certain of the researchers, notably Lidz and Bowen, appear to have been particularly affected by psychoanalytic theory and the then current notions of symbiosis and pathogenic parents. The 1940s and 1950s witnessed a large number of studies on pathological family interaction (Zuk & Rubenstein, 1965).

Lidz, while at Johns Hopkins in Baltimore in the early 1940s, had become interested in the families of schizophrenics. In contrast to much of the early focus on so-called pathogenic mothers, Lidz determined that the father's functioning was often as deleterious to the child as the mother's behavior and attitudes (Lidz & Lidz, 1949). Subsequently, the father in a family with a schizophrenic member became the focus of research (Lidz, Cornelison, Fleck, & Terry, 1957a). After moving to Yale University in 1951, Lidz and his colleagues began studying a small group of hospitalized schizophrenics and their families. He declared that it was not merely the psychodynamics of one parent but that of both that resulted in a pathological family system that produced schizophrenia in a youngster. Disruption of generational boundaries so that marital partners competed for their children's loyalties was one of the major events observed in disturbed families. Concepts of marital schism (in which distance and hostility prevailed between the parents) and marital skew (in which the wife/ mother tends to be destructively domineering) were developed (Lidz, Cornelison, Fleck, & Terry, 1957b). Lidz began to share reports of the Yale work in the mid-1950s, particularly at national professional meetings in 1956 and 1957. *Schizophrenia and the Family* (Lidz, Fleck, & Cornelison, 1965) was a significant outcome of the work of the Lidz group.

Bowen similarly followed a psychoanalytic tradition, beginning his early work by treating psychotic children. He worked at the Menninger Foundation in Topeka, Kansas, from 1946 to 1954. In 1951, Bowen arranged for mothers of mentally ill children to live in the hospital setting with them. After he joined Lyman Wynne at the National Institute of Mental Health in Bethesda, Maryland, in 1954, Bowen started a research project in which the families of hospitalized schizophrenic children lived in the hospital, and he brought seven such families in between 1954 and 1959. Initially he used separate therapists for each family member, but he soon began to use family therapy as the sole therapeutic treatment for families coming into the hospital. Bowen presented reports of his research in the spring of 1957, at two national professional meetings that some family therapists regard as the symbolic beginning of the family therapy movement. In 1959, Bowen moved to Georgetown University, where he continued to do research and treatment, refine his theory, and train others in his particular approach to family therapy, variously called Bowenian systems theory and family system theory (Kerr, 1981).

Bowen's ideas and development are spelled out in a series of papers published under the title *Family Therapy in Clinical Practice* (Bowen, 1978). His major concepts have been the nuclear family emotional process, the family projection process, the scale of differentiation, triangles, multigenerational transmission process, emotional cutoff, and societal regression (Kerr, 1981). Although his therapeutic techniques have changed considerably over the years, one of the hallmarks of Bowen's therapy has been his emphasis on the role of the therapist as "coach." In that approach, the therapist not only serves as a role model for individuals in their process of differentiation from their family of origin but also facilitates their efforts to go back home and deal directly and in person with the family (American Association for Marriage and Family Therapy, 1984). Helping individuals to go home in person in order to differentiate themselves contrasts with the approach used by other family therapists, who encourage or require clients to get their parents and siblings to come in for a few family of origin sessions. Both approaches are, of course, aimed at resolving problems that individuals have carried over into their present lives from their original family relationships.

Lyman C. Wynne brought a slightly different perspective to the study of schizophrenic individuals and their families. Trained originally as a psychiatrist, he subsequently obtained a doctorate in social psychology at Harvard, where he was influenced by the family systems ideas of the sociologist Talcott Parsons. Early in his career, Wynne worked with Eric Lindemann, the pioneering student of grief reactions among family members. In 1947 Wynne first worked with families, instead of just with individuals. When he went to the National Institute of Mental Health in 1952, he began working intensively with families of disturbed patients. Following the influences of Parsonian social psychology, Wynne concentrated primarily on the role relationships and communication disturbances in families with a schizophrenic member. Along with his associates he developed a number of concepts, including those of alignments and splits in families, pseudomutuality, the "rubber fence," and others that were published primarily in book chapters and a series of papers (Singer & Wynne, 1963; Singer & Wynne, 1965a, 1965b; Wynne, 1961; Wynne, Ryckoff, Day, & Hirsch, 1958; Wynne & Singer, 1963a, 1963b). Wynne moved in 1971 to the University of Rochester, where he continues to be a prolific publisher of articles on family relationships and on the research on and treatment of schizophrenia. He is one of the few researchers on the topic of the family and schizophrenia who has continued to do research in that area. In 1982, Wynne was the first recipient of the American Association for Marriage and Family Therapy's Award for Distinguished Contributions to Research in Family Therapy. Wynne has not developed a "school" or practice based on his work as have some other leaders in the field.

The Palto Alto group emerged from a different background than the other early researchers on schizophrenia and the family did. Gregory

Bateson, an anthropologist and philosopher at Stanford University, was the catalyst for the early Palo Alto work. In 1952, he received a foundation grant in connection with the Veterans Administration Hospital in Menlo Park, California, for the purpose of studying patterns and paradoxes in communication. By appointing Jay Haley and John Weakland to work with him, Bateson was able to secure their backgrounds in communication and anthropology respectively. William Fry, who had just completed his residency in psychiatry, was added a few months later. The project lasted until 1954, when the grant expired and was not renewed.

Narrowing their focus and securing a grant from a different foundation, the group began to study schizophrenia. Don D. Jackson, who had just completed a residency in psychiatry at Chestnut Lodge in Maryland where he had been influenced by the late Harry Stack Sullivan and other interpersonalists, was brought into the new project as a consultant in connection with the treatment of schizophrenics in 1954.

At the beginning of the work with schizophrenics, the two major concepts used were the double-bind and family homeostasis (Jackson & Weakland, 1959). Bateson, Jackson, Haley, and Weakland (1956) introduced the concept of the double-bind in a classic paper entitled "Toward a Theory of Schizophrenia," which was offered as a systematic explanation for schizophrenia. A double-bind would consist of a parent sending two messages at two different levels, with one message being disqualified by the other message at another level. Theoretically, a double-bind requires six ingredients: (1) two or more processes in operation; (2) repeated experiences; (3) a primary negative injunction; (4) a secondary injuction, conflicting with the first at a more abstract level; (5) a tertiary negative injunction prohibiting the victim from leaving the field; and (6) a victim who perceives the world in double-bind positions (American Association for Marriage and Family Therapy, 1984; Bateson *et al.*, 1956). Widely hailed in the early years, the double-bind theory today is recognized as not being peculiar to families producing schizophrenics and thus not necessarily an etiological factor in that disturbance. At the time that the schizophrenia project ended in 1962, the group agreement included the statement that "in schizophrenia the double-bind is a necessary but not sufficient condition in explaining etiology and, conversely, is an inevitable by-product of schizophrenic communication" (Bateson, Jackson, Haley, & Weakland, 1963).

"Homeostasis" refers to a dynamic state of a system in which one or more variables are highly stable. For example, the dynamic interplay in a family, during marital conflict or a child's asthma attacks, and the family harmony that occurs while the parents cooperate to take care of their sick child may be quite stable, repetitive, and, hence, homeostatic. Some of the evolving family therapy literature posited an internal mechanism or force within the family that served to maintain its stability and preserve the status quo. Today, most theorists agree that stable functioning arises spontaneously from the ongoing interaction of family members with one another and with their environment. Thus, environmental changes, as in the case of effective therapy, will disrupt the family's homeostatic functioning (American Association for Marriage and Family Therapy, 1984). Both of the concepts, the double-bind and homeostasis, continued to be of major significance in the Palo Alto group's family work (Jackson & Weakland, 1959).

Jackson reported on the schizophrenia project at a national psychiatric meeting in 1957 where he met Ackerman, Bowen, Lidz, and Wynne. The Palo Alto group had come upon family therapy almost accidentally and had not been aware that family therapy was being used elsewhere. As Jackson and Weakland (1959) described it, the group wished to observe the communication and behavior of schizophrenics outside the hospital in a natural habitat and thus turned to the families of the patients. As they conducted their research and talked directly with families with a schizophrenic member, the team members quickly found themselves experiencing pressures from the families for help. So the work in family therapy began, although there had been no clear plans to provide treatment at the outset of the research project.

In 1959, with private financial backing, Jackson founded the Mental Research Institute (MRI) as a division of the Palo Alto Medical Research Foundation. MRI's purpose was studying schizophrenia and the family. Virginia Satir and Jules Riskin joined Jackson. In 1961 Jackson published a paper in which he argued that conjoint family therapy was superior to individual therapy with family members (Jackson, 1961). The Bateson project was awarded a National Institute of Mental Health grant to study schizophrenics and their families as part of the Medical Research Foundation but separate from MRI. Jackson continued to serve as consultant to the project. Also in 1961, Jackson, along with Ackerman from New York's Family Institute, jointly agreed to sponsor a new journal, *Family Process*. The journal began in 1962 with Haley as editor. When the Bateson project closed in 1962, Haley and Weakland moved to MRI. In 1961, Satir began training therapists at MRI with grant funds and continued to provide training there until 1966. Her influential book, *Conjoint Family Therapy* (1964), and the workshops and demonstrations she conducted both while she was at MRI and after she moved to Esalen in Big Sur, California, were instrumental in popularizing the Palo Alto version of family therapy and making Satir the best-known exponent of family therapy (Group for the Advancement of Psychiatry, 1970). MRI continues as a significant center for the treatment and study of family therapy. The early emphasis on communication was subsequently supplemented by the opening of a brief-therapy center in 1967.

Haley, as noted earlier, joined Minuchin at the Philadelphia Child Guidance Clinic in 1967. Haley has been one of the more prolific contributors to the literature of family therapy (Haley, 1962, 1963a, 1963b, 1967, 1971, 1973a, 1973b, 1980; Haley & Hoffman, 1967). His name is most closely associated with strategic therapy, a form of brief family therapy (Stanton, 1981). Most recently, Haley has been at the Family Institute of Washington, D. C.

Ivan Boszormenyi-Nagy and associates at Philadelphia, the last of the family therapy pioneers to be considered here, came essentially out of a psychoanalytic background and has maintained an "intensive therapy" orientation with his associates in Philadelphia. He founded the Eastern Pennsylvania Psychiatric Institute (EPPI) in Philadelphia in 1957 and served as director of the family therapy project there while fulfilling other positions as a psychiatrist. In the early years of EPPI's study of schizophrenia and the family, Boszormenyi-Nagy was joined by psychologist James Framo, psychiatrist David Rubenstein, and social worker Geraldine Spark. Psychologist Gerald Zuk joined EPPI in 1961.

Boszormenyi-Nagy and Framo edited *Intensive Family Therapy* (1965), which quickly became one of the more important books in the field. Fifteen authors, including Ackerman, Bowen, Whitaker, Wynne, Warkentin, and Zuk, wrote original contributions that reflected the field of intensive family therapy as they saw it at the time. Boszormenyi-Nagy and Bowen strongly distinguished intensive family therapy, based on psychoanalytic principles and aimed at reconstructive change in individuals and the family group, from supportive family therapy, aimed at clarifying communication, altering interaction patterns, and facilitating the family's ability to cope with concrete stress situations.

In the late 1960s, Boszormenyi-Nagy became more intensely interested in the importance of transgenerational relationships and the possibilities they hold for working with patients. His book *Invisible Loyalties*

(Boszormenyi-Nagy & Spark, 1973) remains one of the more important sources for transgenerational approaches to therapy. His orientation to family therapy, currently labeled "contextual family therapy" (Boszormenyi-Nagy & Ulrich, 1981), represents one of the major schools of family therapy of the day.

Framo, who started seeing families and couples in 1958, has been more of a marital therapist than a family therapist per se in that he has tended to work primarily with couples. Use of family of origin sessions, in which he sees adults with their parents and siblings as an integral part of therapy, has become a salient feature of his work. Framo has also been instrumental in bringing the object relations theory of Fairbairn and its marital therapy applications developed by Dicks (1967) to the widespread attention of therapists in the United States. Framo's selected papers have been published under the title *Explorations in Marital and Family Therapy* (1982).

Zuk, who organized the first national meeting of experienced family therapists in the United States in the fall of 1964, has contributed a half-dozen concepts from his work in therapy, most of which have been tested through research (Garrigan & Bambrick, 1975, 1977a, 1977b, 1979). The best-known concepts are the go-between role, the celebrant role, and the side-taking role of the therapist. Zuk's work has been explicated in a series of papers and book chapters and in two books (Zuk, 1975, 1981). He is the founding editor of the *International Journal of Family Therapy*.

Other members of the EPPI group were Albert Scheflen and Ray Birdwhistle, who made important contributions to communications theory through the micronanalysis of behavior during therapy sessions, and Ross Speck, who served an internship there and later developed social network therapy (Speck & Attneave, 1973).

In the eyes of some observers (McFarlane, 1983), the high hopes for family therapy as a method of successfully treating schizophrenia do not appear to have been borne out. While it certainly has enjoyed its successes, some would call for its use as part of a broader approach in which more attention is given to biological and constitutional factors than to family interaction and transmission and in which medication and chemical treatment play a primary role (McFarlane, 1983). Certainly, that point of view is far from universal. Refinement of concepts and continuation of efforts to provide understanding of the role of the family through research are still being conducted.

Wynne (1981), in a review of current concepts about schizophrenia and family relationships, has called for continuing research and has made some striking observations on other research and treatment issues. Among the research requirements, according to Wynne, are a continuing need for direct empirical studies that could assess the interaction of genetic and environmental effects in the same families and for studies of families with different role structures—for example, single-parent versus two-parent families—and with different racial, ethnic, and social class backgrounds. Wynne has also made the point that "one should not assume that family variables have the same contribution to the origin and onset of schizophrenia and to its course and outcome" (p. 88). A supportive family system— and the accompanying social network—can be very helpful in making noninstitutional community care of schizophrenics successful, just as an emotionally overinvolved or critical family environment and faulty family communication patterns can precipitate relapse on the part of the patient. Wynne (1981) makes the final point that "although clarification of the possible etiological contributions from the family environment is surely important, such evidence certainly is not required, or hardly relevant, to the obvious need to provide educational and therapeutic support for the family" (p. 88).

In brief, questions about the family's role in the etiology of schizophrenia may not be as important as questions about the family's role in the course and outcome of the difficulty. Family therapy may be helpful in treatment of schizophrenia, regardless of whether the family played a significant role in its onset. Also, it well may be that family therapy has been made possible for dealing with a variety of other disorders and difficulties as a result of the unfulfilled hopes of those who in the early days saw it as a panacea for dealing with schizophrenia. As Winston (1978) has noted, "In retrospect, it is ironic that the family treatment of schizophrenia has probably been the least successful of the range of difficulties treated by family therapy techniques" (p. 32).

Family treatment of schizophrenia has continued to evolve, however. Since 1975, a number of different family approaches—psychoeducational, behavioral interventions, strategic, and systemic—have been devised. These, along with the older multiple family therapy approach, differ significantly from other orientations in that they appear to have significant effects on the schizophrenic process that go beyond those of drug treatment. Also, with the exception of the systemic approach, they widen family systems theory to include factors outside the family (McFarlane, 1983). McFarlane goes on to say that "while the old paradigm saw the task as making the family normal, the new may require the emergence of somewhat abnormal family processes, such as keeping emotion at a low level, artificially simplifying communication, and establishing age-inappropriate control over the patients" (p. 10).

THE CURRENT PICTURE

As family therapy has evolved and become a significant part of the therapeutic world, there have been several attempts to classify the leading family therapists in the United States and the emergent schools of family therapy. Beels and Ferber (1972) separated several of the leading clinicians of the time into "conductors" and "reactors," for example, and Foley (1974) ranked some of them according to how they dealt with eight specific dimensions of therapy. We see little value at this time in attempting to classify family therapists as such. The field has become much larger and more significant than individual figures. Also, classifying therapists on the basis of their orientation always involves some degree of artificiality. Some individuals fit more into one classification and others change their orientation during the course of their career.

The more recent attempts to categorize or classify the different schools fare somewhat better than efforts to place individuals or to describe the field in terms of individuals, but even that kind of classification involves some ambiguity and difficulty. Nevertheless, for the purposes of illustration, we shall give three recent classifications of schools of family therapy and the order in which they appeared.

Guerin (1976) distinguished between "psychodynamic" and "systems" approaches, each of which had a number of subtypes, making a total of seven approaches or schools. Under the psychodynamic he included the *Individual*: dynamically oriented therapists who occasionally see families; *Group*: John Bell, Lyman Wynne, and C. Christian Beels; *Experiential*: Carl Whitaker and Andrew Ferber; and *Ackerman-type*: Nathan Ackerman, Norman Ackerman, and Israel Zwerling. Under the systems rubric were placed *Strategic*: Jay Haley, Don Jackson, Paul Watzlawick, and John Weakland; *Structural*: Salvador Minuchin; and *Bowenian*: Murray Bowen.

Madanes and Haley (1977) grouped the approaches into six categories: *Psychodynamic*: focuses on individual personalities and emphasizes the past; *Experiential*: focuses on family and emphasizes emotional expe-

rience in the therapy session; *Behavioral Family Therapy*: based on learning theory and derived from individual psychotherapy and emphasizes
modification of specific behaviors in the present; *Extended Family*: focuses
on family by either bringing members together in one group or sending
clients home to see family of origin; *Strategic Family Therapy*: focuses on
communication in the present and uses directives from the therapist to
change behavior; and *Structural Family Therapy*: focuses on patterns of
interaction in the present and also is derived from communication theory
as is the strategic approach.

Gurman and Kniskern, editors of the widely used *Handbook of
Family Therapy* (1981), classified approaches to family therapy under four
broad headings: "psychoanalytic and object relations," "intergenerational," "systems theory," and "behavioral." Different authors described
from two to five different forms or approaches under each of the broad
frameworks. Under psychoanalytic and object relations approaches appeared the work of Robin Skynner and Clifford Sager; under intergenerational, the work of James Framo, Ivan Boszormenyi-Nagy (contextual),
Carl Whitaker (symbolic–experiential), and Murray Bowen (family systems); under systems theory, the work of the Mental Research Institute
(interactional), structural family therapy (described by Harry Aponte and
John Van Deusen), strategic (described by M. Duncan Stanton), functional (described by Cole Barton and James Alexander), problem-centered
systems theory (described by Nathan Epstein and Duane S. Bishop), and
integrative family therapy (Frederick and Bunny Duhl); and under behavioral approaches, chapters on behavioral parent training, behavioral marital therapy (by Neil Jacobson), and behavioral sexual therapy.

Another way of describing the development of the field and evaluating the work and contributions of family therapists is through the influence that they have exerted through their writing and publications, whatever their particular orientation. How often an individual is cited in the
writings of researchers and others is one way of assessing the value
attached to his or her work by other professionals in the field. While not
all of the value attached to the works may be positive, frequent citation
may be still regarded as a mark of influence. Several studies have been
made using the Social Science Index as a method for ascertaining the
frequency with which writers in the field are cited during a particular time
period. Four groups of influential figures have been identified: the first-
generation pioneers who published the important sources between 1950
and 1970 (L'Abate & Thaxton, 1980); the first-generation "second wave"

authors, composed of individuals who were born between 1929 and 1939 and who had their major works published after 1970; the second generation leaders who were born in 1940 or later (Thaxton & L'Abate, 1982); and the family therapists whose writings were cited in 1980 and 1981.

Identified as the first-generation pioneers were Ackerman, Bell, Boszormenyi-Nagy, Bowen, Framo, Haley, Jackson, Hans Peter Laqueur, Robert McGregor, Minuchin, Patterson, Satir, Stierlin, Watzlawick, Whitaker, and Zuk. Patterson was the most widely cited of the group by a large margin for the period 1969–1979, followed by Watzlawick and Minuchin (L'Abate & Thaxton, 1980). The first-generation "second wave" authors were Billie S. Abeles, Arthur Bodin, Vincent D. Foley, Ira Glick, Irene Goldenberg, William I. Halpern, Richard E. Hardy, Charles H. Kramer, Luciano L'Abate, Shirley C. Luthman, James F. Masterson, James K. Morrison, William C. Nichols, John C. Papajohn, Robert Ravich, David G. Rice, Jules Riskin, Melvin Roman, Uri Rueveni, Rodney J. Shapiro, Samuel Slipp, Ross Speck, John Sonne, James M. Stedman, Peter Steinglass, Herbert S. Stream, Max Sugar, Robert P. Travis, Alvin W. Winder, and William D. Winter (Thaxton & L'Abate, 1982). The second-generation authors were Donald E. Davis, Sandra Coleman, Allen Frances, Alfred P. French, Alan Gurman, Theodore Jacob, James E. Jones, Kenneth E. Kressel, Barbara Margolin, Thomas W. Miller, David H. Olson, Bruce B. Peck, Jack F. Santa-Barbara, and Howard Stein (Thaxton & L'Abate, 1982). For the 1980–1981 period, the major authors cited in the Index were Patterson, Haley, Minuchin, Watzlawick, Gurman, Bowen, Jacobson, Pattison, Liberman, Selvini-Palazzoli, Stierlin, R. L. Weiss, Wynne, Olson, and Satir (Textor, 1983).

No summary of the present status of family therapy would be complete without reference to the current role of family therapy research in the field. Gurman *et al.*, (1985), whose recent account furnishes the major basis for this discussion, have characterized the role of research in family therapy historically as going "from turning points to consolidation." Briefly, they have described the early beginnings of the family therapy wing of the marital and family therapy movements as coming from clinical research into schizophrenic processes in families (i.e., by the Yale, Palo Alto, and National Institute of Mental Health groups). During the early days of the 1950s, there was a basic fusion between research and therapy (we have noted that therapy arose almost incidentally or accidentally during the course of research by the Palo Alto group). There followed, however, a period of approximately two decades in which family therapy and family research went their different ways, creating a significant research–practice gap in the field (Wynne, 1983). Efforts to reunite the two endeavors were not particularly successful during the 1960s and research appeared to lag behind its early promise.

The first major reviews of research on the two wings of the field were published in the early 1970s (i.e., Wells, Dilkes, & Trivelli, 1972, on family therapy, and Gurman, 1973, on marital therapy). Both reviews, however, were based on data from such qualitatively poor research that they contributed very little to the field in terms of either practice or health care policy materials.

Publication of two reviews of outcome research in 1978 by Gurman and Kniskern (1978a, 1978b) marked the beginning of a reemergence of research as a significant and evidently permanent part of the family therapy field. One of the articles (1978a) involved the review of more than 200 outcome studies and clearly established the efficacy of marital and family therapy. Pinsof's (1981) work, which reviewed process studies (i.e., studies on what happens during the course of therapy, as opposed to outcome studies), also constituted an important step forward in the field. Thus, by the 1980s, there seemed to be no question about the efficacy of family therapy. Questions about efficacy appeared to have been sufficiently resolved and a need demonstrated for more research into change processes and mechanisms in systematically oriented family therapy.

The recent consolidation of research into the family therapy field involves several practical developments that have not only insured its place through the creation of institutes, the establishment of colloquia and consortia to deal with conceptual and methodological issues pertaining to continued empirical research, the provision of organizational recognition and awards for outstanding research, but have also assisted in the movement toward a new and more appropriate epistemological stance among family therapy researchers. Epistemology is that branch of philosophy that concerns itself with the origins, nature, methods, and limits of knowledge (American Association for Marriage and Family Therapy, 1984) and is generally used in the family therapy field to allude to how we know what we know. Adoption of an epistemological stance in which ideas of objectivity in research are replaced with the notion that the knower and what is known are inseparable and influence one another and in which linear causality (A causes B causes C, etc.) gives way to circular causality (patterns in which there is feedback and mutual influence among variables) requires the use of different research orientations and methods from those used in traditional research approaches. A concern with how the parts of what is being studied are connected means that the researcher is committed to studying not only the structure but also the process of the problem under study.

The most recent and comprehensive review of research (Gurman et al., 1985) addresses such philosophical issues as those mentioned and others currently under debate in the field. The authors call for a systemic perspective on human behavior processes to be used in family therapy research. The review also deals with the efficacy of family therapy for specific kinds of clinical disorders/problems and populations, the efficacy of the major schools of family therapy, questions pertaining to change, the present state of process research, the training of family therapists, and the relationships between research and practice in family therapy. The authors list 44 reviews of family therapy research published between 1970 and 1985. Covered in the reviews are various approaches to marital and family therapy, marital enrichment programs, marital communication skills training, parent effectiveness training, premarital counseling, and divorce therapy. During recent years, research reviews have been published at an increasing rate; approximately half the reviews that are cited have appeared since 1979.

Among the major findings, conclusions, and observations offered by Gurman and colleagues (1985), as we have freely adapted and interpreted them, are the following:

• Approximately 71% of the cases of childhood and/or adolescent behavioral problems treated by any one of several well-defined family therapy approaches or eclectic methods can be expected to improve.

• Almost no evidence has been offered on the efficacy of the "systemic" family therapies (e.g., Family Systems Therapy, Strategic Family Therapy, and the Milan Model) for schizophrenia. Current data would, by default, favor the use of psychoeducational approaches.

• Conjoint couples treatment in groups may be the preferred method for alcohol-involved marriages and may be superior to individual therapy of the alcoholic spouse.

• Nearly all studies of the effectiveness of conjoint marital therapy for affective and anxiety disorders among adults have involved behavioral therapy and have challenged the assumption that such symptoms should routinely be reframed as systemic functions.

• Studies of nonbehavioral marital therapy would support the use of conjoint marital therapy over "individual" therapy for marital problems.

Even though the research has some methodological problems, the data provide a defensible rationale for public policy decisions in favor of marital therapy. They do not offer clincians much help with specific decisions in everyday practice.

• Research on behavioral marital therapy shows that it may be more effective with younger couples and those who manifest evidence of continuing commitment and caring. On the basis of empirical evidence, the authors disagree with others' conclusions that behavioral marital therapy is equally effective to systemic or psychodynamic marital therapies.

• Mediation has received the strongest and most consistent support of those major forms of "divorce therapy" that have been investigated empirically.

• With regard to preventive intervention techniques, a common finding has been the appearance of rather short-lived "highs" among the couples participating in a variety of enrichment experiences. Researchers have recommended that distressed couples be more carefully screened out of encounter programs, that leaders of such groups be trained in crisis intervention techniques, and that referral to follow-up marital therapy be done as needed.

• When family therapy methods have been rigorously tested, they have been found to be effective, although proponents of the major "schools" have provided little or no empirical evidence of the effectiveness of their therapy (an interesting "impressionistic estimate" of the effectiveness of 14 marital and family therapies for specific disorders/problems is given by the authors).

• No *direct* research evidence exists that proves that training experiences in marital and family therapy increases trainee effectiveness, but there are indirect, suggestive indications of such effectiveness.

• With regard to the assessment of change, too little attention has been given to the study of therapeutic process in family therapy and researchers continue to use inappropriate measures. There is a need for assessing change from multiple perspectives.

• Treatment outcome studies should routinely include evaluations of system-level variables and these should be evaluated with regard to their hypothesized linkage with and relevance to presenting problems.

• The authors call for a new conceptual understanding of research process, which includes study of small "chunks" of therapy in which there is elucidation of the relationship between process and outcome variables that are closely linked in time, attention to the psychotherapeutic alliance between therapist and clients, and use of instruments that seek to measure specific interventions at specific points with patients who present specific problems.

• Very little process research has been conducted in family therapy.

• Research findings should be presented in forms that make sense to clinicians.

• Family therapy research is done for both political reasons pertaining to public policy and for scientific reasons aimed at improving understandings of how people change.

An example of the latter point is furnished by the argument of Russell and colleagues (Russell, Olson, Sprenkle, & Atilano, 1983). They have argued that family therapy research "linking family system functioning with individual symptoms via an analysis of their functional consequences for the family and using that foundation to organize both treatment and outcome evaluation" (p. 11) is greatly needed. They claim that such a strategy would help in the discovery of whether linking system dynamics more explicitly to therapy is more cost-effective and efficient than basing treatment on symptoms only. In addition, they view the maintenance of the dual system *and* symptom focus through stages of diagnosis, treatment, and follow-up evaluation as a challenge for the next decade.

The present picture with regard to professionalization, including the status of organizations, journals, licensure/certification, service delivery, education/training, and related matters, will be addressed in Chapter 10.

SUMMARY

The roots of family therapy are many and varied. In addition to the mainstreams that we have described briefly, group therapy, Gestalt therapy, transactional analysis, encounter group approaches, and psychodrama, among others, have contributed techniques to family therapy. Group therapy and family therapy remain separate fields. Families, which have a history and intimate ties stretching over generations, are very different from ad hoc groups of strangers assembled for therapeutic purposes. Some of the differences have been illustrated in empirical research (e.g., Strodtbeck, 1954, 1958). Family interaction can only be understood in terms of the family's history (M. Nichols, 1984).

Our discussion certainly has not included all of the influential figures, but it has illustrated the variety of backgrounds out of which major and representative individuals came to family therapy. As Hoffman (1981) has pointed out, the early researchers and clinicians who worked with family groups and who all focused on the family as a social system came from varied backgrounds. Some, for example, Lidz, Bowen, and Boszormenyi-Nagy, were from a background in psychotherapy. Others, for example, the Palo Alto group (with the exception of Jackson), came from a background much more influenced by communications theory, cybernetics, General System Theory, and related developments from the scientific world than from experiences in psychotherapy.

Other influential figures who should be mentioned include research psychiatrist John Spiegel, whose publications and organizational activity greatly influenced psychiatry, and Otto Pollack, a sociology professor who was concerned with applying role concepts to the diagnosis and treatment of the family. As early as 1949, Pollak served as a consultant to the Child Guidance Bureau of the Jewish Board of Guardians in New York City, where he was acquainted with Ackerman. He later had contacts that evidently contributed to the thinking of Satir, Bowen, Harold Lief, and others in the marital and family therapy field.

Parloff (1961) has described three stages leading to the emergence and development of family therapy as a method of study and treatment. The pattern he has described is essentially accurate for psychiatry. In stage one, during the zenith of psychoanalytic orthodoxy, contact was discouraged and virtually forbidden between the analyst and members of the patient's family because it was thought that such contact would contaminate the patient–therapist transference and countertransference relationship. The second stage was concerned with the study of the negative effects of the behaviors of significant persons such as mothers. The third stage was concerned with an increasing emphasis on the influence of culture and current life experiences on human personalities, as spelled out in the theories of Harry Stack Sullivan, Erich Fromm, Karen Horney, and Erik H. Erikson. At the same time, new techniques, such as Moreno's psycho-drama, were diminishing concern about the possible deleterious effects on transference and countertransference of involving persons besides the therapist and the identified patient in the treatment situation.

Another way of looking at the general developments, viewing things much more broadly than from the perspective of psychiatry, shows that the development of methods for dealing with problems of marriage and family life proceeded essentially as follows: First, individual counseling and psychotherapy were seen as the approach of choice for such difficulties. Second, it was seen as possible to treat marital discord by dealing with the two partners directly and, subsequently, by dealing with their interaction and transactions as well as with their individual personalities. Third, after many years of treating families in piecemeal fashion, it finally was deemed possible and, later, desirable in many cases to see the entire family unit together and to regard the family as the context of treatment regardless of the number of persons present for interviews. By the 1950s, all three methods—individual, marital, and total family—were seen as valid approaches by different groups of clinicians. In some senses, each approach still has its own adherents, devotees, disciples, and apologists.

Recently, there has been an increasing movement in the direction of convergence. As Lief (1980) has put it:

Until recently, marital and family therapies were not received warmly by psychiatrists who placed great emphasis on intrapsychic processes and who tended to look down on the nonmedical therapists engaged in marital and family therapy.

Today, marital and family therapy are going through a process of convergence. . . . conceptually the merger of the two fields has great merit.

The conceptualization of marital and family therapy depends on a systems approach, which incorporates psychodynamic, communication, and behavioral concepts. The unification of these approaches is based on the belief that relationships are at least as important in human behavior and therapy as are intrapsychic events. (pp. 240–241)

The task of combining approaches that include two bodies of knowledge, personality dynamics and multipersonal systems dynamics, is not complete. As the 1970 Group for the Advancement of Psychiatry report on family therapy noted, "The thorough integration of these two system levels into a comprehensive theory is a long-range task" (p. 565).

CHAPTER TWO

An Approach to Family Therapy: Systems and Systems Thinking

Jay Haley, in giving a theory-oriented history of the development of family therapy, has been quoted as saying that until the mid-1950s, therapists thought that in order to bring about change they needed to center on the "ideas" that people had. That is, the therapist used an intrapsychic approach. Haley termed this a "vertical model," meaning that the therapist had to penetrate "deeper" or farther down into the psyche of the person in order to change ideas and, consequently, to alter behavior. The focus changed during the 1960s, first to how people communicate, and, subsequently, to how they organize, according to Haley. The move was from an intrapsychic to a systems approach.

However the advent is described, systems perspectives and systems thinking have emerged as major conceptual and practical changes in the scientific and clinical worlds in the 20th century. This is not to imply that all scientists and all therapists use systems perspectives and think in systems terms. That certainly is not the case. However, systems orientations do occupy a preeminent position in the field of family therapy, although the task of integrating systems and other orientations into a workable blend is very much an issue facing family therapists, as we have indicated.

One of our purposes in this chapter is to set forth a systems perspective that will help the reader to "think systems," to begin conceptualizing more explicitly and more effectively in systems terms. Rather than posing a dichotomy between "depth" psychodynamic historical orientations and systems orientations, we hope to introduce the reader to an integrative family therapy approach in which historical, interactional, and existential perspectives all have a place and blend into a coherent systemic framework for study and treatment.

This chapter is divided into three sections. The first provides an introduction to General System Theory (GST) and some of its salient concepts, and also sketches the background out of which GST arose. We feel that in order to view a family as a system it is necessary to know something about systems theory in general. We do not attempt to apply GST specifically to families, but to examine families as systems, using those parts of GST that do have relevance for the study and treatment of families. The third section describes some of the important facets and issues inherent in taking an interactive approach to family therapy.

GENERAL SYSTEM THEORY: AN INTRODUCTION

GST's emergence represents, as we have noted, one of the major conceptual and practical changes in the scientific and clinical worlds in the 20th century. Although named by the eminent biologist Ludwig von Bertalanffy, who made significant contributions to the concepts, GST emerged from long-term evolutionary developments. Many persons in several different scientific fields were working on similar conceptions when von Bertalanffy published his concept of GST in 1945. Consequently, his ideas found widespread acceptance in the scientific world, where the major research orientation previously had been that of mechanism/reductionism.

A brief sketch of the background out of which GST emerged is helpful in understanding the significance of this new approach to scientific work, which soon became accepted as a major new orientation to clinical work as well.

For some 1900 years, Western thought tended to be dominated by Aristotelian teleology. "Teleology" is variously defined as the study of final causes, as the fact or quality of being directed toward a definite end, and as a belief that natural phenomena are determined by an overall purpose in nature. When Aristotle's view of nature was combined with medieval theology and ethics, the basis for the scientific outlook of the Middle Ages was established. Founded on both reason and faith, this organic world view carried as its major goal understanding the meaning and significance of things, rather than prediction and control as in later scientific approaches. The Aristotelian/medieval outlook generally discouraged the

empirical study of natural phenomena and the formulation of explanations of other than a teleological nature.

Beginning approximately with the 17th century, a new scientific
approach developed. Variously referred to as Galilean, Cartesian, and
Newtonian, this mechanistic outlook ruled Western scientific thought and
explanation for the next 300 years. According to mechanical theory,
everything in the physical world is governed by the inexorable laws of
mechanical or linear causality. Galileo's (1564–1642) major contributions
included his emphasis on an empirical approach to nature and his use of
quantification, that is, studying nature mathematically. Descartes (1596–
1650) made significant contributions to the general framework of science
with his view of nature as a machine governed by exact mathematical laws
and with his analytic method of reasoning in which ideas and problems are
broken into pieces and arranged in logical order. Newton (1642–1727)
effectively synthesized the work of Galileo, Descartes, and others and
provided the mathematics for the mechanistic view of nature. Newton's
invention of differential calculus gave physics a mathematical basis for
measuring natural phenomena and behavior and completed the Scientific
Revolution, and Newtonian physics provided the model to be followed. As
the mechanistic viewpoint became solidly established, physics became the
basis of all the sciences (Capra, 1983).

Mechanistic/analytic thinking became the scientific approach. The
scientist's goal became that of reducing reality into ever-smaller units in
order to determine the causes of individual events or units. Scientists
attempted to discern the rules or laws governing the parts and then to
understand the complex phenomena as a result of understanding the
elementary parts. That approach has been characterized briefly as "the
whole is nothing more than the sum of its parts" (Beavers, 1977, p. 11).
The best-known example of the resultant linear thinking probably is the
stimulus response explanation in psychology. A leads to B, B leads to C, C
leads to D in a chain of linear causality. Reductive analysis thus became
the operational procedure used in the physical sciences. Eventually, it
became evident that reductive analysis is not appropriate for use in certain
instances. Analytic procedures, for example, are not applicable to situations in which the actions or behaviors are not linear in nature. Some parts
of reality are not explained as a result of efforts to reduce them to ever-
smaller units.

The breakdown of what we are calling the classic mechanistic/reduc-
tionist outlook began in the 19th century with the discovery of evolution in

biology and with other developments that pointed to the inadequacies and shortcomings of the Cartesian–Newtonian views of the universe. The major blow came, however, early in the 20th century, with the introduction of two theories that focused on the nature, function, and relationship of objects. Einstein's revolutionary theory of relativity and further developments in physics that resulted in quantum theory became a major part of scientific explanation. These developments spelled the end of the reign of the mechanistic view of the universe as the only way of explaining and dealing with nature. Newtonian physics was joined by a new physics embodying a world view using holistic, organic, and ecological concepts. This systemic approach set the stage for the development of GST (Capra, 1983).

While these scientific developments were occurring, another factor was evolving. This was the emergence of organismic theories in several different fields. Organismic theory calls for the study of the organizing principles or relationships that result when the entire entity is taken into consideration. This approach obviously is very different from a reductionistic perspective in which isolated parts of processes are studied. Reductionism deals with parts in isolation. Organismic approaches focus on the entire entity and on the relationships that result from the dynamic interaction of the parts of the whole. Any organism is considered as a living system. Goal-directed behavior, including growth and creativity, can be considered and accounted for by the dynamic interaction among the components of the living system.

At the risk of being repetitive, we note again that GST arose in the biological sciences as a result of attempts to provide better and more appropriate explanations of natural phenomena. Linear thinking had some definite and demonstrable effects and advantages. By relying on a series of linear cause-and-effect occurrences, one could predict outcomes by linking such sequences, or one could start with an event and work backward until a basic cause was discovered. However, such an approach left many things unexplained. Frequently, much of the phenomena being studied had to be left out of consideration in order to predict outcomes or find beginning causes (Steinglass, 1978). Life phenomena, living things, do not yield easily to study under the analytic methods of the physical sciences (Rapoport, 1968).

As GST theory developed, organization rather than reductionism came to be regarded as the unifying principle in science. Briefly, "the whole is different from the sum of its parts" is a systems approach. That is, when parts or components are examined separately, the results or findings cannot simply be added together in order to determine what the whole will look like. The whole must be examined as a whole, as a system, rather than as the sum of a number of parts.

Parenthetically, we would like to note that the emergence of GST did not render previous scientific work invalid. There are still uses for reductionistic work in modern technology. The point is that neither reductionistic thinking nor systems thinking should be accepted as the only possible way of regarding the world.

The early work of von Bertalanffy in biology led him to adopt the organismic principle. This means that organisms are organized things and must be regarded as such by scientists. Subsequently, he began to lecture and write about GST in an attempt to provide a theory that would account for systems and organization in general. By the time he made a published presentation of GST following World War II, von Bertalanffy found that parallel developments were appearing in cybernetics, information theory, game theory, decision theory, typology or relational mathematics, and factor analysis (von Bertalanffy, 1968). To some extent, the phenomenon of independent invention was functioning in the area of scientific explanation as systems approaches were emerging in several different areas simultaneously. Nevertheless, it was von Bertalanffy who developed GST and led the way in introducing its concepts to the psychiatric and psychological world in particular. At the same time, he noted that there were many organismic developments in psychiatry that could be traced back to Adolph Meyer and that in American psychiatry and psychology organismic/systemic approaches could be found in the work of Goldstein, Menninger, Grinkler, Carl Rogers, Arieti, Gordon Allport, Maslow, and Brunner (von Bertalanffy, 1968). Similarly, Gregory Bateson (1980) was dealing with human life in terms of a systems approach when he emphasized "the pattern which connects" (p. 8). Sullivan (1953), the interpersonal psychiatrist, was using a kind of systems approach when he defined personality as "the relatively enduring pattern of recurrent interpersonal situations which characterize a human life" (pp. 110–111).

Concepts for Family Therapy

The new organismic world view introduced such relevant concepts for family therapy as "systems," "organization," "ecology," "open systems," "complexity," "positive feedback," "negative feedback," and "negative entropy." We shall make no attempt to define all of the important concepts found in GST, but shall give some attention to a few that have the most relevance for systems thinking and family therapy (see American Association for Marriage and Family Therapy [1984] for a glossary of family therapy terms). The following definitions of GST concepts serve both to introduce the reader to their salient meanings and to provide an in-context glossary of terms used throughout this book.

System

A system was defined by von Bertalanffy as a set of elements standing in interaction. Others have referred to a system as something that is put together in such a way that whatever affects one part of it affects other parts. GST involves a search for "general structural isomorphisms" (Gray & Rizzo, 1969, p. 7).

We have described the family as a system whose various members and subsystems interact much like the organism of the human body, with its ongoing interaction of organs, blood flow, and nerve endings, does. An injury to a portion of the body summons the resources of the entire organism to combat the danger and ensure survival, just as stress experienced by a member or subsystem of the family requires adjustment and accommodation of the remainder of the system. For example, when a member of the family is injured, the entire family system may flock to the hospital, change their schedules, and otherwise help and give indications that they are affected by that member's difficulty.

Organization

This is to be considered the first concept among the concepts of living systems. As Steinglass (1978) has put it, "If a *system* is defined as a set of units or elements standing in some consistent relationship or interactional stance with each other, then the first concept is the notion that any system is composed of elements that are *organized* by the consistent nature of the relationship between the elements" (p. 305).

The organization of the family defines its basic structure—its coherence and fit. It tells us how the various members and subsystems are arranged in an interactive field. A family may be organized, for example, around a rigid, dominant male head, his compliant and passive wife, and a group of either rebellious or compliant children.

Subsystem

A subsystem is part of a system that carries out a particular process in that system (Miller & Miller, 1980). The major subsystems identified within the nuclear family, for example, are spousal, parent–child, and sibling. The individual also may be considered a subsystem within a family system. We regard a marriage as both a system in its own right and as a subsystem of a family.

Subsystems have their own organization, boundaries, and interactive patterns. The marital subsystem is composed of husband and wife; the parent–child subsystem, of the parents and children; and the sibling sub-system, of the children in the family. The children will have their own patterns of relating, their own rituals, and their own difficulties and competences as a sibling subsystem.

Wholeness, Boundaries, and Hierarchies

These are key notions within the concept of organization (Gurman & Kniskern, 1981). *Wholeness* has to do with seeing patterns rather than with reducing entities to their parts in a reductive fashion. For example, the family system may be described as "depressive" as a result of observations of the enmeshing characteristics of the system, rather than of observations made only of an individual member's reactive depression or of other individual characteristics.

The concept of *boundaries* describes who is to be included within a certain system and the quality of the interactive process and feedback that occurs with other related systems. Boundaries serve to regulate the flow of information and feedback to the systems so that a family with "closed" boundaries would allow limited information to come in and would restrict the outward flow of information. An isolated family that had little to do with outside systems would be described as one with relatively closed boundaries. Clinically, it might not provide much helpful descriptive information.

The concept of *hierarchy* refers to the fact that living systems have several different levels in which the simpler, more basic system levels compose the more advanced and complicated higher level systems. Miller and Miller (1980) have indicated that seven such levels may be conceptualized easily in living systems: cells, organs, organisms, groups, organizations, societies, and supranational systems. In the family, the "simpler" individual, spousal, parental, and sibling subsystems compose the more complex nuclear family system that is part of the even more complex intergenerational system.

Open Systems

A living system is relatively open. That is, it exchanges information and other material with the environment, with other systems in the environment. The relatively open family system not only processes information freely but also allows its members to come and go within a balance of both protecting and engaging mechanisms. The school, the community, the church, and various other groups influence and are influenced by a relatively open family system.

Closed Systems

A closed system would be one in which there was no exchange with the environment and the system components were not influenced by the environment. Families are relatively open or relatively closed. As noted or implied above, a family that maintains a very low interchange of information and interaction with the schools, or the workplace, or other parts of the community would be described as a relatively closed family system.

Living systems exist in a "steady state" rather than in a state or condition of equilibrium or homeostasis. In a steady state, there is a combination of homeostatic and viable or adaptive mechanisms operating. This concept is difficult to illustrate clearly, but a clinical example would be a family in which the fluctuations between behaviors that would maintain the status quo and actions that would deal with new challenges in the environment keep the family system going in a kind of dynamic tension. A family, for example, struggles to maintain desired family participation and behaviors on the part of its teenage members at the same time that it permits them to leave the family unit to be with their friends and to adopt behaviors that are different from those of the family elders and even from those of the younger children. Viability, which refers to spontaneity, growth, creativity, and general capability of living, is necessary for the system's survival. We can also refer to the steady state as the means by which the organism maintains the disequilibrium that produces growth and development while continuing as a viable organism.

Equifinality

This is an important characteristic of the steady state. Equifinality refers to the fact that the same results can be obtained by different means and by starting from different beginning points. The nature of the systems' organization determines the outcome. For example, there is no single kind of "good parent" subsystem that will produce healthy children. Westley and Epstein (1970) found that healthy offspring come from families with healthy parents as well as from families with disturbed parents. Equifinality is related to "circular causality" and the fact that feedback may cause changes in a process and provide corrective mechanisms that make it unnecessary to proceed from a beginning point to a predetermined outcome in a mechanistic fashion. "Linear causality," by contrast, results in the ability to reach only a given conclusion as a result of starting from a particular beginning point, e.g., A leads to B. The concept of equifinality has immense practical value for clinicians in that one may start from any one of several different points in many cases or use any one of a variety of different methods, techniques, or approaches in order to obtain a desired result. It obviously is quite different from a mechanistic, reductionist approach in which, for example, a given symptom would be considered derived from a particular earlier condition or cause and treatable only by dealing with that presumed prior cause.

Feedback

The concept of feedback means that there are two channels carrying information in such a fashion that one loops back from the output to the input, feeding back into the system information that affects succeeding outputs from the system. The understanding and use of feedback loops has shown the way away from the old deterministic/teleological debate in which there had to be predetermined outcomes. Systems can have both deterministic and goal-seeking characteristics that can be explained in terms of self-correcting behavior on the part of the system through the use of feedback (information). In a family, the children's socialization experiences in school provide new incoming data that the total system must process and attempt to accommodate to and adjust to adequately. In a relatively closed system, of course, the feedback from the school may be perceived as threatening and potentially dangerous in that it threatens to pull the children away from the family system.

Feedback may be either negative or positive. "Positive feedback" makes things change. The positive feedback loop may even set up a runaway situation in which the system moves beyond its limits of functioning and self-destructs. Positive is not to be interpreted here as desirable but merely as descriptive of a feedback loop that increases deviation in a system and causes change. Clinicians sometimes encourage the use of positive feedback in ways that are intended to break up the existing system or patterns of relating and behaving. "Negative feedback," in contrast to positive, provides information that decreases the output deviations and helps to achieve and maintain stability in relationships (Watzlawick, Beavin, & Jackson, 1967). Negative feedback, in short, cancels errors and helps to maintain a steady state in systems. This, also, is a concept frequently used by family therapists in their interventions that are aimed at stabilizing systems. The study of methods of feedback control, "cybernetics," is a significant part of GST.

Negative Entropy (Negentropy)

This concept is the opposite of the idea of "entropy," a major concept in thermodynamics that holds that over time, there will be a gradual loss of energy. The degradation of energy occurs because over time, heat energy cannot be converted into an equivalent amount of work. As such change occurs, the system becomes disorganized and even chaotic. In contrast to entropy in a closed system, an open, living system secures energy through an exchange with the environment. This leads to an increased degree of organization and more complex patterning. The concept of negentropy is essentially the same as that of "information." The influx of information into a system provides a kind of "energy" that leads to the reduction of uncertainty within the system, and thus helps the system to become increasingly organized and complexly patterned, rather than becoming disorganized and perhaps chaotic (Steinglass, 1978). For example, a family that is isolated from its context and has very little interaction and communication with its community may become suspicious, fearful, and disorganized.

Nonsummativity

The family system cannot be understood merely by summing up the attributes or characteristics of the individual members, although characteristics partially determine the nature of the family. As noted, the family as a whole is different from the sum of its parts and one must attend to the pattern, not merely to the parts. A clinician who separately interviewed five members of a family, for example, would not get the same picture, the same understanding and comprehension of the family, that the clinician would who brought the five members together and observed them in interaction.

Communication

All behavior is considered communication, since one "cannot not communicate." Communication defines relationships and establishes roles in the family system through the setting of rules. The transactional nature of the family system, including verbal and nonverbal communication, shape the behavior of members of the family. Patterns of communication among family members and with external sources are indicative of the relative openness of both internal and external boundaries. For example, the manner in which family members organize themselves around a dinner table or seat themselves in a therapist's office defines boundaries, hierarchies, coalitions, and triangles. The look of a parent toward a child or the tone of a wife's voice in addressing her husband are indicative of roles, rules, and moods.

Stability and Change

Feedback loops that bring information and other forms of input into the system operate so as to promote both stability and change in the system. Families are thus self-regulating in that any input that affects a member is modified during the process of feedback. Family stability is maintained by means of negative feedback mechanisms and family change is brought about through positive feedback mechanisms in the most simple explanation of stability and change. In most cases, change in a system is a result of accommodation to new input. The change may at times be dramatic but is usually gradual, often with a step forward followed by a step sidewise or backward.

Structure

Two very important concepts that we use with our students and that we shall emphasize in succeeding chapters are structure and process. Structure can be defined in several different ways, for example, as in the common dictionary meaning of the "arrangement or interrelationship of all the parts of the whole" or "the manner of organization." The Millers'

(1980) emphasis on the structure of a living system as "the arrangement of its parts in space at a given moment in time" is important, as is their notation that structure refers to the arrangement of both subsystems and components, and that a structure may be either fixed or changing.

Process

As defined by Miller and Miller (1980), process refers to change over time and includes the ongoing functions and history of a system. Again, as with the structures of a system, process may involve one or more subsystems. As we use the term, process describes an organic-like quality that undergoes movement, growth, and change. Erikson's description of an epigenetic principle in individual developmental theory provides one example of a process, although it is much more narrow than what we think of when we talk about family process. Similarly, we are not using process to refer simply to the movement through various life cycle stages or substages, as the concept is employed in some textbooks.

The processes or functions in a living group such as a family may be subject to change; that is, they may be reversible. A living system carries its history with it in the altered structures of the system and the consequently altered functions (Miller, 1969). In human groups, communication or information exchange and processing is an exceedingly important process, contributing, as noted above, to change in either positive or negative directions. "Process," of course, is a neutral term and may refer to desired change or undesirable change, depending on the values of the viewer.

Steinglass (1978) distinguished between process and structure as follows: "Organization or patterning observed along a spatial dimension is called structure. Patterning along a temporal dimension, on the other hand, is referred to as process or function" (p. 317).

In subsequent chapters, we shall spell out more clearly and completely the meaning of structure and process as we apply these concepts to the family system.

FAMILY SYSTEM MODELS

There are different ways to begin "thinking systems" and different ways to operationalize systems concepts. We do not intend in this section to describe various therapeutic theories for dealing with families, for example, family of origin, structural, strategic, or symbolic–experiential.

Rather, we shall provide an introduction to a model for approaching families as systems and illustrate some of the ways in which systems concepts can be used in forming models for understanding families.

Various attempts have been made to establish models that can be used in family research, theory, and clinical practice. Two that have involved extensive efforts to integrate the multiple and diverse concepts in family theory and family therapy are the *Beavers Systems Model* (Beavers, 1976, 1977, 1981, 1982; Beavers & Voeller, 1983) and the *Circumplex Model* of Olson and associates (Olson, Russell, & Sprenkle, 1983; Olson, Sprenkle, & Russell, 1979; Russell, 1979; Sprenkle & Olson, 1978). The Beavers Systems Model was derived from clinical practice and associated observation and research. The Circumplex Model was developed from a theoretical perspective. The differing starting points and emphases in the two models have contributed to some differences between them. The authors have continued to work in a cooperative fashion to provide correctives to difficulties perceived or discovered in the models through comparison.

Although the Beavers Systems Model and the Circumplex Model have several conceptual features in common and both are relatively new and require more testing before being considered totally finished products, they also continue to have some significant differences. They both emphasize family adaptability and family cohesion as important conceptual factors in family systems, although they emphasize them in different ways. Beavers relates adaptability to competence and places it on a continuum; that is, the more adaptability and competence the better it is for the family. The Circumplex or Olson model defines adaptability in terms of change, using a systemic concept of change ranging between morphogenesis (continual change) and morphostasis (no change). The goal in such an approach or process is to attain a dynamic balance for the family system between the extremes of morphogenesis and morphostasis. Family cohesion also is regarded as having a curvilinear dimension by Olson. That means that too much cohesion or too little cohesion is not considered desirable for the functioning family system (Beavers & Olson, 1983; Olson *et al.*, 1983).

We find both models helpful, but our preference is for the Beavers model because we think that it more accurately reflects the clinical realities that we see. Furthermore, it seems to integrate systems theory more adequately with family development theory and to offer greater opportunity to incorporate ideas and offerings from psychodynamic theory. The Beavers model, it should be noted, is a model of families, of family organization and family process. It is not a model of family therapy.

The Beavers Systems Model uses a continuum for family adaptability. On the horizontal, adaptive axis of the Beavers model, families can be placed on a continuum from dysfunctional to optimal. There is a negentropic approach. The more negentropic the family—that is, the more flexibility and growth potential actualized—the more the family can function and deal effectively with stressful situations, changing the structures as it needs to do so. As adaptability occurs, there is a complex interaction of morphostatic and morphogenic features. As noted, the Beavers model relates adaptability to competence. The more competence and adaptability the better.

Autonomy, maturity, and degrees of health or illness are seen as falling on such a continuum, from dysfunctional to optimal. An optimal family that is well differentiated will encourage individual family members to differentiate and to develop increasingly higher levels of autonomy. Beavers views differentiation of the self of the individual as an outgoing, infinite search (Beavers & Voeller, 1983).

Family cohesiveness, the second major concept emphasized in both models, is not seen by Beavers as falling along a continuum. Instead, it is construed as curvilinear. Too much or too little cohesion can cause difficulties. Cohesion is dealt with in the Beavers Systems Model along the vertical or family interaction style axis. Families vary between centripetal (directed toward a center) or centrifugal (directed away from a center) features. In centripetal families, members view their relationship satisfactions as coming from inside the family and tend to be held too tightly within their family. They are not adequately "differentiated" or "individuated," to use terms employed by others. Centrifugal families, on the other hand, are characterized by the tendency to expel members, and view their relationship satisfactions as coming from outside the family. The most competent families seek to avoid either extreme and to change as needed in order to meet family members' needs, for example, becoming more centrifugal as the offspring move toward adulthood and departure from the home.

The Beavers model distinguishes nine types of families: optimal, adequate, midrange centripetal, midrange centrifugal, midrange mixed, borderline centripetal, borderline centrifugal, severely disturbed centripetal, and severely disturbed centrifugal families.

The model deals with cross-sectional approaches to families and does not deal with historical–multigenerational data, although it could be integrated with such data. Similarly it appears to be highly adaptable to a theoretical–clinical orientation meshing family development and the developing competence of its children as they move toward increased autonomy.

The materials that we have described here from the models illustrate ways in which the family can be viewed as a system and refer to ways in which systems concepts can be applied to the understanding of families. As Beavers notes, capable families approach relationships with an intuitive systems understanding, appreciating the interchangeability of cause and effect, for example, recognizing that harsh discipline causes rebelliousness and that rebelliousness brings harsh discipline in a circular pattern of causality. Families that are not tied to rigid behavior patterns have the ability to change and differentiate in a growing manner (Beavers & Voeller, 1983).

SYSTEMIC FAMILY THERAPY

Family therapy is characterized by a number of "schools" or approaches to treatment, each of which tends to be connected with the name of a given individual or treatment facility, as we noted in Chapter 1. The emergence of schools of therapy is an expected, predictable development in the maturational history of family therapy. When any field of thought or practice has been in existence for a sufficient period of time, the theories and techniques in that field will develop to the point that such schools emerge and disciples cluster around the leaders of the schools.

Often the differences among the various approaches are more apparent than real, the similarities greater than the gurus and their followers wish to admit. At other times, there are genuine differences that make it impossible to integrate all of the schools into one single approach or integrated theory. Whatever the realities, the picture often presents itself to the neophyte as one of great complexity and general confusion. Consequently, it is very tempting to identify oneself with one approach and become a dedicated follower of one of "the great men" or major schools of the field. The advice of Hall and Lindzey to students of personality to immerse themselves in one single theory of personality from among the large number available and to branch out eventually has been followed in spirit by many students entering the family therapy field.

We do not give such advice to students or teach in that fashion. Instead, we urge our students to grasp a wide range of concepts and to begin trying to integrate them as best they can from the outset. There is no comprehensive theory of marital and family therapy that embodies all of the relevant concepts, but the absence of such an overarching framework should not drive us to embrace uncritically a limited approach, no matter how attractive, and to freeze our learning endeavors into an explication of the work of a master or a school. As we shall endeavor to illustrate later, the first field to master is family. Therapy comes second.

It is much harder and, yet, much more rewarding and growth producing in the long run to strive to remain open and to integrate as best we can old knowledge and new findings into a constantly developing framework with both solidly established and heuristic elements in it.

As one of us (Nichols) has put it:

For many years I insisted that students, trainees, and supervisees devise their treatment strategies on the basis of theory. My statement, as sincere and straightforward as I could make it, was that I did not need them to follow my path or pattern of treatment. What I asked, and required of them, was that they have a solid and valid reason for doing what they did and that they be able to tell me why they were doing what they were doing. In other words, they had to have a valid and defensible reason for undertaking the particular course of action that they followed. I wanted the theory to come first and insisted that the technique be devised from theory. All of this was particularly important, I felt, during a period in marital and family therapy in which there was tremendous ferment and experimentation, much of it without defensible and rational underpinning.

More recently, we have recognized that few psychotherapists or marital and family therapists operate from a firm, consistent, and comprehensive theoretical base. Rather than having a solid connection between theory and practice and rather than expecting therapists to function on the basis of a complete theoretical underpinning from which techniques are drawn, it is more realistic to expect marital and family therapists to operate on the basis of a set of guiding concepts. For example, there are several GST concepts that can be applied to marriage. Marriage can be described as an organized system characterized to some degree by wholeness and circularity. However, systems theory, as it has been applied to marriage, remains essentially a number of loosely connected concepts rather than an integrated theory of marriage and marital disorder (Steinglass, 1978).

What we expect, therefore, of students, trainees, and supervisees at this point is that they function on the basis of commitment to an understanding of a series of reasonably well-articulated concepts. Those concepts or underlying assumptions should, insofar as possible, be related to theoretical explanations of the phenomena with which they are dealing, as well as to their ethical components and to emotional understanding of themselves and the families with which they are working.

The present state of epistemology with regard to marital and family behavior and marital and family therapy, however, permits only a partial integration of knowledge and incomplete structuring of a basis for explanation and intervention/treatment. In our judgment, only the true believer in a particular approach that blurs the distinctions between differences and ignores alternative explanations is able to put together a theoretical approach that is complete and consistent. The remainder of us must struggle with the often horrendous task of trying to live with different explanations of phenonema. Not all of the "lumps in the oatmeal" of theoretical concepts can be dissolved so that there is a smooth blend of theoretical understanding.

Rather than having a homogenized blend of theoretical understanding and explanation that covers all of our dealings, we generally are faced with the question of putting together as best we can a series of concepts based on theory, observation, and experience.

The challenge we cast before our students is to steer clear of premature commitment to any single school or set of techniques and to continue the emotional and intellectual struggle to integrate what can be integrated from diverse sources into an ever-deepening understanding of the richly complex phenomena with which we are grappling.

Happily, we are not alone in our wish to integrate concepts toward the development of a more comprehensive approach to family therapy. Although others are not necessarily conceiving the task in the same way as we, there are family therapists seeking to integrate concepts in the field. Framo (1975), for example, has written that he sees "the real task of the psychological sciences over the next century as a deepening understanding of the extraordinarily intricate relationship between the *intrapsychic* and the *transpersonal*" (p. 20; italics added).

Others have attempted to integrate various psychotherapeutic approaches or aspects of such approaches to marital therapy (e.g., Berman, Lief, & Williams, 1981; Feldman, 1979; Gurman, 1978, 1980, 1981b). Most of the attempts have involved efforts to blend psychodynamic approaches or concepts with behavioral and systems concepts.

Recently, still others have begun to develop an integrated approach to family therapy. Included are the Duhls (1979, 1981) and Moultrup (1981).

The latter has noted the advantages of identifying primarily with one school, that is, of having a group with which to identify and exposure to an integrated and reasonably consistent approach to family therapy. He notes that the main disadvantages may be the adherence to a "party line" that ignores data from other schools and the possibility of being unsystematic in deciding what to include in one's approach to therapy.

The systemic approach to family therapy that we teach is not one in which we study the major schools and seek to fit them or various parts of them together into an integrated whole. Rather, we take a much broader and more general approach. We start with the clinical data with which we are faced and deal with it in the light of our general knowledge of family functioning and human behavior. As noted earlier in our "lumps in the oatmeal" metaphor, there are sometimes several equally valid pieces of information available to us that cannot be readily reconciled, so we hold them in our awareness and use them as we can, hoping that eventually we may be able to smooth out some of the conflicts among them. To a significant degree, we function as pragmatists in doing therapeutic work, being quite eclectic in our use of techniques, as we suspect is the case with many therapists.

Our attempt toward integration in family therapy has evolved over the years. We do not try to secure an integrative or integrated family therapy by taking psychotherapeutic approaches originally developed for work with individuals and melding them into one approach to be applied to families. Nor do we seek to apply the same set of techniques and interventions to all families with which we work. As we have long pointed out to our students, therapists have the choice of fitting the family to the treatment or the treatment to the family. Our systemic approach is a prescriptive one in which the interventions are based on our ongoing assessments of the family process, problems, and needs.

We do not model "the way" interventions should be made, but take very seriously the implications of the principle of equifinality, particularly the idea that several different paths may be taken in order to reach a desired treatment goal or outcome. The choice of approach at any given stage in therapy should be determined on the basis of the ongoing assessment and the therapist's ability to take appropriate steps within the constraints and possibilities of the situation, including the therapist's own strengths and limitations.

The systemic family therapy approach that we use and teach our students calls for therapists to think, feel, and act in continually changing and complex patterns as they deal with a family. Therapists, in our judgment, need to be able to think about and understand relevant past events and issues, to think about and respond appropriately to current family interaction, and to be adequately empathic and emotionally responsive to the family and the therapeutic situations with which they are involved. We are concerned with the history of the family, with its interactional patterns, and with its emotional life, all over at least three generations, as well as with our interaction with the family in the current therapeutic situation and relationship.

Conceptualizations remarkably close to those that we have developed over the past decade or more were published recently by Grunebaum and Chasin (1982). The major difference seems to be that their endeavors were produced as a result of efforts to help students who had been taught different theories in their earlier education to integrate such theories as they began to work with families. That is, it seems that their efforts stemmed from trying to help students use concepts previously learned as if they were from "mutually exclusive or incompatible schools of thought" (p. 403) in an integrated way to understand and influence families. Our efforts have involved working with students from the beginning to approach families from the three perspectives: the historical, the interactional, and the existential. We stand rather close to those authors in perceiving that treatment approaches may be based on understanding, transformation (change), and identification, all of these being ways in which learning can occur and behavior change. Generally, all three will be involved to some extent in our work with a given family.

Historical Perspectives

Historical perspectives view family functioning and difficulties in relation to what has happened in the past, either to some member or members or directly to the family as a whole. How did the family reach its present state? Our concern with history is not, of course, a matter of preoccupation with the facts of the past as such. Hence, we do not consider it essential to spend several sessions taking a history except in most unusual circumstances. We are concerned with what needs to be dealt with—past or present—in order to improve the family's current situation and point it toward a better future.

A question frequently used as an opener either with couples or with families is "What brings you here?" Beyond that request for statements of the presenting problem(s), we may do some exploring of what has contributed to the problems in the perspective of the clients and how they have tried to deal with the problems in the past. There are cases in which the uncovering of facts (and attitudes) is exceedingly helpful in eradicating fears, lessening anxieties, and resolving long-standing grief reactions. Families do carry their history with them, even though the members may not be aware of important events and feelings that strongly influence how they live.

As we have pointed out to our clients many times, being aware of something, knowing what has transpired, and dealing with it in therapy does not alter what happened in the past, but it very well may change its impact on the current family system and on the clients' lives. This is particularly true in those instances in which there is an emotional reenactment or other development that permits emotional energy to be released for more productive use in the family system.

Let the reader note that we are not indicating that insight is necessarily a goal in family therapy. In some instances we may decide that an insight-oriented approach is desirable with a particular family or subsystem of the family, whereas in other cases we may consider it preferable to deal with uncovered materials in other ways. What we are indicating is that the review of historical situations and data creates an emotional milieu that helps to connect the family with its living history.

Generally, history is important in family therapy, although to different extents and in different ways with different families. We do not know whether we are behind or in front of those family therapists who omit the historical and dynamic factors in family assessment and treatment, but we certainly are not even with them. Individuals, as well as the historical setting in which they developed and the current context, are part of the important whole with which we must deal.

Interactional Perspectives

We noted in Chapter 1 that family therapy is concerned with change. It is greatly involved with the contemporary interactional patterns of families and particularly with recurrent interactions and structures that are causing problems for the family. The goal is not necessarily to help the family to understand what is going on, although this may be part of the manner in which a therapist tries to reach the goal of transforming or changing the undesirable or dysfunctional patterns of behavior or family structures. Sometimes therapists intervene in ways that bring about systemic change without making family members aware of what they are doing, for example, by means of imposing paradoxical tasks or directives that result in alteration without a direct connection being apparent to the clients.

Of course, some family interaction patterns can be addressed without reference to past events. Securing changes in faulty communication patterns among family members occasionally can be achieved by simple, direct interventions into what is happening in the here and now. Frequently, this involves helping family members to monitor their communication techniques and teaching them how to communicate more effectively and appropriately.

Some family therapists may decide to make a historical examination of patterns of family interaction as part of their assessment and treatment of the problems. Simply by definition, whenever the therapist begins to explore the background of a phenomenon or to trace its development, he or she has at least momentarily adopted a historical perspective and has at the very least implied that what previously transpired is important to understanding and perhaps dealing with it in the present.

Other family therapists may act to effect changes in the present family structure without explicit reference to the past. Minuchin's structural family therapy, for example, is essentially an ahistorical approach. It is directed toward altering, where necessary, current family boundaries, coalitions, affiliations, or heirarchies (Minuchin, 1974).

Existential Perspectives

This perspective refers to the efforts of the therapist to apprehend the emotional life of the family and its members, as well as his or her own emotional experience and reactions when working with the family system. Taking the existential perspective involves being adequately responsive and sufficiently differentiated from the family at the same time so as to be able to carry out the related tasks of being empathic with family members while consciously playing roles and conducting tasks appropriate to the therapeutic needs of the clients.

Taking the existential perspective and joining the system emotionally, understanding what it means to the clients to be a member of their family, and serving as a model for identification, while managing to avoid entrapment in the family is far from easy. Beginning therapists, or any therapist who has not adequately resolved problems of individuating from his or her family of origin will find the varied aspects of dealing with the existential perspective much more challenging and potentially problematic than adopting the historical or interactional perspectives.

Whitaker, in his writings, filmed interviews, and other presentations, has described and modeled very creative and effective ways in which he takes the existential perspective with families. Whitaker's work illustrates how *he* is able to function, not how anyone else may take the existential perspective. He cannot be copied. The part that seems most remarkable about Whitaker's work, and the portion to which we recommend that our students attend, is the way in which this canny and avuncular clinician uses his own personality and understanding of himself to deal with families. He stands as a reminder of the better meanings of the idea that the person of the therapist can be a significant factor in therapy, particularly if one keeps in mind, as Whitaker always seems to do, that one is dealing with a complex living system.

DIFFICULTIES WITH INTEGRATION

There seems to be no simple answer or easy solution to the question of how to teach students to think in dynamic, systemic, and existential terms, and how to blend all of these into an integrated systemic approach. The best that we can do with students is to give them a start. Our own attempts to understand how best to do this and our efforts to implement our understanding will continue to evolve and change.

There is some agreement in the field with our stance that no single theory or school of family therapy can claim superiority in terms of clinical effectiveness and that integration is needed. There also is agreement by some that integration is not an easy task to accomplish (e.g., Liddle, 1982; Pinsof, 1983). As Liddle (1982) has put it, "Systematic eclecticism, or the orderly application of theory and technique from differing but compatible schools of thought, cannot be taken as a simple task" (p. 247). This is illustrated by a recent integrative effort by Stanton (1981) in which he sought to combine structural and strategic approaches. Even though the difficulties of integrating those closely related models are much less than those of blending therapies with greater diversity, it was still deemed necessary to provide a set of rules for guidance in making decisions about when to apply one approach or the other.

The issues involved in implementing an Integrative Problem-Centered Therapy (IPCT) described by Pinsof (1983) are much more complex than in implementing the structural and strategic models. The IPCT approach calls for the blending of three different orientations (behavioral, communicational, and psychodynamic) into an integrative model for dealing with problems brought to psychotherapy. Therapists following the IPCT approach play a variety of therapeutic roles and use several different therapeutic styles. The role may call for the therapist to function initially like a behaviorally or structurally oriented family therapist who focuses on the reinforcement contingencies or structural characteristics of what Pinsof terms the "patient system" (all of the human systems—biological, individual–psychological, familial–interpersonal, social–occupational, and other—that may be involved in the maintenance or resolution of the presenting problem). Subsequently, the therapist focuses more on communication and the relational history of the system and begins to function more like a psychodynamically oriented family therapist who may include family of origin members in the sessions. At points, the therapist may work like an individually oriented psychodynamic therapist.

All of the therapist role taking and functioning referred to above calls, of course, for shifts in the members of the patient system who are seen in treatment. The total family may be seen at some points, individual members at others. Pinsof does not spell out in further detail the criteria to be used in making particular kinds of interventions or taking specific roles. We suspect that this is because the reasons for making such decisions and the criteria for making certain interventions may be related more to the "art" than to the "science" of therapy at this time in family therapy history. That is, they are more readily determined and understood in the context of clinical supervision than they can be set forth in lists of indications and contraindications and clearly described.

For a therapist to function in the ways Pinsof envisages requires that one be competent and conversant with behavioral, communicational, and psychodynamic orientations as well as with individual and family modalities of therapy. Such role shifting requires "considerable time, energy, training, and personal maturity" (Pinsof, 1983, p. 33) on the part of the therapist. Not every therapist should be expected to deal with all of the demands with equal expertise.

To the foregoing, we would add the caution that therapists cannot easily switch approaches with families, no matter how talented and experienced as clinicians they may be. Each shift can be expected to require preparation of the family for the change in approach or modality of treatment. One cannot, for example, simply decide to use an insight-oriented form of treatment after having customarily employed a behavioral approach and expect the family to make a smooth transition to the new treatment. Similarly, if one has been using "direct" methods in which the family members are informed about the changes they are expected to make and the things they are to learn and do, one cannot replace such an approach with "indirect" or paradoxical treatment techniques without careful preparation of the family for the alteration, if, indeed, such a change can be made successfully at all.

Pinsof notes that IPCT currently is based more on principles and premises than on scientifically valid data and that it should be modified over time so that it can deal with what he terms the specificity question. As he puts it: "As science replaces dogma within psychotherapy, scientifically valid answers will begin to emerge to the specificity question—what intervention, for what problem, with whom, at what point in treatment. Eventually, therapeutic eclecticism will be based on a scientific foundation" (Pinsof, 1983, p. 34).

Liddle (1982) has argued that attempts should not be made to develop a supertheory that would help all populations with all kinds of presenting problems. He posits two reasons why such an approach should not be attempted. First, it is unrealistic for most therapists to believe that they "should immediately be capable of skillfully blending several therapeutic approaches in a unified, consistent, and effective way" (p. 246). The complex, difficult matter of systematically integrating complementary therapy models has barely begun in the family therapy field. Second, even if it could be assumed that most therapists could, with work and proper training, become experts at integration, the status of most contemporary schools of therapy is such that they do not lend themselves to ready integration. Liddle describes most contemporary schools of thought as "pretheoretical and in dire need of clarification, specification, and verification" (p. 247). That is, he sees the concepts and techniques themselves as being too vague and poorly defined and inadequately specified to lend themselves to ready integration.

Given the political issues involved in adopting a particular model, the role of theory in everyday practice, and the problems of eclecticism as he views them, Liddle (1982) has suggested that therapists concerned with monitoring and improving their effectiveness should periodically make an "epistemological declaration." That would be "*our own idiosyncratic statement of what we know and how we know it, what and how we think, and what and how we make the clinical decisions we do*" (p. 247).

Liddle (1982) suggests five interrelated questions that therapists should address in determining where they stand on important issues. As adapted, these include:

1. *Definition.* This relates to the therapist's assumptions about human nature and about therapy. How does the therapist define and view therapy? How does the theoretical orientation adopted by the therapist fit with his or her assumptions and beliefs about people?

2. *Goals.* The therapist's beliefs about goals, their nature and importance, will place him or her closer to some theoretical orientations than to others. Some orientations call for specific behavioral goals; some call for symptom relief or problem resolution. How should goals be defined, if at all?

3. *Therapist Behavior.* The therapist's personal comfort and compatibility with an orientation's prescription of desired therapist behavior will affect the attraction–rejection of that particular approach. This also relates to the therapist's theory of change, its nature, and the mechanisms that permit or cause it to occur.

4. *Dysfunction–Normative Behavior.* This refers to the therapist's theory of normative family functioning and pathology. Subquestions involve the therapist's view of whom to include and the role of the past. All of these, of course, influence the theoretical approach taken by the therapist.

5. *Evaluation.* How therapists should evaluate their work and their responsibility for assessing treatment outcome are the focus here. To this we would add the matter not only of evaluating therapy's effectiveness but also of assessing the value of various therapeutic techniques and the conditions under which they are effective and could be used by the therapist.

These are all very similar to questions that we pose with students as we try to help them grapple with such issues during their academic work and supervised clinical experience. We also encourage them to continue trying to find answers to these questions in subsequent stages of their careers.

We are aware that teaching from an integrative perspective is not easy for either the teacher or the student. It may be necessary at times to make compromises with our ideal approach. For example, it may be necessary for some students to maintain a stronger attachment to a particular school or set of techniques than we would consider desirable because of the student's personal needs for security and certainty at that point in their career. Similarly, it may be deemed expedient with certain students to help them master and use easily taught techniques during early exposure to the field of family therapy, rather than to burden them with the kind of responsibility for adopting therapeutic techniques that we typically place on and seek to develop in students. At the same time, we try to help students remain abreast of findings in clinical and empirical research that would assist them in answering the specificity question of what intervention, for what problems, with whom, and at what point in treatment.

Obviously, we also believe that despite its difficulties, the use of an integrative approach is superior in the long run to education and training in a single orientation. At the very least, using an integrative approach of the kind that we are describing and that we teach to students seems to us to prepare them for flexible functioning and future development much better than following a single model does.

We shall have a great deal more to say about assessment in treatment perspectives and approaches in subsequent chapters. We wish to close this chapter with another reminder that taking a systems approach and thinking systemically is not done in any standardized fashion. Fortunately, taking a systemic outlook and approach also follows the principle of equifinality and provides a variety of ways to reach the goal of furnishing effective family therapy with a systemic orientation to the family system. It is the family with which we are concerned, because understanding families as systems, not systems theory as such, is at the heart of family therapy.

CHAPTER THREE

The Family as
an Integrative System

The major focus in this chapter is on the family as an integrative or shaping force in the formation and maintenance of human personality. Just as we emphasized "thinking systems" in Chapter 2, so we underline here the importance of "thinking family." Rather than thinking about "disease" or about an "isolated individual" when there are difficulties in human development, interactional functioning, or mental health in general, we think first about the family as the most appropriate unit for assessment and possible intervention. Although there are a few exceptions to this general rule, whenever psychotherapeutic work is considered necessary or desirable, we generally start with a family approach because of the salience of the family as a shaping force for human beings throughout their life cycle. Similarly, we think in family terms whenever we think about the formation of personality and its integration. The relationship of mother and infant, for example, in early personality formation represents not merely a one-to-one relationship but the impact of the mother as family representative on the child.

Defining "family" to the satisfaction of all has proven impossible even for such experts as the specialists for the White House Conference on Families convened during the Carter Administration. We shall attempt to describe rather than to define family. A family is composed of a collection of interrelated individuals. It is an organized group that has the kinds of intimate personal emotional attachments and meanings among its members that cause social scientists to describe it as a primary group. A family also is a subsystem of the larger social system in which it is located. As such, it communicates through its structures and functions with other subsystems of the society. The roles taken by family members in particular serve to link society's other subsystems, such as the educational, with the family. The family also is a most important agency for the transmission of the culture's major values to individual members of the group. These values are always filtered through the family's own orientations, whether brought to children through parents or to children through direct encounter with cultural values in educational, media, or other subsystems and institutions of the society. Families also occupy some specific geographical location, such as urban or rural, that affects how the unit is organized and encounters the cultural and social system in which it is set (Papajohn & Spiegel, 1975). It is possible to discuss families in terms of any one or more of these aspects, from individual members to value orientations. We shall attempt in the next few paragraphs to sketch briefly how we go about "thinking family."

Working from a family perspective, in our judgment, means thinking in multigenerational terms. One's experience in family living is typically a multigenerational experience. Thus we seek to assess individuals, family systems, and family subsystems in such terms. This means that most factors are considered with regard to the complex involvements and transactions of at least three generations. It is those transgenerational phenomena that define both the family process and the integrative nature of the system.

The understanding of families as systems means that historical or situational events or changes that occur throughout the generations will have an influence on all living members of that system. For example, the death of a grandparent has ramifications for that person's living spouse, for the sons and daughters, and for the grandchildren. A daughter's struggle with grief reactions to the loss of her father may draw her closer to her mother and siblings and away from her husband and children, thus affecting three generations. The surviving grandparent may pull back dramatically from family and other social ties or may take up residence with one of the children and become an intrusive force in that child's marriage and in the rearing of the grandchildren.

We are defining "family" operationally as *a multigenerational system characterized by several internally functioning subsystems and influenced by a variety of external, adjunctive systems.* It is not sufficient to focus on a nuclear family and its subsystems, no matter how important the nuclear family may be considered. To understand and assess the scope of family functioning, one must attend not only to the spousal, parental, and sibling subsystems of the presenting family unit but also to the extended subsystems of each spouse in terms of their respective parent–child and sibling subsystems in their families of origin.

In addition, one must comprehend the role and effects of significant external systems, such as occupational or educational, that influence and may actually compete with the family system for time, resources, and commitment of emotion. These external systems may also be integrative or shaping for the individual. The shaping nature of occupations is well-known, for example. However, because the family system is primary in time and emotional salience and because the family member's involvement in external systems brings some reciprocal influence to bear on the family's functioning, we have chosen to identify the outside entities as "adjunctive systems." They both influence the individual and the family and, as we have indicated, are affected to some extent by the family's reciprocal interaction with them. For the individual, we essentially consider the family primary and the others adjunctive.

All of our emphasis in this chapter or in our therapeutic work cannot be strictly on families as systems or on the adjunctive systems that affect people. The Duhls' felicitous statement that "it is hard to kiss a system" (Duhl & Duhl, 1981, p. 488) serves as a reminder that in the final analysis one has to work with people. They are members of systems and may be regarded as systems within themselves, but they remain persons. What is integrated or shaped in the complex interaction between the human organism and the environment is human personality. Whatever definition of personality is chosen from among the scores available, therapists generally expect their work to effect positive changes among the persons with whom they interact and labor. We consider it necessary to the performance of good family therapy to have a sound understanding of how human personality is shaped and sustained in both its normal and abnormal manifestations within a given sociocultural setting.

The family is an integrative system because of its developmental role in the formation and functioning of persons both while they live within their nuclear family and long after they have left their family of origin. A family systems approach does not merely take the point of view that what continues to affect and influence the person after departure from the family of origin is basically what he or she stored intrapsychically. Rather, the family is integrative because of the family processes that work over several generations and that continue to operate long after one has physically "left home."

PERSONALITY FORMATION

There are nearly as many definitions of personality as there are students of personality. When the various definitions are lumped together and analyzed, two emphases emerge. That is, personality definitions tend to stress the "internal" or the "external" aspects of personality, depending largely on the orientation of the person making the definition. Psychologists have tended to focus on the internal aspects, the psychological and psychophysiological factors in personality. Sociologists and cultural anthropologists understandably have emphasized the external portions that can be related more straightforwardly to cultural and social forces. Some theorists combine both the internal and the external aspects in their definition and understanding of the meaning of personality. The psychiatrist–family therapist Ackerman (1958), for example, proposed a biopsychosocial model of personality in which attention was given to intrapsychic events and interpersonal events, the real and the unreal, the unconscious and conscious organization of experience, related modes of social adaptation, and a person's view of both the future and the past. Rather than choosing one from among many definitions or adding one more definition to an already overcrowded field, we shall not be concerned here with definition but shall emphasize instead the fact that understanding personality is impossible apart from comprehending the context in which it is formed and sustained as a system and subsystem in a hierarchy of systems.

Traditionally, discussions of personality development have involved arguments over "heredity versus environment" or "heredity and environment," or some related way of attempting to deal with the recognition that a biologically endowed human organism functions in a physical and sociocultural setting. By this time in history, we assume that most serious students of human personality acknowledge the fact that both heredity and environment and their complex interplay must be considered in dealing with personality. As the psychologist Gordon Allport (1961) put it, "The most important point of scientific agreement is that no feature or quality is exclusively hereditary and none exclusively environmental in origin" (p. 67). The old arguments concerning heredity versus environment are essentially meaningless, because the two sets of forces cannot be separated in any meaningful way. Genetics and environment both provide potential and both set limits for human development and functioning. The question of what determinants shape and sustain human personality has to be refocused and framed in other ways.

One of the most comprehensive frameworks for understanding the factors that determine personality formation has been provided by Kluckhohn and Murray (1956) in connection with their explanation of how "every man is in certain respects like all other men, like some other men, and like no other man." They discussed four classes of determinants—constitutional, group membership, role, and situational—that along with the interaction of the four help our understanding of the ways in which every person is like all, some, and no other members of the species. We have borrowed their list, changing the last category from situational to idiosyncratic experiences. The discussion that follows was influenced by the Kluckhohn and Murray material but essentially reflects our views and understandings, not theirs.

Constitutional Determinants

Important constitutional determinants that influence not only a person's needs and expectations but also how that individual is treated by other people include age, sex, and physical traits such as stature and physiognomy. Some would include temperament as a significant constitutional factor. Temperament refers to the individual's mode and intensity of emotional response, for example, whether lethargic and phlegmatic, "laid back," or intense and highly active, "hyper"; quality of prevailing mood, for example, whether one tends to be optimistic and lighthearted or pessimistic and gloomy; and susceptibility to emotional stimulation, for example, whether quickly or slowly emotionally aroused. Although there is a lack of consensus about the role temperament plays in human behavior and precisely how to define temperament, the more solidly a personality disposition is rooted in one's constitution, the more likely it is to be referred to as temperament (Allport, 1961). Attempts to tie temperament and bodily physique together so that a given body type would be expected to manifest a characteristic type of temperament have been made since the time of the ancient Greeks, and are included in the work of Sheldon in contemporary times (Sheldon, Dupertius, & McDermott, 1954; Sheldon & Stevens, 1942; Sheldon, Stevens, & Tucker, 1940). Such efforts do not appear to have been very successful.

A major implication for family therapy, in addition to the difference of behavior and reaction related to age and sex, is that temperamental differences among children often affect in significant ways the reactions of parents to their offspring. A compliant "good baby" may be handled differently than a colicky "difficult baby," for example, and a "responsive child" rewarded differently than a "hyperactive" youngster.

Group Membership Determinants

By this label, we refer to any lasting organized group from at least the national level down to small local units such as the family. Membership in a group or organized entity such as those tends to shape individuals in both general and specific ways and to expose them to both general and specific influences. That is, there are general cultural patterns and social dimensions that impinge on individuals, as well as things that are mediated to the individual through agents of the society or groups such as parents or teachers.

A society is composed of people and the ways in which they are organized and linked together in a system. Their system of relatedness is partly ideational; that is, they behave and think in ways that are normative for their group. Culture, simply defined, is the shared, learned behavior that forms a characteristic way of life for the society. Culture includes, of course, material aspects and artifacts as well as nonmaterial components such as ideas, values, and concepts. As implied above, individuals learn about a culture or learn a culture from other individuals and through participation in small groups, as well as from general exposure to the culture. The subsystems of the society such as the family, school, peer groups, and work groups provide filters through which important aspects of the culture and social order are mediated to the individual. Socioeconomic class or social class also serve as a highly significant filtering and shaping factor in one's development and living. There are many possibilities of deviation from the norms of a culture, and there are many important subcultures within the confines of a large and complex nation such as the United States.

Despite the existence of filtering groups and factors and the possibilities for idiosyncratic learning as a private individual, there are many things that can be predicted on the basis of group membership. For example, one can make some informed guesses about Mr. Smith by knowing that he is American, a lawyer, Protestant, middle-class, Southern, and a lifelong resident of Tampa, Florida. Similarly, some predictions about Mrs. Jones could be made from the knowledge that she is Irish-American, a nurse,

Roman Catholic, middle-class, and a resident of Boston, Massachusetts. Add race and the possibilities of making informed guesses or accurate predictions about attitudes and behaviors of individuals are increased still further. One can make informed guesses also about families on the basis of social class, occupational level, ethnicity, and other factors related to culture and value considerations.

Two sources of information and assistance for the family therapist regarding ethnicity are Papajohn and Spiegel's (1975) work and the edited volume by McGoldrick, Pearce, and Giordano (1982). The former work deals with generational conflicts and conflict resolution among Puerto Rican, Greek-American, and Italian-American families. A major focus is on the value orientations. McGoldrick and associates have collected chapters on Native American, Alaskan Native, black, Afro-American, West Indian, Mexican, Puerto Rican, Cuban, Asian, French Canadian, German, Greek, Iranian, Irish, Italian, Jewish, Polish, Portuguese, and Norwegian families, and provide a number of useful concepts for understanding and working with such families.

One additional set of factors that strongly influences families and how they function and mediate the culture to their members should be mentioned. That is the set of demographic or population factors surrounding the family and providing its context. The density of population may profoundly affect families. For example, life is different in an urban high-rise setting with a population density of 25,000 persons per square mile than it is in a rural area with 40 persons per square mile. Also, the sex ratio of a population area—the number of males per 100 females—affects life, as does the total number of persons in a given city or state. Family therapy in rural Wisconsin may be very different for these reasons, as well as others, from family therapy in New York City.

We find it virtually impossible to overestimate the relevance of understanding culture and its varied influences in understanding personality and working with families. Most of the behavior of human beings is learned, and comprehending not only how it is learned but also what is learned becomes of vital importance in working effectively as a therapist.

Instinct is not as important for human beings as it is for the lower portions of the animal world because in the process of evolutionary development *homo sapiens* attained the capacity for symbolic functioning language that permitted the development and transmission of culture. Man became a "symboling" creature *par excellence* who could think abstractly and communicate with other members of the species verbally.

Planning, self-observation, introspection, and other ego functions became possible. It was no longer necessary to pass along what had been learned through direct training or observation. Ideas and descriptions could be expressed through words. Nor was it necessary to act only on the basis of instinct. It was not necessary for all members of the species to carry within their nervous system the means for instinctive patterning to emerge at necessary points in order for the species to survive. What was necessary for survival and what was valued could be learned and stored through symbolization and thus transmitted to succeeding generations.

Human interaction was greatly facilitated by the accomplishment of language. Role taking and role playing, which will be discussed below, were both made possible or easier by the acquisition of language. Object relations became possible because of the new ability not only to form images and internalize models of relationships but also to reflect on the meanings of those models of relationships and to contemplate and plan how one would deal with and relate to the reciprocal object (person).

Parenthetically, one of the interesting and important contributions of family therapy has been the renewal of an emphasis on communication, including nonverbal communication, in human interaction. The use of words and language to obscure communication, rather than to facilitate direct and clear understanding, in schizophrenic behavior was, of course, one of the early foci of interest among those who found themselves becoming family therapists.

Role Determinants

Role determinants are determinants of personality in that playing a distinctive role for a long period of time becomes the basis for differentiating or distinguishing personalities within a group.

Roles have been defined in many ways, including the expectations (rights and obligations) that accompany a given status in a social group. Role playing is different from role taking, another important behavioral science concept. Role playing involves organizing one's conduct in conformity to the norms of the group. Role taking has to do with placing oneself in the position of the other, imagining how a situation looks from the standpoint of another person. Role taking is much closer to empathic functioning and empathic relating to another person or persons. Role playing is expected to be fairly standard for all players (persons) who occupy a given position in a social system.

Roles also may be characterized in several ways. In addition to "conventional" roles, which are learned through participation in the life of an organized group and which involve fulfilling modes of conduct appropriate to that group, roles also may be described as "situational" or "interpersonal." Situational roles are peculiar to given social circumstances and situations and, again, would be considered standard for all role players encountering such situations. Interpersonal roles are defined by the personal characteristics of individuals participating in reciprocal relationships. There is overlap, of course, in that there are conventional ways of being a husband and special interpersonal ways of being a husband in relation to the particular other person who is one's wife. John Jones is expected to behave in certain general conventional ways as a middle-class husband, but he also is called upon to be a husband in certain specific ways in relating to Mary Jones. In almost all group transactions, persons act as both conventional role players and as unique human beings at the same time, although the mixture of conventional and personal–interpersonal behaviors will vary widely from situation to situation. Therapists have to attend to both the conventional and the unique aspects of the situation and the behavior and make the interventions in terms of both dimensions.

Within families there are role determinants of both varied natures and varied functions. One may have the role of older child, family pet, family scapegoat, decision maker, as well as parent, child, sibling, and many others. Playing any one of these for an extended period of time generally makes a distinct impression upon the personality of the person playing the role.

Idiosyncratic Experiential Determinants

These refer to things that individuals experience that are not normative for the group in which they live. That is, the other members of the group do not undergo such experiences as a result of being a member of the group. The events or experiences may occur on a single occasion or on many occasions and can be regarded as idiosyncratic experiential determinants so long as they are not common to the experiences of the other group members.

Examples would include having a physical accident, being physically handicapped, being adopted, and a long list of other possibilities, all of which could be expected to have a strong impact on the formation of personality.

Not only the four classes of determinants but also the interaction or interrelatedness of the determinants has to be taken into account in understanding the foundations out of which personality is shaped and sustained. Personalities of males and females differ because of physical differences and because of different cultural expectations and demands at various points of the life cycle. There is an interactive or interrelatedness component among all four determinants through the life cycle of the individual. Those who undergo similar experiences and who have similar constitutional makeups will tend to exhibit some common characteristics. Culture, as well as society (including its organizations and groups), tends to play a significant integrating, shaping role in the formation of personality in continuing and complex ways.

The human organism, in our judgment, should never be considered merely as something being acted upon by the environment in which it develops. Neither should it be regarded as developing inexorably in some predetermined fashion, regardless of the setting. Allport's idea of a proactive organism that interacts with its environment, instead of being merely reactive or a passive recipient of environmental impress and pressures, has considerable explanatory merit. A child in a family is not merely a passive organism molded by its family, peer group, or culture into some kind of standard predictable personality. Neither is the child something whose personality will develop in certain "angelistic" or "bad seed" directions, regardless of the efforts of the parents. The outcome of the interrelatedness of organism and setting in dynamic interplay is what determines the kind of personality that emerges and that appears in situation after situation.

THE NUCLEAR FAMILY

Although there are several group membership determinants of personality, as we have indicated, we focus on the nuclear family as the most significant formative force on the human organism as it develops into a distinctly human personality. As noted, the nuclear family is basic and primary both in terms of coming first in time in the life of the developing person and in the sense of being foremost in importance and influence during those early years in particular. Without a nuclear family or some adequate and appropriate substitute, the infant and small child literally would not survive.

As we shall continue to emphasize, the biological needs of human infants are such that they must absorb a culture in order to survive and must be cared for in a protective group while developing to the point of being able to function on their own. Caring persons who not only look out for the purely physical needs of the infant and child but who also provide an adequate supply of affection, touch, and general emotional sustenance are also needed for healthy development. The lengthy period of dependency and the intense attachment to those caring persons provide the developing child with powerful shaping forces. The ways of thinking, acting, believing, and relating that children observe and participate in during their formative years are almost literally the only ways of thinking and so on that the child knows. It is only with the passage of many years, for most persons, that they begin to witness and experience different patterns.

The functions of the nuclear family today are not the same as they were in the American nuclear family a few generations ago. Families have changed their role dramatically in a relatively short time. When this was a more simple society, essentially agrarian and rural, many important social functions such as the protective, productive, educational, and others were fulfilled directly by the family.

With the coming of the Industrial Revolution in the 19th century and the rise of the factory system, important changes took place. Production tended to move off the farm and out of the cottage industry of the home into the factory. Education shifted to the school, particularly with the development of the public school system beginning in Massachusetts in the 1840s and continuing with the advent of universal compulsory education through age 16. Protective functions shifted to the state through various components of government. Much of the health care formerly assumed by the family is provided today in a multibillion dollar health care delivery system that constitutes one of the major industries of the nation.

By the 1920s and afterwards, sociologists and other social scientists were concerned about what was described as the decreasing functions of the family. A number of myths arose among both academicians and laypersons about what the family had been in the past. Families never had been as large as they generally were remembered to have been, and the nuclear family had always been the significant unit, according to family historians (Harevan, 1982).

It does appear to be true that the nuclear family is more adaptive to an industrial system and urban living than a three-generational family unit would have been. It also seems to be true that the rise of the factory system and an accompanying commercial and business system make the possibility of family units functioning together as productive units far less likely than if families lived on farms. On the farm, for example, a 10-year-old could work and help to produce for the family and earn his or her own way economically. During a time of more simple technology, children could be economic assets when they could work as field hands or in the kitchen with food preparation and preservation. In most urban settings, children are economic liabilities.

Families of a few generations ago did tend to include more adults than do contemporary nuclear units consisting of only the husband and wife, and certainly more than single-parent units. Households often included boarders, who were not necessarily relatives (Harevan, 1982). Especially during time of economic difficulty, even urban families might "double up" in their living arrangements temporarily. Those and other factors, including value orientations, frequently resulted in different patterns of childrearing than often are found today. Whatever the form, childrearing was important in the past as well as today.

Social scientists seem to have demonstrated that the idea of a so-called isolated nuclear family in contemporary urban living is not and has not been an accurate portrayal of families. Most urban families have far more contact and involvement with relatives and portions of the extended families out of which the nuclear family was formed than the concept of an isolated nuclear family would imply. Nuclear families are not isolated and functionless.

Parsons and Bales (1955), for example, concluded that the nuclear family has two irreducible functions: the primary socialization of the young and the stabilization of adult personalities. They note that human personality is not born, but is made in families that serve as a kind of "factory" where socialization occurs. Human infants do not automatically become integrated personalities. A great deal of work is required on the part of those who would provide for their socialization. As the infant develops into a child, the child into an adolescent and teenager, the teenager into a youth, and the youth into a young adult, different and ever-changing responses are required on the part of parents. The parenting functions as well as the occupational and marital endeavors of adults have the potential for contributing to the stabilization of the adults in the nuclear family.

Certain characteristics of the nuclear family contribute to the forms that the two functions described by Parsons and Bales assume. It has, of course, two sexes represented. Traditionally, the functions and roles of the man and woman in the nuclear family have been different but complementary. Currently, with more than half of the married women in the United States working outside the home and a good portion of them opting for a long-term extrafamilial occupational role or for a career, there is change going on with regard to how the family roles are to be organized. The nuclear family also has two generations, each having different needs and responsibilities. Affectional and erotic ties bind the members together in a unit that to some degree protects them from the larger society (Lidz, 1980).

Families require the ability to perform certain essential functions in order to conduct the childrearing tasks adequately. As adapted from the work of Lidz, these are: a dynamic organization of the family that helps to channel the children's drives and guides their movement toward personality integration; nurturant parental capabilities that meet children's needs in an appropriate manner at each developmental stage; enculturation abilities to provide children with essential instrumental techniques of the culture; a social system that provides opportunity to learn social roles and values of the society; and a clear communicational system for two-way communication (Lidz, 1980).

The nuclear family is serving both the needs of the society of which it is an articulated subsystem as well as the multigenerational family system of which it is a part. One does not have to espouse any one of several traditional religious values to recognize that the orderly replacement of population and citizens is a powerful need for all societies and the family has a preeminent role in that process. The entire socialization process is not entrusted to the family. Other social agencies, such as the various parts of the educational system, assist with the socialization task of teaching the developing child the basic roles demanded by the society and with the enculturation task of teaching such essential techniques needed for adaptation and survival, as knowledge of the language of the society. Families obviously handle these tasks with varying degrees of skill and success, depending in large measure on the particular position in the society held by the family and the degree of competence attained by the family. Minority families, for example, may not be able to provide their children with the same kinds of skills that mainstream families are able to give to their progeny.

The physical and emotional needs of the infant and small child are such that a social group that provides protection and permits total investment of emotions is essential. At the beginning, children need to be totally dependent. In dealing with their children, parents are faced with the task of starting with a totally dependent organism and helping it to move toward independence. The developing individual has the task of moving from dependence to relative independence to interdependence in a stable adult relationship with a partner of his or her own in a new nuclear family, if the line is to be extended and the social function of reproduction and replacement of citizens is to be fulfilled. The launching pad toward later independent functioning is a solid experience in dependency, as many psychologists have pointed out. The parents must be concerned from the beginning with putting themselves out of a job. As they do so, the original marital dyad that became a family turns once again into a marital dyad without children residing at home.

In order to provide adequately for the needs of the developing person to first be totally immersed in the family and then to move toward appropriate emancipation, the family unit must be a relatively open system that adequately buffers the child from the outside world while permitting increasing attachment of the youngster to values and relationships outside the family. Families as subsystems of their society must have boundaries that are semipermeable, that permit the exchange of appropriate information between the family and other systems in the society. Boundaries that are too rigid can result in the family being too isolated and too dependent on its own idiosyncratic ways of thinking, feeling, valuing, and acting. An extreme example of such a family would probably be regarded in its community as strange and different. As Parsons and Bales (1955) pointed out several decades ago, the family must be a differentiated subsystem of a society and not what we would call a closed "little society" or anything resembling such an entity. Research appears to have demonstrated clearly enough that the presence of very rigid and impermeable boundaries between the family and the outside world cut off the entry of information from the outside that might contribute to healthy functioning (cf. the research of Lidz and Wynne in particular).

At the same time, if the boundaries between the family and the outside world are too wide open and there is too great a commitment of family members to the outside world and too great an involvement of such members in the outside world, there is likely to be an underorganized family, one with insufficient cohesion to produce healthy family relationships and personalities.

Adults, in order to fulfill their dual responsibilities to the family and to the society, need to have "roles other than their familial roles which occupy strategically important places in their own personalities" (Parsons & Bales, 1955, p. 19). They need roles outside of the family, such as occupational and social roles, that put them into contact with relevant portions of the society and culture. Such roles, in our judgment, are very important to the self-esteem and general mental health of most adult males and females in our society. With the rise of the womens' movement, there has come an awareness that not only males but also females desire and require the opportunity to play significant roles in the social world outside of the home and family. It is difficult to continue one's own emotional development and to maintain a firm sense of selfhood and personal identity if one is essentially dependent on the accomplishments of others. Women who live vicariously and obtain their identity through their husband's position and their children's accomplishments generally encounter difficulties in middle or later stages of the family cycle.

Not only do both men and women need to occupy significant places and play important roles in relation to the outside world, but also they need roles other than the parental one inside the family. First and foremost, they ideally need to consider their marriage, rather than their jobs or their parental roles, their major source of emotional sustenance. The nuclear family has its origin, of course, in the attractions of two persons who subsequently mate and produce offspring. Personal fulfillment and other emotional reasons are the basic motivating forces in the movement into marriage for most persons. Marriage has the potential of enabling them to complete their lives through the provision of a stable emotional and social relationship and the provision of children, the rearing of which brings into play portions of their personalities not otherwise utilized. The marriage relationship becomes much more complex and a nuclear family emerges when a child comes to the marital unit. The major point for many adults to remember is the primacy of the marital relationship.

Inside the nuclear family, it seems necessary for the adult marital partners to form a solid coalition between themselves and to maintain the boundaries between the generations, that is, between themselves as marital partners and parents, and their offspring, in order to provide maximally for the development of children. This has been demonstrated not only clinically (Ackerman, 1958; Bowen, 1960; Minuchin, 1974; Zuk & Boszor-menyi-Nagy, 1967) but also through research with competent families producing healthy children (Lewis, Beavers, Gossett, & Phillips, 1976; Lidz & Lidz, 1949; Westley & Epstein, 1960, 1970). Not only the health of the children but also the general functioning of the family unit is strongly influenced by the nature of the relationship between the parents and the strength of the marital coalition.

Strong marriages and marital coalitions have been shown to have clear distributions of power and leadership, open and direct communica-tion, and high levels of marital complementarity and need fulfillment. Who provides leadership is not so important as the clarity of the power structure and the generational lines. Power in the most competent optimal family units is not arbitrary but is shared between the parents. The children's ideas are considered. The adults remain in charge but share leadership and being in charge according to situational and contextual factors (Lewis *et al.*, 1976; Mishler & Waxler, 1968; Spiegel, 1957; Westley & Epstein, 1970).

Minuchin (1974) has appropriately called the family "the matrix of identity," noting that human identity has two elements, a sense of belong-ing and a sense of being separate. The sense of being separate cannot be adequately developed unless there is opportunity for the child to separate from the parents and to be separate from attachments to the parents within the framework of the family. The maintenance of a strong marital coalition and generational boundaries contributes importantly and essen-tially to the child's need for freedom for development.

The family is an integrative system in the development and main-tenance of human personality in two ways: because of its historical devel-opmental role and because of its ongoing processes.

Developmental Role

We have already been illustrating the fact that the nuclear family is integrative in the personality of the human being because of its develop-mental role. This developmental role is not confined to what occurs when one is an infant or young child. Much early personality theory, particu-larly that influenced by psychoanalytic ideas, emphasized the strength of early life experiences. Not only ideas emanating from psychology but also traditional Western religious thought seemed to imply that what happened in the first 5 years or so of life was fixed and essentially unchangeable. Although many personality theorists, particularly those with a developmental orientation such as Erik Erikson, stressed that the capacity for change remained present throughout the life span, the general idea seems to have prevailed that what was learned in the early years tended to be sealed within the psyche of the individual.

The boundaries of the psyche are like those of all open systems, semipermeable. There is a continuous interchange between the internal processes of the human organism and the external social environment. There is a feedback system involving organism, environment, and the interpersonal relations between human beings, between self and other persons.

Personality is not fixed. Although the family has the task of providing a secure base from which the developing person can be launched into the outside world as a relatively autonomous personality, it must be recognized that personality is only relatively autonomous. The autonomy varies according to the situation and the environment (Ackerman, 1958).

Social role was seen by Ackerman (1958) as forming a bridge between the processes of intrapsychic life and the processes of social participation. It is through playing social roles that the social identity of the person is established and manifested in the contexts of various life situations. At the same time that one is playing various social roles he or she is also involved in acquiring age-appropriate skills and knowledge that contribute to social and personal identity.

The extensive extrafamilial influences on the developing and functioning personality are, as we repeatedly emphasize, exceedingly important but mediated and/or moderated by the impact of the family. The family, in other words, serves an integrative role for individual and interactional processes throughout the life cycle. No other system is more influential, for better or worse, on the individual's life as a child, youth, adult, spouse, or parent. Thus, the family is integrative not only in a cross-sectional but also in a developmental sense.

Parsons and Bales's identification of essential functions—primary socialization of the young and stabilization of adult personalities—emphasizes the long-range nature of the integrative role of the nuclear family. The interlocking of generations in the developmental tasks is something significant to which we shall return later in this chapter.

It is necessary to have some solid understanding of a framework of individual development and to fit this into a framework of family development and broad social process. Freely adapted to a family systems perspective, Erikson's (1950) "eight ages of man" approach is a useful framework. We approach the framework with the understanding that the dominant forces in personality development are located in the family and in the ways in which it deals with the lives of its members and that external events are major among the various forces determining behavior. The dominant forces are the family transactions and the social transactions that affect the developing child and person, rather than intrapsychic events and dynamics. In terms of the early experiences of infants, for example, what they are affected by is not merely impressions or perceptions of a relationship with the mothering one, but by the contacts with the family system as mediated through the mother who, in turn, is affected by such things as the kind and degree of need satisfaction being experienced in her marriage.

Our adapted version of Erikson's approach (see Table 3-1) is based on several presentations he has made over the years but primarily on a 1959 lecture.

The life stages in the Eriksonian framework vary chronologically among societies. Our primary concern is with the stages as they occur in

Table 3-1. An Adaptation of Erik Erikson's Stages of Personality Development

Life stages	Radius of interaction (interpersonal mutuality)	Psychosocial primacies (basic struggles)	Related elements of social order
Infancy	Maternal person(s)	Basic trust versus basic mistrust	Cosmic order
Early childhood	Parental combination	Autonomy versus shame and doubt	"Law and order"
Play stage	Basic family unit	Initiative versus guilt	Ideal prototypes
School age	Neighborhood school	Industry versus inferiority	Technological fundamentals
Puberty and adolescence	Peer groups	Identity versus identity–diffusion	Ideological perspectives
Young adulthood	Partners	Intimacy and solidarity versus isolation	Patterns of competition and cooperation
Adulthood	Divided labor	Productivity versus self-absorption	Currents of education and tradition
Old age	My people "mankind"	Integrity versus despair	Wisdom

North American societies. At each stage, a developing person encounters a new area of interaction or interpersonal mutuality. This does not mean in most instances that the old areas of interpersonal mutuality cease to be of importance but rather that new units become important as well. In addition to the family system, the radius of interaction named for each life stage essentially occupies the central position for that stage.

During infancy, the maternal person or persons, referring to the biological mother and others who take on a mothering or closely related interactive role with the infant, is the focus of interaction or interpersonal mutuality. Originally the tie between the infant and mother is largely biological in nature, the baby having developed in a symbiotic physical relationship with its mother. The original tie shifts through interaction and socialization into a deep and enduring emotional attachment and relationship in a normal course of development. Infants who cannot, for whatever reasons, develop such an emotional attachment with the mothering one do not achieve the capacity for physical and emotional closeness with others. They do not, in other words, develop out of the condition referred to as autism (Cohler & Geyer, 1982). Autistic children are severely damaged and retarded emotionally and developmentally.

No discussion of human development would be complete without some attention to that part of attachment referred to as "object relations theory." As used here, this conceptualization refers to the ways in which persons internalize the behavior of significant figures by creating models or abstractions of those figures in their psychic world and using those models to guide subsequent behavior in relation to those or other significant figures. The term also may be used to refer to models of relationships such as the models of marriage witnessed and internalized during one's development. The models thus may provide guidance for playing roles as well.

These internalized models are not stereotyped "rigid pictures in the head." Instead, they are composed of dynamic sets of perceptions, beliefs, and attitudes that are continually being altered and recast into new combinations, based on the interplay of the original perceptions and whatever new information has accrued through subsequent life experiences. Bowlby's (1969, 1973) term "working models" reflects the dynamic, changing nature of these images.

Our first experiences with model learning or object internalization occur, as noted, as an infant in relation to the mothering one. The infant begins at a very early age to form abstractions in its developing mind as a result of interaction and contact with the mothering one. These internal-ized images may be based on parts of the mother as perceived by the infant. When such splitting of the original mother object occurs, the mothering one is regarded as a "good mother" and as a "bad mother," depending on whether she is felt to be gratifying or frustrating by the infant. The learning about the world external to oneself that goes on in object relations learning occurs in ways that remain obscure. Much of this kind of learning evidently takes place outside conscious awareness.

The early development and attachments of the infant have been studied intensively. Mahler (1979) provides one of the better sources of theory and information based on research. She has described three stages of development occurring during the first 3 years of life, the autistic, the symbiotic, and the separation–individuation phases. During the first phase, the infant is objectless. During the period of normal autism, the infant appears to be completely concerned with its own omnipotent, autistic orbit and in a state of primitive hallucinatory disorientation, according to Mahler (1979).

About the 2nd month of life, the infant becomes aware of a need-satisfying object outside itself. Beginning with approximately the 3rd month, it normally enters into a symbiotic relationship with the mothering one. "Symbiosis," a term borrowed from biology, refers to a condition in which two dissimilar organisms live in a union or very close association that is beneficial to both organisms. It is not merely parasitism, which is advantageous to only one of the organisms. Mahler considers symbiotic gratification necessary to human development. It involves a blurring of boundaries and a kind of fusion of the organisms in both psychic and physical delusional, hallucinatory senses. A mature adult version would be the symbiotic relationship that partners enter into temporarily during times of extreme closeness in sexual relations. When the mother–infant symbiosis is optimal, the first subphase of separation–individuation be-gins.

Separation–individuation has four subphases. The first, differentia-tion, begins during optimal symbiosis, when the infant, after having been assured of the satisfactions and reassuring safety of symbiotic attachment, gains the locomotive ability to be more mobile and begins to be expansive, moving outside the symtiotic orbit. The practicing subphase occurs from approximately 10 to 16 months of life. The youngster uses locomotive abilities to explore wider realms of the environment and reality. This period of relative indifference to the mothering one is replaced in approximately the second 18 months of life with the rapproachment subphase. During that subphase, the child begins to approach the mother actively but on a more realistic basis than previously. During the final subphase of separation–individuation proper, the youngster in optimal development forms a discrete identity, holding a firm sense of separateness and individuality. Mahler does not refer to physical separation but to the child's psychological awareness of its separateness from others (Mahler, 1979).

Object learning or model internalization is very important in early life, but it also can occur at later stages including adulthood. Bettelheim's (1943) observations of behavior in Nazi concentration camps during the late 1930s manifest examples of such learning by adults. Such learning also is reflected in a number of other instances in which individuals are placed in situations of extreme dependency with strong authoritarian figures holding control over them. Understanding such object relations patterns is important in assessing issues of mate selection and marital interaction.

During infancy, the major struggle of the young organism as it relates to the outside world, including the total cosmic order as everything outside of itself tends to be experienced, is between basic trust and basic mistrust. Is the outside world as experienced directly and as mediated through the mothering one to be trusted? Is the setting in which the infant is existing a harmful, painful, untrustworthy place, or is it benign, caring, and trustworthy? The same struggle goes on with regard to the infant's own impulses, according to the Eriksonian framework. How does the infant acquire faith that it can be expansive and attach and not have to stay within itself? The basic trust versus mistrust struggle, therefore, involves both what is inside and what is outside the infant. We have already noted the importance of successful resolution of this early struggle.

In the Eriksonian framework, the infant gradually moves into the second stage of life, where, from our point of view, two important things happen. First, during early childhood, the youngster's world of interaction expands to include not merely the mothering one but also the father, the total parental combination. Typically the child must learn to share the mother, just as earlier it had learned to separate from the mother and to deal with the loss of the mother as a perceived part of itself. The father must be added as a separate object with whom the child interacts and must cope in both reality and psychically as a part of the family system and the mediated social system.

Second, during this stage, the child encounters limits and acquires from the parents some sense of the laws or rules by which they guide and limit him or her. Among the issues emerging are the dichotomies of freedom of self-expression and its suppression, willfulness and cooperation, and love and hate. Early discipline in terms of both guidance and punishment conveys to children a picture of what "law and order" are and how they affect their ability and freedom to function. The basic struggle for children in this period, therefore, is between autonomy, the freedom to function according to their own wishes and in accordance with their own feelings of confidence and certainty, and feelings of shame and doubt.

According to Erikson, if a person can form a sound sense of self-control without loss of self-esteem, he or she acquires a lasting sense of pride and autonomy. If self-control is not experienced and a person feels impotent and overcontrolled, a lasting sense of shame and doubt result. Although the picture is complex, it is essentially accurate to say that if the sense of restriction, limitation, and punishment experienced by children is too strong, too harsh, they will come to feel shame and doubt in relation to themselves. Youngsters may feel ashamed of their own bodies and impotent with regard to control of even such basic bodily functions as elimination of feces, for example, because of the ways in which they are treated by the parents. Ideally, the period gives the child an opportunity to explore freely and confidently and to feel an adequate sense of self-direction and autonomy.

The next stage, the play stage, involves interaction with the basic family unit. For younger children, of course, older siblings are an important part of the family and must be incorporated into areas of interpersonal mutuality. As contact is made with other persons, youngsters portray and emulate those whom they admire. Initially this includes primarily parents and other family members, but eventually admiration and emulation are extended to other individuals whom the child witnesses in daily living, such as the mail carrier or the garbage collector, or personalities encountered through the mass media. Much of the play stage is taken up with pretending or "playing like" one is a mother, a pediatrician, a fireman, or other admired figure. The child is trying out roles and in so doing working on developing a sense of self as a distinct person.

It is during this stage that the basic struggle with regard to taking the initiative occurs. The ability to take initiative sufficiently to override feelings of guilt is exceedingly important. As Erikson has pointed out, now that the child has become solidly convinced that he or she is a person, the youngster must find out what kind of person he or she is going to be.

During the school-age life stage in North American societies, the child is intensely concerned with acquiring the basic technological skills necessary for social functioning. Children begin to sharpen the basic skills of literacy. Language development began, of course, in the family much earlier, but is improved upon and added to with acquisitions from other technological areas within the formal learning environment of the neighborhood school. Depending on how successful they are in the mastery and use of necessary skills, children either develop a sense of industry and enjoy the rewards of industry as these are perceived by parents and conveyed to the child, or they develop a feeling of relative failure and inferiority in relation to the tasks and perhaps to their peers.

Societal pressures frequently impinge on the child through the parents, who may be upset because their youngster is not achieving at a level or proceeding at a pace in the mastery of skills and utilization of them that the parents feel is normative or desirable for that age level. Clinicians often encounter rather competent adults who carry a lingering sense of inferiority because they "never could measure up" to parental expectations. "An A− never was good enough, it had to be an A+, and if it was an A+, nothing was said because that was expected."

As with the other stages, successful mastery of the primary struggle at this stage—industry versus inferiority in this instance—prepares the developing child for the struggles of the succeeding stages. Erikson uses the epigenetic principle as part of his explanatory scheme. This principle, borrowed from embryology, holds that the critical tasks of each of the developmental stages must be mastered at the appropriate time and in the appropriate sequential order. The epigenetic principle forms limitations to what can be learned or mastered at any given stage.

The epigenetic principle certainly is illustrated during the stage of puberty and adolescence. Children cannot deal with certain physically based characteristics until they have reached the stage of develoment at which those physical changes have occurred.

During this period in American society, the peer group comes to occupy a position of central importance as the arena of interaction. This is due in part to constitutionally based physical changes and developments that are occurring in the bodies of boys and girls and due in other ways to the peculiar nature and shape of the culture and the form of social organization that tends to isolate children and teenagers from adult, mainline society. The long gap between the attainment of biological maturity and social majority in complex cultures intensifies the sense of isolation from mainstream life and enhances feelings of being a misfit and out of phase with life for many teenagers.

The struggle of the teenager between identity versus identity diffusion is well-known. It is at this point that youngsters typically begin to wrestle most earnestly not only with who they are as a person, as a masculine or feminine being, but also as a member of society. The ideological perspectives of the culture and the ways that they are conveyed to the adolescent frequently add to the young person's struggle and confusion. From a larger perspective, the confusion of the larger society and its culture are reflected in the vicissitudes of the adolescent's life and stage of development. Identity efforts are not solely a matter of internal working and striving. Real and imagined hypocrisies and contradictions between professed values and actual behaviors on the part of adults often become foci for intergenerational conflict.

Again, in this life stage, the family unit continues to serve a vital mediating role for the developing person, filtering the culture and easing or making more difficult the teenager's movement toward departure from home and assumption of a place in the world as a young adult.

From a family systems perspective, the question of whether a young man or woman emerges from the earlier years and the parent–child context as an individuated young adult is not an indication of unresolved internal conflicts such as oedipal struggles. Rather, it is more likely to be a reflection of marital tensions and difficulties in which unconscious attempts to fill voids in the marital relationship have resulted in a distorted and problematic parent–child relationship. This may be manifested at either end of a line, in an overinvolved and intense parent–child attachment or in a loose relationship in which there is neglect and little emotional investment.

Erikson's last three stages of personality development are important, but our feeling is that our space will be better used by refraining from additional discussion here and referring the reader to subsequent sections in which we discuss mate selection and marital interaction.

Erikson's scheme hints at but does not make adequately clear the fact that while the individual is developing along certain lines, there is concurrent development in the family system, and in the social system. At the same time that the individual is moving successively from early adulthood to middle adulthood to middle age, he or she also is moving within the family system from child to parent to grandparent. Within the society or the social system, an age cohort sequence may be identified in which one is developing from youth into established adulthood, and so on (Troll, 1975).

Erikson has pointed out that it is important to notice the "cogwheeling of generations." As children move from childhood into adolescence, their parents move from adulthood into middle adulthood, and their parents' parents (their grandparents) simultaneously move from middle adulthood into middle age or, in some cases, into old age. Comprehending what is happening in the complex interlinking of generations is very important to the therapist. This leads us into a second way in which the family is integrative.

Process Role

"Process," again, describes an organic-like quality that includes change, movement, and growth. It is not always simply linear or simply circular. The changes and growth in family process come together for the family in an ebb and flow of movement. Erikson's epigenetic principle is an example of process, although more narrow in focus than what we mean by the concept.

As the generations link together, very important transgenerational processes become part of the dynamic picture of individual and family life. As we have indicated, we consider it vital to view persons and systems in terms of the transactions and various interlocking processes that are in effect across generational lines. For example, we approach parent–child difficulties from at least a three-generational perspective. When we consider what the parent is expecting of the child, we automatically think about what the parent's own parents expected of him or her, either in reality or in his or her perception. Symbolically, and at times in reality, we think in terms of who the parent feels is "looking over his or her shoulder" and what they expect of him or her with regard to childrearing.

Patterns of thinking and feeling, hurting, fearing, and so on are passed down through the generations in what has been referred to as "nongenetic transmission." The child has an emotional and intellectual heritage that is every bit as real in its consequences as the genetic heritage that has been passed on by his parents. Preceeding generations are actively represented in the individual's life through those "non-genetic transmissions" that are transmitted and maintained through a variety of verbal and nonverbal communicational modalities.

One version of transgenerational processes has been described by Bowen in his attempts to account for schizophrenic behavior. In his early work, he had a three-generational hypothesis to account for the development of schizophrenia in a family member. That is, he thought that it took at least three generations to develop schizophrenia in an individual (Bowen, 1960). More recently, Bowen has replaced this idea with a multigenerational transmission-process concept. The parents will, on whatever basis or bases, select one of the children who is immature—the parents themselves are immature—and try to keep that child fused into the family system. That child, the most strongly attached of all the children in the family to the parents, will differentiate himself or herself less than his or her siblings and will function less effectively. Bowen thinks that if this process is followed over several generations, the lines of descent will produce persons with lower and lower levels of differentiation. If the family hits severe stress, schizophrenia may occur in an early generation. Sometimes the process may slow down or even remain static for a generation or more. As a result, it may take ten generations to produce schizophrenia (Bowen, 1976). Incidentally, Bowen notes that most persons select a spouse who is at or near their own level of differentiation from their family of origin. This is basically consistent with what some of the remainder of us have observed in terms of "marital complementarity."

Beavers and Voeller (1983) also have noted that it is difficult for a person to move much beyond the level of competence of their family of origin in their individual development. Further development can occur if the individual is fortunate enough to encounter a particularly helpful environment, a family with greater possibilities, or a therapeutic relationship that is helpful.

It may be useful here to return to an idea that we touched on previously, namely, that much individual difficulty or pathology is not carried by the individual intrapsychically. Accordingly, when the family therapist works with families, he or she is not concerned primarily with reworking the psychic life of the individual but with altering the relationships in the family.

A FINAL NOTE

We shall not attempt to spell out at this juncture the details of how personality development prepares one for marriage and parenthood. It is sufficient here to note that both marital strengths and marital problems often have their roots in the developmental experiences of satisfaction and vicissitudes that individuals have undergone. A given experience or set of experiences can, of course, cut either way, providing the basis for good marital experiences and expectations or for poor adaptation and adjustment. Symbiosis, in our judgment, is one of the more powerful experiences that one undergoes during the developmental years. It provides the kind of experience that one wishes to return to, either to enjoy additional pleasure or to try to secure an adequate amount of what one tasted in not quite fulfilling and satisfying terms. Similarly, one may wish to avoid the closeness of a symbiotic relationship altogether.

Once again we wish to emphasize the understanding that it is the family transactions that are most important in preparing one for marriage and family living. Also, we wish to underline once again the fact that human personality continues to change, as do all open systems.

CHAPTER FOUR

The Family as
an Interactive System

While the integrative aspects of systems refer to a system's origins and functions, and the developmental deal with its history, the interactive pertains to its present organization.

The interactive approach is concerned with what a system looks like and how it behaves. It is the interactive nature of the system that comes the closest to disclosing its "living" characteristics and the power of its collective components and subsystems. The interactive aspect of a system is that part that is in a continual and reciprocal interrelationship with the external environment and that processes informational feedback. It is the interactive nature of a system that conveys its organization.

It is important to note that it is the interactive aspect of the system that the family therapist encounters, contacts, and perturbs (see Chapter 7). The interactive nature of a system provides crucial experiential and empirical descriptive data for the therapist to use in determining where, how, and in what manner to engage, form an alliance with or "join," and enter the system in order to effect therapeutic change. It is the clinician's responsibility in assessing and treating family dysfunction to recognize and understand the complex interactional factors throughout the broad family system that distinguish normative from dysfunctional family patterns.

As Rapoport (1968) has said, one may generalize from the concept of organism to that of an organized system. Each family displays its own idiosyncratic interactive patterns in the ways in which its members organize themselves into roles, the manner in which power is distributed, the fashion in which separateness and connectedness are handled, and the way in which love and grief are experienced. As these patterns are blended into the family's ongoing behavior, dysfunctional elements may occur at vary-

ing historical and developmental stages and at different locations throughout the broader systemic network. However, even with the diversity of
styles and shapes of patterns that are possible, the interactive aspects of
each family system can be dealt with descriptively around two concepts:
structure and process. Understanding these elements of a system is crucial
for the family therapist in conducting an accurate clinical assessment and
developing an informed treatment strategy with a family.

In this chapter, we shall deal with structure in terms of subsystems,
boundaries, and triangles. We shall discuss eight concepts or pairs of
concepts in explaining family process. These are: continuity and change,
separateness and connectedness, enmeshment–disengagement, communication, parentification, scapegoating, myths and secrets, and power. These
certainly do not exhaust the supply of structure and process concepts that
are available, but they constitute the major ones in our judgment and are
adequate for our purposes in this book.

FAMILY STRUCTURE

The structure, as we noted earlier, outlines the basic organizational
"shape" of the family system. It is the structural aspect, the arrangement of
the internal components, that the outside observer first notices. Miller
(1969) has defined the structure as the "arrangement of subsystems and
components in a three-dimensional space at a given time" (p. 83). Structure, as contrasted with process, is static. In reality, however, structural
shifting and reshaping occur as the system accommodates to its own
internal tensions as well as to external influences. Thus, while the basic
properties are static, the structure must be seen as both fixed and changing
over time.

It is the structure that offers critical preliminary clues regarding a
family's functioning and dysfunctioning and provides the clinician with a
"checklist" of features for assessment.

Subsystems

Practically, it is useful to conceptualize and graphically characterize a
system's structure by subdividing it according to three basic subsystems:
spousal, parent–child or parental, and sibling. These subsystems delineate

interactive patterns among family members based on the roles and functions that are expected of them. Most family systems display aspects of
this basic three-subsystems organization, although the actual makeup
varies, for example, in single-parent families and stepfamilies. The variable
structural shapes of these subsystems combined with their interactive
features provide the early-assessment clues mentioned above.

Spousal Subsystem

This subsystem in the nuclear family is composed of the husband and wife
who make up a marital dyad. It is central to the life and survival of the
family system in the early stages and generally continues to be important.
The spousal subsystem is a product of the individual spouses' personal
development, family of origin and general life experiences, and mate-
selection processes. The formation of the nuclear family begins with the
establishment of the marital relationship. The uniqueness of each nuclear
family system is forged by the new linkage that occurs when the two
spouses come together with their respective intergenerational experiences
and relationships (see Figure 4-1).
    The functioning of a family system is highly dependent on the success-
ful formation of the spousal subsystem. Formation of a viable spousal

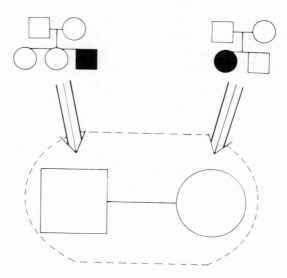

Figure 4-1. Formation of the spousal subsystem.

subsystem involves bringing together realistic expectations, clear role definitions, and adequate emotional bonding between the two people. The complex interplay between the horizontal and vertical loyalties of the two spouses (Boszormenyi-Nagy & Spark, 1973) may deter or prevent the achievement of adequate and appropriate expectations, role definitions, and emotional bonding. In marriages in which both spouses have difficulty leaving home (separation) and remain highly enmeshed with the family of origin (vertical loyalties), their ability to bond with the other spouse emotionally (horizontal loyalties) and form a solid spousal subsystem is impaired. Similarly, if one spouse has achieved relative independence from the family of origin and the other has not, the resulting imbalance in the relationship will find expression in chronic conflict over loyalties and attachment. (The observed tendency for mates to be differentiated to approximately the same degree is a tendency, not a universal fact.)

Impairment in the establishment of the spousal subsystem represents or leads to an intrinsic weakness in the family-formation process and in the resulting family structure. When this occurs, it becomes necessary for the spousal subsystem to compensate for the weakness by forming other structural alignments/coalitions (triangles) to offset the systemic imbalance. For example, the development of bonding and intimacy in the new spousal subsystem of young adult first marriages may be weakened by the continued attachment and failure to separate from family of origin ties on the part of both husband and wife. Or in another instance, a spousal subsystem imbalance may result from a situation in which the husband is excessively tied to his family of origin while his wife displays a relatively greater distance in relating to hers. An early or "unplanned" conception may result, perhaps through secret sabotaging of birth control procedures by the wife in an effort to provide for her own needs for attachment through acquiring a baby, or through unconscious collusion on the part of the partners who have the fantasy that "having a baby" will take pressure off the early imbalance. In such circumstances, further dysfunctional patterns arise, but their symptomatology will not necessarily be witnessed within the spousal subsystem. More typically, the symptoms will be seen in the parent–child subsystem in a child who later acts out the systemic conflicts.

Parent–Child or Parental Subsystem

This subsystem is formed, of course, with the conception of the first child. The pregnancy, not the birth as such, begins to diffuse the former primacy of the spousal subsystem for the couple and begins to refocus their emotional energy toward the expansion of their marital boundaries to include parental responsibilities and a new member. Because it is a dramatic transitional period reflecting both emotional and structural shifts, entering this subsystem involves the potential for new dysfunctional issues to emerge.

As the parent–child subsystem forms and expands to include the first child and then subsequent children, the interactive complexity of the system increases manyfold. The parents' performance of normative roles ranging from the provision of nurturance to discipline often is shaped or at least colored not only by the role models provided by their respective parents but also by the caretaking or dependency roles that they experienced within their own sibling subsystems in their family of origin. In addition, vertical loyalties that were not resolved during the formation of the spousal subsystem may help to produce either deficiencies or excesses in their performance of parental roles.

All of these factors contribute to an increasingly complex system of interactive alignments/coalitions. Extreme examples are reflected in Figure 4-2, in which the father's continuing family of origin attachment may render him unavailable for parenting and the actual introduction of the infant into the system may push him farther away from the spousal

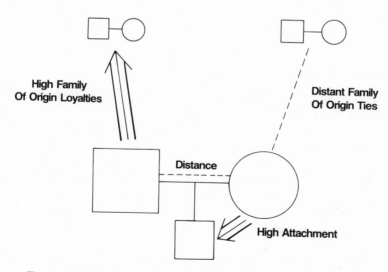

Figure 4-2. Imbalance of spousal and family of origin loyalties.

subsystem and closer to his family of origin. The mother may experience the infant as an emotional substitute for both her absent husband and the lack of closeness and contact with her distant family and thus may become excessively involved in her parenting role, even to the extent of encouraging overdependence and regressive behavior on the part of the infant.

In a large number, perhaps a majority, of dysfunctional families that the family therapist is asked to treat, the primary conflict and symptoms will be displayed within the parent–child subsystem. The entry and attempted integration of a child into a spousal relationship colored by the mutual idealization and varied expectations of mate selection may dramatically trigger the emergence of latent growing up and separation issues in relation to the families of origin, often setting off various kinds of fears and fantasies in the marital partners. The relatively sudden shift to child-related issues, particularly for young adult marriages, challenges immediately each spouse's own degree of individuation and dependency, and may result in either facilitating the consolidation of their parenting efforts or aiding their retreat back into family of origin alliances. Thus, it is the entrance of a child into a system that may create an interactional imbalance, and it frequently and reciprocally is the child who then carries the resultant stress through a variety of patterns systemically calculated to rebalance the system. Many such families live out their family life around the issues and needs of the children created by such situations. In such "child-centered" families, the enormous preeminence of the parent–child subsystem serves to camouflage stress or deficits in the spousal subsystem and often at various other levels in the intergenerational network.

Sibling Subsystem

The sibling subsystem reflects the interactive patterns among the children in the family system. This subsystem generally has been overlooked in the literature on families and family therapy and still tends to be disregarded very often in clinical assessment. One significant exception is the work of Toman (1976) who has descriptively characterized the influences and impacts of one's ordinal position within the family and within the sibling group. After extensive research, he has suggested, for example that being the oldest, middle, or youngest child in the subsystem has clear ramifications for future role performance and for one's expectations when selecting a mate.

The sibling subsystem provides early and continuing experiences in both socialization and peer attachment. In terms of the overall family structure, it is the least powerful subsystem and generally remains dependent on the evolution of alignments/coalitions among the other subsystems. Nevertheless, interactive patterns within this subsystem may have powerful influences on the remainder of the family. The traditional concerns of parents over "sibling rivalry," for example, can be understood more clearly where the oldest of three children has been parentified (see Figure 4-7). The parentified child in such situations is pulled inappropriately into the parental alliances and frequently is given excessive responsibility for taking care of the parents, the household, and the siblings. By virtue of being cast into the parentified role, the child gains great amounts of favors and attention. This establishes basically confrontational interactive patterns between that child and the siblings. The other children cannot compete for attention with that child and feel left out, hurt, and often angry.

At times, the family therapist may wish to consider involving siblings in the therapy experience instead of or in addition to simply working with parents from the family of origin. Recreating the sibling subsystem in therapy with adult clients may be more acceptable and less threatening to many who harbor strong fears about bringing their parents into therapy. Much of the same family of origin data that generally are obtained from parents can be relived and worked through just as easily and effectively with siblings. This may have long-lasting effects also by improving formerly poor sibling relations. The sharing of early experiences and perceptions among siblings engenders a useful kind of bonding among them despite the differences that they experience growing up in their family of origin. For example, one isolated and depressive 45-year-old woman whose husband was contemplating divorce learned for the first time in therapy sessions with her three siblings about the jealousy and anger with which they had regarded her because of her parentified role as cartaker for their alcoholic mother. The emotional cutoff that she had experienced from her siblings when their mother had died 15 years ealier was overcome. The reunification of the sibling subsystem brought on constructive changes for the woman in her marriage as well.

Boundaries

Boundaries mark the shape of the family system and its subsystems. They are like invisible lines circumscribing the system and delineating who is within it and who is not. Boundaries also define the quality of the system's interactive process and determine its reception of feedback from external sources such as vocation, school, and the intergenerational network. In this respect, boundaries serve both to differentiate and to protect the nuclear family system from the external social environment.

The family therapist must be able to identify both the internal and external boundaries of a family system. The "external boundaries" circumscribe the entire nuclear family and differentiate it from its social milieu. These boundaries also serve to define and regulate the interaction between the nuclear system and the intergenerational network (see Figure 4-3).

The "internal boundaries" serve a similar function by differentiating the subsystems from one another. It also has been suggested that the individual members of the system possess quasi-boundaries that differentiate one member from another.

The qualitative structure of boundaries can be described as relatively open, relatively closed, or diffuse (see Figure 4-4). "Open boundaries" represent the normative ideal in that they allow a manageable and tolerable level of interactive input and output for the system. It is a misconception that open family boundaries allow a maximum of interaction and information exchange and processing. Too much interaction and exchange would be overwhelming. A boundary is not a fixed state but a dynamic process of monitoring and controlling internal systemic comfort and balance (homeostasis) with external feedback and interaction. A boundary may be evaluated in terms of its relative "flexibility" and "rigidity." Boundaries that move toward rigidity in the face of internal or external crisis and relax when the threat has passed may be described as possessing an appropriate blend of rigidity and flexibility. In many chronically dysfunc-

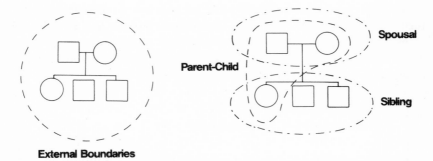

External Boundaries

Figure 4-3. The location of external and internal systems boundaries.

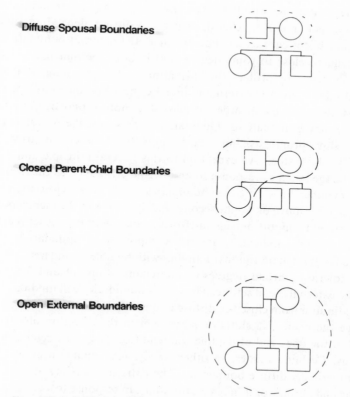

Diffuse Spousal Boundaries

Closed Parent-Child Boundaries

Open External Boundaries

Figure 4-4. Diffuse, closed, and open boundary patterns.

tional systems, the boundaries appear to be rigidly closed or diffuse. The ideal, in other words, permits the boundary to close at times and thus to protect the system from external threats and, alternatively, to open sufficiently for members to leave the system and return, as well as to permit the flow of information that we have mentioned several times.

"Closed boundaries" restrict the processing of feedback and limit the system's interaction with external systems and entities. Families with relatively closed boundaries tend to be isolated from external elements and appear to cling together for self-protection.

"Diffuse boundaries" are minimally drawn. The system is poorly differentiated and thus vulnerable to external influences. Diffuse boundaries reflect poor organization or sometimes underorganization on the part of the family system.

The quality of boundaries for any system may move among being relatively open, relatively closed, or perhaps diffuse, depending on situational and historical factors. For example, the external boundaries normally tend to close to some degree shortly after the marriage of young adults in order to protect the formation and functioning of the new spousal subsystem. The external boundaries may become more open after the first child is born in order to allow for more supportive interaction from the new grandparents. Qualitatively, however, the movement normally is slow, progressive, and consistent with the patterns of growth and change in the system. An exception to this general principle and pattern would be the system's response to an internal crisis such as the death of a family member. In such cases, boundaries would either close tightly in a self-protective move or would become widely diffuse as the members of the system sought support outside in efforts to deal with their grief reactions.

As we have indicated, another component of boundaries is their relative flexibility and rigidity. Families with flexible boundaries are capable of tolerating broad degrees of interchange—output and feedback— with the external social setting. Thus, their boundaries will modulate along the continuum from closed to diffuse to open. Families that are not able to manage the respective shifts or movement in the direction of either the closed or the open end of the line will tend to evolve more rigid boundary patterns. Certain families, in other words, may maintain either rigidly closed or rigidly diffuse boundaries. The pattern of rigidity may be either historic and chronic or it may be situational, in response to a crisis or some unpredictable change. For example, in a family in which one spouse has had a history of depressive episodes, the other mate along with the children and even family of origin members may pull together defensively in an effort to protect the vulnerable member and thus the family itself from external influences and forces that are perceived as potentially disruptive and threatening to that family member. Such families may display a chronically rigid and closed boundary. In a situationally based pattern, events that tend to render the family system vulnerable—loss of a job, an extramarital affair, or the death of a child—may create temporarily rigid and even closed boundaries.

Triangles

The array of alignments among family members across generations often appears complex and overwhelming to the beginning family therapist. Most such structural alignments, with the exception of alignments in which two members are in a supportive relationship because of common interests or concerns, occur in patterns in which three members are involved. Early research in social psychology and group behavior indicated that when difficulty occurs between two members of a social group a third member typically is pulled into the interaction in order to diffuse or refocus the tension away from the dyad. This process provides something of a homeostatic or steady-state function for the system, rebalancing the dyadic system when the stress gets too high, thus ensuring the system's survival.

Alignments were defined in early family therapy literature by Haley (1967) in terms of coalitions in which two members pull together in order to protect themselves or to move against a third member who is threatening the system. Haley characterized the "perverse triangle" as an intergenerational coalition among members that breached the generational boundaries. For example, a wife may align with her mother or with a child against her husband. Bowen developed his family of origin and differentiation theories around these concepts. He observed clinically that dyadic systems turn into triadic systems or triangles under stress and that over a period of time, the roles in a triangular arrangement become stable and functional positions within a system. He thus termed the triangle the smallest stable group.

Normative developmental, transitional, and situational events all engender stress and conflict in a family system. Thus, triangular alignments become basic interactional building blocks in a system's structure. They serve to balance the system at both the nuclear and the intergenerational levels. As building blocks, triangles may serve in both functional and dysfunctional ways. In families with great conflict and high vulnerability, for example, the triangles may appear to be very rigid, much like the protective aspect of rigidly closed boundaries, and may endure in that form over many years and across several generations.

Some theorists have suggested that many, even hundreds, of triangular arrangements are possible within a three-generational system. It is our view from clinical observation that each nuclear family system tends to possess at any given time a *central triangle* that serves to provide structural balance for the system. Such central triangles may involve intergenerational members; that is, they may include not merely one (as in the case of sibling triangles) but two or three generations. Clearly, other triangles exist in nuclear families, but they are secondary in function and power to the central triangle. The central triangle dominates the structure of the family system and often contains either a parentified or scapegoated family member. In some highly rigid systems, the membership of the central triangle may remain constant and endure over many years, even after children have left home and married. In other systems, membership in the central triangle may vary according to developmental and transitional patterns, such as those that occur when children are successively scapegoated as each one either reaches an age to leave home or is legally removed from the home. Recognizing the central triangle and its functioning and power is critical to early structural and process assessment.

Fogarty (1975), an early student of Bowen, has illustrated very effectively the fact that triangles come in different sizes and shapes. His model is reflected in Figure 4-5. In the balanced triangle A, all members are equidistant from one another. The isosceles triangle B demonstrates a close coalition between two members, with the third member located equally distant from the two of them. The other isosceles triangle, C, shows a pattern in which there is a considerable distance between two members and an equal distance between two of them and the third member. Triangle D illustrates a variable pattern in which the two members to the left in the diagram are distant from the third member but not equally distant from that member.

Fogarty (1975) has also defined the nature of the interlocking triangles that cross generational boundaries. In Figure 4-6, issues from the family of origin triangle ABC spread into and influence the mate selection and marriage of A to D, just as the triangle DEF affects the mate selection and marriage of D to A. With the birth of the child G, the new triangle DEF becomes the product of ABC and DEF and is reciprocally influenced by changes and patterns in those triangles.

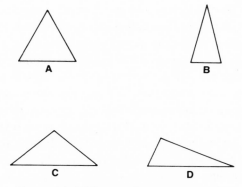

Figure 4-5. Different triangular patterns.

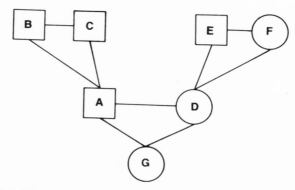

Figure 4-6. The intergenerational linkage of triangles and individuals.

Obviously, it is important for therapists to be able to recognize and assess the role and function of triangles in the clinical system with which they are working. Personal exercises that aid family therapists in recognizing and understanding the central triangles in their own families of origin are useful. For example, beginning family therapists may develop a genogram (see Chapter 6) of their family of origin network. Here they would identify major triangular relationships in which they participated.

FAMILY PROCESS

The energy and movement of a system are reflected in its process, which appears in both recurrent and singular, infrequently appearing interactive patterns. Patterns of family process may appear in an inflexible fashion across several generations or may arise reactively in efforts to accommodate to or manage external influences. Again, the structure refers to the shape of the system and the process to the actual interactive sequences and emotional milieu of it.

When the family therapist first makes contact with a family in a clinical situation, the family process makes it possible for the therapist to engage the system. It is the elements of process, therefore, that the therapist must encounter and recognize experientially, because it is through them that it is possible to form an alliance with the system.

While structure and process are linked together and function in a reciprocal fashion throughout a system, we have found it useful to deal with process in terms of eight concepts or pairs of concepts. These shall be discussed in the order in which we listed them earlier in this chapter.

Continuity and Change

Every system is engaged in a struggle for survival and continuity that is intrinsic to systems. A crucial question facing every system is that of how much change it can tolerate and still survive. A tension is always present when maintaining the status quo or allowing the influx of sufficient information to push the system toward new levels of behaving and functioning. The steady-state concept of General Systems Theory is the best reflection of this sense of polarity and tension within a system.

During the earliest days of the family therapy movement, it was thought that the major therapeutic goal was the reestablishment of a state of homeostasis for the family system (Jackson, 1957). This means that the presenting symptoms would be reduced or eradicated and the system returned to a condition of balance or tension management in which the system was "at rest." Further developments in systemic epistemology have suggested that the goals of family therapy more appropriately may involve pushing the system beyond restoration of a previous condition of equilibrium to a place where it must accommodate by making substantial changes so that it functions at a new level (Dell, 1982; Elkaim, 1981).

More recent developments make more explicit the differences between "first-order change" and "second-order change" (Ashby, 1952). First-order change refers simply to making corrective changes in order to return the system to a balanced or functional level, as in the familiar analogy of the household thermostat that keeps the temperature within a prescribed range. Second-order change involves altering the nature of the system itself so that new levels of functioning are achieved, as, for example, when the dial on the thermostat is moved to a new setting. These patterns of potential change also are related to the associated concepts of "morphostasis" (system constancy) and "morphogenesis" (system redefinition) (Hoffman, 1981).

These issues of systemic change will be addressed further in Chapter 7. Here it is sufficient to note that every family system experiences an internal tension regarding the management of influences that would create change. Often, it is the perceived threat of change that causes some systems to withdraw behind protectively rigid external boundaries and other systems simply to split into disconnected chaos. The intrusion of the therapist into the family is an initial step in potential systemic change.

Separateness and Connectedness

At the same time that a tension between first- and second-order change exists within a system, a similar tension plays itself out within the family around the emotionally laden theme of separateness and connectedness. These concepts dramatically highlight the interplay that occurs for families with regard to emotional closeness and distance. Each family evolves its own unique and idiosyncratic pattern that defines both for individuals and subsystems the allowable degrees of intimacy, openness, autonomy, and differentiation. Such patterns do not constitute family typologies, as in the case of enmeshment–disengagement, but form an internal theme perceived and accepted by all members as a guide for their integration.

Perhaps more than most other concepts the separateness–connectedness theme represents pure family process. The pattern of separateness–connectedness in a family cannot always be determined from the verbal data presented by a family or characterized by a family's verbal productions. Often the family therapist must experience this theme as he or she comes into contact with the family's "dance" (Hoffman, 1981). The concept of separateness–connectedness is introduced here both in order to provide a description and in order to help the reader to begin thinking more explicitly and conceptually about family process. For example, how tolerable is the separateness when the first child is ready to leave home? How powerful is the connectedness when a parent contracts a terminal illness?

Enmeshment–Disengagement

The concepts of enmeshment and disengagement were introduced initially by Minuchin and colleagues (1967). They used them as descriptors in their early work in identifying parent–child dynamics among low-income families with delinquent children. However, the concepts have become generic to the family therapy field as an effective classification typology or continuum regarding a family's interactional processes.

These concepts refer to an emotional level of interactive functioning within families. The enmeshment pattern involves an identifiable emotional intensity among family members in terms of attachment, frequency of interaction, and reciprocal dependency. The individual member of the system will share a common, although not always explicit, personal survival need for the maintenance of the family process. In an enmeshed system, external or internal events or situations reverberate quickly and profusely throughout the entire system. One member may speak as if he or she were speaking on behalf of another member(s). Toward the extreme of the continuum, the highly enmeshed family may display either closed and rigid external boundaries that isolate the system from external influences or diffuse external boundaries that allow the enmeshment to spread unchecked across several generations. However, the internal subsystem boundaries are diffuse and ill defined, allowing many intrusions to occur, such as that of a child into the spousal subsystem.

Enmeshment should not be confused with emotional closeness, intimacy, or issues of communication. The intensity of enmeshment actually may create emotional withdrawal on the part of certain members of the family as a protective defense for their autonomy and individuation. Adults coming from enmeshing families of origin may limit their capacity for interpersonal intimacy as a result of being fearful of replicating enmeshment patterns and losing autonomy. Overall, members of enmeshing families have experienced close affective attachment and carry both the result of such attachments and the expectations that relationships should be of that nature in mate selection and in their adult relationships, even though the cost of enmeshment often is limited individuation and difficulties with separation from their family of origin.

The disengaged pattern of family process involves a remarkable absence of affective intensity in family attachments. Relationships throughout the subsystems are characterized by emotional distance, lack of sensitivity to individual needs, and a high frequency of independent activities. Families falling toward the extreme end of the continuum lack cohesion, something that is reflected in rather diffuse external boundaries. Internal boundaries in such families may be either rigidly set with little relationship to other internal subsystems or completely diffuse with individual family members each going in their own separate direction. Individuals in such systems evolve independence and autonomy early but often at the cost of experiencing emotional loss or a severe limitation of personal affective ties with parents and siblings.

While Minuchin's enmeshment–disengagement concepts have been criticized as being more "linear" than "circular," they offer the family therapist an important descriptive mechanism for use in assessing and understanding the quality of a family's interactive process. The reader is referred to other authors who have attempted to offer similar descriptive concepts: Hoffman, borrowing from Ashby, has talked about the "too richly cross-joined system" (1975) and the "too poorly cross-joined family" (1981); Aponte (1976), in discussing low-income families, has described the "underorganized family"; Stierlin (1974) has written of "centripetal" and "centrifugal" separation patterns in families with adolescents; and Wynne (e.g., 1958), as a result of his research with families of schizophrenics, has referred to the concepts of "pseudomutuality" and "pseudohostility."

Communication

When "communication" is mentioned, most of us think of the verbal aspects of interaction. The family therapist, however, must view communication from the broadest possible stance that can be taken with regard to human interaction. Perhaps the verbal interaction that we engage in so routinely is but the "tip of the iceberg" when the totality of the verbal, nonverbal, and other expressive ways of human communication is considered (see, for example, the exploration of the contexts of speech and meaning by Scheflen, 1974, in which he deals with kinesics, posture, interaction, setting, and culture). As Watzlawick and colleagues (1967) have noted, "one cannot not communicate," meaning that all behavior communicates something of ourselves to others. Beginning clinicians can fall rather easily into the trap of hearing and responding only to the words and problems expressed by clients rather than attending to the myriad underlying and subtle meanings that are being expressed.

Communication in the family is pure process with multidimensional meanings. The themes, codes, and innuendos of a family's communication are difficult for the family therapist to decipher because the family's private meanings have evolved from years of history and are bound by uniquely patterned rules and references to family subsystems, coalitions, and triangles. The family therapist takes on the risky task of entering the system and becoming part of it in order to experience the power and meaning of the family's "code."

The early studies of communication between schizophrenics and their parents illustrated dramatically the patterned levels of communication.

The Palo Alto group made familiar the concept of a "message" level and a "meta" level in which the sender gives a message about the communication, for example, how to interpret it. The classic paper on the double-bind theory of Bateson and associates (1956) emerged from such study. Laing and Esterson (1964) illustrated similar phenomena with their collection of case studies of schizophrenics and their families. Others have elaborated on communication patterns in families (e.g., Satir, 1964; Selvini-Palazzoli, Boscolo, Cecchin, & Prata, 1978; Watzlawick *et al.*, 1967).

Jackson's (1968) early use of symmetrical, complementary, and reciprocal "modes" of interaction popularized the use of categories that have often been used to characterize specific patterns of family interaction. Symmetrical communication is at an equal, "head to head" level, with each person assuming equal control and authority. Such a pattern tends to lead to competition, confrontation, and escalation, as in the case of two professors arguing a point or both spouses paying the bills. The complementary pattern is something of a "one-up, one-down" pattern in which one individual is identified as being "in charge" and given authority and acknowledged expertise by the other. An example is a normative parent–child relationship. There is less competition in this pattern, although in certain families it can become rigid and lead to authoritarianism and undue dependency. Jackson believed that the reciprocal pattern, which represents a mixture of the former types, was more functional and offered greater flexibility to the family.

Parentification

Where stress exists within a system, particularly in a dyad such as a marriage, a third member may be triangulated into the group in order to maintain the continuity of the system or to restore its balance. In a nuclear family system it frequently is a child or children, who, in a serial fashion, may be pulled in as the third member of the troubled subsystem. When children are involved in family triangles, in particular if it is with the parents, they frequently function in the role of either a parentified child or a scapegoat. Many family systems tend to have children who play such roles, sometimes interchangeably. The development of such patterned roles occurs in a circular and reciprocal fashion with the parents and system needing the child to perform the function and the child gaining a certain amount of status and emotional reinforcement as a result of playing the parentified child role. The greater the vulnerability of the family system to stress and the greater the need for balance in the system, the more likely the role is to take on a quality of rigidity and emotional drama that becomes central to the family's emotional process.

Parentification may occur between adults when one spouse "parents" the other. The parentification of a child generally occurs when the system's internal boundaries are diffuse, the spousal subsystem poorly defined, and the parents, due to marital stress or overly strong ties to the families of origin, cannot perform the executive parental function for the system. The resultant triangle usually is formed among mother, father, and one child (see Figure 4-7). As noted earlier, the child in such a role is given an inordinate amount of responsibility not only for the care of the household and the siblings but also in many cases for the emotional and physical well-being of the parents. Similar responsibilities are assumed in intergenerational patterns such as those between mother, child, and grandparent.

The child who assumes the parentified role, particularly if it takes on the role as an infant, is pulled out of the normal developmental experiences, becomes a pseudoadult, and may give up childhood play and peer attachments. In one such case, a precocious little girl had slept in her parents' bedroom for the first 2 years of her life and subsequently slept immediately across the hall from their bedroom. From the time that she went into her own bedroom, however, neither her door nor that to her parents' bedroom was ever closed. In early family therapy sessions, that 6-year-old child ordered her 3-year-old brother around, protected and de-

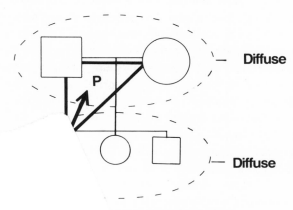

The parentified child.

fended her parents, and attempted to speak for both the family and the therapists.

Children who are parentified frequently develop adjunctive symptomatology, such as adolescent depression, problematic self-differentiation, school phobia, separation problems, or emotional cutoff. As adults, they often manifest an inability to relinquish control in adult relationships.

The parentified child performs a homeostatic function in the family by returning the system to an often tenuous balance and maintaining it in a balanced state. The role may be performed by the same child even into the adult postseparation years, or it may be bequeathed from one child to another in a kind of succession. The entire family process tends to revolve around the central triangle involving the parentified child. Therefore, it should not be surprising to the family therapist that it is not merely the parents who are reluctant to give up this pattern but also the child, who may resist returning to an age-appropriate position in the sibling subsystem.

Scapegoating

Scapegoating, like parentification, involves a systemic dynamic in which one member is triangulated into a subsystem in order to alleviate stress and rebalance the total system. Unlike parentification, where the third member of the triangle functions within the troubled spousal subsystem, the scapegoating process involves an attempt to dissipate or remove the stress by pushing it away and placing it outside of the subsystem. While scapegoating may occur throughout the intergenerational network, it most often is seen in a parent–child triangle (see Figure 4-8). In such situations the scapegoated child takes on or absorbs the stress from the marital dyad and carries it away from that family subsystem. The tension is then acted out through school misbehavior, inappropriate sexual activities, or a variety of delinquent actions.

The classic statement on scapegoating was made by Vogel and Bell (1960). They identified "an emotionally disturbed child as an embodiment of certain types of conflicts between parents [and recognized that members of the family] are able to achieve unity through scapegoating a particular member . . . " (p. 412). Ackerman (1964) defined a similar three-person process that embodied roles of "persecutor," "victim," and "rescuer." The victim performed the scapegoat role by seemingly binding the family

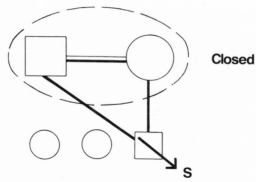

Figure 4-8. The scapegoat child.

together. As that role took on greater proportions, however, it would begin to impair family functioning significantly.

Scapegoated children typically are brought to clinical services as the identified client, the source of the presenting problem. The parents often are willing to relate stories of the child's misdeeds in a seemingly unending fashion, carefully keeping the focus away from themselves. At the same time, the parents' own relationship is presented as calm, reasonable, and stable. Typically they will resist all efforts to have them take a close look at their own relationship. Many inexperienced family therapists are misled by the apparent tranquility in the spousal subsystem and throughout the total family system. The role of the scapegoat in the family is accepted and reinforced by the siblings who see their brother or sister as "bad" or "crazy." Beginning therapists in particular may fail to recognize the function that the family scapegoat performs in balancing the system. Similarly, many therapists and treatment programs do not comprehend at the outset the systemic etiology of the presenting problem and proceed to accept the parents' designation of the scapegoated child as the source of the family problems and then to treat the child and his or her behaviors in either individual or group therapy.

The system's homeostatic power to resist change should never be underestimated. Despite the parents' complaints about the child who is identified as the major problem and their pleading to the therapist to correct the behaviors, there typically is great resistance to change, particularly when the remainder of the family is not involved in therapy. In fact, it is to be expected that as the child's behavior improves, the parents will attempt to sabotage the therapy, either overtly (by changing therapists, dropping out of therapy, and so on) or covertly (by aiding in the commission of additional inappropriate behavior by the child).

Removal of the scapegoated child from the family, as in cases of serious juvenile delinquency, may set off a reactive sequence of events within the family system. First, the dissolution of the central triangle through the removal of the child may result in instability and some degree of chaos in the system. Second, the marriage may begin to manifest stress and conflict may erupt. Some marriages may be so vulnerable once the extruded stress and conflict have returned that the partners move quickly to divorce. Third, there generally is a move to recreate another central triangle in order to restore a homeostatic balance to the family system. Consequently, another child in the family may be triangulated into the marital subsystem in order to handle the liberated tension through assignment to either a parentified role or to a scapegoat role. In one such family that was treated in a mental health center by traditional psychotherapeutic means, a family of eight children headed by a controlling mother and an alcoholic father produced six scapegoated children, one after the other in serial fashion. Prior to the entry of the identified client into the role, the scapegoats had included a 26-year-old daughter who had become pregnant at 17, a 23-year-old son who had been convicted of robbery, a 21-year-old daughter who had become pregnant and suicidal at 17, a 19-year-old son who had been convicted of drug charges, and a 17-year-old son who had been convicted of vandalism. The role of scapegoat had passed from one child to the next as the scapegoated one either left or was removed from the home.

Myths and Secrets

A subtle and often hard to detect process in families revolves around secrets and myths. Often, such components of family life can be identified and their power recognized only after the family therapist has engaged and joined the family system. Most families have secrets regarding such issues as premarital pregnancy, the suicide of an uncle, the criminal conviction of a grandfather, or some other matter considered shameful. The clinical significance of a secret is the hidden power that it exerts within a nuclear or intergenerational family system. Certain secrets may conceal a vulnerability in one member, embarrassment in another, or a provocative indiscretion in another member.

The role of the secret is to stabilize and protect the family system. This is not simply a matter of keeping information from being disclosed. A family secret actually functions to shape the structure of the system in a protective manner around what is hidden. Considerable amounts of energy go into shaping and maintaining the structure so established. An interesting fact about secrets is that they often are present at a conscious level among the family members—although usually they are present at a preconscious level—and although most family members know about the secret, the secret is never mentioned within the system.

Family therapists who work in the family of origin, parent–child, or sibling subsystems are the most likely professionals to discover secrets that have been hidden and passed down across generations. In one case in which the female client's two female siblings were attending the therapy session with her, it was discovered that all three shared protective feelings regarding their deceased mother. When the issue was pursued, it was revealed that all three had some knowledge that their mother had been conceived premaritally. They were amazed that all had access to the knowledge but had not spoken about it to the others, although all were more than 40 years of age. None knew where they might have learned about the secret. When discussing the situation, they did come to recognize that it explained certain things for them, such as why their mother and grandmother "fought and never got along."

Myths in a family are even more difficult to identify than secrets because they normally are not based on fact or reality. Their function is similar to that of secrets in that they provide a unifying conceptualization of the entire family that serves to promote stability and continuity. Myths are pervasive beliefs about what and who the family is, how it should behave, or what each member is like or should be like. They pervade the entire system and are accepted emotionally and often cognitively as reality by *all* members of the family.

One of the best-known myths is the "suicidal myth," identified initially by Gehrke and Kirschenbaum (1967). This myth often is found in an enmeshing, isolating family system that has rather rigid, closed boundaries. The shared belief in the family is that if any member were to leave the family, the system itself would not survive. Consequently, children come home directly after school, there are few social contacts for adults or children, and growing up and separating from the family are not expected or planned. Reciprocally, individual members of the family carry the belief that "if I were to leave home I would not survive." In one closely knit

Midwestern family, four of the five adult children were married and lived along with other members of the nuclear and extended family within a 1-mile radius of a small town. The exception was the oldest daughter who had joined a religious order and lived in a convent on the West Coast. The youngest son and his wife had lived for 2 years in a Southern community where he had attempted to start a business similar to the one in which his father and brothers worked together. When his business began to fail economically, he said that he knew that he should not have left home and that it was "too dangerous" being so far away from home. The weekend after verbalizing those feelings, he packed up and moved his family back home, originally going into his parents' household. Eventually he purchased a home two blocks from his parents' home.

Power

Power is an exceedingly important factor to assess in dealing with a family. Understanding the power arrangement and distribution within a family enables a therapist to explain not only the hierarchical organization but also certain of the structural patterns of triangles and coalitions that exist within the system. A distinction between power and authority is in order at this point. Authority refers to the legitimate right to do something. Power refers to the ability to use force in order to accomplish whatever tasks or reach whatever goals one is seeking to achieve.

Family therapists should never regard power as existing solely within the boundaries of a nuclear family system because power often is transferred and expressed intergenerationally. For example, a mother may possess power within a nuclear system because power has been transmitted to her through the females in her family over several generations. Her familiarity with power and the propensity to use it in interpersonal family situations would have affected the mate selection and spousal subsystem processes as well as the parenting behavior. Females in such family systems could be expected to select weaker and more dependent male spouses in order to reinforce their own power and perhaps to manifest overly dominant behaviors in serving as a parent to male children. Similarly, therapists should not routinely assume that the power in a family system resides with those who occupy the positions of authority. As we have noted, for example, the roles of a parentified or scapegoated child carry great power within a family by helping to maintain its balance and survival. Such power has been given to an individual who does not have the normative authority to function in a parental role.

Clinical issues regarding power will be discussed further in Chapter 7, particularly with regard to the family therapist's need to recognize where the actual power lies and to utilize this knowledge to enhance his or her ability to effect therapeutic change. The other concepts and patterns defined and described in this chapter will be operationalized further in the discussions on assessment and treatment in Chapters 6, 7, and 8.

CHAPTER FIVE

The Family as
a Developmental System

Family therapists, in our judgment, should be educated and trained in the area of family from the beginning of their graduate and professional education. To start with the study of individuals and then to deal with the family in a hurried and skimpy fashion does not provide the family therapist with the depth and breadth of knowledge that is required in order to be an effective family therapist. Family study is not something to be added on as an afterthought. Rather, the study of the family in depth is an essential part of the preparation of the family therapist. So, also, is the study of the individual, but the study of the individual in the context of the family is crucial to good preparation and to good therapy.

As we have pointed out many times over the past 2 decades, it is possible to learn as much about the plasticity and functioning of human beings from cultural anthropology as from dynamic psychology. Fortunately, it is neither necessary nor desirable to omit the study of either individuals or the contexts in which they function and are shaped, but the study of the family is at least as important as the study of the individual. In this chapter, we shall focus on one approach to the understanding of families, because we think that the orientation to families discussed in this chapter is the most useful one available to us.

THE FAMILY DEVELOPMENT APPROACH

More than 2 decades ago, family specialists distinguished five conceptual frameworks that often are used in the study of the family. Named were the institutional–historical, the structure–function, the symbolic–interactionist, the situational, and the family development approaches (Hill & Hansen, 1960).

We find the family development approach to be the most compatible with our need for understanding and working with families and clinical populations. It embodies not only systems concepts for helping us to deal conceptually and practically with whole families but also appropriate concepts for understanding individual development and functioning in a family context.

The family development conceptual framework developed by Reuben Hill and associates used four major concepts in its conceptualizations. First, the family is a system that is relatively closed, boundary maintaining, equilibrium seeking, adaptive, and purposive. Saying that it is a relatively closed system means that the family tends to close in on itself while dealing with some issues, but that it has semipermeable boundaries that do permit interchange with the environment; it is not a totally closed system but not a wide open system either. Second, it uses structure concepts such as position, role, and norms, which help in examining the internal occurrences in the family. Third, it employs concepts of goal orientation and education to elucidate the functioning and task-performance aspects of the family. Fourth, such concepts as stages of development, role sequences, and careers of family positions are used in the observation and understanding of events over the life history of the family (Hill, 1971).

Historically, the family development perspective emerged from collaboration between Evelyn M. Duvall and Hill, beginning in 1943. The work was refined in the preparation of background papers they prepared for the National Conference on Family Life held in Washington, D.C., in 1948. As noted by Duvall (1971), their work involved bringing together the life cycle approach that was already well-known among sociologists and the developmental task concept that was emerging in (individual) human development research and theory. The life cycle began to be viewed as involving a series of developmental tasks throughout its span. The formulation of the concept of family developmental tasks was accomplished by a work group in family development research at a workshop on marriage and family research assembled and led by Duvall in 1950 (Duvall, 1971). Subsequently, the family development approach was popularized among students and professionals alike by the writings of Duvall, Hill, Roy Rodgers (1973), and others. Duvall's widely used textbooks on family development, which began to appear in 1957 and have continued to be published in revised editions to the present, have presented the material to several generations of students. Recently, the work has been discovered by mainstream family therapists (e.g., Carter & McGoldrick, 1980; Glick & Kessler, 1974; Haley, 1971).

The family development perspective, simply stated, holds that families "go through predictable stages of development that can be understood in terms of the development of the individual family members and of the family as a whole" (Duvall, 1971, p. v).

Each individual has developmental tasks to perform at given stages in life. Those tasks have been defined as tasks that arise at or around a certain time in the individual's life. Successful completion of the tasks leads to happiness and subsequent success with later tasks, and failure leads to individual unhappiness, social disapproval, and problems with subsequent tasks (Havighurst, 1953). There are many such tasks to be performed by the individual, and they have been variously described and grouped into stages.

Duvall (1971) has described developmental tasks in ten categories for seven stages in the individual's life. The stages are infancy, early childhood, late childhood, early adolescence, late adolescence, maturity, and aging. One of those tasks, for example, is the task of achieving an appropriate dependence–independence pattern. As adapted from Duvall's (1971, pp. 108–109) work, this task in three of the stages would be as follows:

- In *early adolescence*, the task is to establish one's independence from adults in all areas of behavior.
- In *late adolescence*, the task is to establish one's self as an independent individual in an adult manner.
- In *maturity*, the task is to be interdependent—now learning, now succoring others as need arises.

Others have freed the concept of developmental tasks from its strong ties to biological roots and have related it more closely to role theory and systems theory. Rodgers (1973), for example, redefined a developmental task as a set of norms or role expectations arising "at a particular point in the career of a position in a social system" (p. 51).

Family Developmental Tasks

The concept of family developmental tasks is best described in the words of Duvall (1971):

Family developmental tasks run parallel to those of the individual. A family developmental task is a growth responsibility that arises at a certain stage in the life of a family, successful completion of which leads to satisfaction and success with later tasks, which failure leads to unhappiness in the family, disapproval by society, and difficulty with later family developmental tasks.

Family developmental tasks are those growth responsibilities that must be accomplished by a family at a given stage of development in a way that will satisfy its (1) biological requirements, (2) cultural imperatives, and (3) personal aspirations and values, if the family is to continue to grow as a unit. (pp. 149–150)

Developmental tasks for a family range from those that are critical to a particular stage to those that are less significant and certainly not critical to that stage. A stage-critical task for a family with a teenage child would involve balancing freedom with responsibilities for teenagers as they mature and emancipate themselves. For the adult, a stage-critical task would be that of establishing postparental interests and careers (Duvall, 1971).

The Family Life Cycle

Various divisions have been made of the family life cycle. Duvall (1971) divided the cycle into eight stages, each of which has some stage-appropriate developmental tasks. The eight stages delineated by Duvall are as follows:

- *Stage 1.* Married couples (without children)
- *Stage 2.* Childbearing families (oldest child birth–30 months)
- *Stage 3.* Families with preschool children (oldest child 2½–6 years)
- *Stage 4.* Families with schoolchildren (oldest child 6–13 years)
- *Stage 5.* Families with teenagers (oldest child 13–20)
- *Stage 6.* Families as launching centers (first child gone to last child's leaving home)
- *Stage 7.* Middle-aged parents (empty nest to retirement)
- *Stage 8.* Aging family members (retirement to death of both spouses).

Each family is viewed by Duvall (1971) as going through the stages with the oldest child and essentially repeating the process with subsequent children. She has noted the conceptual problem involved in establishing the family life stages in connection with the progress of the first child, indicating that there is no simple way to deal with the conceptual difficulties posed by families with more than one child (pp. 116–118).

Rodgers (1962) modified Duvall's schema into a model that included 24 stages or categories, making room for the movement of several different children through the family life cycle.

Hill (1970) has emphasized the three-generational properties of the family life cycle, much as we have done in this book. The marital pair in the nuclear family form a "linkage bridge" between their own parents and their children's generation. There is, therefore, a linking and mutual interdependence among the generations as they move through the life cycle in a linking and kind of cogwheeling fashion.

Others have modified the number of stages for clinical purposes. Howells (1975, p. 94), for example, has described the family in terms of seven stages or phases. Each of these involves changing structure and functions. As we have adapted them, they are:

1. The phase of courtship to marriage (informal partnership).
2. The phase of early partnership in marriage (formal partnership). The adults in the family continue alone from marriage until the birth of the first child. This phase ends with the start of the family's expansion.
3. The phase of expansion. This one lasts until the birth of the last child.
4. The phase of consolidation. The family continues with no more additions to its members and ends when the first child moves out to live elsewhere or to found his or her own family of procreation.
5. The phase of contraction. The decline of members sets in as all the children leave and the founders of the family find themselves alone as a couple.
6. The phase of final partnership. The life of the family continues with the founders alone as a couple.
7. The phase of disappearance. During this phase, first one partner and then the other dies. The family is no more, except that it lives again through its representatives in other families.

Barnhill and Longo (1980) have adapted the family life cycle concept but have emphasized the transitions from one stage to the next. They attempted to set forth nine key issues in the transitions, as follows:

Commitment. This is the key issue in the transition to stage 1 (establishment of the family). This transition includes late courtship, wedding, honeymoon, and parenthood. Commitment is made as the partners in the new family deal with breaking away from their respective families of origin and developing an attachment to the new family.

Developing new parent roles. In stages 1–2, the transition from spousal to parental roles involves the development of several new interrelated roles.

Accepting the new personality. Transitions 2–3 involve acceptance on the part of the family of the development of a new personality in the family.

Introducing the child to institutions. In transitions 3–4, the child needs to be helped with the task of establishing independent relationships to school, sports groups, church, and so forth.

Accepting adolescence. In transitions 4–5, the family has to face several new role transitions and developmental issues as a youngster in the family deals with puberty and early adolescence. Youngsters struggle with developing their sexual identity and integrating themselves into a peer-group culture.

Experimenting with independence. The family needs to permit independent and related adult strivings to emerge as the oldest child moves into young adulthood.

Preparation to launch. Permitting the oldest child to accept an independent adult role in transitions 6–7 involves several role transitions for the family. There is an overlap between this transition for the family of origin and transitions 0–1 for the child's generation as it begins to form a new family.

Letting go—facing each other again. Stages or transitions 7–8 have to do with the transition of the parents as they let go of the children and begin to face each other as spouses who are alone again for the first time since the early marriage, prechild days. Also, they begin to enter into grandparental roles and to take part in a new three-generational pattern.

Accepting retirement and/or old age. In transitions 8–9, the older generation is faced with moving into an entirely new lifestyle in which career and related issues are absent. The middle generation often has to begin planning for caring for the older as well as for the younger generation.

A major point to be made with regard to the transitions discussed by Barnhill and Longo is that symptoms appearing in one or more family members at such times, for example, depression or delinquent behavior, often indicate that the appropriate life cycle tasks are not being mastered. To state it conversely, disruptions or failures in the achievement of family developmental tasks may result in the appearance of symptoms and symptomatic behavior in a family member. This has obvious implications for both clinical assessment and intervention. Changes in family size, for example, frequently are accompanied by the appearance of symptoms. That is, losses from the family or additions to it may produce symptomatic reactions in one or more family members. While this is far from universal, it occurs often enough to warrant careful attention by the clinician at both the original assessment and the ongoing assessment–treatment stages.

Another clinically oriented framework, one that includes a developmental task conception, has been proposed by Solomon (1973). Each of the developmental family stages that he proposed poses a life crisis situation that must be resolved if adaptive growth is to be continued by the family. Solomon broke the family life cycle down into five stages:

Stage 1—The marriage. Marriage involves two tasks: ending each spouse's primary ties with his and her own parents and redirecting the energies formerly invested in the family of origin into the marriage.

Stage 2—The birth of the first child and subsequent childbearing. This stage requires the consolidation of the marriage as well as the establishment of parental roles. Sacrificing marital roles for parental roles is a difficulty frequently encountered in this stage.

Stage 3—Individuation of family members. During this broad midrange of family life, the task becomes that of the continual modification of roles and the evolving individuation of each member across time.

Stage 4—Departure of the children. The adults in the family during this period are faced with the primary task of reworking their parental roles so that they can establish a position for themselves as parents of adult children.

Stage 5—Integration of loss. During this stage the adults in the family have to deal with accepting social, economic, and physical changes that accompany old age.

A specialized adaptation of the family life concept has been made by McGoldrick and Carter (1980). They started their coverage of the stages of the family life cycle at the "Between Families: The Unattached Young Adult" stage. For each stage in the cycle, they describe the key principle of the emotional process of transition and the second-order changes in family status that are required in order for the family to proceed developmentally. As a person makes the transition from the family of origin into the stage of being an unattached young adult, he or she must deal with the emotional process of accepting the parent–offspring separation. At this point, second-order changes that are required, according to McGoldrick and Carter, include the differentiation of self in relation to the family of origin, the development of intimate peer relationships, and the establishment of oneself in work.

Parenthetically, in our discussion in the latter part of this chapter, we do not choose to make this into a separate stage but include it under the somewhat broad rubric of formation of a family. We acknowledge that the path followed by McGoldrick and Carter is valid, but point to the fact that a considerable amount of overlap exists between differentiating from one's family of origin and forming a marriage and new nuclear family of one's own. The process of realignment of relationships with one's own family of origin that usually begins with an increasing differentiation of self in late adolescence is advanced by marriage. We choose, in other words, to treat the entry into marriage more explicitly as part of an ongoing process of detachment–reattachment (detachment from one's family of origin and reattachment to an opposite-sex peer for the purpose of forming new marriage and family relationships) rather than as a more separate and discrete stage. Leaving the old family is a process more than a stage, in our judgment.

There are other uses and adaptations of the family life cycle concept. Those that we have mentioned are among the more important and useful for the family therapist. The advent of the women's movement and changes in the roles of females have resulted in corresponding changes in marital relationships and a need to revise marital developmental tasks. Conceptualizations beyond those made earlier are required (e.g., Zemon-Gass & Nichols, 1981).

Also, as Fisher (1977) has noted, the use of a developmental stage concept for the classification of families has some definite implications for the consideration of family pathology. Two fundamental views concerning the nature of family pathology emerge. The first, as illustrated in the work of Haley (1971), Duvall, and others, is that family pathology is based on a combination of life-stage events and external circumstances. The second point of view derives from the more clinically oriented work that has been done in this area and suggests that pathology stems from the family system itself, the developmental stage simply defining the nature of its symptoms or coloring the particular expression that it takes. Fisher also notes that the two views point toward somewhat different foci for clinical intervention. The first focuses on environmental manipulation in conjunction with working with specific family members. The other emphasizes intervention that involves all family members and dealing with the family structure. It embodies a stronger emphasis on a systems conceptualization, according to Fisher.

We shall not attempt to list the various developmental tasks facing those persons occupying the different family positions throughout the family life cycle. That would be too extensive a listing for our purposes in this book. Rather, we refer the reader to the latest edition of Duvall's *Family Development* (1971) for a comprehensive listing and discussion, and shall restrict our discussion in the second part of this chapter to some issues that have particular relevance for therapeutic work.

FAMILY STAGES AND TASKS:
A DEVELOPMENTAL–CLINICAL APPROACH

For our purposes, we shall divide the family life cycle into five stages, as follows:

1. Formation: Mating and marriage
2. Expansion: Parental beginnings and subsequent years
3. Contraction: Individuation and eventual separation of youth
4. Postparental stage
5. Other stages

The fifth stage or category, "Other stages in the family life cycle," shall be dealt with in Chapter 9, where the focus is on marital breakup, single-parent living, remarriage, and stepfamily functioning. The first four form the framework for the remainder of this chapter.

The marital subsystem formed at marriage constitutes the normative basis for family stability and continuity in the nuclear family. Its functional role within the broader nuclear system is central to the unique characteristic patterning of each family's structure and process. Thus all displays of family function and dysfunction must be assessed by the clinician in relation to the role of this subsystem. It is with this understanding in mind that we are setting forth the descriptions and analyses of the mating and marital processes that follow. The two central components of the marital subsystem involve the mate-selection process and what we term "marital complementarity." By the latter term, we refer loosely to the ways in which the mates "fit together," to how they are attached and relate on the basis of their needs for the other.

Formation: Mating and Marriage

The central role of mate selection in understanding family formation and potential dysfunction is too often overlooked in the clinical literature. While mate selection has been alluded to as a distinct developmental stage, it is more accurate clinically to identify it as a transitional process at the time of the first marriage. The process, functionally and symbolically, becomes an attempt to replace early attachment patterns and personal needs gained by each individual in his or her family of origin experiences with fulfillment in an adult interactional relationship, and to integrate the residues of the past with present experiences and interpersonal relationships. It represents a dramatic psychosocial transition for the young adult from former parental identifications and family dependency through separation from the family of origin to the establishment of a new level of adult attachment and expected intimacy. The process of selecting a mate, while colored by cultural romanticism and family expectations, nevertheless serves to link each individual's level of personal development and historical need patterns with those of a selected mate in a new and explicit dyadic process.

The process is further dramatized by fantasies and idealizations and unconscious needs for personal fulfillment. These may take the form of expecting that a new spouse will help one separate from the family of origin or replace a nurturing parent. Whatever the fantasy, this transitional process provides the clinician with critical data with regard to family formation and subsequent function and dysfunction.

Characteristics of this process are identifiable and clinically predictable. However, as clinicians, we must learn to extricate ourselves from our romanticized cultural socialization so that the mate-selection process can be more objectified. This often involves looking at one's own courtship and mate-selection process. Such introspection and consideration should be characterized by a careful analysis of one's own and one's spouse's family of origin parental models, as well as of the attachment and interactive patterns in our present marriage. The identification of additional issues in this chapter should assist the reader in this process.

We have seen some of our students fall into a clinical trap because of their overidentification with the process of "being in love" on the part of their clients. Younger students, for example, when questioned about the viability of a marriage with which they are working or when asked why a particular couple have remained together despite destructive patterns of relating, have responded with, "But they are in love," or "I can tell that they love each other." If we are to work effectively with marital and family issues, an understanding of the processes of mate selection and marital interaction not only in an intellectual sense but also in terms of how such processes function in one's own family seems vitally important. The idealized concept of love in real relationships too easily becomes contaminated by cultural, family, and personal factors. The process of selecting a mate is not magical or mystical but an expression of each individual's own personal needs and development in a particular sociocultural context.

Marital relationships are different from other kinds of relationships. It is not accidental that disappointments and frustrations in family interactions and relationships frequently elicit strong, often violent reactions. Both object relations theory and multigenerational family theory provide explanations and illustrations of the fact that in marital interaction the feelings that operate between the spouses are not confined to the present situation. From the multigenerational perspective, for example, mate selection can be explained in terms of individuals seeking to regain a lost parent through marrying a person who seems to embody some crucial attributes of the lost parental object. By replacing the missing parent, one strives to rebalance obligations and loyalties in the family ledger (Boszormenyi-Nagy & Spark, 1973). From an object relations standpoint, one projects onto the individual with whom one is intimate certain important images from earlier relationships with parents. This is particularly evident in conflict areas, where one may project part of the earlier conflict into the mate and act out the other side of it. Psychologically, one acts both defensively and in pursuit of satisfaction when seeking a mate. Even if a therapist has difficulty understanding all of the object relations patterns that may be present with a couple, he or she should be able to note how individuals seek out what is familiar when they seek close interpersonal relationships.

Another way of putting this is to note that when pairing, coupling, or mating moves into marriage, there is a coming together of more than simply two individuals. Marriage involves the joining of two families and two ways of life. Each partner brings not only the ways of believing, thinking, valuing, and acting of the family of origin but also issues in relating that were not resolved in the family of origin. What the partners are bringing from their families and how they are leaving their families form an important part of the mate-selection and marriage process.

The relationship issues and tasks are not merely those of dealing with a parent or with parents but also those of dealing with an entire family unit. Getting married may be a major way, or in some instances the only way, an individual perceives that they can separate from the family of origin. If there is enmeshment, if the family is trying to hold on and not permit the person to depart, the young man or woman may seek to find a way out by marrying and gaining the support of a spouse to replace the family ties or to attenuate their force.

Marriage may entail a severing of ties, a cutting off emotionally and behaviorally from the family of origin. Again, this may be perceived as the best or only way one can be free of parental and family dominance and control. Other young persons may find it both necessary and possible to put some distance between themselves and their new partner and the respective families of origin without totally severing the family relationships. The marital and individual task here appears to be that of securing and maintaining an appropriate distance that involves some contact and closeness but not so much that it interferes with individual and marital development. It seems obvious that successful resolution of the relationship issues with one's family of origin is essential to the formation of a marital relationship that has adequate opportunity for growth and resolution of its own tasks and problems.

North American mate selection is conducted essentially in an open choice manner. That is, young men and women do not have their marriages arranged for them, as is the case in many traditional societies. Presumably, they are free to choose a mate on the basis of personal preference and to "marry for love." It is true that there is a great deal of room for implementation of personal choice and selection on the basis of mutual attraction. However, it is equally true that there is no such thing as completely free choice in selecting a mate.

Folk wisdom has reflected some of this complexity with the espousal of two different, conflicting statements about mate selection. On the one hand, there has been the popular view that "opposites attract," and on the other, the opposing view that "like marries like." Placed in the proper perspective, both views have considerable validity. It has long been demonstrated by sociological researchers that "like does marry like" in that individuals generally select a mate from similar racial, religious, educational, and sociocultural groups. Hollingshead's (1950) description of mate selection as fishing in a pool of eligibles on the basis of race, religion, education, and similar factors still appears to hold true for the most part. There has been some diminishing of barriers between potential partners from different sociocultural groups and categories in recent decades, but the general bias against mixing is still evident. The tendency to marry a person from a similar social and cultural background is understandable in terms of propinquity and opportunity, as well as in terms of being comfortable with the familiar.

When psychological and emotional factors, in contrast to social and demographic criteria, are considered, the picture becomes much less clear and definitely more complex. There is no simple and clearly delineated picture of the theories explaining psychological and emotional factors in mate selection.

The idea that individuals select a mate on the basis of need complementarity has been a significant part of psychological theory from at least the time in which Sigmund Freud published some of his ideas early in this century. He theorized that the selection of a love object often occurs because people strive to gain a perfection perceived in the lover that they have not been able to attain on their own. In his writings on narcissism, Freud indicated that narcissistic persons select anaclitic (dependent) persons and conversely. Such object choices (other persons) may hail from similar racial, religious, and other backgrounds, despite the fact that they are psychologically different.

More recently, sociologist Robert Winch (1958) sought to analyze the love that attracts individuals into mating relationships. Winch reported that in mate selection, each individual will seek within their field of eligibles to find that mate who gives the greatest promise of providing maximum need gratification. Such need patterns in the attraction process were viewed as complementary by Winch. The actual selection process was seen as varying in the degree of conscious and unconscious awareness present. Winch suggested that the complementarity operated in a reciprocal fashion. That is, a dependent person would likely be attracted to a nurturant individual because of the dependent needs that the nurturant partner could gratify. Reciprocally, the nurturant partner would receive gratification in the process of taking care of the dependent partner.

Winch came up with four types of complementary couples and relationships. These included the Mother–Son marriage in which the husband is childishly dependent and the wife nurturant and dominant; the Ibsenian couple in which the husband is dominant and nurturant in a motherly fashion and the wife childishly dependent; the Master–Servant Girl pattern in which the husband is overtly dominant and covertly dependent and the wife subservient and strong, holding a traditional view of the status of women; and the Thurberian marriage in which the husband is inhibited in the expression of emotion and the wife highly expressive.

Winch's research aroused a considerable amount of interest and controversy in family sociology, social psychology, and related fields. The thesis that the need pattern of each person in the selection process is complementary rather than similar remains an intriguing idea but one that is far from being demonstrated definitively as a central rule in mate selection. Clinically, selecting a mate may be seen not as a magical or mystical matter but as an expression of each individual's own personal needs and development as they are put into play in a particular sociocultural context. Winch's theory, even though it has not gained substantial sociological verification because of the difficulty of collecting empirical data on unconscious needs as compared to demographic factors, does provide an important and provocative set of ideas for use by clinicians. The complementary patterns he described may be witnessed clinically in some couples, but are not demonstrable in others.

There have been other authorities who have suggested that the individual tends to marry someone with similar needs, rather than complementary needs (e.g., Murstein, 1961). Framo (1980), a clinician, has pointed out that both the need complementarity and the need similarity theses may be accurate and true, depending on the depth and length of inference one is making about mate selection.

The classical psychoanalytic view that mates are selected on the basis of a combination of conscious and unconscious needs and perceptions has been widely expounded. The discrepancy between the conscious and attainable and the unconscious and unattainable in one's expectations has been seen as a major, if not *the* major factor, in subsequent marital discord. (Kubie, 1956).

Two special instances of object relations and unconscious determinants have been reflected in the writings of Napier and Dicks. Napier (1971, 1978) has postulated that individuals tend to marry someone who seems to represent an opportunity for them to master their fears. This is very close to Kubie's (1956) statement about marrying to wipe out old pains or to settle old scores, for example, marrying the alcoholic friend of one's alcoholic brothers at whose hands suffering had been experienced, thus attempting to achieve mastery of an old problem. Dicks's (1967) observations about the selection of a partner who enters into an unconscious interlocking collusive process in order to make certain that the unresolved issues from earlier in life are never resolved but that the marital relationship is never ended also may be regarded as referring to a particular form of complementarity. Closely related to the foregoing is the idea that persons tend to marry someone who is functioning at approximately

the same level of personality differentiation but whose defensive patterning is organized in an opposite fashion (Bowen, 1966).

A particular concern of research with regard to mate selection has
been the manner and process by which a relationship is formed. Several
theories regarding the attraction and commitment process in particular
have been advanced by both psychologists and sociologists in support of
either homogamy or heterogamy. Murstein (1976) has attempted to build
on earlier theories and to advance a comprehensive theory of choice in his
stimulus–value–role theory of marital choice. In the stimulus stage, one
person is attracted to the other because of social, physical, mental, or
reputational attributes. If this, in effect, is successful and viable, it is
followed by a value comparison stage that is negotiated mainly through
verbal interchange. The role stage essentially refers to the functioning of
the couple in compatible roles. At all of the sequential stages, a principle of
exchange that is subjectively experienced by the man and woman is in
operation and must operate successfully if the relationship is to be viable.

The role of marital expectations has been dealt with in a creative and
clinically useful manner by Sager (1976). He points out that each partner
enters marriage with three levels of expectations for the relationship,
spouse, and self: conscious and verbalized expectations, conscious but not
verbalized expectations, and expectations that are held outside of awareness. Those that are conscious but not verbalized may be withheld from
the spouse because of embarrassment or a fear that they will not be
fulfilled even if they are communicated. Some of those that are outside of
awareness may not come into effective operation until the marriage moves
into a particular stage of the life cycle. Sager described the expectations as
constituting a kind of unspoken but powerful "contract" in which each
spouse expects the mate to fulfill a reciprocal part of the assumed bargain.
The contract idea has been used as the basis for an approach to marital
therapy by Sager.

Another feature of the mate-selection process in American society
that deserves attention is what has been described as the tendency toward
remaining permanently available as a mate. The tendency to remain
permanently available for mating, to be ready to marry again following
divorce or widowhood, involves some obvious differences with the old
pattern followed by many of selecting a mate on the basis of lifelong
mating intentions (Farber, 1964). A corollary to the permanent availability
tendency, one that both enables the operation of the tendency and that is a
reflection of it, is the fact that increasingly we not only can enter marriage

by choice but also that we can end it by choice and seek another relation-ship. No-fault divorce, longer life, greater affluence, and a number of other factors including changed values make for continuing alterations in the role of choice in mate selection and marriage. The precise effects of the part played by permanent availability on marriages in general are difficult to assess. Effects on a particular marital relationship, however, often can be observed as part of the dynamics of the marriage, operating on either a unilateral basis with one spouse holding the permanent availability value or on a bilateral basis.

Typically, marriage occurs in North America in early adulthood. In the United States, there has been a tendency in recent years toward later marriage. Despite dire predictions in the 1960s and early 1970s about the doubtful future of marriage and family life, the overwhelming majority of adults do marry, although they are doing so on the average at a later time in their lives than did several preceding generations.

A framework that combined individual and marital stages of develop-ment and broke the adult years down into seven stages was constructed by Berman and Lief (1975). The stages and individual tasks for each individ-ual period that they adopted from Levinson's work (Levinson, Darrow, Klein, Levinson, & McKee, 1974) are as follows:

- Stage 1. 18–21 years: Pulling up roots
- Stage 2. 22–28 years: Provisional adulthood
- Stage 3. 29–31 years: Transition at age 30
- Stage 4. 32–39 years: Settling down
- Stage 5. 40–42 years: Middle life transition
- Stage 6. 43–59 years: Middle adulthood
- Stage 7. 60 years and up: Older years

The stages and tasks published later from Levinson and associates' (Levin-son, Darrow, Klein, Levinson, & McKee, 1978) longitudinal studies of men are slightly different from those given here. We shall treat stages 1 and 2 together for our present purposes.

The individual task in the Berman–Lief framework in the first stage involves developing autonomy and in the second involves developing intimacy and occupational identification. The marital tasks for the first two periods are, respectively, making the shift from the family of origin to a new commitment and making a provisional marital commitment, a commitment that will either deepen or begin to fragment in subsequent years. In Havighurst's (1953) familiar developmental tasks approach, the developmental tasks of early adulthood include selecting a mate and learning to live with a marital partner, as well as managing a home, getting started in an occupation, and several others.

Marriage occurs in the Eriksonian framework at a time in which the individual's basic struggle is between intimacy and isolation. Intimacy does not occur automatically or develop naturally. Lest it be unclear, we refer here to emotional intimacy, involving trust, risk, and reciprocal exchange of ideas and affection, and not merely physical closeness and genital apposition. "Instant intimacy" is a contradiction in terms in our judgment, because trust and closeness do not arise except through a process of give-and-take, testing out over a period of time.

Intimacy involving mutuality of attachment and communication is a deep emotional need for most of us. At the same time that we seek to establish such a relationship—one that sometimes may approach the ideal of our early symbiotic experiences—we need to do so while retaining a firm sense of identity, knowing who we are ourselves internally and outside in the world in which we function (Daniels & Weingarten, 1982). "Intimate involvement supposedly reaches its peak when orgasm is experienced with a beloved sexual partner. Ego boundaries are dissolved and result in blissful ecstatic fusion. Thus, fusion is an important psychic mechanism which is fundamental to the achievement of true intimacy in a loving and mature object relationship" (Giovacchini, 1976, p. 432). In order to be able to let go for such intimate fusion on a temporary basis, for such "regression in the service of the ego," to use Kris's (1934) felicitous term, it is necessary to have a firm sense of identity and a belief that the ego boundaries will be restored.

People wish to be married for many reasons. In addition to social and cultural pressures and their desire for a suitable mate and a continuing relationship, people seem to marry in an attempt to gain a new symbiosis. That is, we make an attempt to secure what we once had or sought to have during infancy in relation to the mothering one. Such feelings from early life either were reinforced or were not reinforced during one's later experiences in life leading toward marriage. In saying that we seek the kind of relationship that we once had, we are not implying or saying that there is a simple one-to-one connection between past and present. But there does seem to be significant linkage between the adult desire for closeness, intimacy, and a relationship embodying symbiotic elements and the drive of most of us for a mate and the kinds of experiences that we had in early life.

We are not always comfortable with the intimacy that we secure or seem to be getting from the other person. Two factors or clusters of factors that can be detected clinically seem to be related to our difficulties in obtaining and maintaining closeness. One is the pattern of closeness between the person and the mothering one and parenting ones during infancy and early childhood. The second factor or set of factors pertain to close relationships—relationships of intimacy—that one has experienced subsequently. Clinically, one needs to check out both sources—the early mothering and parenting experiences and relationships and the subsequent close attachments that the person has had. How did he or she experience and handle the later relationships? How much closeness was sought? How much and what kind of intimacy has the person been able to tolerate and sustain?

As couples move into marriage in either the first stage of young adulthood or in the latter part of their 20s and begin to try to deal with each other as spouses, there are different issues in both intimacy and power that must be addressed. During the first stage of the Berman–Lief framework, the intimacy between the mates tends to be fragile. There typically is a deepening of intimacy during the second stage, but the closeness is still characterized by ambivalance.

Other important issues for the first two stages of adulthood in the Berman–Lief framework revolve around power, marital boundaries, and marital conflict. Early in marriage, the original family ties tend to conflict with marital adaptation. The marital boundary question—who is to be included and who is to be excluded—typically produces conflict over the inclusion and/or exclusion of in-laws. Do the partners go to his parents or to her parents for Sunday dinner or do they stay home and otherwise go their own way? Who is to be turned to for financial advice or support in times of stress? During the second stage, the marital task of securing a provisional marital commitment is hampered by conflict over uncertainty about the choice of a marital partner—Is this the right one? Did I make a mistake?—and stress over parenthood.

The boundary questions again have to do with who or what is to be included or excluded, particularly with reference to friends and potential lovers and with regard to work versus family life. The power dimension in the earliest stage involves a testing of power. Here a clinician generally can observe intimations of the power relationship that prevail in the marriage of the families of origin of the spouses. Sometimes the struggle is on the level of crude and raw gender differences. In other instances, there may be an intellectual or ideological commitment to equality but an emotional need and behavioral attempt to gain dominance by either or both of the young persons. Frequently, the struggle has some of the characteristics of a symbolic dance in which the partners are following different dance manuals or choreographed routines. Typically, when the spouses are in their late 20s, the power issue becomes that of establishing patterns of conflict resolution.

At the same time that the new partners are forming their marital relationship, the family of origin of each of them is having to include a new member. That is, the new spousal system typically has to be accommodated or attached in some important ways to the families from which both the young man and the young woman originated.

Expansion: Parental Beginnings and Subsequent Years

Parenthood generally becomes part of the marital partners' life experience for the first time during the second stage of adult years (years 22–28 in the framework we are using). For many persons marrying today, the marriage is occurring later than formerly and parenthood is being postponed in many cases, thus pushing the birth of the first child much closer to age 30. Hence, in many instances, the problem of establishing a pair intimacy and working relationship may be given as much time or even longer than formerly was the case.

Some research has bolstered the common clinical impression that the important question is not whether the child comes early or late, but the quality of the readiness of the husband and wife for the experience of parenthood (Daniels & Weingarten, 1982). Adequate separation from one's family of origin and ties to parents, possession of a clear sense of identity, and establishment of a strong relationship of intimacy with one's mate all are important ingredients in readiness for parenthood.

At the same time that young adults are concerned with intimacy and other issues, they are, in Erikson's framework, dealing with the individual struggle of generativity. Primarily, generativity has to do with one's concern for establishing the next generation (Erikson, 1950). This is the side of parenthood that has to do with caring for the offspring rather than merely being identified as a parent. Parenthood has, along with its pain and toil, the potential to help men and women tap into sources of growth-producing experiences and activities that are not likely to be found elsewhere in their lives.

Generativity is not the property of one sex or the other. Rather, it is an experience that can be enjoyed by both parents. In recent North American society, however, there has been an underinvolvement of many fathers in the experiences and processes of childrearing, leading to a lack of growth and development for the fathers in those areas. To the extent that men have been underinvolved in socialization and caring activities with their children, they have been shortchanged on this dimension of stabilization and growth in their own personalities and, in our judgment, have been cheated, along with their children. The trend that started in the 1960s for more men to be involved emotionally and practically as parents is admirable in our estimation. As clinicians, we now find that we cannot predict how men will be involved in parenting nearly so easily as we could a decade and a half or so ago.

Decision making about having a child may follow any one of several paths, ranging from not making a conscious decision and assuming that children will come if and when they come, across the scale to a path of deciding not to have children at all. Some young partners follow the "natural" path and do not make a decision one way or the other but simply "let nature take its course." Others decide to defer childbearing for some definite or vaguely defined period of time, for example, "until we get better acquainted" or "until we get settled a bit." Sometimes there is a more specific reason for the delay, such as, "We wish to wait until we get established in our careers." The major difficulties between the partners are likely to come when they have different expectations or wishes. For example, one wishes to have a child later or not at all and the other desires to have a youngster as soon as possible. Similarly, problems arise when there is poor communication or no communication between the spouses about their wishes, and the issue is not clarified.

At any given time in the United States, an estimated 15% of married couples in the childbearing years have fertility problems, the great majority of which have a physical basis (Daniels & Weingarten, 1982). Among those who are childless, a small number that is difficult to ascertain precisely are voluntarily childless. Professional literature has given an increasing amount of attention to those married persons who do not wish to have children (e.g., Veevers, 1973, 1974, 1975), as have popular writers (Peck, 1971; Silverman & Silverman, 1971). Pressure for having children has lessened. Clinicians need to give more attention to the feelings of the partners about having or not having children than frequently is given in clinical work. Feelings of stigma about not having children or having too many, feelings of resentment about the same issues, and related attitudes sometimes play significant roles in marital and individual adjustment.

Advice long given to young couples to "have a baby" in order to help them cement their marriage or otherwise cope with adjustment problems flies in the face of research showing that the addition of a child brings more, not fewer, coping issues and stress. The childbearing and childrearing years are not the times in which couples report their highest amounts of marital satisfaction. Some research shows that couples report their highest amounts of marital satisfaction in the early stages of marriage, before the addition of children (Campbell, 1975). Researchers also find the marital satisfaction curve rising again after the children have departed (Rollins & Feldman, 1970). The point here is that childbearing, which issues in a period of childrearing covering approximately one-half of the family life cycle (McGoldrick, 1980), brings new adjustment problems for the couple.

Reactions to the birth of a child may need to be explored with a couple prior to the birth of the first or subsequent child, as well as later. Sometimes, difficulties in marital or personal adjustment that contribute to family problems may be traced back to dislocations in the family system that occurred at the time of the birth of a child. Such dislocations may go unnoticed at the time.

There are many reactions that can be felt by either the wife–mother or the husband–father with regard to the birth of the first child or a subsequent youngster. Particularly if the child is unwanted or is obviously physically damaged, there may be parental reactions of denial, embarrassment, guilt, failure feelings, grief, and similar feelings. In subsequent years, reactions of overprotection, scapegoating, or even emotional and physical abuse may be forthcoming toward a damaged or disabled child (Tymchuk, 1979). Even among parents of presumably desired and healthy babies, reactions of anxiety in mild to moderate forms are not uncommon, although seldom recognized at the time.

Earlier research (LeMasters, 1957) described the birth of the first child as a crisis. More recent family studies literature does not support such an interpretation. Rather, it seems more accurate to refer to the birth of the first youngster as constituting a time of transition (Hobbs & Cole, 1976; Rossi, 1968). The addition of the baby transforms the relationship from dyadic in nature to triadic in nature, from a twosome to a threesome and potentially brings into play all of the various possibilities for triangulation.

The birth of subsequent children tends to be viewed differently by both parents than the arrival of the first. Common observation shows that a couple may be unhappy with an early arrival, or not ready for a second child, or may be upset by the arrival of a child after having thought that their family was complete. Just as the addition of the first baby may put a strain on a marital relationship, so may the advent of a second, third, or subsequent youngster. An insecure husband, for example, may be able to cope reasonably well with the addition of the first child but be unable to share any more of his parentified wife with a second child and begin to exhibit symptomatic behavior that may or may not fracture the marriage. A number of factors typically enter into how the newborn's addition to the marital or family unit affects the husband and wife.

Obviously important to the family are reactions of the child or children already present to the arrival of a sibling. Much of the parenting material in the popular pediatric materials and mass circulation magazines is devoted to helping young parents find ways of making the experience an acceptable and nontraumatic one for the children already in the family. Preparation of the child and such actions as bringing the child a gift from the new sibling are common parts of this picture. As Toman (1976) has pointed out from his extensive research into family constellations, attitudes toward the arrival of a sibling may vary according to the number of years between the siblings, the sex of the newcomer, the number of children already present, and the position of the child already present. These attitudes and affects emerge over the years.

According to Toman, the age difference between the children tends to produce some definite patterns of reaction. If the baby arrives only 1 or 2 years after the older child, the older typically sees the sibling as a rival for the affection, care, and attention of the parents. If the second child comes 3 or 4 years after the first, the older seems to be less threatened in his power and control over the parents. If the older child is 4 or 5 by the time the baby makes its advent, the older youngster generally has learned how to respond to the different sexes and the reactions depend in large measure on the gender of the baby. In brief, the older child tends to be considerably more civilized by this time in its life. The family balance is affected by the gender of the new arrival; a family of two males and two females generally functioning more smoothly than one in which there are three members of one sex and one of the other. In the latter case, the older child is likely to seek the affection and attention of the parents more strongly. If the age difference between the children is 6 years or more, they belong in our terms to different generations. The older child is hardly affected by the younger. As a general rule, the small age differences tends to pull siblings more strongly together (Toman, 1976).

Toman's research is an excellent resource not only for understanding the meaning of new arrivals but also for comprehending many other feelings, attitudes, and behaviors that stem from the particular ways in which families are structured on the basis of age and sex differences and similarities among the children. We find it helpful not only for the clinician or student but also for the client. For a client to learn that certain "mothering behaviors," for example, are found in his sister because of her ordinal position sometimes provides a beginning point for effecting attitudinal and behavioral change. "Migawd! That's us!" has been the reaction of more than one client to the reading of a few paragraphs of Toman's descriptions, followed by less defensive and more protective behaviors.

Sibling relationships are just beginning to be studied seriously on a significant scale with respect to the lifelong impact that such connections have among brothers and sisters (Bank & Kahn, 1982).

Among all family members—mother, father, or child—the reaction to the birth of a baby and the addition of a new member to the family is conditioned and moderated by all the intimate and important relationships that they have encountered in their family living. The nature of the family system and family processes that prevail have important effects on the reactions of any and all family members to the birth. As we have noted, for example, the mother's reactions to her new baby and her relationship with it cannot be understood apart from her marital relationship. The same observation holds for the father as well.

The period of family life from expansion to launching, for families not altered by divorce or death and family reorganization, typically begins when the partners are in their middle to late 20s and lasts until their middle adulthood. Beginning with the first child, the nuclear family expands so long as children are coming and then has a period of consolidation before the launching of the children into the outside world begins. That is, this period begins with the birth of the first child and lasts until the last child leaves home. As the children begin to depart, the nuclear family begins the process of contraction that continues until death eventually takes the partners and marks the end of that unit in the family chain.

As emphasized earlier, the partners need to establish and maintain clear and firm generational boundaries in order to rear children adequately and to produce healthy relationships and appropriate autonomy in their offspring. The maintenance of boundaries is not an easily accomplished matter. For the couple, during their late 20s and early 30s (stage 3 in the Berman–Lief framework), there may be temporary disruptions in the marital boundaries while the partners seek to make up their minds about each other, vie for power and dominance, perhaps become restless and suffer a commitment crisis, and on occasion come into conflict over how they relate (Berman & Lief, 1975).

A new stage of the family life cycle, referred to as the "termination of the intergenerational hierarchical boundary," has been proposed by Williamson (1981, 1982). During approximately the 4th decade of life, the adult seeks to terminate the hierarchical boundary between self and the older parents. Power is redistributed and the younger generational member seeks to give up a need to be parented and to relate to his or her parents as a peer. This process involves accepting the older generational members as they are while giving them up emotionally and psychologically as parents. Williamson has spelled out a number of specific guidelines for working with those clients who can be helped to achieve a successful negotiation of this proposed stage.

During their 30s, while the husband/father may be settling down (Levinson et al., 1974), the wife/mother may be undergoing a crisis of her own as an individual. She frequently goes to work or returns to work outside the home when the youngest child enters kindergarten or begins to stay at school all day in the first grade. Not infrequently, by the time she hits the mid-30s, today's middle-class wife/mother in particular may be asking the now familiar questions, "Is this all there is?" and "Who am I?" As a result of the changes that she requires as a human being in order to find both a secure personal identity and a firm sense of self and a sense of meaning and satisfaction, a marital crisis often occurs. At the very least, if the wife/mother does not abort her struggles and strivings, a new marital task that does not appear in the published literature surfaces for the couple. Briefly put, it becomes necessary for the couple to restructure their marriage so that there is room for both the husband and the wife to have their own identities (Zemon-Gass & Nichols, 1981). There typically are other reasons for the couple to begin restructuring their relationship during this period. By the time the first child enters adolescence, for example, the parents are in a position to be reminded that the youngster will be leaving home in a few years and that eventually they will be on their own once again. What is called "midlife" may be felt at a different point for each couple and may last several decades in some instances (Pincus & Dare, 1978).

The midlife transition for the male, sometimes popularly and somewhat incorrectly referred to as a midlife crisis, typically comes around age 40 (Levinson *et al.*, 1978). At that juncture, he may be involved in a significant struggle to come to grips with where he is in relation to where he would like to be in fulfilling his aspirations. For some men this period involves withdrawal not only from their spouse but also from their family and engagement in erratic patterns of behavior including moodiness, outbursts of temper, and other actions that have not been typical of them.

Unfortunately, both the wife/mother's struggles and those of the husband/father often occur at approximately the same time that one or more of their children has undergone or is undergoing puberty's changes and the later vicissitudes of the teenage years. As others have remarked, the "fit" between the needs and behaviors of the parents who are entering the 40s or in some cases reaching middle-adulthood and those of the teenagers in the family is not a smooth one in many instances. To the extent that a parent may be going through a "second adolescence" while the child is going through a first, a recipe for difficulty is being cooked up in the family.

At all stages through the childrearing years, it is important for the clinician to be alert to the relationship between the expectations of the parents regarding their children and the actual behaviors of the children. Typical social expectations of parents for children beginning with the school years and subsequently may include good performance in school during the elementary period, continuing advancement in school during the years 12–18, some interest in the opposite sex, and an increasing evidence of responsibility and self-sufficiency; at approximately 18, increased separation from the parents, greater self-sufficiency, departure from home, and perhaps marriage (Tymchuk, 1979). There are, of course, social-class, ethnic, and individual family variations on those themes.

How the boundaries of the marriage are maintained with regard to the children and in relation to other systems in their environment seems to be strongly related to how the partners deal with the issues of intimacy and power. The power task of spouses in their 30s pertains to establishing "definite patterns of decision making and dominance." In "good marriages" there is a notable increase in intimacy during those years and in "bad marriages" a gradual distancing between the spouses (Berman & Lief, 1975). Conflict in the marriage likely comes from different approaches to productivity in terms of how the couple deals with their children, work, and friends, as well as their marriage during those years (Berman & Lief, 1975).

At the end of that decade and into the 40s, there is a simultaneous need to sum up and evaluate where things are and a tendency to be questioning and to consider leaving marriage, changing job, and making other changes in living. It truly is a time of transition not only for the male but also for the marriage. If the wife/mother has a career of her own, there probably will occur a similar midlife transition regarding vocation.

Contraction: Individuation and Eventual Separation of Youth

This period "starts before it starts." That is, the preparation for the launching of the young into the outside world to live their own lives begins long before the actual departure day arrives. In a very real sense, parents are putting themselves out of a job from the beginning of their days as parents. Childrearing involves a continual and sometimes tenuous balancing of the dependency scales, providing the youngster with adequate amounts of support and dependency while at the same time encouraging autonomous and independent functioning. The idea that complete independence ever occurs on the part of either parent or child is generally erroneous. More accurately, we probably could refer to the healthy goal as being that of mature interdependence.

By the time that the young man or woman leaves home, whether to go to school or to work and to a separate residence, he or she has had several years of experience in orienting toward the world outside the family. Both the psychophysiological push of adolescence and the structure of the society that groups teenagers in age peer groups largely isolated from the mainstream society have facilitated movement away from their parents. As noted, at the same time that this development is occurring with the adolescent/teenager, the parents often are struggling with their own midlife or middle age difficulties. Faced with changes in themselves that include the passing of their own youthfulness at the same time that their children are beginning to move toward their own physical maturity and departure from the home, the parents invariably have to cope with loss. For some adults who are discouraged and deeply concerned about their own future, the loss that they face may be experienced as unbearable. The power relationship between child and parent shifts in terms of who is needed by whom as the movement toward relative mutual individuation continues (Stierlin, 1974).

Stierlin (1974) has delineated three ways in which the forthcoming departure affects parents. Drawing from his clinical work, he found them either denying that the departure was coming by refusing to talk or think about the matter, reacting with feelings of gloom and deep depression, or anticipating being lonely and depressed when the children left but indicating that they could cope with the situation.

Parents send out messages to their offspring with varying degrees of clarity that contribute to either a relatively easy separation or to hard and difficult struggles. Whether the messages indicate that the parents can live without the child and how they will live without him or her or convey that living in the absence of the child will be impossible is, of course, crucial to the youngster's ability to depart without undue guilt or fear if, indeed, the youngster is able to depart at all. Families, as mentioned in Chapter 2 in connection with Beavers Systems Model of the family, have been characterized by Stierlin (1974) as being either centripetal or centrifugal. Again, centripetal families orient the children toward the inside, toward staying in the family, whereas centrifugal families do not serve as such a magnet. In extreme form, as we are using the concept, such families are underorganized and have a minimum of relatedness prevailing among members.

There is a need on the part of the husband and wife to recognize and deal as appropriately as possible with the loss that they sustain as a child leaves home. There are guidelines for predicting the severity of the loss of a person. Among those are recency of the loss. That is, the passage of time does help with the diminishing of the pain of a loss, unless there is active blocking of the mourning process so that the grief work cannot be completed. Previous experiences with losses, their number, and their severity also provide indications of the probable severity of present or forthcoming losses. The smaller the family and the greater the imbalance in the family resulting from the loss, the more severe it is likely to be (Toman, 1976).

For the marital couple, the need is to work through the feelings of loss and to detach sufficiently from the departing and departed child so that appropriate amounts of emotion invested there can be reinvested in the marriage or in other pursuits and interests. Just as the individual task for middle adulthood involves restabilizing, so a major marital task has to do with stabilizing the marriage for "the long haul" (Berman & Lief, 1975).

How do the partners handle the vacuum left by the departure of their children? Intimacy may increase or it may decrease, depending in large measure on the foundations built prior to the launching time. Similarly, conflicts may increase or decrease when there is no longer the buffering or instigating presence of a child or children. Marital partners may find the "empty nest" stage a depressing, threatening, and nonfulfilling time of their life, or it may be treated as a time of significant activity for mutual enjoyment and fulfillment with the spouse.

At no place in the family life cycle does the "cogwheeling" of generations become more evident and the tasks for the generations more numerous and complicated than at the launching and contraction period of the nuclear family. A three-dimensional perspective is essential here, if the therapist is to deal intelligently and effectively with the issues presenting themselves in many cases at that time period.

Recent decades have brought forth a three-generational situation that is unprecedented. A major factor in the emergence of the new situation has been the increased longevity of the population. That is, large numbers of persons are living into their 60s and beyond, as contrasted to earlier generations when it was rare for one or both of the marital partners to live through their 40s and 50s. Today, both partners typically are living at the time that the children are launched from the home. As recently as three generations ago—couples marrying around 1890—the odds were approximately 50–50 that one of the partners would have died before the launching stage was reached. That means, in brief, that the grandparents—the parents of the parents doing the launching—are likely to be present and to live for many years after the youngsters have been launched. Frequently, this faces the "middle generation" with the task of dealing with important dependency needs and support issues of both their offspring and their parents, causing them to be a "caught generation" (Vincent, 1972).

Although it is not universal, this three-generational situation is common enough so that it must be regarded as the typical picture today. (It may be complicated farther by disruptions in the family life cycle such as those brought about by divorce and remarriage, but our concern at the present is with uninterrupted family development, as we have noted.)

We have already described briefly the tasks that the parents (the middle generation) face in relation to their children and in relation to themselves and their marital relationship at the beginning of the contracting stage. To this we must add another facet at the beginning of the stage and several others near the latter part of it. The additional task at the beginning is related to dealing with their own parents, the grandparental generation.

The older generation, the grandparental, faces impending decline in physical abilities and health and the eventual death of first one spouse and then the other. Retirement and financial security are issues for most older couples. Retirement may bring problems in terms of how they relate to the other and how they use their newly found leisure time, if appropriate patterns of dealing with the other have not been formed previously. These and other changes may result in shifts in the dependency–independency relationship between the grandparents and their own children. The loss of autonomy may become a significant issue for the older couple and the question of how much and what kinds of responsibility to take with regard to them may become a matter of major concern for their children (the middle generation). The familiar "reversal of the generations" in which adult parents assume roles vis-à-vis their parents that the older generation formerly occupied in relation to them most frequently occurs during the launching–contraction stage of the family life cycle, although there may be intimations of such changes earlier.

At the same time, the middle generation is faced with the need to work out new patterns of relatedness with their departing and departed children. The younger generation (the children/grandchildren) simultaneously has the task of implementing educational, vocational and friendship/marital goals of their own while appropriately detaching and rerelating to their parents and family of origin. For most of the younger generation, the task involves learning to relate to their parents on an adult-to-adult basis as a single person first and, subsequently, with some more changes in the relationship, as a young married person. The departure of the children from home and the recasting of the parent–child relationship is complicated on the part of those who are subsidized while pursuing graduate or professional education or buying a home or beginning a business.

During the latter part of what we are dealing with here—the period of contracting—the transition to another family life stage begins. Another generation is born and the older (grandparental) one passes from the scene. The parental generation becomes a grandparental generation and begins to cope with the issues of retirement, declining physical health, and other matters that their own parents faced years earlier.

There is no easy dividing line between the launching stage and the postparental stage. Some families have a period in which there are four living generations, whereas others lose the grandparents early and may not go through a period in which three generations of a family are living simultaneously.

Postparental Stage

This stage of the family life cycle, as we are construing the cycle, involves a continuation of tasks that began in the launching stage. The middle generation has the dual tasks of reintegrating the marriage following the departure of the children and of coping with loss. Some of the important parts of this stage we anticipated in the previous section in our mention of the "cogwheeling" of generations. Much of the activity discussed under that rubric continues into this stage. There is no discrete, disjunctive break between the launching stage and the postparental stage. We have chosen to select the departure of the last child from home as an arbitrary marker for the dividing line between stages. While doing this, we recognize that active parenting behavior may continue for some years after the last child has left home and that there may be reversals of the launching process when a child later returns home, as happens on occasion, for example, following a divorce.

Our focus in this section is on the middle or parental generation as it moves into its final years. During this stage, the third or older generation typically dies, and the younger produces offspring. Thus, there is a shifting of generations, the middle moving into the position formerly occupied by the older and the younger entering the place formerly held by the middle generation.

Loss is a major issue during this portion of the family life cycle. It is to be presumed that the loss of the children generally has been faced and managed, for better or worse, by the parents during the launching stage. The death of their parents faces them with another kind of loss, carrying with it as concomitants the necessity of recognizing that they, the survivors, are truly orphans, and aging orphans who are themselves mortal. As they, the parental generation now becoming a grandparental generation, cope with such strong emotional realities, they also find themselves facing the same issues with regard to forthcoming retirement, health changes, declining physical strength and ability, and others that their own parents encountered some 25–30 years earlier. If this sounds familiar and repetitious, it is because there is a cycle present that keeps repeating itself.

The most significant loss, however, in the typical family life cycle as it moves onward toward the eventual disappearance of the generation that we are discussing is the loss of one's spouse. Although the loss of a parent or child by death may be painful and personally disruptive, it typically does not produce the disjunctive practical outcomes that accompany the death of one's marital partner and does not require the same kind of rearrangement and restructuring of one's life.

Most of the emotional reactions that we shall discuss below would be found in relating to any important loss, particularly loss resulting from the death of a close love object. Consequently, the discussions and understandings given here with regard to emotional reactions and adjustments to loss by death apply elsewhere. The discussion is placed here for purposes of convenience and will not be repeated in detail in other places where it also would be applicable.

Loss of a loved one by death typically produces a crisis in a marriage and a family. Crisis-intervention understandings and techniques typically are appropriate background for dealing with loss of a spouse by death, as one works with the surviving partner.

Additional understanding is required, however. In our judgment, a comprehension of bereavement and grief and of the entire mourning process is essential to dealing with this stage of the family life cycle. "Bereavement" refers to the loss itself, to being robbed as it were of something valuable to oneself, and to being left sad and lonely. "Grief" pertains to the feelings engendered by the loss, the emotional reactions of the bereft person, including anger, hostility, fear, depression, despair, and others. Grief is used in our understanding as part of the larger process of mourning, which includes not only the emotional reactions of the person but also the total behavioral pattern exhibited by the survivor from the time of the loss onward (Bowlby, 1969). Mourning processes may be considered essentially concluded when the survivor has accepted the loss and reinvested emotions in new objects and pursuits and is restructuring his or her life in a reasonably stable and functional manner.

There are several good studies and discussions available of the reactions of survivors to loss. The pioneering work in this regard was done by Lindemann (1944), who worked with and studied victims and survivors of a night club fire tragedy in the 1940s. Other studies have been provided by Kubler-Ross (1969) and Parkes (1973). A useful formula for understanding acute grief reactions can be constructed from the available empirical research reports and clinical observations. Lindemann's work is the primary guide in the following description, but the work of Oates (1955) and our own observations and experiences with bereft individuals and families also are included.

1. The initial reaction to the loss or to being informed of the loss is one of shock, followed by numbness. Going numb appears to be nature's

way of providing for protection against the pain. This initial reaction may last from a day to several days, depending on the circumstances of the loss—whether expected or unexpected, the psychodynamics of the bereaved person, the nature of the relationship with the dead person, and a number of other issues.

2. Next, a period of denial typically is evident. Expressions such as the following are frequently heard, "I don't believe it." "It can't be true." The denial generally is accompanied by a range of agitated behaviors, including difficulties in settling down physically and problems in sleeping. These reactions may or may not include outbursts of tearfulness and crying. For some persons, most of the crying comes later, after the original walls of disbelief and defenses of denial have been breached.

3. Surprising emotional reactions may be forthcoming as the denial breaks down and the next stage begins. Not only the survivor but also others around that person may be shocked and upset by the emotional reactions that erupt. Anger, rage, bitterness all may pour out in alternating patterns that seem beyond the boundaries of reason. "I'm going crazy!" is a common fear and feeling. Guilt reactions because one is feeling angry toward the deceased are common. Similar outcries against others and the Deity may be forthcoming, followed by reactions of guilt or bitterness over the loss. Eventually, most persons come to feel that they are not crazy. If they are able to accept the fact that a loss has occurred and that it is all right for them to have strong emotional reactions to the death and departure of the spouse, they move into the next stage.

4. Although this stage does not occur in the same way for all survivors, it is common for the person to think about and talk about the events of the death over and over. Sometimes they spend a considerable amount of time trying to determine whether they could have done anything to prevent the death, or make the deceased more comfortable, and so on. "Was it my fault? Could I have done anything?" These and similar questions may be voiced as the survivor turns over and over the memories of the death and last day. Many survivors repeat such questions internally, struggling with them themselves without voicing them aloud or sharing their concerns with others.

5. Eventually, with most survivors, there comes a time in which the loss has been accepted and much of their living is done in the present. At odd moments and at unpredictable times, when they are reminded by circumstances that they formerly had a mate present but do not any longer, there will be a return of the pain. This has been called poetically

and accurately "selective memory and stabbing pain" (Oates, 1955). By this phase of the reaction, the survivor typically has withdrawn most of the emotional investment in the deceased spouse and has begun to invest in other pursuits and other persons. In pathological cases, individuals may continue to worship the deceased, to act as if he or she really has not died, or to take other paths that involve denial of the experience of loss and the nature of the relationship with the deceased partner.

Throughout the period of mourning, the survivor's abilities to function may vary widely. Endeavors that were routine in earlier days may take a significant amount of effort to accomplish. Sticking with a task may be difficult and sometimes impossible for the grieving individual. Talking may be done on a kind of compulsive basis. Aimless behavior may mark the days of individuals who improve, and would be expected to improve, as the grief work is accomplished. New patterns of organization may be evolved over a period of time, patterns that do not involve interaction with a mate who no longer is present.

The loss of a loved one by death brings a crisis that needs to be met with reorganization as the survivor works through the grief and begins to complete the process of mourning. Family relationships are altered by the death, and additional accommodations and alterations are required in response to the loss. What kinds of living arrangements have to be made? Can the survivor live alone? Should he or she move in with one of the children, rotate living with several of the children, live alone, or get a live-in companion, if that is economically feasible? Should the survivor move into a nursing home? What about remarriage for the survivor? These and many other predictable questions are raised as the loss is faced and the need for reorganization of life without the deceased becomes part of the life cycle.

In the foregoing discussion, we have dealt with the reaction of a spouse on an individual basis, partly because that is where it is experienced most and partly because very little that is clinically helpful is known about systemic response to the death of a spouse. Families generally do not consciously prepare their members for dealing with death. Also, we have not discussed situations in which there is a high degree of ambivalence and even relief at the death of a spouse or deaths in which there was something unsavory or shameful involved. Those situations pose challenges for the individual and for the family system that require great sensitivity on the part of the clinician and must be handled on a case by case basis.

Other Stages in the Family Life Cycle

For the sake of convenience, we have carried the family life cycle through various stages to the point of decline and disappearance in the postparental stage without referring to disruptions by earlier death of one of the spouses or marital breakup through divorce. We are well aware that a significant number of families do not go through a complete cycle such as we have described without disruption. Couples divorce before having children. Others divorce after having children. Remarried families have become a major form of family in North American society. For many persons, there is a pattern of dating, marriage, separation and divorce, single-parent living, remarriage, and stepfamily living, with or without additional children. This process is significant enough and difficult enough to cope with to warrant separate treatment. We shall address the issues involved in Chapter 9.

CHAPTER SIX

Clinical Assessment
of the Family System

A concern for clinical assessment is often neglected in the technique-oriented approaches to family therapy. There exists an unfounded assumption that the therapist can move into a family system with a dazzling array of maneuvers and evoke change. This approach to family therapy may indeed provoke the system to accommodate to the therapist, but the resultant change may be potentially random, defensive, and/or regressive. It is our strong belief that system assessment provides the basis for the most useful and responsible clinical strategies. Clinical assessment is, by definition, the process by which clinicians gain understanding that is necessary for making informed decisions (Korchin, 1976). Moreover, it is our experience that teaching the beginning family therapist to conduct a thorough and careful clinical assessment provides the student with the tools and necessary discipline for integrating theory and practice.

We have seen too many family therapists emerge from recent training experiences armed only with a "bag of tricks." Some family therapy training programs have developed approaches that emphasize plunging the learner directly into clinical work with families. Such programs de-emphasize grounding in both broad family theory and in knowledge of psychopathology and personality development. Students who are trained in such programs lack the ability to think systemically and to understand family structure and process. It has been observed by many leaders in the field that individuals trained in that fashion have serious limitations not only in growing as family therapists but also in their ability to interact and function in interdisciplinary clinical settings.

Clinical assessment in this field as in others provides the central linkage for translating theoretical conceptions into practice. It is our belief, as we have noted previously, that sound practice is based on solid grounding in theory. To this we would add that the most effective way to acquire a substantial grounding in theory is to master the relevant substantive content, moving into practice only after having delved deeply into the body of knowledge on which family therapy is based. Reading books, listening to recorded interviews, watching videotapes, or attending workshops may serve as appropriate continuing education, but such activities do not provide the basic theoretical grounding necessary for the practice of family therapy. Nor does launching into practice uneducated and untrained and "learning by doing" prepare one to be a family therapist. Rather, one proceeds systematically to learn about theory, cognitively and experientially.

Similarly, a responsible therapist does not make a therapeutic intervention or undertake a given course of treatment because "it seems like a good idea" or because it looked good when demonstrated at a workshop or conference. Veteran clinicians sometimes appear to the observer to make moves quickly, without going through the process of assessing the situation with which they are dealing. Some of those who entered the emerging field of family therapy in the 1950s and 1960s have expressed impatience with theory and assessment. A closer examination of how they function and how they were trained usually discloses that they do operate from a theoretical base, one that has become so familiar and ingrained that it forms a kind of "second nature" for them. They draw upon it without necessarily being aware that this is happening. Much of their impatience with theory and formal assessment stems from the fact that they were trained originally in theoretical and practical orientations that were not appropriate for family therapy. Sucn reactions are understandable in those who had to fight their way out of a traditional psychoanalytic background.

DIAGNOSIS AND ASSESSMENT

Some distinctions need to be made at this point between "diagnosis" and "assessment." While they are related, they are not the same. Diagnosis is the more narrow and restricted of the two terms.

"Diagnosis" comes from two Greek words, *dia* which means "between" and *gnosis* which refers to knowledge or knowing. Literally, diagnosis has to do with "knowing between" or distinguishing between and implies that one classifies the situations or conditions into types. The widely used expression and concept "differential diagnosis" is somewhat redundant in that any diagnosis is by implication a differential diagnosis. Historically, the concept of diagnosis has been associated with disease and physical medicine.

"Diagnosis" has been adapted for use in other fields; for example, in organizational study, reference is sometimes made to organizational diagnosis. Essentially, however, diagnosis is an individual concept and one related to individual disease or disorder. Attempts to relate individual diagnostic categories and disorders to families and family process have not been particularly successful or significant. Use of the term "family diagnosis" is often made, in spite of the fact that it is an imprecise use of terminology and something of a misnomer. Diagnosis in family therapy has been defined as a special way of knowing that involves diagnosing, researching, and doing therapy (de Shazer, 1983).

"Assessment," as noted, is a broader term than diagnosis. It has to do with estimating or determining significance, importance, or value, rather than classification into categories of disease and lacks that sole individual rootage associated with individual diagnosis. Although it is hard to do so, it seems sensible to restrict the use of the term "diagnosis" to the classification of individuals and their manifestations of problems and difficulties into psychological nosological categories and to use the concept of "clinical assessment" when referring to family system, subsystems, processes, and functioning.

Individual diagnostic labels may be necessary in family therapy work, even though "symptom diagnoses such as those provided by Axes I and II of the *Diagnostic and Statistical Manual of Mental Disorders*, 3rd edition (DSM-III) [American Psychiatric Association, 1980] are clearly inadequate for treatment planning" (Wynne, 1983, p. 252). As Wynne (1983) points out, a formulation of the problem that also includes contextual circumstances and other factors such as what the persons affected believed should be done "is a far more appropriate starting point for treatment" (p. 252). At the very least for family therapists, the widespread use of DSM-III and the *International Classification of Diseases* (ICD-9-CM) (World Health Organization, 1979), both of which classify disorders only in individual terms, require that they be able to affix a standard diagnostic label on an identified patient or client in order to communicate with other professionals. Those who work in medically oriented settings that use such classificatory systems have no choice about the use of individual diagnostic labels.

The study and treatment of pathology is an integral part of the education, training, and practice of family therapists. As indicated earlier, the understanding of pathology in family therapy is that it results from occurrences in family interaction and is not simply an intrapsychic event (Bell, 1975). Symptoms seen by family therapists are the same as those witnessed by individually oriented therapists, but the explanation of their source and maintenance is different. Psychoanalysts, for example, view symptoms as resulting from repressed conflict between the ego and the id or between the conscious and unconscious of the individual. Other forms of individual psychology also regard symptoms as stemming from internal conflict and consider the environment only as a source of stress that serves to activate the symptom formation. The resulting treatment is primarily concerned with dealing with intrapsychic mechanisms (Robinson, 1979).

Family therapists, by contrast, while looking at the same behaviors as individual therapists, regard symptoms from a family transactional viewpoint, as coming from relationship events occurring between intimately related persons. To focus on "obsessive–compulsive" or "hysterical" pieces of behavior in individuals and to label these as the "symptoms" may be necessary from a practical standpoint, but from a family therapy perspective, one may be dealing only with minor parts of a larger complex whole. Not only is the context, particularly the family context, taken into consideration by family therapists during assessment but also treatment concepts are broadened to include attempts to change the relevant portions of the context (Framo, 1972).

We are not suggesting here that the differences between orientations are insignificant, but that certain amounts of accommodation to the realities of functioning in the current mental health milieu may be necessary.

Assessment may or may not lead to family therapy, or to therapy of any kind, for that matter. One of the purposes of clinical assessment is to determine what kind of help, if any, is needed. If therapy is indicated, what kind and with whom? Is another kind of intervention required and, if so, what kind and with whom? Clinical assessment is undertaken, again, for the purpose of gaining understanding that is required in order to make informed decisions. Careful assessment may lead to the conclusion, for example, that an adolescent who has been marked by his parents as "a problem" or as having problems needs academic tutoring and other forms of practical help and not therapeutic assistance.

Parenthetically, there are a number of different approaches to diagnosis and assessment taken by leaders of the various "schools" of family therapy. An interesting summary and comparison of six approaches or schools—Bowen theory, symbolic–experiential (Whitaker), structural (Minuchin), strategic (Haley), brief therapy (Mental Research Institute), and systemic (Milan associates)—has been made by Liddle (1983). Again, the approaches taken in the various schools appear to relate not only to the theoretical stances of the individuals representing each school but also in several instances to the personalities of the individuals, thus making it difficult for the beginning family therapist in particular to differentiate between what is generic to family therapy and what is idiosyncratic to the individual whose work is described.

A more general approach is taken by Reiss (1980) who indicates that there are some choice points in assessing families. He describes those as: developmental versus cross-sectional (focusing on current family functioning or longitudinal family functioning); family direction versus environmental direction (tracing the impact of the broader network of relationships on internal patterns in the family or focusing primarily on shaping forces within the family); crisis versus character (focusing on immediate difficulties or on the family's enduring patterns of defense and adaptation; pathology versus competence (focusing on disorder or on the family's competence; and thematic versus behavioral (focusing on the underlying experience and motives or on the surface phenomena). Much of what Reiss discusses corresponds with our understanding of the issues in assessment. We would simply point out here that assessment for us often involves emphasizing and giving attention to both sides of some of the dichotomies involved, for example, focusing on both pathology and competence.

THE FAMILY ASSESSMENT PROCESS

With regard to family assessment in general, three important points need to be identified.

First, assessment is an ongoing process. One does not make an initial assessment of the problems, strengths, needs, and potentialities of a family and then forget about assessment from that time forward. Rather, assessment is something that is done continually, as the therapist continues to work with the family. Assessment is undertaken for the purpose of understanding the problems of the family and making suitable interventions both at the onset of one's contact with them and subsequently. Assessment in some ways is an existential–experiential process involving both the family and the therapist and their interactions. As de Shazer (1983) has pointed out, not only the family's descriptions and the therapist's descriptions of their problems, but also the interventions of the therapist, the family's reported response to those interventions, and the therapist's response to the family's response constitute the bases of the therapist's knowing the family's situation. This process is repeated in recursive fashion in the continuing contacts of therapist and family. There are two broad approaches to therapy with a family: fitting the family to a treatment modality (i.e., everybody is dealt with in the same way) or fitting the treatment to the family (i.e., tailoring the treatment strategies to the family). Our preference clearly is for the latter course of action. It is indefensible for a clinician to attempt to fit clients into his or her singularly narrow approach or orientation to therapy on the basis of an inadequate assessment.

Second, there generally is a tension between assessment and intervention, between the therapist's need to gather information in order to be helpful and the client's need to be helped without undue delay. Many beginning family therapists, particularly those moving into the field from other, traditional disciplines, sometimes are seduced or overwhelmed by the drama and array of the presenting problems. The tendency is to become pulled into the intervention crises and conflict and to respond with "band-aid" interventions, rather than giving themselves adequate time and opportunity to understand the system and develop a therapeutic alliance with the family. There are, of course, exceptions, such as life-threatening situations that must be attended to before further assessment and treatment can proceed. Our focus generally is on the enduring patterns of adaptation utilized by the system. What are the patterns of interaction, the role relationships, and the family rules that generally organize the shape of the family members' life together? At the same time, we find it necessary to look not only at the dysfunctional elements, but also for competence, for the abilities of the family to use what material, psychological, and social resources that it possesses in adapting to its environment and securing its goals (Reiss, 1980). As the therapist begins to understand and think systemically, he or she begins to operate with a certain minimal "need to know" construct or check-list. One learns to determine clinically that when certain issues and data are identified, they provide reliability for clinical decisions concerning intervention. It is not always possible in training situations or in certain clinical settings for a complete assessment to begin with the first contact. However, the veteran clinician recognizes that assessment begins with the initial contact, which is usually by telephone. Since assessment is such an integral part of treatment, the clinician cannot take shortcuts and rely on data from other sources and reports, but must begin his or her own family assessment process as early as possible and continue it throughout the course of treatment.

Third, when we speak of systemic assessment, we are alluding to a process that is much more complex than routine or perfunctory history taking. Individual therapists traditionally have relied on formal case history data gathered by way of straightforward questioning and probing. Therapists from such orientations have had to focus on verbally recounted histories because they have had access only to the individual from the system who is displaying symptoms, not to the system itself. In contrast, the family therapist chooses to have access to the entire system and must rely first on engaging and joining the system and dealing with its members in order to understand it. Historical data are evolved progressively and in stages most of the time, but securing them is secondary to the therapeutic process of engagement. Two fundamental principles of family assessment noted by Reiss (1980), observation of the family as a unit and integrated system and careful attention to the patterns of interaction among the members over time, illustrate further the complexity and ongoing processual nature of family assessment. Systemic assessment thus involves the blending and interplay of both interactive and developmental data. The beginning family therapist must learn to "read" aspects and dynamics of the system's process. As experience is gained, the therapist learns to perturb the system carefully in order to assess more quickly its structure and range of accommodations to its environment. Ackerman (1958) anticipated the evolution of systemic assessment well when he advised early family therapists not to rely on verbal data but to let "a live history" of the family emerge.

Keeping these general principles in mind, we shall now consider some of the questions to be used in approaching a case. The family therapist uses a series of reflective questions when approaching a beginning case. Such questions must be evolved by each therapist as part of his or her systemic thinking. They form the basis of early clinical hypotheses that inform the therapist about the general structure and process of the family system and the best methods by which to engage the family in a therapeutic relationship. For informational purposes and in order to aid beginning family therapists in developing their own questions, we include a list of questions that we use in our own clinical practices.

1. How does the family member who called to make the appointment "represent" the system?
2. How is the presenting problem or the identified individual's symptomatology connected to the remainder of the system?
3. What recent event(s) prompted the present level of system dysfunction?
4. Does this dysfunction express an acute (crisis) situation or a long-standing (chronic) pattern of functioning?
5. How amenable will the system, beyond the identified member, be to engagement in the therapy process?
6. Is it an enmeshing or disengaging system?
7. What are my skills/resources for engaging such a system?
8. Is there immediate evidence of significant intergenerational influences?
9. Which subsystems or members may seek to collude with me or to sabotage the therapy in other ways?
10. Are there subjunctive issue pertinent to initiating therapy, for example, prior therapy, additional therapists involved, medical concerns, or legal concerns?

DEVELOPMENTAL FAMILY ASSESSMENT: A TRANSGENERATIONAL MODEL

Beginning family therapists often become frustrated by the inability to determine what to look for when they begin to assess a family system. This is manifested, for example, by reactions of confusion or indecisiveness on the one hand or the making of premature judgments on the other. For the veteran clinician, the identification of major issues normally may occur within the first 30 minutes of contact in an initial session. The ability to make such rapid and important practical judgments can only be acquired through experience and clinical seasoning. For the beginning therapist, the first step is to focus on doing a careful initial and continuing assessment that will provide a solid foundation and discipline for all clinical work.

Again, the ongoing assessment process involves a thoughtful examination of a broad range of individual and multigenerational components. This means that the therapist seeks to recognize the role of individual family members, their levels of personal development, and the meaning of any symptomatology that they may manifest. Along with the assessment of each individual member, the clinician examines the dyadic interactional patterns within the spousal, parent–child, and sibling subsystems, as well as the broader interactional patterns within the nuclear family group. In addition, one attempts to identify specific patterns of multigenerational coalitions, triangles, and forms of scapegoating that were identified in Chapter 4.

A resource that is invaluable to the family therapist in the assessment process is the genogram. Derived originally from anthropology and geneological studies, this provides diagramatically the position and location of family members, their births, deaths, marriages and divorces, over several generations. The family map (Minuchin, 1974) is often differentiated from the genogram by the inclusion of systemic patterns such as coalitions and triangles. The descriptive value of the genogram for assessment is the visual impact of locating both roles and interactional patterns which exist for members of a system over several generations. For the purposes of this text we use genogram to be inclusive of both locations and patterns.

We also have evolved a modified genogram that may appear somewhat unfamiliar to the reader. The traditional genogram (see Figure 6-1) connects all individuals by vertical lines to their respective families of origin. For training and supervision purposes, we have found that depicting the family of origin and nuclear systems separately allows for the clearer identification of clinical patterns within both systems and the visual recognition of transmission patterns between the generational systems (see Figure 6-2). This is true particularly with large or complex three- or four-

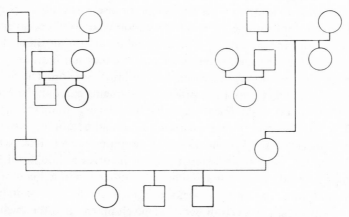

Figure 6-1. Traditional three generational genogram.

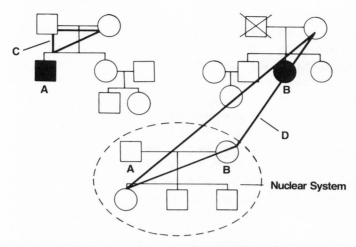

Figure 6-2. Modified training genogram.

generational systems. Thus in our model the figure for an adult spouse will appear both within the nuclear system and as a shaded figure within his or her respective family of origin system (see Figure 6-2, A and B). Similarly a triangulation pattern may be depicted both historically (see Figure 6-2, C) and presently across intergenerational boundaries (see Figure 6-2, D).

We are providing the following developmental overview in an effort to give students some "handles" and to encourage the development of their own assessment check-list. As discussed in Chapter 3, taking such an overview is not only highly compatible with systemic thinking, but also reinforces the conceptualization of family structure and process in trans-generational terms. It is our experience that learning to understand family life in a developmental fashion facilitates systemic thinking and the incor-poration of a rich core of relevant history in ways that are not possible in more mechanistic approaches to family therapy.

A Transgenerational Model

One must learn to blend an understanding of the immediate presenting problem with a comprehension of events and influences in a broader and more powerful context of transgenerational forces in order to grasp fully and appreciate the complexity and reciprocity of family systems. Presenting problems should always be examined for the presence of transgenerational influences. This does not mean, however, that simply putting the historical pieces together will solve the problem. The roots of most systemic dysfunctions do not arise overnight but are evolved through a variety of interactional patterns that may span many generations. To understand the "life" of a system that is being treated, one cannot be satisfied only with viewing its present visage. Rather, it is necessary to understand the growth of the system by filling in its joys and tragedies, its secrets and means of survival. Those who would challenge the family system with mechanical interventions fail to touch its humanity and should not be surprised when treatment is aborted or symptoms recur.

The value of a developmental transgenerational model for assessment is twofold: first, it provides a structure for the family therapist to use in understanding and tracing the patterns and locations of the dysfunction throughout the system and beyond the drama of the symptomatology; and, second, it places the immediate stress of the presenting problem for the family within a broader and more understandable context that diffuses the crisis and makes the problem seem much more manageable. In addition, such an approach redefines the presenting problem according to what we term "systemic developmental disruption." This means simply that we relate the symptomatology back to the patterns and history of the family system and place symptoms within the context of the system's natural growth and development. Most dysfunctional patterns evolve, prior to their presentation as symptoms, from disruptions in the system's normative processes. The system's relative effectiveness or ineffectiveness in accommodating such disruptions determines the magnitude and character of future symptoms. It is important to remember that though some families may present themselves for therapy at the onset of the disruption, others may not feel that there is a problem until disruptive events have accumulated or until additional transgenerational influences have occurred and have resulted in severe symptomatology. These systemic disruptions may occur in three forms (see Table 6-1).

"Normative developmental transitions" involve the movement between expectable family life stages (see Chapter 4). These include marriage, childbearing, career changes, children leaving home, and others.

"Systemic shifts" involve more subtle changes in the internal balance of relationships within the system. They may be triggered by transitional stages or may occur independently. Transitional stages are illustrated by

Table 6-1. Three Aspects of Developmental Disruption

Systemic developmental disruption
1. Normative developmental transitions
2. Systemic shifts
3. Systemic trauma

the decision of a traditional wife to return to school as the teenage children begin to "leave the nest." Their departure and the wife's decision may disrupt the existing collusive patterns and the complementarity in the marital subsystem, leading to a crisis. Independent shifts may be seen when, for example, a husband's controlling mother dies and he begins to move away from the marriage emotionally and behaviorally and into extramarital involvements.

"Systemic traumas" are unpredictable life events such as the death of a child, major physical illnesses/disabilities, or the termination of a career position. While such events are crisis producing on their own, their effects may produce subtle and disruptive reactive patterns as the system attempts to accommodate to them and survive.

These three categories describe and constitute most of the developmentally disruptive phenomena that underlie patterns of family behavior. The events or situations, whether they are predictable transitional events or unexpected happenings, occur naturally within the life of a system. Some family systems may accommodate to such events by evolving new structures and interactive patterns, thus creating a new systemic level of behavior (second-order change). Other systems may react to such events in a manner that redirects conflict and stress through a symptomatic member or through a rigid coalition in an effort to rebalance the system. It is the latter case that the family therapist will be asked to treat.

The following content areas are organized here in a manner that is designed to provide a structure and sequence for the assessment process. In an effort to operationalize the content areas and issues in the assessment process, each section is followed by a listing of areas of *interactive inquiry* and *process observation*. The questions associated with the inquiry and observation areas are intended to provide the beginning family therapist with specific content issues to explore as well as with patterns of systemic process to observe. It may be helpful for the student, rather than thinking of a case, to draw a three- or four-generational genogram of his or her own family and to imagine responding to some of the issues addressed under each section with personal family data.

Family Separation

The traditional period of family separation for adolescents and young adults often displays important central characteristics of the family system in a dramatic fashion. It is valuable to recognize certain features of this period when assessing cases involving adolescents or when assessing adult issues of maturity, individuation, and intergenerational loyalty.

In the case of referred adolescents, one needs to look first at the family in which the adolescent has emerged. Prepubertal patterns in the parent–child subsystem tend to reflect either parental overinvestment in the child or underinvestment and emotional disconnectedness. Overinvestment tends to accompany family enmeshment that circularly reinforces dependency. The child enters puberty and adolescence with a protracted dependency on the parents, and the parents are reciprocally committed to hanging onto the child. Underinvestment is found in disengaging families in which the parents are more distant and withholding. The child often pulls away from the family's influence and may have already formed rigid patterns of opposition to the parents prior to puberty. The child will enter puberty feeling alone and confused, with little parental support.

These early patterns, unless interrupted, present potentially dysfunctional issues throughout the family's movement during this period. When assessing the adolescent's role in the family system, it is important to differentiate early versus later stages of adolescence. Early adolescence is characterized by dramatic physiological changes and struggles with psychosexual impulses. It is a period in which peer attachments are becoming increasingly important to the youngster. Its conclusion generally is marked by the achievement of genital maturity. Later adolescence is characterized by a general integration of both personal identity and sexual maturity. The drama of puberty typically is replaced by heterosexual attachments and growing urges to disengage from dependency on the family.

Crises in the family during this period often reflect the system's struggle to accommodate the adolescent member. However, the beginning therapist must recognize that separation issues are always reciprocal. Too much attention often is focused by clinicians on the drama of the adolescent's behavior without adequate regard for the inability of the parents to facilitate their child's autonomy or for the parents' subtle vicarious identification with the child's misbehavior or delinquency.

Systemic struggles in families with early adolescents focus on issues of premature autonomy strivings of the youngsters and the increasing power of their attachments with peers. Adolescents from disengaging family systems are more involved with peer attachments than family and those from more enmeshed families are just beginning to undertake some movement away from parental controls. Struggles in families of later adolescents focus on matters of sexual maturity, growing physical independence, and more serious heterosexual attachments, although the struggles may present in terms of quarrels over "hours," the friends of the teenager, and use of the family car. In some systems, the sexual maturity of children may create either intrusive or distancing reactions by parents, and may trigger latent sexual difficulties within the marital subsystem.

Attention to the centripetal and centrifugal patterns described by Stierlin (1974) is helpful in the assessment process. The centripetal pattern follows Minuchin's (1974) enmeshing system in which the adolescent is bound by rigid and isolating family boundaries. Gratifications appear greater within the system than outside, and personal growth and separation are experienced with great ambivalence. In the centrifugal pattern, the adolescent is expelled early and forcefully. The system has little internal cohesion and members find greater gratification outside of the family. It is important to assess such patterns early because they tend to be repeated across generations. In addition, young adults who separate prematurely or who never achieve adequate autonomy may carry significant adjustmental and adaptive issues with them into the stage of mate selection.

The focus of the inquiry and observation of two types of cases in the following illustrative material is on the issue of family separation. These are cases in which the identified client is an adolescent and cases in which the attention is on the adult marital subsystem. The inquiry portion pertains to questions to be asked and areas to be explored. The process observation portion deals with what the therapist observes, reflects on, and intervenes into for the purpose of assessment–therapy.

Interactive Inquiry: The Adolescent Family System

1. Explore the types and frequency of activities that the family participates in together or separately in order to determine the family members' level of involvement.

2. Look at the peer, school, and dating involvements of each child in the system in order to determine their relative autonomy and differentiation from the family.

3. Explore the amount of time and emotional energy invested by the parents in the adolescent children's activities in order to determine the relative amount of family enmeshment or disengagement.

4. Ask specific questions in order to determine aspects of the family's everyday life patterns, such as "Do all of you usually eat dinner together?" "Tell me what it's like."

Observation of Process: The Adolescent Family System

1. Look for patterns of separateness and connectedness in the manner in which the family members seat themselves in your office.

2. Monitor the family's verbal, emotional, and affective interaction in order to determine its intensity as well as its cohesiveness or randomness. The interaction will suggest enmeshment or disengagement tendencies.

3. Reflect on your own emotional response to engaging the system. Does it feel closed and protected or diffuse and unbounded? These reactions generally provide clues about the system's external boundaries and suggest strategies for further engagement of the system.

4. Perturb the system by testing its relative tolerance for separation. For example, engage one of the adolescents in a dialogue regarding future issues, particularly getting married. Use your own style to do this in a playful and prodding manner, and then observe the remainder of the system's accommodation of your intervention.

Interactive Inquiry: The Adult Marital Subsystem

1. Explore each spouse's high school peer and dating activities in order to determine their relative differentiation from their family of origin.

2. Ask about the length and quality of their courtship in order to determine early attachment with each other or impulsive reactivity against their family.

3. Discuss how their family responded when older or younger siblings left home in order to determine their family system's tolerance for separation. Identify on a genogram how far from home each of their siblings are at the present time.

4. Review the extent to which their parents supported their decision to marry in order to determine patterns of reactivity.

5. Ask about the specific frequency of their present contact with their parents (telephone and physical visits) in order to determine the continuing enmeshment and vertical loyalties.

6. Explore their activities following the death of a parent for reactive behaviors.

Observation of Process: The Adult Marital Subsystem

1. When meeting only with the marital partners, use 1, 2, 3, from the previous section, looking for patterns of separateness and connectedness, monitoring the interaction, and reflecting on your own reaction to engaging the marital subsystem.

2. Monitor the relative comfort and discomfort of each spouse as they discuss historical data concerning their leaving home and talk about their present contact with their parents.

3. Use a gentle or playful manner to challenge the spouses' respective family of origin loyalties in order to determine both the intensity and rigidity of those ties and the accommodation resources of the marital subsystem for dealing with them.

4. Plot the relative family of origin loyalties on a genogram for each spouse and look for imbalances which may influence both attachment to the mate and marital complementarity.

Mate Selection

This period, as does the phase of family separation, carries dramatic systemic influences. Perhaps more than any other developmental period, it provides the link between the personal styles and family of origin experiences of each mate with the unique interactive patterns of complementarity in their relationship. In Boszormenyi-Nagy and Sparks's (1973) terms, it provides the interchange between vertical and horizontal loyalties. For the young adult struggling with separation issues, marriage often is fantasized as a replacement for the structure and security of the family system. Under such circumstances, marriage often is entered into impulsively with the young person bypassing normative courtship and mate-selection experiences. Such marriages become a forced coalition between the rescuer and the rescued with each using those pseudocomplementary roles in an effort to survive the stress of separation from their family of origin.

Blanck and Blanck (1968) defined three developmental levels at which individuals may approach their first marriage. First, and most ideal, is the level at which they are at their "peak" and are emotionally ready to marry and to cope with the inherent adjustment demands of the relationship. Second, others approach marriage with "unresolved or partially resolved" developmental tasks from earlier stages. There are, for example, individuals who carry excessive dependency on their family of origin through the process of separating from the family and consequently fail to achieve much individuation. This situation adds pressure to the mate-selection process in that a partner must be found with whom these earlier developmental issues can be met and partially worked through. Depending on the mate actually selected, it is expected that personal growth will continue for both individuals with their reciprocal need patterns being nurtured by their relationship. However, it also is possible that certain mate-selection patterns and decisions will block further growth for the individuals, at least within that relationship. Third, there are individuals who display either "blocked or incomplete" achievement of earlier developmental tasks (e.g., characterological or borderline personality conditions). Unlike individuals at the second level who seek mates in order to continue their growth, these individuals must search for a partner who promises to satisfy those predominating basic gratification needs. When such early developmental failures are present, the gratification of those major needs takes precedence over the interactive and bonding dimensions of the marital or mating relationship.

Information and understanding about the developmental level of the mating persons are very useful to the therapist in identifying the personal resources that each of them brings to the mate-selection process. Further assessment of the mate-selection process also gives the therapist important clues to the relationship's potential for bonding, intimacy, openness, and independence from family of origin constraints. In fact, discovering how the persons met and evolved a commitment to each other often provides more critical clinical data than simply exploring the early stages of their marriage. Again, the family therapist needs to know clinically the pattern and extent of bonding in the marital subsystem, because this subsystem is central to the remainder of the nuclear family system.

The assessment of mate selection involves examination of at least three components: demographic variables, emotional maturity, and couple complementarity. Although these issues were discussed in earlier chapters, we shall review them again briefly. With regard to demographic variables, early family sociologists adequately documented that persons tend to select mates from within a range of similar demographic characteristics such as race, religion, educational level, and socioeconomic background. These factors serve to narrow one's "field of eligibles" to the point where more emotionally based and psychological mechanisms take over. In demographic terms, individuals still tend to marry homogamously, that is, to marry persons with similar demographic characteristics. The second component of mate selection involves the frequently made clinical observation that persons tend to select mates who either fall within or approach a level of personal growth and maturity or ego development equal to their own. This means that it is to be expected generally that individuals will marry within Blanck and Blanck's (1968) developmental categories, rather than across them. The third component, complementarity, has to do with the patterns of emotional needs and need gratification that exist between the partners. Early psychoanalytic literature defined some complementary patterns in a variety of colorful terms: dominant/sadistic–passive/masochistic (Mittelman, 1944, 1948); folie à deux (Oberndorf, 1934); and the "love sick" wife and the "cold sick" husband (Bird & Martin, 1959). More recent efforts to research mate selection (Murstein, 1961; Winch, 1958) have come up with findings that indicate that both the "opposites attract" and "likes attract" theories are to be found (see Chapter 5 for a discussion of this topic). Again, we use the term "complementarity" to refer to the manner in which the partners need each other emotionally and how they "fit together" in the satisfaction of their needs.

It is important for the family therapist to examine the extent to which the mate-selection process has occurred within these normative patterns. Obvious relationship stresses may occur where imbalances are evident about religious, ethnic, and educational factors. Subtle but more powerful disruptive issues may arise where persons with "incomplete" emotional development select someone who is at a "blocked" level. The former will become disillusioned and frustrated at his or her mate's inability to offer much emotionally to the relationship. Conversely, the "blocked" individual will become angry that his or her spouse will not meet emotional needs in the total, complete manner expected. The complementarity factor, particularly in cases in which quite different individuals fit together strongly, is a major component in marital bonding. It helps to explain how people fit together and maintain apparently dysfunctional and conflicted marriages for years without significant change, until growth and change in one partner upsets the balance in the relationship.

Interactive Inquiry

1. Explore each spouse's family of origin separation patterns and the dating and courtship experiences in order to determine whether there was either a continuity of patterns or reactive impulsivity involved for them in selecting a mate.

2. Ask each spouse to reflect on their emotional closeness with each of their parents and to specify notable characteristics in order to determine same-sex and cross-sex identification and use of role models. Note these patterns on a genogram for each partner.

3. Explore the mate-selection process, giving particular attention to their idealization of the other and the process, in order to determine their expectations, disappointments, and aspects of complementarity. Ask in a playful manner, "Tell me how you met one another?" "Do you remember what attracted you to him (her)?"

4. Inquire about the actual decision to marry in order to determine both power and control patterns, as well as potential intergenerational influences.

Observation of Process

1. Observe the frequency and intensity of their interaction, both verbal communication and how they look at and physically act toward the other, in order to determine the quality of affective interaction and bonding.

2. Observe the relative "fit" and balance between the spouses in both their verbal and nonverbal interaction in order to determine relevant aspects of their respective maturity and the complementarity of the marital subsystem. As part of this, examine your own emotional intuitive feelings and reactions to the couple with regard to comfort and availability for emotional attachment.

3. Observe the extent to which discussion of their early courtship experiences triggered forgotten, camouflaged, or latent aspects of romantic idealization. Playful dramatization of the early romantic experiences may be helpful in mobilizing latent romantic idealization in the present relationship.

4. Observe and compare the relative openness and congruency between the spouse's respective recollections of their courtship in order to determine both the reliability and continuity of their recall. Discuss the discrepancies with the couple, *observing their interaction more than the content of their responses.*

Family of Origin Patterns

While examination of family of origin patterns is somewhat out of a logical developmental sequence at this point, it is important in the assessment process to look back historically to the spouses' respective family of origin data. This task must be done at the same time that an examination is being made of their relationship. Hence, we include the discussion at this point. It is our experience that by looking at separation and mate-selection factors first, the clinician gains more definitive data to use in discovering or confirming historical patterns. It also generally is easier to engage clients initially at the stages of their early courtship and mate selection than by "digging" around in their family of origin history and risking stumbling upon secrets prematurely.

It is important to look at the three components of mate selection within the parental marriage of each spouse. Such examination will define the character of their family of origin systems and the roles that those systems played throughout the parent–child and sibling subsystems in which they were reared. It is equally important, of course, to look at structural patterns regarding internal and external boundaries, coalitions and triangles, and process issues of complementarity, enmeshment–disengagment, scapegoating, and parentification (see Figure 6-3).

These family of origin patterns are important at two levels. First, they offer a qualitative view of each spouse's early growth experiences within their family of origin, experiences that will be reflected in their expectations and perceived roles as they begin to form their own nuclear family system (Napier, 1971). Second, those patterns will form equally powerful and often inherently dysfunctional intergenerational linkages. For example, a young woman who has been parentified in her family of origin and thus involved in a triangle with her parents, may carry this enduring triangle and pattern of interaction with her in a manner that not only influences her mate selection but also operates explicitly to limit the formation of adequate boundaries around her new marital subsystem. Depending on reciprocal patterns brought to the relationship by the

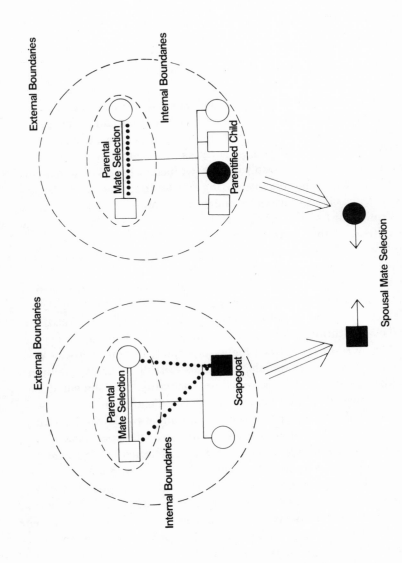

Figure 6-3. Family of origin pattern in mate selection.

External Boundaries

Internal Boundaries

Parental Mate Selection

Parentified Child

Spousal Mate Selection

External Boundaries

Parental Mate Selection

Internal Boundaries

Scapegoat

husband, that intergenerational pattern may help to explain either the wife's excessive need to "nurture" and control the husband or her emotional unavailability due to her continued parentified role in her family of origin triangle.

Interactive Inquiry

1. Ask how the parents of each spouse met, the length of their courtship, and how they complemented each other in order to determine the relative aspects of parental mate selection, couple complementarity, and relationship boundaries.

2. Explore the specific roles taken by each person within each parent–child subsystem in order to determine patterns of closeness, distance, and triangular alignments. Note these on a genogram for each spouse.

3. Ask each spouse to compare their present marital and parental roles with those of their parents in order to determine continuity of patterns or reactivity in role models and expectations.

4. Compare and integrate for yourself this information with the data on separation from the family of origin and mate selection previously obtained in order to gain a preliminary composite picture of what each spouse has brought to the marriage.

Observation of Process

1. Give careful attention to the relative ease with which each spouse recalls family of origin data. Note the areas of sensitivity or repetitive role patterns that would indicate the existence of former and/or continuing loyalties and triangles.

2. Test the suspected potential for occupying scapegoated or parentified roles by dramatizing aspects of these roles historically within family of origin experiences.

Family Formation

A marriage brings together all of the prior historical experiences and influences of each spouse and forms the nucleus of a new family system. Unfortunately, many clinicians fail to recognize the importance and role of the developmental consequences and powerful intergenerational pressures that influence the formation of a new system. The early experiences of the partners in the marital subsystem, built on top of earlier developmental, separation, and mate-selection factors and experiences, become critical to the future and structure of the new marital subsystem. The earliest tasks of establishing a comfortable range of reciprocal intimacy and bonding will establish bases for and influence the establishment of future internal subsystem boundaries and the relative need for triangulation of other members into the marital subsystem. For example, if the early period of bonding is interrupted by a pregnancy within the first 6 months of marriage, the family therapist can expect to find more diffuse boundaries around the marital subsystem than would be expected if the first pregnancy occurred after several years of marriage. The diffuseness renders the marriage more vulnerable to problems associated with lack of privacy and external intrusive influences, for example, from family of origin influences.

The interplay between vertical and horizontal loyalties, between loyalties with the family of origin from above and loyalties with the mate on the same level, is critical in the family-formation stage. For young adults in their first marriage, the years of vertical family of origin loyalties generally far outweigh the more recent historical ties to the spouse. Thus, a central task of the first year or so of marriage is the balancing of those loyalties in order to form a viable marital subsystem. If both spouses carry intense vertical loyalties into the marriage, they will have difficulty forming protective marital subsystem boundaries and will struggle with limited early emotional investment in the mate and marriage (see Figure 6-4).

Where one spouse brings strong vertical loyalties and the other strong expectations/needs for horizontal loyalties into the marriage (see Figure 6-5), an immediate imbalance is present in the new subsystem. The former will display more emotional investment in the family of origin and the latter will be expecting more closeness and intimacy in the marriage. This early imbalance creates high levels of disillusionment and conflict. Where the disparity in loyalties is great, early marital dissolution could occur. Relationships with less disparity that also are influenced by other factors such as children and career issues may achieve a stable balance in spite of the disparity in loyalties.

Another important assessment clue in the formative stages of a relationship is the gradual and normative breakdown of romantic idealization. Even though our culture reinforces high romantic expectations in marriage, the result of everyday life together takes its toll and erodes both the early romantic expectations as well as the deeper fantasies of the individual

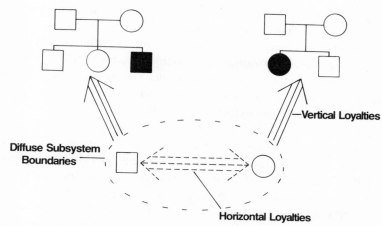

Figure 6-4. Excessive vertical loyalties, weak horizontal loyalties, and diffuse spousal subsystem boundaries.

for need gratification. This erosion generally occurs within the first 2 years of marriage and often within the first year, and is evidenced in angry reactive and regressive behavior evolving from the disappointment that the partner cannot be all that was idealized or fantasized prior to marriage.

Spouses who survive this early dose of reality begin to form an underlying collusive structure that was present at least in embryonic form during their mate-selection process. Such collusion is a normative ingredient of bonding and forms a protective substructure for the relationship.

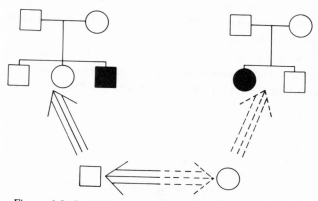

Figure 6-5. Imbalanced vertical and horizontal loyalties.

Each spouse implicitly and at least preconsciously, sometimes unconsciously, agrees to support the other and in essence promises not to tread into vulnerable and sensitive areas of personal growth. This collusive agreement may involve covering up everything from underlying fears of dependency and intimacy to secrets of former sexual liaisons and incest. Collusive processes may be helpful and growth enhancing in some instances and malignant and dysfunctional in others.

Recognition and clinical assessment of the nature of the collusive bonding is important. Where either the relationship is tenuous or individuals have significant vulnerabilities and developmental deficits, the clinician can expect to find highly rigid collusive patterns. The partners will bond together not only to make the bonding work as best it can but also to protect it from discovery and interference by outsiders. In fact, the greater the underlying deficits, the greater the need for a rigid protective structure. Discovery of collusive bonding patterns alerts the family therapist to interactive patterns in the marriage as well as to issues of resistance in treatment that will be discussed in Chapter 7.

Interactive Inquiry

1. Explore the relative emotional involvement (in family of origin and in the marriage) of each spouse at the beginning of the marriage by discussing issues of geographical distance from their families, frequency of contact with them, reciprocal responsibilities, and economic giving and receiving. Integrate these data for yourself with information on earlier family of origin and separation patterns in order to determine the availability of each spouse to the marriage and the balance of loyalties.

2. Compare the spouses' respective expectations with regard to intimacy, responsibilities, and marital roles in order to identify early inhibitors to bonding in the marriage.

3. Review specific patterns of sexuality and sexual interaction during the early phase of the relationship prior to conception of the first child in order to determine the quality of intimacy and bonding and changes that have occurred.

Observation of Process

1. Look for early areas of ambivalance or discomfort in the relationship in order to determine relationship issues and deficits in bonding and levels of protective and defensive collusion.

2. Note the relative degrees of privacy and the nature of the boundaries that protected the relationship in its early stages.

3. Test the current protective collusion in the marital bonding by gently probing a sensitive area for one of the spouses and observing the extent to which the other spouse attempts to intervene, protect, or rescue the spouse.

Family Development

As the emotional dimensions of the marital subsystem evolve, the relationship also must begin to manage additional factors in the world of everyday living such as education and career issues, geographical movement, involvement in social networks, and the potential for pregnancy. Conception and the birth of the first child bring to an end the exclusivity of the marital subsystem and mark the beginning of the second nuclear family subsystem, the parent–child subsystem. As noted previously, when conception occurs premaritally or within the first 6 months of marriage, the clinician can expect to find weak marital subsystem boundaries. Even a planned conception after a year or more of marriage brings dramatic changes. New boundaries must be formed and for the young adults who are inexperienced in childrearing, the new roles often will replicate those with which the spouses grew up in their respective families of origin. Where early bonding is tenuous, the formation of the parent–child subsystem will challenge the privacy of the couple and may serve to diffuse at least temporarily aspects of marital stress.

The accommodation of the marital subsystem to the birth of a child offers important assessment clues regarding both the individual spouses and their early interactive patterns. The birth of the first child often serves as a triangular glue that holds tenuous marital relationships together at that time by deflecting the spouses' attention toward the parenting role. On the other hand, the birth of a child can trigger intense resentments, jealousies, and competition for attention between spouses, particularly on the part of dependent husbands (Pincus & Dare, 1978). Reactive and dysfunctional patterns that occur at this stage of family formation usually can be predicted from earlier assessment data.

Similarly, the clinician should not overlook the influences of second and third children. Addition of second, third, or subsequent children presents the system with the task of systemic accommodation to an increasingly large subsystem. As the family moves through these childbearing and childrearing years, additional external factors also may intrude on the system. Such influences may be predictable, for example, career changes or relocations, or unpredictable, for example, serious illnesses or the death of a spouse's partner. In assessment, the therapist should always be sensitive to the system's resources for accommodating to such influences and the reciprocal structural and process changes that are necessary. For example, the decision by a traditional wife/mother to return to school or work outside the home may not only require serious adjustments in the parent–child subsystem but may also threaten early collusive agreements for her to remain in the household. Her exposure to influences external to the system may encourage new personal growth that could upset the marital balance and jeopardize the existing complementarity of the couple. Similarly, the death of a parentified husband's mother may launch a new developmental sequence for him that could either give him more freedom for intimacy with his wife and emotional availability as a husband and father or propel him into a series of sexual liaisons outside of the home in a reactive and regressive manner.

As the children reach adolescence and begin preparing to "leave the nest," formerly latent issues may be brought to the surface. Most apparent in clinical referrals at this stage are tenuous marital subsystems that survived despite covert difficulties so long as the parent–child subsystem was present to be predominant in the family. For approximately 20 years or so, spouses may have related to each other primarily as parents of their children. With the children leaving the system, the ability to diffuse and obscure differences and potential conflicts diminishes, and suddenly the marital system is threatened. Although some spouses begin to manifest difficulties early and engage in a variety of covert behaviors that are designed, at whatever level of awareness, to prevent the children from leaving them alone to deal with one another, many couples experience a shock reaction when the departure date draws near. Such parents begin to realize that they have done so little interpersonally over the years and have, in fact, grown in different directions and may have been held together only by the presence of the children. The potential for postparental restructuring of the relationship thus is exceedingly important to assess.

Such assessment is especially important when extramarital relationships become prominent. The liaisons must be assessed by the clinician as if they were a subsystem within the family's network, as indeed they are in some instances. Beginning family therapists often are reluctant to ask about such relationships and thereby miss major systemic influences, or become caught up in the drama of the "affair" and fail to understand its actual meanings for the family. Overall, the clinician needs to know both the emotional meaning of the relationship for the individual who is involved, that is, sexual, impulsive, situational, reactive, need gratification, and so on, and its role within the marital subsystem and broader family system. For example, some extramarital relationships may be relatively benign with regard to their influence on the system and function as a balancing factor for a spouse whose partner retains excessive vertical loyalties. Some are malignant in that they provide major sources of pain and stress for the other spouse and for the children. Some extramarital involvements, as in the case of the wealthy business or professional man whose paramour and out-of-wedlock child live 2 miles away from his wife and three other children, may be known to all of the persons affected. Others may be kept "secret," but trigger various kinds of reactions and "acting out" behavior among the children.

Interactive Inquiry

1. Explore whether or not the pregnancies were planned and discuss the responses/reactions of each spouse to the conceptions.

2. Follow the developmental thread of both the marital and parental roles from the conception of the first child to the birth of subsequent children. Integrate this information with other relevant situational data such as career or geographical moves and family of origin influences in order to determine the relative "ups and downs" of the relationship and the major shifts. Note these moves on a genogram.

3. Compare the relative changes in spousal and parent–child boundaries over the developmental life span.

4. Compare the specific parenting patterns of the spouses with those of their own parents. Relate this material to the early complementarity of the couple and identify shifts and incongruities that appear.

Observation of Process

1. Observe the relative affect displayed by each spouse with regard to sensitive issues while you are dealing with the conceptions and pregnancies.

2. Look for reciprocal patterns of accommodation by each spouse

individually and in the marital subsystem following the birth of each child in order to determine patterns of rigidity or new growth.

3. Throughout the developmental span, look for shifts in couple complementarity or differential growth between the spouses.

4. Test the present spousal subsystem boundaries by playfully looking at areas of privacy, intimacy, and sexuality with them.

5. Where triangular patterns of parentification or scapegoating are suspected with children, test the primacy or power of the parental alliance by dramatizing the relative power of the identified child in the system.

The model of developmental assessment that we have presented here is intended to provide a means of operationalizing theoretical concepts regarding the family's structure and process and to provide some guidelines for use in organizing salient and expectable features of a family system's development. It should provide the beginning family therapist with a preliminary conceptual check-list and a format for clinical inquiry. No attempt is made in this model to address traditional areas of individual diagnosis and to provide material for psychiatric nomenclature. It is expected that students entering practicum in graduate programs or post-degree training programs shall already have been exposed to personality theory and psychopathology and be acquainted with the assessment and diagnosis of pathology for individual classificatory purposes.

Once again, we wish to be clear that systemic family therapy does not ignore or rule out as unimportant the recognition of major psychiatric conditions such as psychosis, depression, or borderline conditions. As noted above, in order to function effectively and responsibly, the family therapist must be able to perform traditional diagnostic work and be familiar with DSM-III and the ICD-9-CM categories. However, the family therapist also seeks to bring to cases a broad systemic and contextual view of etiology and symptomatology that will affect treatment issues dramatically.

CONSTRUCTING A FAMILY ASSESSMENT

A written family assessment is useful not only as a teaching tool but also as a means of organizing clinical data and understanding systemic patterns throughout treatment. It provides the basis for deciding on treatment strategies and serves as a continually updated composite picture and collection of hypotheses regarding the family case. In our training programs, beginning and advanced family therapy students are asked periodically to write a three- to five-page assessment of a selected training case. Normally, students are expected to select a case that they are just beginning and to compile data for the assessment following the third or fourth session. The requirement that such an assessment be written may appear to be routine and the performance a perfunctory matter. However, it is our experience that the process of collecting data and organizing it in the form of a written presentation facilitates the development of conceptual abilities and the enhancement of the student's clinical discipline. It enhances the student's clinical inquiry work, gives the supervisor immediate data to monitor, and supplements the student's resources and deficits.

Conceptual tasks are blended with experiential learning in such education and training in order to help the student achieve an adequate level of systemic thinking ability and integration of theory and practice. It has been our observation that family therapy students trained exclusively with live and experiential methods tend to become intensely technique oriented. Their conceptual abilities in assessing family process often are limited and they adapt poorly to working with varying clinical populations and in clinical settings different from those in which they were trained. We require our family therapy students to pay the price of learning how to think, conceptualize, and continually assess the family and human processes that they encounter so that *family* and not technique is emphasized.

The following example of a family assessment outline is structured for training purposes and is illustrated by a former student's[1] assessment of an ongoing case. Permission was obtained for use of the material and names and facts have been disguised so as to provide protection for the clients.

Description of the Family

1. *Demographic Profile*. Give a reasonably detailed description of the identified client(s), and of all significantly related nuclear and extended family members. Attach a three-generational genogram (see Figure 6-6).

2. *Family Developmental History*. Trace the highlights and transitions from the spouses'/parents' own families of origin through adolescent separation and courtship to mate selection, family formation, and birth and rearing of children. Identify significant losses, illnesses, geographical changes, and so on.

---

1. We are indebted to Michael Denny, Ph.D., for the use of this material.

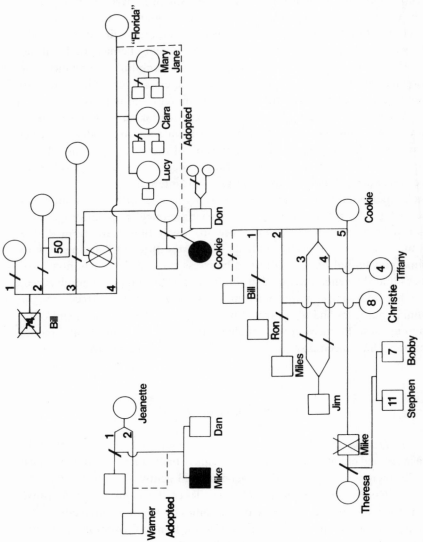

Figure 6-6. Family assessment: The Smith family genogram.

The Smith family consists of the mother, Cookie, and four children. The two boys, Stephen, age 11, and Bobby, age 7, are the stepsons of Cookie and the stepbrothers of Christi, age 8, and Tiffany, age 4. Cookie was married in January 1983, to Mike Smith. Both were aged 32. Mike died of cardiac arrest in March 1983. Following the death of the boys' father, they continued to reside with their stepmother and stepsisters. Stephen and Bobby's biological mother, Theresa, divorced their father in 1975, and gave custody of the boys to her exhusband. Since that date, she has not had any contact with either her exhusband or her biological sons. The other significant biological relative of the boys is the paternal grandmother, Jeanette, who is remarried to the boys' stepgrandfather, Warner Smith. Cookie's exhusband, Jim, was her third husband, and is the adoptive father of Christi and the biological father of Tiffany. Both girls maintain continuous contact with their father. Cookie Smith is a fraternal twin who was reared by her biological grandfather and stepgrandmother, whom she refers to as mother and father. The biological grandfather is deceased, having passed away when Cookie was in her early teens. Cookie and her brother, Don, were the biological children of Nancy and Bill Jones. She and Don were given up by Nancy, who placed them in the custody of the biological grandfather and stepgrandmother after divorcing Bill Jones and denying that he was the biological father of the children. Cookie's biological grandfather was married approximately four times; the first and second marriages resulted in two children each; the third marriage was to Julia, with two female children being born to the union, the youngest of whom was Nancy (Cookie's mother); the fourth marriage for the biological grandfather was to Florida and three daughters were born to this union. Cookie refers to those three girls as her sisters. The oldest is Lucy, the second Clara, and the youngest Mary Jane. They were approximately 10–12 years older than Cookie and her brother, Don. Cookie Smith maintains contact with her stepgrandmother, Florida, and her three biological aunts, whom she considers her sisters. Her brother, Don, has married for the second time and is an optometrist in Tennessee.

Very little is known about Mike's early years, other than the fact that his adoptive father, Warner, married Jeanette when the boys were in elementary school. There is some indication that Mike and his brother Dan, who lives in Ohio, did not get along well with their adoptive father. Warner and Mike's biological mother, Jeanette, indicated that Mike was an unruly son who left home early and joined the armed forces. Both parents refer to him as a chronic liar and manipulator. Cookie has confirmed this, indicating that he kept his medical condition from her. Throughout Mike and his brother Dan's upbringing, their mother was considered an alcoholic, and she has continued to drink excessively in the later years of her life.

Cookie Smith grew up on a small farm in North Florida with her fraternal twin, Don, and her three aunts. Cookie and Don were named by their biological grandfather, whom they refer to as their father. He named them after two characters from the Don Quixote story. Cookie despises her given name, Chiquita, and prefers to be called Cookie. Throughout her upbringing, she was considered the little princess who would get most of her needs met through either her stepmother or her oldest aunt, Lucy. Cookie dated various young men through high school and, after graduation, went to business school in Jacksonville, Florida. There she met an older man, with whom she ran off to St. Louis. After reaching age 20, she returned home and began dating a young man her own age. She eventually married him, but the marriage was annulled after 4 months. She described Ron as quite violent and highly attached to his own family of origin. She left home after the marriage was annulled and moved to South Florida for 6 months, but returned home, began dating again, and worked as a chiropractic assistant. Although she was taking birth control pills, she became pregnant with Christi and eventually married Miles. They divorced within the first year of marriage. She reared Christi alone and received little help from her own family of origin. Eventually, she met her third husband, Jim, who was married at the time and had two children, a boy and a girl. Jim divorced his wife, married Cookie, and adopted Christi. Cookie reported that they married for income tax purposes and had the marriage annulled within the first year; however, they remarried and lived together until after the birth of their child, Tiffany. After divorcing Jim, Cookie moved to Tallahassee, Florida, and took a job as an orthopedic assistant. When she began dating seriously, her exhusband Jim moved from South Florida to Tallahassee in order to maintain continual contact with her and his two daughters. In 1981, Cookie began dating Mike and continued to do so for approximately 2 years, until they married in January 1983. After they were married, she and the two girls moved into Mike's home with him and his two boys, and attempted to settle into a reconstituted family. However, Mike's untimely death left her with the care of the two boys and her own two girls.

Comment. This case illustrates the value of using a multigenerational genogram in order to identify historical patterns and sequences in the family system. Many cases lend themselves to the use of further intergenerational data. The developmental history description in a family assessment should be focused initially on the evolution of the spousal subsystem, with significant events and patterns from each spouse's family of origin traced to present marital interaction patterns. Significant transitional or crisis data provide a background to understanding family structure and process. The outline is designed to delineate the essence of the family's structure (demographic profile) and its process (developmental history), prior to focusing on the presenting problem(s). The illustrative data in this case illustrate well the need for the clinician to sort out and identify structural and process issues where there are continuing intergenerational influences as well as multiple marriages and multiple caregivers for children.

Presenting Problem

Give a concise statement of the clients' reported reason(s) for seeking clinical services, the referral source, and a summary of prior treatment, relevant medical history, and court or school reports.

On April 4, 1983, Cookie was seen individually at her request in order to help her cope with rearing four children and dealing with her grief over losing her husband. In the first interview, she reported that the older son, Stephen, age 11, was experiencing difficulty in middle school and was being extremely recalcitrant. She was seeking family therapy in order to help the four children and herself to settle into a family. The suggestion that family therapy be sought had been made by the middle school. There had been no previous therapy or court involvement, and no significant medical data had been identified.

Comment. The presenting problem should be stated concisely according to the client's remarks. Beginning students need to pay attention as objectively as possible to what the clients report without either becoming pulled into problem solving or interjecting their own interpretations prematurely. In the Smith case, the client identified a blend of issues involving the sudden and unexpected loss of her husband (spousal subsystem), as well as the distruptive behavior of a child and her difficulty in reorganizing the family after the crisis (parent–child subsystem).

Clinical Assessment

Give a summary of your early clinical impressions at four levels:

1. Give clinical impressions of each family member's own individual development with regard to maturity, personality integration, ego development, capacity for intimacy and bonding, and management of stress and anxiety.

2. Evaluate interpersonal dynamics within the spousal, parent–child, and sibling subsystems. This would include patterns of coalitions, triangles, parentification, scapegoating, internal and external boundaries, and enmeshment–disengagement.

3. Identify broad family system and transgenerational patterns such as myths, secrets, and coalitions.

4. Characterize the system's social network patterns including residential environment, career, school, religious, and other social contacts.

1. Following the second session, which Cookie, Stephen, Bobby, Christi, and Tiffany attended, it was determined that this was a highly disengaged reconstituted family. The mother's fragmented family of origin attachments carried over into her multiple marriages and into her present inability to nurture the children effectively or to stabilize the system following the sudden loss of her husband. With a lack of family of origin supportive network, she has relied on tenuous male relationships in an effort to meet her continuing needs for structure and nurturance. Cookie's two daughters appear well adjusted to the divorce of their biological parents, but grief stricken about the recent death of their stepfather. The boys have "acted out" the problems of the system, probably due to the mother's difficulty with male figures. Overall, the children appear to be developmentally immature, although this is covered by a pseudoautonomy due to the lack of nurturance. The disengaged patterns in this family have made it difficult to assess the boys' grief responses to the loss of their father.

2. This appears to be a disengaged system with the mother providing little nurturance or support for the children, particularly for the boys. She relies on strong control tactics such as spankings and unrealistic restric-

tions. The two boys are highly enmeshed with their parental grandparents. This appears to be a reciprocal source of nurturance for them, probably encouraged covertly by the mother. The parent–child subsystem boundaries are diffuse, with the boys displaying greater bonding with the grandparents than with the mother. The older boy, Stephen, tends to be the scapegoat of the family. Additional evidence of this was found when the therapist had the grandparents in treatment and found them also scapegoating Stephen. The younger son, Bobby, was favored by the grandparents, who primarily reared him.

3. The fragmented nature of the mother's family of origin has provided little support or influence. However, the boys' paternal grandparents continue to play a predominant role with them. It was determined that the grandparents did not wish to seek custody of the boys and preferred to have them live with Cookie. However, it appears that the boys would prefer to live with their grandparents. There are no data at this time regarding explicit coalitions or family myths.

4. The father's death will add more economic pressure to the system, which in turn will put more pressure on Cookie's employment role. Previously, her employment had been sporadic. These factors could increase the level of disengagement in the system as well as increase the power of the grandparents to gain control of the boys, should the grandparents desire to do so.

Comment. The clinical assessment is the "meat" of the paper and requires the blending of individual, subsystem, intergenerational, and social network data. It is important here to operationalize systemic concepts and to begin clinical speculation regarding the family's style and functioning. In the Smith case, the mother's own developmental deficits and problems with nurturing stand out in the scapegoating of the 11-year-old boy, Stephen. The disorganized, disengaged nature of the system made it difficult to identify major triangles or underlying themes or myths in this early phase of assessment.

Etiology

Give a statement of the probable level of conflict in the family:

1. In which *subsystem* does the basic conflict reside? (Note: This refers to the basic conflict, not to the presenting problem.)

2. Determine the level at which the conflict *originated* (e.g., developmental transition, present situational influences).

3. Are present conflicts acute, transitory, or chronic?

1. While the presenting problem identified the scapegoated child, the basic conflict appears to be with the mother's ineffective role behavior in the parent–child subsystem. This behavioral ineffectiveness predated the death of the husband and reflects deficits in her own personal development and the absence of adequate and appropriate role models in her family of origin. A secondary level of conflict resides in the intergenerational system in the form of the influence of the paternal grandparents.

2. The roots of the conflict lie in the mother's family of origin. These deficits have been dramatized in the present system by the sudden death of the spouse.

3. The effect of the husband's death represents an acute crisis for the system, while the underlying deficits in the parental role appear to be chronic.

Comment. The etiological statement involves an effort to identify the source of the conflict structurally according to the involved subsystems and by process according to the historical onset and patterning of the dysfunction. The goal of the clinician here is to move away from the presenting problem and to conceptualize the stress according to the broader life of the system. The Smith case illustrates very well the involvement of multiple subsystems and the effect of severe chronic patterns in the ongoing life of the family unit.

Treatment Goals and Strategies

Provide a statement of what can be accomplished realistically with regard to first- and second-order change and identify individual, interactional, and family system variables of significance. Project a recommended treatment of choice, identify the primary system or subsystem to be treated, that is, total family, parent–child, marital, individual, intergenerational, network, blended family network, and so on. Identify the expected pattern, frequency, and duration of the projected treatment and provide a rationale for it.

The initial goal will be to return the system to some level of balance, which will of necessity require structural reshaping in order to accommodate to the loss of the husband/father. This will involve both first- and second-order systemic changes. The mother will need to begin developing a positive interactional relationship with the boys and to reestablish greater control over the system, with the backing of the grandparental system. Custody of the boys will need to be cleared up so that Cookie's efforts in creating a family context for herself and all four children are not sabotaged. Scapegoating of Stephen will be challenged by putting the problem into a family context and by educating the mother with regard to the creation of the present system. Assisting her to differentiate from the therapy system will be the final treatment goal. The treatment strategy initially will involve a blend of conjoint family sessions and individual work with the mother. It was decided that the initial approach would be to bring the level of problems into a family context and to begin treating the entire reconstituted family system. It was further indicated that eventually the mother would be involved in individual sessions in order to assist her to recognize her own emotional needs and patterns resulting from her family of origin and how those patterns and needs have influenced her formation of adult relationships. As soon as possible, the grandparents should be invited to participate in the therapy process.

Comment. The treatment goals and strategies should state clearly what the therapist anticipates with regard to first- and second-order change. They should identify relevant issues at the individual, subsystem, and intergenerational levels. The Smith case illustrates an implicit need for second-order change with regard to the system's normative accommodation to the loss of a central member. It also illustrates the need for working at certain times with one member—in this case, Cookie, the mother—and with the entire intergenerational system.

Predictions

Anticipate issues that may occur in the treatment process and/or reciprocal behavior by clients and/or the system outside of treatment, for example, sabotaging, resistances, and acting out behaviors.

The potential sabotaging with regard to the scapegoated child may come both from the mother and the grandparents. The goal of assisting the mother in establishing firmer parental boundaries and closer emotional ties with the children may meet with resistance and could trigger an impulsive search on her part for a replacement mate.

Prognosis

Project the family's potential for homeostatic renewal (stabilization) and/ or systemic change.

The family's potential for restabilizing appears good if the grandparents support the mother. If they sabotage the mother's already weak role in the system, the prognosis appears quite poor. Goals for further restructuring of the system and redefinition of the mother's role are guarded at this time.

Comment. The areas of prediction and prognosis are included in an effort to facilitate the therapist's anticipatory "instincts" and conceptual understanding of systemic change. It is important for beginning therapists to "practice" and to test clinical speculations with their supervisor. Gradually, this improves their accuracy and the reliability of their projections, thus increasing students' trust of their clinical "instincts." The prognostic statement should, of course, interface with the previously stated treatment goals. The Smith case illustrates well how the relationship between systemic hypotheses made earlier and family dynamics facilitates the therapist's ability to predict and estimate the potential in the family for therapeutic change.

Role of the Therapist

Identify where you have had previous experience with similar cases, issues of personal enmeshment, management of resistances, control issues, and how you expect to use supervision.

While disengaging families are somewhat more difficult for me to connect with, I have worked with enough by this time to anticipate issues that will arise. I think that I have established good rapport with the mother and children, but need to examine the best ways to invite and involve the grandparents in therapy.

Comment. The statement concerning the role of the therapist should be introspective and reflective. It is intended to link the person of the therapist with the idiosyncratic nature of the particular case that is being assessed and treated. Beginning therapists may have difficulty responding personally and not theoretically to these issues and will need to rely on the supervisory relationship for assistance in identifying many of the significant issues. The Smith case was developed by a family therapist who was particularly experienced in dealing with the kinds of chaotic and disorganized cases that present at mental health centers. His treatment plan and predictions, although presented succinctly according to instructions given students, were well thought out and were appropriately based on the assessment data. The statement on the role of the therapist was not as complete or as clear as is desired. Such incomplete or unclear segments of a family assessment provide particularly important material for the supervisor to take up with the students in supervision, pressing them for clearer and more complete thinking.

The Smith case was in treatment for nearly a year. Good progress was made in redefining parent–child roles. However, as the clinician had predicted, the dependency needs of the mother, Cookie, pushed her into involvement with another male, and she soon began to make plans to leave the community with him. The grandparents, who became only marginally involved in the family therapy, were advised by their attorney to "snatch" the boys from Cookie. They did take the boys and proceeded with a custody suit which Cookie chose not to challenge.

Briefly, the overall assessment framework is intended to serve as a means for organizing salient and expectable clinical features in a family system's development into a comprehensive although succinct statement for assistance in treatment and supervision. It should provide the beginning family therapist with a wealth of data from critical areas that aid understanding and a format for pursuing the clinical inquiry. The ability to conceptualize, abstract, and organize data into succinct statements from among the plethora of detail and observational material available to the student therapist is the first thing that we seek to enhance by the use of a family assessment outline.

The relationship of assessment with treatment will be pursued additionally in Chapter 7.

CHAPTER SEVEN

Family Therapy

We have given a considerable amount of thought to the writing of this chapter. On the one hand, we do not wish to present an oversimplified "how-to-do-it" approach that does not reflect an adequate relationship between clinical intervention and theoretical orientation. The field is already overburdened with such materials that lack an adequate grounding in theory, that rely too much on technique and do not provide enough understanding of content. On the other hand, we do not intend to provide a review of how family therapy is done by adherents of various schools or competing clinical orientations in the field. Once again, a solid understanding of family development and family structure and process is the appropriate basis for performing family therapy. Given such a foundation, one can learn how to assess family and individual needs and to intervene in family difficulties in therapeutic ways. Many different techniques may be used in making effective therapeutic interventions, provided one uses them at appropriate places and in suitable ways. Conversely, the best techniques in the world may be used and the most respected orientations may be followed with ineffective outcomes or disastrous results if the clinician does not have an informed appreciation of the functioning and needs of families and of the particular family with which he or she is dealing.

Our hope is that we have laid a substantial theoretical foundation with regard to family development, structure, and process and to clinical assessment in the preceding chapters so that the production of clinical interventions and strategies will evolve as a natural extension from that base. We are aware that the process of developing knowledge and skills is not a matter of simple linear causality. One does not, in other words, simply learn about family content from research and study, then learn about family assessment, and then learn how to make appropriate interventions and to do family therapy. It is very important to establish a solid, comprehensive knowledge of the substantive materials on family as a starting point. Such comprehension, however, is enhanced and expanded in a recursive fashion as one begins to work with families in clinical assessment and treatment. That is the place where cognitive learning comes alive and responsible and effective experiential learning occurs.

Once the beginning family therapist has acquired a basic orientation to family, there is no substitute for supervised learning experiences and relationships with competent and seasoned family therapists. We use a plural term here because of our observation and belief that the best learning occurs when the student has the opportunity to work with several supervisors, rather than "majoring" in one mentor. In the final analysis, we believe that clinical skills are developed and perfected in ongoing clinical practice performed under good supervision. The clinical work of assessment and intervention take on significant meaning, rather than being perfunctory mechanical tasks or sterile actions to be done because one has read about or observed them being performed by a master therapist or teacher.

What we shall try to do here and in the following clinically oriented chapters is to blend the theory that we presented earlier with crucial issues in practicing family therapy. A major part of our intent is to provide frameworks and discussions of issues that can be used by family therapy students and their supervisors as part of an ongoing learning process. Here, we shall attempt to take the reader through a sequence of issues and tasks regarding preparation, engagement, and termination in conducting family therapy.

PREPARATION FOR FAMILY THERAPY

This section provides an introduction to some of the issues that the family therapist needs to address prior to meeting with a family. The model that we are offering for consideration is one in which there is room for making decisions about a number of components within the framework of a systemic approach to working with families. The issues that we identify here are offered in an attempt to further the reader's experience in thinking systemically and to provide a reflective interrelationship with the pragmatic concerns of "doing" family therapy.

Defining Therapeutic Directions

Issues of family system change with regard to homeostasis and first- and second-order change have already been discussed. We also have covered assessment issues with regard to etiological and developmental factors that influence the potential for change. With these factors in mind, it should be clear that the primary goals of family therapy do not stop simply at symptom relief (although occasionally this may be a necessary condition for the family to enter therapy). The family therapist is always monitoring the system's pattern of accommodation around the presenting dysfunction as well as the system's potential for rebalancing and achieving new levels of accommodation that would mark systemic change. Such potential therapeutic change can be seen as either returning the system to a presymptomatic homeostatic level of functioning (first-order change) or moving the system to new levels of interaction beyond their prior functioning (second-order change).

It is important to recognize that both first- and second-order change constitute viable treatment directions. Unfortunately, some family therapists have promoted an idealization of second-order change, thereby implying that family intervention cannot be successful unless second-order change has occurred. It is our opinion that it is clinically naive to idealize second-order change over first-order change. The potential for either is grounded intrinsically within the developmental history and human process of each system. An analogy from individual psychotherapy is useful. Occasionally, when treating an individual with rigid defenses, the therapist may decide that to dig out or tamper with the tenuous ego development under the surface could be more destructive than therapeutic. Similarly, some family systems simply do not have the interactive resources or energy to accommodate to new levels of functioning.

It should not be surprising, despite implications by some therapists to the contrary, that the potential for systemic change is based more on the intrinsic nature of the system than on the skills of therapist. The family therapist need not make an early decision about whether first- or second-order change is to be sought and, in fact, often may shape his or her interventions so as to move back and forth between the two directions in order to test the system's resources.

Related similarly to the issue of direction of goals is that of when and where to use family therapy. Most technical treatment discussions deal with the "indications" and contraindications" for use of an approach. In the preceding discussion of learning to think systemically, we have evolved a definition of family therapy around an orientation (epistemology) with regard to human behavior and interaction and not one that is dependent on techniques or what the therapist does. Therefore, concerns regarding indications and contraindications for a systemic family therapist are irrelevant, because it is assumed that the therapist approaches not only clinical situations but also life in general from this new epistemological orientation. This does not mean, of course, that there are not good reasons to choose certain systemic interventions at certain times (e.g., structural, strategic). However, the systemic approach to the family remains the same, the therapist approaching the situation systemtically whether the presenting problem begins with an anorectic child, a delinquent adolescent, or a depressed spouse.

Formulating Therapeutic Goals

Keeping the first- and second-order directional issues in mind, it is important for the family therapist to recognize the interplay between his or her general goals of family therapy and the actual direction and conduct of the treatment process. Therapists always must balance their goals for therapy with the idiosyncratic needs and resources of each family system. This interplay establishes and defines the new "therapeutic system" evolving between the therapist and the family. As the beginning family therapist learns to monitor the interaction, he or she will gain respect for the life of the system and will be less likely to impose therapy goals disconnected from the system's concerns and resources. In fact, the therapeutic goals will emerge from the "life" of the new therapeutic system, if such monitoring is carefully done.

Therefore, one of the most important issues at the onset of contact with the family is the matter of clarifying both what the family is seeking and what the therapist can offer, and whether these are compatible enough to make therapeutic work viable. The family or family representative making contact with a therapist will have expectations that may range from the highly specific ("Fix up this teenager") to the very general and even vague end of the spectrum ("The school said we should call, for some reason . . ."). Family expectations may be very practical or exceedingly impractical, realistic or unrealistic. Obviously, there may be a wide discrepancy between the family's goals and purposes and what the therapist thinks is necessary or possible in working with the family. From these two levels of expectations, it is important to establish very early a sufficient amount of agreement regarding goals to make therapeutic cooperation possible.

However, establishing adequate compatibility between the goals of the therapist and those of the family often requires an interim step early in the therapeutic relationship. The individual requesting the initial appointment, for example, frequently is the overcommitted member or caretaker of the system, whose stance may not be representative of what the other family members expect or desire. Thus, the task of the therapist may involve recognizing and dealing with different goals and different purposes among various family members. A husband/father, by way of additional illustration, may wish to have something done about the behaviors of the children, and his wife may place the source of the problems in the marriage and wish to have something changed in the marital relationship. Sometimes it may not be necessary to try to resolve such differences in outlook among family members directly, provided that it is possible to follow treatment approaches that permit simultaneous attainment of seemingly discrepant goals and purposes (Feldman, 1976). On other occasions, it may be appropriate to point out to a family that "it is necessary to deal with x-issue before we can get to y-issue. We can get there, but in my judgment, this is the best way to proceed in order to get what you want."

There appears to be fairly general agreement among family therapists on two points regarding therapeutic goals: first, that there should be symptom relief without the emergence of new symptoms in any family member (Green & Framo, 1981); and, second, that therapy should help the family achieve appropriate developmental tasks in the family cycle (Carter & McGoldrick, 1980). Both of these would be labeled "outcome goals." They are goals that would be expected to result from the therapy as an ultimate outcome. The first of them, symptom relief or elimination, is at least an expressed part of most families' reason for contacting a therapist. Whether the family actually desires change in the fundamental systemic conditions that may be producing the symptomatology may, of course, be another question. However, with regard to the second goal, families are less likely to demonstrate an awareness of the need for help in achieving mastery of ongoing developmental tasks than they are to seek symptom relief, simply because family members do not view their lives in the broad conceptual framework of the family life cycle. When specific developmental tasks are highlighted as issues, many families quickly grasp the practical and immediate importance of those tasks.

It should be clear that the formulation of therapeutic goals occurs on several levels, that is, the immediate goals of the family regarding the presenting problem, potential longer range goals of the family pertaining to permanent changes, the therapist's immediate goals for symptom relief, the therapist's overall outcome goals, and the therapist's various subordinate goals. It is the task of the therapist to balance and revise these goals continually, according to the progress of the therapy.

Conceptualizing the Role of the Therapist

The therapist approaches the family system as an outsider who has been asked in one way or another to intervene in the life of the family. From our perspective, the therapist comes to the family with the task of assessing the family system and engaging the family in treatment for the purposes of alleviation or elimination of symptoms and making changes that will assist the family in achieving improvement in its ongoing functioning. Within this broad framework, the therapist has many tasks to accomplish and numerous roles to fulfill. One may be called on to serve as a role model, a perturber (disturber) of the system, a go-between and side taker (Zuk, 1976), and in many other ways, depending on the situation and on his or her orientation, needs, values, and abilities.

As family therapists approach a new case, they bring to the event not only the range of explicit clinical knowledge and skills that have been developed but also their own personal history of family ties and experiences. This combination may prove to be a blend of both invaluable clinical resources and at times burdensome baggage, depending in part on the nature of one's family and personal experiences.

As therapists move to initiate a new therapeutic system with the family, they must continually monitor the degree of emotional and physical contact that is required with the system, that is, noting the times to move in and the times to pull back. The therapist's own personal resources provide the therapeutic bridge to engaging the system. A therapist's own role earlier in life as a parentified child in an enmeshing family of origin provides grounds for an immediate identification with a depressive parentified child as well as inherent caution and awareness of the importance for balancing the engagement with the remainder of the parent–child triangle.

The role of the family therapist is by definition intrusive into the life of the family system. Its influence spreads far beyond contact with the identified or "sick" member and, if effective, mobilizes resources that have not been recognized previously as available within the family to aid change. While intrusive, this role should be performed with a human and not a technical quality and manner, and with respect for the life and integrity of the family system.

The role of cotherapists has been the focus of a considerable amount of discussion over the years. During the early stages of family therapy, attention was given to the power and complexity of family systems, especially those severely disturbed family systems containing a schizophrenic member, and the ability of such systems to confound and overwhelm even a seasoned therapist. The perceived need for the "lone" therapist to have outside support and feedback in order to avoid being "swallowed" by the system was one of the reasons why some family therapists pioneered in the use of "live" supervision in which the supervisor actively intervened in the ongoing treatment process. (Observation of therapists performing individual psychotherapy had been done for a long time through one-way observational mirrors, but typically without the use of active intervention by the supervisor.)

Advantages ascribed to cotherapy are that this approach can accomplish systemic changes faster than a therapist working alone, that the combined presence and efforts of two therapists give more power vis-à-vis the system than one therapist possesses, and that the interactive styles of the therapists and their potential for taking various roles vis-à-vis each other and the family offer them greater possibilities for engagement and movement with the family system and subsystems. Experienced family therapists find that roles can be strategically divided so that, for example, one therapist aligns with the parents and the other with the children. Both the ability to take various roles and the interactive styles have the potential for creating considerable leverage and power in conjoint family sessions. Cotherapy roles can be defined also with regard to rebalancing power between subsystems (Everett, 1976; Everett & Volgy, 1983). Napier and Whitaker (1978) have provided a good study in the implementation of complementarity by cotherapists and Keith and Whitaker (1983) have given an interesting discussion and rationale for taking a cotherapy approach. We recognize that typically clients cannot afford cotherapists in private practice, and in many agency settings cotherapy is not considered to be efficient in terms of either cost or time. Similarly, reviews of available research indicate that while cotherapy may be especially appropriate for some clinical problems, "at present there is little substantive basis for the routine use of cotherapy teams in family and marital therapy" (Kniskern &

Gurman, 1980, p. 222; see also Todd & Stanton, 1983). Nevertheless, family therapists in training should avail themselves of cotherapy team experiences in order to recognize the issues of power and balance within the therapeutic system.

Therapists working alone, which is the way most therapists work outside of subsidized research and training facilities, should be aware of their own resources and skills as well as knowledgeable about the structures of therapy in order to make realistic decisions about where and how to intervene and work with family systems and subsystems. Such awareness and knowledge is added to what they know about family and learn about the structure and process of the particular family presenting itself for therapy.

The explicit tasks of the therapist will be delineated further when we deal with engagement and systemic change.

Deciding Whom to See and When

Family therapy cases may present in several different ways. That is, an initial request for help may take any one of several forms, including a request for help for the total family, an identified client, parent–child problems, or marital difficulties.

Occasionally, and perhaps in increasing numbers, the total family may be identified by those requesting help as the source of difficulty. Such families seem to identify either a general cluster of family problems or a specific, identified family member as the source of tension. In the former instance, the family often will say, "There are a lot of things not going right. We don't get along. We don't have time for each other. We don't communicate. We just need some help in straightening things out." In the latter case, the family tends to identify one member as "having problems," but also recognizes that "Johnny's problems are not the whole picture. The whole family is involved."

Many families request help for one member, either an adult or a child, who is seen as having individual problems that are not perceived as being related to the family. That is, such problems are viewed by family members as belonging to that person and not to the family as a whole. Such members often are referred to by mental health professionals as "the identified patient." The "identified patient" may be self-referred, as in the case of a depressed husband or wife, or referred by the family or school, as in the instance of a child manifesting school phobia. Requests for assistance for identified individuals probably are still more common than calls for help for the total family, although, as we have noted, requests for the latter type of assistance have increased markedly in recent years.

It also is rather common for a parent to identify a problem or set of problems as existing between himself or herself and a child or adolescent. Sometimes, the problem is described in triangular terms as involving a conflict between the parents on one side and the youngster on the other. "He is rebellious, argues with both of us about anything and everything. He won't do a thing that he is told to do. He acts like he hates us sometimes. We just don't have a relationship with him. He seems to get along fine with his friends and all right with his brothers and sisters, but not with us." At other times, a parent will call about problems among the siblings, noting that they do not seem to be able to do anything to bring about a cessation of the sibling conflict.

Clinical experience indicates that, in general, both involvement and engagement of the father are likely to be crucial when dealing with a two-parent family. Typically it has not been easy to get fathers involved for a number of reasons, including the tendencies for fathers to leave childrearing details to their spouse, their reluctance to see problems in psychological terms, and their general opposition to involving themselves in therapeutic work that includes discussing "personal" and "private" situations with an outsider and relating to him or her in a dependent fashion. A number of clinicians and researchers (Berg & Rosenblum, 1977; Kressel & Slipp, 1975; Napier, 1976; Shapiro & Budman, 1973; Slipp, Ellis, & Kressel, 1974; Teissman, 1980) have emphasized the importance of involving and engaging the husband/father in family therapy.

As noted above, one of the most common areas of presenting problems involves the marriage explicitly. Because the marriage is so important and forms the initial and central family subsystem, Chapter 8 will be devoted entirely to marital therapy.

Whatever the form of the original request for help—total family, identified client, parent–child problems, or marital difficulties—the family therapist should always monitor the relationships between the various subsystems, their boundaries and relative power, and the manner in which the presenting problem is embedded within them. From this broad systemic perspective, the family therapist has innumerable choices of patterns and sequences of clinical interventions. Some of these are suggested in Figure 7-1.

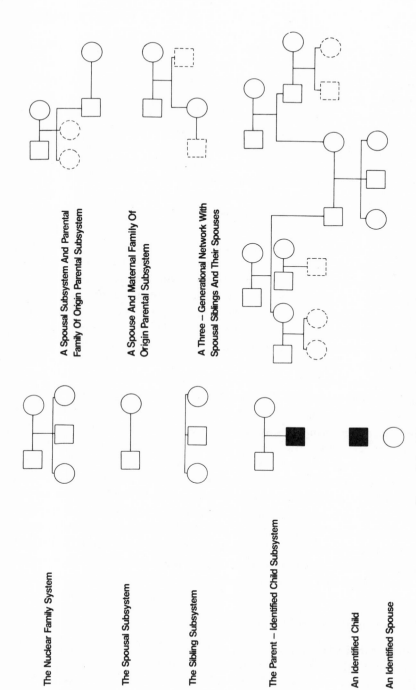

The Nuclear Family System

The Spousal Subsystem

The Sibling Subsystem

The Parent – Identified Child Subsystem

An Identified Child

An Identified Spouse

A Spousal Subsystem And Parental Family Of Origin Parental Subsystem

A Spouse And Maternal Family Of Origin Parental Subsystem

A Three – Generational Network With Spousal Siblings And Their Spouses

Figure 7-1. Alternative units for systemic intervention.

225

Clinical Options Based on the Presenting Problem

In the early phases of family therapy, clinicians must make a rapid assessment of the presenting symptomatology relative to the structure of the family system. Initially, they must make decisions regarding whom to invite to the first session. There are many options available to therapists, depending on the circumstances of the case and their level of experience and training. One can begin with an individual or a subsystem of the family or with the entire nuclear family or even with portions of the extended family. Rigidity certainly is not the principle that we follow or that we would advocate for our students to use as a guideline in deciding how to start with a case.

As we discuss some of the options open to therapists, it is with the understanding that they may make changes about who comes to the sessions following the initial appointment or appointments, regardless of who is present for that meeting. It is not necessary, again, for therapists to adhere rigidly to the opening format. What occurs in the opening appointment with the family or with whomever is present for the session, as well as what happens subsequent to that meeting, often causes an alteration in the composition of the group gathered together for later therapy sessions. Skynner (1981) and Stanton (1981) have discovered from quite different perspectives some of the issues present with regard to who is to be in charge of the sessions and who is responsible for the outcome. We shall allude to the control or power issues in the discussion that follows. Our major concern here, however, is with the options open to the clinician at the beginning of contact with a client or with a "patient system," to use Pinsof's (1983) term. We also are concerned with the flexibility that may be exercised as the therapists proceed to deal with the family system on the basis of the presenting problem and the issues that emerge from their initial contacts with clients. Not all family therapists view the issues in the ways that we do and some have very strong and understandable reasons for taking other approaches, for example, requiring that all members be present for the first appointment.

The Issue of the Total Family

A significant issue that arose in the early history of family therapy and that has continued to be controversial is the question of whether the entire family unit has to be present for the initial appointment and what to do if a member or members decide not to attend the session. Numerous family therapists (e.g., Bell, 1983; Minuchin, 1974, Napier, 1976; Napier & Whitaker, 1978; Whitaker & Miller, 1969) have either suggested or indicated flatly that it is important or even essential to have all family members present from the beginning of treatment. Bell (1983), who describes his approach as rigid even to himself, staunchly refuses to proceed with therapy unless all family members are present for all sessions. In such an approach, in particular, the therapist in starting treatment is faced with the issue of refusing to go ahead with treatment and to delay until all members are present, as Bell and others would do, or to proceed with those family members who do come to the meeting.

If the decision of the therapist is to delay until reluctant members can be brought into therapy, there is the question of how the task is to be accomplished. The responsibility for securing the participation of the reluctant member can be taken by the clinician, who can make telephone calls, write letters, or, perhaps, in extraordinary circumstances, even visit the individual. Teissman (1980) has described the risks—that if the therapist is successful in getting the reluctant member to attend therapy, the family may conclude that the therapist rather than the family is responsible for change in the family system. He also has described and summed up the enabling moves of the clinician under the headings of increasing the attractiveness of attending and decreasing the attractiveness of not attending. Teismann considers the potential benefits of attempting to involve the refuser by direct action on the part of the clinician worth the effort and the risk that such moves entail.

The responsibility for bringing all family members to the initial session can also be given to the family. For some therapists, the question of whether or not to meet with the family unless all family members are present is a simple one, as we have indicated—they simply will not do it. This throws the responsibility directly on the family and makes the question of control of the therapeutic relationship and process a simple and straightforward one. That is, the therapist assumes and maintains control at the outset by refusing to proceed until his or her conditions for beginning therapy are met by the family. Whether it is possible to delay treatment until all family members agree to be present is a matter of practicality and reality. Therapists who work in agencies, for example, may not have the luxury of imposing such strictures as "no therapy without total family attendance."

Whether it is necessary to have all family members present in order to conduct effective and responsible therapy is essentially a matter of opinion. Some available research (Berg & Rosenblum, 1977) indicates that very few family therapists will refuse to see families unless all members are present. Certainly, there has been an accrual of a large amount of clinical experience that would support the idea that treatment can be launched successfully without all nuclear family members being present for the initial sessions or even for succeeding meetings (Selvini-Palazzoli, Cecchin, Prata, & Boscolo, 1978).

In our opinion, the decision regarding whether to proceed if all family members are not present and what to do if they do not attend sessions is best handled on an individual basis, rather than on the basis of inflexible principles and guidelines. Beginning family therapy students should examine the question carefully in supervision, where they can also look at such other issues as the motivation of the family member who makes the first contact, that member's role within the system, and the nature of the presenting problem. Napier (1976) has suggested that the most general guideline to be used in establishing the structure for beginning family therapy is to try to "keep each generation intact, avoiding splitting the marital pair or the children" (p. 5). It is our belief that given the limited experience of beginning family therapists and their need for broad training exposure, the directions for initiating family therapy should follow issues surrounding the presenting problem. As we have indicated elsewhere, family therapy represents an orientation (epistemology) regarding behavior and not a "technique." Thus, family therapy may be conducted effectively whether the therapist is seeing one or eight family members.

The Identified Individual

When the presenting problem is focused on a child displaying difficulties and disturbances of the kinds that are referred to as symptomatic (e.g., depression, delinquency, school phobia, and so on), the family therapist must decide whether that child or other children should be invited to the initial session. The therapist, for example, needs to ascertain at the time of the initial telephone contact whether the child's symptoms indicate the possibility of such life-threatening situations as anorexia or threats of suicide that would warrant the child's being seen by the therapist immediately.

Adults often will present themselves with specific symptoms such as depressions, obsessions, or phobias. Basically, the family therapist wishes to treat such situations as he or she would cases of scapegoated children, that is, with the initial assumption that the adult probably is carrying the symptom for a family dysfunction, in this instance one that is embedded in the intergenerational network with his or her family of origin. The less the clinician does to overreact or to reinforce the symptom, the greater will be the possibility of understanding and redefining the symptom systemically. Often one wishes to involve the spouse of the presenting client as soon as possible and perhaps other nuclear or extended family members as well. The principle to be followed here is that one should observe and deal with the symptoms in the broader context of the family system.

The Parent–Child Subsystem

Important decisions concerning who should be seen first also have to be made when the presenting problem involves a parent–child situation or a complaint that the siblings are causing trouble by their modes of behaving and relating. The therapist may decide to see the entire family together or to see only the parents initially and perhaps other family members later. If an apparent scapegoating situation is present, the clinician can anticipate that the parents will reenact a process of blaming the child to some degree in the first therapy session. Some therapists may wish to allow such a pattern to evolve and then seek to interrupt the scapegoating interactive sequence in the first session. Our tendency is to proceed in a more controlled and cautious fashion. We are more concerned at the outset with engaging the family, and particularly the parents at that point, in the therapeutic process. Also, if the scapegoating process has been going on for a long time, for example, since a 14-year-old child was 6, the power of that sequence of behaviors will be such that even the most experienced therapist may not be able to accomplish both engagement and interruption in the first session. If the parents and the children are seen together and the scapegoated child is "dumped on" in the interview, it is very difficult for the therapist to avoid getting caught in an undesired early coalition as a result of either moving in to protect the child or by siding with the parents. For either of those actions to occur early in the therapy would jeopardize the possibility of engaging the system.

By understanding and anticipating such interaction and dynamics in the system from the time of the initial telephone contact, the clinician can be prepared to avoid dealing with them directly at the outset by structuring the early sessions so that only the parents are included. A general rule of thumb to be followed is that where the symptom is embedded in the parent–child subsystem, the therapist should consider forming an early alliance with the parents in order to begin the therapy. This does not mean forming a coalition with them in a session against the child but refers instead to seeing them solely as a subsystem and forming a sense of bonding with them so that they perceive the therapist as an ally who can help them "fix" their child. It allows the therapist to move into the system immediately without directly challenging the scapegoating process and, because he or she is not present, diffuses the process of blaming the child.

The next step may be to request to see all of the siblings together without the parents. This action responds to the parents' concern that the therapist "see" their child, yet continues to diffuse the focus from the identified child by not singling him or her out to be seen alone. Working with the sibling subsystem separately from the parents gives the therapist an opportunity to engage the children independently of the parents and to continue to interrupt indirectly the reenactment of the scapegoating sequence in the family. The manner in which the clinician structures the early session, if done with a quality of finesse, can permit the clinician to provide a powerful challenge to the family system at the same time that he or she is involved in collecting necessary assessment data.

At this point, there are two options open to the clinician. The first would be to move into conjoint sessions with the parents and all of the children, following the initial separate subsystem sessions. Experienced therapists rarely wish to convene only the central triangle of father, mother, and identified (scapegoated) child in their office. The power and energy of this triangular structure would be expected to shut out the therapist. Generally, it is a much wiser move clinically to include other aspects of the system, in this case the siblings. Such action tends to diffuse the central triangle and to give the therapist other components of the system with which to connect.

The decision to move to conjoint sessions with the entire nuclear family system is indicated where interactive patterns require interruption and where issues of separation–individuation are prevalent with adolescents, or where systems have triangular or scapegoating patterns so rigid that the parents are unable to move away from the identification of a given child as "the problem" in order to deal with their own role in the dysfunctional family process.

The second option would be to move within the parent–therapist alliance and to gradually shift the focus from the child to parenting, then perhaps to family of origin parenting models for each of the child's parents, over to the parents' responses to the conception and their integration of each child into the family, on to the courtship and mate-selection period during which they formed their relationship with each other, and finally to their privacy and bonding in their marital interaction. This circuitous clinical route from the presenting child to the marriage could involve from 1 to 20 hours of therapy. Although systemically we know that where both parents are involved in the central triangle with a parentified or scapegoated child, the child's symptomatology typically is a reflection of deficits in the spousal subsystem, we also know that to move in and focus too quickly on such issues would prematurely challenge the protective collusion of the marriage. It is often a matter of poor timing when beginning family therapists move in too quickly on the marriage. Understandably, the parents in such situations will often defend themselves and their subsystem by countering, "We came to you to help Susie, not to answer all these questions about our personal life." The effect is that they may perceive that the therapist is blaming them for the child's problems and may leave treatment as a result of this perception.

When the clinician can engage the system through an alliance with the parents and eventually move to treating the marriage, it may sometimes prove unnecessary to even see the children in therapy. Shifts that occur within the system and in the spousal subsystem, such as moves that strengthen subsystem boundaries, will have ramifications for the parent–child subsystem. As the marriage makes changes, the pressure on the symptomatic child may be relieved. Seeing the parents together from the beginning may be particularly good strategy to use for young children, who may never need to be brought into therapy or may need to be brought in only for the purpose of consolidating systemic changes conjointly at the conclusion of therapy. However, the therapist should be aware that the symptomatic child may be reluctant to "give up" the symptoms, such as the intrusive access by a parentified child into the marital boundaries, even when the original systemic dynamics have changed. We wish to reiterate that there are conditions that may involve life-threatening illnesses or threats among children that would warrant their being seen by the therapist immediately. We do not wish to portray "one way" of engaging the system, but rather to provide the reader with a basis and model for thinking through clinical strategies.

The Marital Subsystem

The other major area of presenting problems involves the marriage explicitly. This may be identified by clients in terms of problems in communication, "getting along," sexuality, in-laws, or financial conflicts.

Within the context of clinical engagement, an important systemic concern is to make every effort to involve both spouses at the outset of therapy. To begin marital work with only one spouse sets up an immediate imbalance and perhaps establishes an unwarranted collusion between the therapist and the spouse making the initial contact. Working with only one spouse raises significant ethical problems. At the very least, both the spouse who is present and the spouse who is absent should be informed of the potential risk to the marriage that is inherent in therapy when only one mate participates (Gurman & Kniskern, 1978b).

Often, one spouse will say that the other "will not come," hoping thereby to gain attention and perhaps support from the therapist against the partner. Beginning therapists sometimes learn to their surprise that a spouse coming individually for therapy will tell the mate that the therapist has agreed with everything that he or she has been telling the other for years. One young male therapist, after six individual sessions with a woman who said that her husband was not interested in therapy, received an angry telephone call from the husband reporting that the wife had packed a suitcase and was planning on going out of town for the weekend with the therapist. The manipulative wife thus succeeded in gaining both the husband's and the startled therapist's attention. After the crisis subsided, the clinician learned that the woman had engaged in extramarital affairs previously in efforts to maneuver the husband out of his alcoholic pattern and that she had never invited him to participate in the therapy with her.

Therapists use various methods, including telephone calls or letters, of ensuring that the client's spouse is informed and invited to come to therapy. Some clinicians may refuse to see one spouse without the other being present, at least at the beginning of the therapy. Our experience over the years has been that practically all individuals whose spouse has requested assistance will respond to an invitation to attend one session, either alone or in the company of the mate, for the purpose of helping the therapist to understand the client. If the spouse is invited to a session for such consultative purposes, it is vital that the clinician be honest and stick to the purposes that were announced. If the invited mate begins to change the focus, it is the clinician's responsibility to point out what is happening. The session can be moved back to following the original purposes or can be moved into an examination of the invited spouse's concerns and problems, but if the latter course is followed, it should be done with informed consent on that individual's part. On some occasions the invited spouse decides that he or she wishes to become part of the therapy.

If a clinician should decide that the other spouse is genuinely unavailable and there is reason and need to proceed individually with the presenting mate, several precautions should be taken. First, the client needs to recognize that by pursuing therapy on his or her own there is created the risk that any changes made as a result of therapy may either help the marriage or harm it. That is, such therapy has the potential either to enhance the relationship or to create a destructive imbalance that may jeopardize the future of the marriage. One's growth in therapy may be quite healthy for him or her as an individual but dysfunctional in the relationship (Gurman & Kniskern, 1978b). Second, the client needs to recognize that the therapy sessions are not intended to serve as "gripe sessions" for ventilation about the mate. Third, both therapist and client should be aware that the absent spouse may become intrigued or frightened after a few weeks and may decide voluntarily to enter therapy.

To have an absent spouse decide to enter therapy after his or her mate has met with a therapist for several sessions creates an imbalance that needs to be recognized. The more time that the clinician has spent with one spouse, the more likely that there are issues about alliances that must be addressed. Not only may the client spouse feel that he or she has a prior relationship with the therapist but the absent spouse who decides to enter therapy may also have that feeling. Similarly, no matter how objective the therapist feels himself or herself to be, the fact is that there is a likelihood that feelings of protectiveness toward or alliance with the original client may be present if the treatment relationship with that person has gone on for an extended period before the second spouse enters therapy. The therapist has to make the judgment as to whether he or she can realistically become therapeutically involved with the spouse who is entering therapy late and thus achieve an equitable balance as the move is made from individual to conjoint sessions. Some therapists attempt to ease the anxiety of the new client and work toward creating a balance by seeing the newcomer for several sessions alone. It may not be necessary to balance out the sessions meticulously so that each of the spouses has been seen individually by the therapist the same number of times, but sufficient time is required to establish a cooperative and working therapeutic relationship.

Beginning therapists in particular may have difficulty in attaining a balance in conjoint work if one spouse has already been seen for six or eight individual appointments. One alternative to be considered is that of referring the spouses as a couple to a colleague who can begin conjoint work with them, seeing them together from the beginning.

By way of summary, many families today are presenting themselves as a whole for therapy, giving generalized complaints. In most cases, such families are amenable to beginning therapy with the entire nuclear family system present, at least until the dysfunctional processes are identified.

How the presenting complaint is treated depends in part on the nature of the complaints and in part on the orientation of the family therapist who receives the complaint. How therapists perceive and treat problems ranges across a spectrum. On one end of the line is a stance that regards the presenting problem as *the* problem. The problem is treated for itself and not as a symptom of anything else. Other therapists may regard the presenting problem as indicative of the fact that the family is having trouble negotiating one of its developmental tasks or stages as it tries to move through the family life cycle. Still other therapists may assume that the presenting problem is causally related to the structure of the family unit. At the most remote end of the spectrum from the problem-as-problem end is the orientation that regards the presenting problem as symptomatic of family dysfunction. The difficulties that are manifested are systemic efforts to solve a deeper family system problem (Segal & Bavelas, 1983). Our understanding and approach is that the presenting problem may be any of these things. Determining which one it represents is a matter for the clinician to ascertain during assessment.

The Intergenerational Network

When to include members of the intergenerational family network is one of the more important issues that may be decided after treatment has begun. As we have indicated repeatedly, it is important to view the family system from the perspective of three to four generations. This broadens the effect of the presenting symptomology into interactive models and patterns that have been transmitted and maintained over several generations (Boszormenyi-Nagy & Spark, 1973). The family therapist should always be alert to identify intergenerational patterns, even when working with an individual. Moreover, the decision to include members of the intergenerational network in the treatment process requires some careful strategic consideration. The systemic principle or guideline to be followed here is similar to that of avoiding isolating the central triangle of the father–mother–scapegoated child in the therapist's office. The more access the therapist has to other parts of the system, the more he or she enhances therapeutic control and diffuses the power of the presenting conflict.

In systems that present either child-centered or generalized family symptoms and where there are members of the extended family, such as one of the spouse's parents, living in the household, that individual should be included in the early consultations with the parents or in conjoint family sessions in order to make contact with them and to determine their actual role within the family system. A member of the extended family may be part of a central triangle involving child–mother–grandmother, the father/spouse being effectively removed from participation because of the effects of his wife's continuing ties to her family of origin, and perhaps because of his own passivity (see Figure 7-2). In similar situations in which parents of the spouse live nearby and play active and intrusive roles in the nuclear family's everyday life, consideration should be given to involving those persons in the therapy at an early stage. Therapists should never underestimate the power of grandparents to facilitate or sabotage family

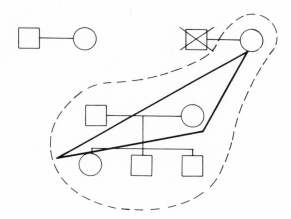

Figure 7-2. Intergenerational central triangle with maternal grandparent living in the nuclear household.

change, particularly in the case of enmeshing family systems with weak external boundaries.

Live-in extended family members can be invited to family therapy sessions routinely as regular members of the family system. Family of origin members living nearby can be invited on the same basis or as "consultants" to the therapist and family. Taking the consultative role often softens the threat perceived by both the spouses and their parents to having the parents present in the treatment sessions. Resistance to having a parent or sibling present in therapy sessions is to be expected on the part of clients. The clinician should be prepared to work through this decision in treatment with clients, as well as being ready to give consideration to the impact of timing in making such a move. The therapist needs to be clear as to whether the invited family-network members will be part of the therapy or will be consultants. The original designation of consultant may change either at the request of the parent or of the therapist, but such changes should be made with the clear understanding of all parties. Invited parents in all cases must be protected from direct verbal assaults by their children and from being made the "object" of therapy without their having agreed to become clients.

We believe that in working with marital dysfunction, every opportunity should be taken to involve relevant family of origin members. This may include any or all of the family or origin members. The power of intergenerational loyalties and patterns can hardly be overestimated as forces shaping dysfunctional elements in marital interaction. Such issues can be dealt with verbally by reflection or recall, by "coaching" the clients to return home to work on significant issues with their family of origin (Bowen, 1978) or by bringing family of origin members into the therapy sessions with the identified clients. If the parents reside at a distance from the place of therapy, some therapists may have the parents of spouses fly in on one occasion or routinely for 2- to 4-hour sessions. Others may schedule periodic conference calls in which distant parents are heard through telephone speakers in the therapist's office. Other clinicians simply have to be alert to possible opportunities in which the parents and/or other relatives will be in town for a visit. Therapists may find that many holiday periods and weekends can be used profitably by planning ahead with their clients and scheduling special appointments to accommodate the visits of relatives.

We have focused primarily on the impact of spouse's parents, but the therapist must be alert to the possible inclusion of other members of the extended family who by their presence can "bring alive" important family data. In one such case, a wife's parents were too elderly to make the distant trip to visit her. She had been dealing with long-standing guilt feelings over the physical and emotional distance that she had experienced with her parents since her marriage and had associated those feelings with an inability to be close to them while growing up. An older sister, who lived only 4 hours away, came to visit her, making possible the scheduling of a joint session with the two sisters. They had not been particularly close due to an 8-year difference in age, but the session was dramatic. The client learned that her sister had been in therapy for similar issues several years earlier. The sisters shared similar feelings of guilt and anger, but the older revealed some family secrets to which the client had not been permitted access. Before the client had been conceived, the mother had experienced a series of miscarriages and a painful stillbirth. The parents had pulled their relationship back together but in doing so had withdrawn emotionally from the two older children, drawing tight boundaries around their spousal subsystem (see Figure 7-3). It was reported by the sister that the client's conception had not been planned. This brought on an intense, tearful period for the client which was worked through with the sister over two additional therapy sessions. The client was able to understand something of her parents' grief and to get in touch with the distance and unavailability of feelings that she had felt while growing up in that system. She was finally able to stop waiting to get more emotionally from her parents and to become more emotionally available to her own spouse. Those changes also opened up a new degree and new quality of closeness and sharing between the sisters.

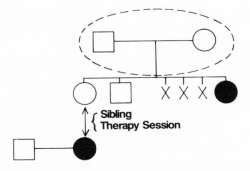

Figure 7-3. Sibling therapy session and family of origin boundaries.

Marital therapy with only the spouses present may require many months to reach a point of emotional impact that can be achieved the moment a parent enters the therapy room. It is not simply a question of efficiency to include extended family members but also a matter of dealing directly with the ongoing problematic issues as well as the historical components of life from the family of origin.

ENGAGING THE FAMILY SYSTEM

The earliest and primary task of the family therapist is to engage the family or subsystems of the family in such a way that therapy can begin. This endeavor includes establishing a working relationship with the family system as well as getting family members involved in treatment sessions.

The Engagement Process

The literature on psychotherapy traditionally emphasized the importance of establishing rapport and a therapeutic alliance with clients at the onset of therapy. Developing a therapeutic bargain with an individual client is a matter of dealing one-on-one and "hooking" one person into a working relationship aimed at helping with his or her individual problems. Securing an adequate amount of trust between therapist and client and dealing with the emotional and intellectual relationship between two persons and the motivations of an individual for change are the hallmarks of the engagement process in individual psychotherapy. Engagement in group psychotherapy is somewhat similar, except that the individual members of the group have to work out their reactions and attachments to a group that is composed of persons with no previous shared relationships and history, as well as with the therapist.

The engagement process in family therapy is different from individual and group psychotherapy for both the therapist and the clients. The issues of rapport and therapeutic alliance are relevant and generalizable to family therapy, but at a more complex level. Instead of encountering a focused relationship of intense emotion with an individual client, the family therapist must "read" and respond to a broader spectrum of emotional styles and systemic patterns. To use an athletic analogy, engaging an individual could be described in terms of facing an opponent in the boxing ring and reading, anticipating, and responding to the moves of that individual. Family therapy is better represented by the analogy to a quarterback "reading" a defense in football, attending to and responding to cues from various individuals and from the defensive team as a whole or to a defensive signal caller anticipating and planning to interpret and respond to the cues manifested by various members of the opponent's offensive team. As noted, the family therapist cannot make a therapeutic alliance simply with one member of the family system. Ideally, the family therapist must engage the entire family system by inviting to therapy as much of the available system as possible.

Engagement of the family system goes on at the same time that the family therapist is attempting to assess the system and determine its therapeutic needs. This involves assessing quickly the crucial aspects of the various subsystems' boundaries and relationships, the emotional availability of the system, and the system's patterns of power and its hierarchies of influence.

Kniskern and Gurman's (1980) research indicates that active and structuring behavior by the therapist in early sessions is important not only for engaging and holding families in treatment but also for affecting therapy outcome. They appropriately indicate that the therapist must achieve a therapeutic relationship with the family before confronting the tenuous family defenses. The therapist who moves in too quickly and too strongly often damages the family situation.

Some of the active and structuring behavior of the therapist may include not only defining the problem as residing within the family system and not merely within a particular client but also may indicate verbally and nonverbally how he or she will deal with the family and its members. Also, as Kniskern and Gurman's (1980) research discloses, the person of the therapist and the quality of the therapist's relationship skills often transcend his or her technical interventions and techniques in their effectiveness.

A significant part of what the therapist must do in the initiation of family therapy is to establish instrumental coalitions with relevant parts of the family. Such coalitions must be shifted as necessary (Sluzki, 1975). To make the necessary assessments and attachments to the family, the family therapist must learn to use resources and skills of finesse, humor, power, and establishment of control when confronted by family fears, resistance, and manipulations. For the beginning therapist, many of the important and essential skills will begin to evolve in supervisory relationships in which the developing clinician is challenged to recognize and operationalize personal resources and interactional skills.

Resistance

Individual psychotherapy literature, particularly that pertaining to psychoanalysis and psychodynamic psychotherapy, has given a large amount of attention to resistance in therapy. The expected resistance defenses of the individual have to be overcome and the cooperative ego of the individual has to be enlisted in the therapeutic effort in order for therapy to proceed effectively. Technically, resistance in psychoanalytic therapy refers to opposition to making conscious that which is unconscious. Much of the resistance in such treatment is to the interpretation of the therapist. The concept of resistance can be used in a general sense to refer to opposition to treatment itself and it frequently is used in just that fashion.

Other individual psychotherapists do not necessarily regard resistance as coming from intrapsychic struggles of the individual. Most emphasize to some degree the reality of the difficulties inherent in establishing an emotionally charged and intimate working relationship between therapist and client. From a practical, commonsense perspective, there is no good reason why an individual should not be uncomfortable, anxious and, hence, resistive to walking into a treatment setting and opening up his or her thoughts, feelings, and problems with a stranger. The more painful the secrets and struggles that the person is expected to expose and face, the more difficult the task could be expected to be for the client. The fear of facing the unknown as well as the painful known can always be expected to be anxiety producing for human beings, singly or in family groups.

Although all therapists encounter resistance, resistance in family therapy is different and in our judgment more complex than it could ever be in individual psyhcotherapy. Individual family members may not see the necessity or even the desirability of getting involved in therapy, especially if they perceive the problems troubling the family to be located in and belonging to one symtomatic family member. In addition, the family members as a unit may be resistive to undergoing therapy, exposing private family matters including strongly held family secrets, and making changes among themselves and in their family structure and process. Resistance in family therapy may be open and very direct, or it may be indirect, covert, and passive. One or more individuals may express in action the resistances of another family member or members. Children, for example, may be serving as "missionaries" for their covertly resistive but ostensibly cooperative parents, to use Stierlin's (1977) term for youngsters who carry out a mission or task on behalf of their parents.

Deciding whether to interpret the resistance as in the case of individual psychotherapy, whether to face it directly, or whether to ignore it and work around it represent some of the possibilities and extremes of the possible approaches to resistance in family therapy. Within the field of family therapy, psychoanalytic or object relations, three-generational, structural, behavioral, and strategic approaches to resistance have been identified and described (Anderson & Stewart, 1983). A pragmatic approach has been taken by Anderson and Stewart (1983, p. 24), who have defined "resistance" as all the behaviors in the therapeutic system that interactively prevent the therapeutic system from achieving the family's goal for therapy.

The major issue in resistance in family therapy, in other words, does not have to do with opposition to bringing issues into awareness but to making changes. The "struggle over treatment" in family therapy has been characterized by Napier (1976) as basically involving anxiety concerning change. Struggling with the therapist is seen as a "behavorial question" by which members of the family try to learn more about the kind of human being the therapist is and more about the nature of therapy. The large question is, "Dare we expose our family to this stranger?" (p. 4).

In an effort to operationalize clinically the important early-phase engagement, we have identified two sets of therapeutic variables. These variables—separateness and connectedness, observation and activity—are used in an attempt to define aspects of the family therapist's role in engagement that must be continually balanced with the system.

Separateness and Connectedness

Initial engagement calls for the therapist to be available to the family and to move in to "join" (Minuchin, 1974) the system at certain places ("connectedness"), and also to maintain a reciprocally balancing stance of thoughtfulness, objectivity, and control ("separateness"). We do not see being related to the family as being an all-or-nothing matter in which one "joins" and becomes a family member, as some interpret Minuchin's concept, or stays completely outside the family and works from there, as

Bell (1983) indicates that he does. Rather, it is a mixture of connectedness and separateness. Each therapist must learn how to establish and maintain his or her own comfortable and effective range of functioning between connecting with the family and remaining separate. There are significant variations in styles among therapists and in the mixture of the two factors. One certainly can err in the direction of being too close, too involved, and even enmeshed, and one can err along the line of being too remote, too distant, and too separate from the family.

For the therapist to err in the direction of excessive connectedness will result in the seduction or entrapment of the therapist within the system and the loss of objectivity and effectiveness. For example, the beginning therapist may unwittingly become pulled into an intensely enmeshing family and begin to try to function as if he or she were another member of the system, guided by the ongoing patterns of interaction and transaction in the family. When we view video tapes of such situations in supervision, we often will turn off the audio portion and ask the trainee, "Who is the therapist here?" Frequently, it is not possible to tell from the actions and bodily postures and expressions which party is the therapist because of the trainee's extreme connectedness with the family system. For the therapist to err in the opposite direction and to remain or become too distant and often analytical and to take an intellectual stance toward the family prevents him or her from establishing a working relationship with the family system. Here the therapist often steps back, remaining professionally and personally aloof, perhaps giving pieces of intellectually based advice while the family reenacts its typical conflicts or seems to flounder about without appropriate direction in the unfamiliar setting of the therapy room.

Observation and Activity

With the second set of variables, observation and activity, as well as with the first, each clinician must learn his or her own pattern of balance with a family system. Observation includes experiencing and "reading" the forms and patterns of interaction in the family system as well as learning from direct inquiry and data collection. It involves processing verbal and nonverbal data, historical and current interactional material. We hope that we have made it abundantly clear that simply asking questions and writing a social history is inadequate and ineffective. In order to understand how the system is functioning, the therapist must make contact with it, experience it, and begin to push on its boundaries. If one observes seasoned family therapists carefully, it becomes apparent that they "know" much more about the family system from personal interaction and engagement with it than from the questions asked. In many instances, the questions are asked by the therapists in such situations for the purpose of verifying a "hunch" that they have as a result of the personal engagement with the system or with a portion of it. The experiential part of engagement can hardly be overemphasized, but it is used in a meaningful and responsible way when therapists reflect on their experiences and combine them with theoretical understanding.

The action or activity element of engagement must be monitored closely by the therapist. Many beginning clinicians err because of their need to "do something," to cause something to happen, or to alleviate the symptoms either because of their expectations of themselves or because of their discomfort and anxiety. The result of such actions is likely to be "band-aid therapy" in which only superficial changes are accomplished. Activity cannot be separated from observation without a large price being paid. In fact, one's observational impressions should evolve in large measure from active engagement with the family. However, activity should be understood as being much more than either planned or random behavior. It has been our observation that well-intended strategic interventions by beginning therapists early in the therapy process tend to be mostly random activity. Beginning therapists often employ such techniques in order to decrease their own anxiety and try to control the therapy simply by doing something. Something "paradoxical" may be attempted, for example, because they read about strategic interventions or saw such techniques demonstrated at a workshop. Unfortunately, they fail to recognize the breadth of observational or experiential foundation that a seasoned family therapist draws from in order to finesse a family system in a metaphorical manner. For the beginning family therapist, such an approach becomes a "trick" that may confuse the system momentarily. However, without proper assessment data and understanding, the beginning therapist does not comprehend the meaning of the system's reciprocal response/reaction and thus is not equipped to predict what would ensue or to plan what should be done next.

Perturbation

Earlier in this chapter we referred to "perturbation," a term meaning in simple dictionary terms "disturbance," to refer to the interactive actions taken by the therapist toward a system. "Perturbation" is a term borrowed from astrophysics. It is a useful systemic term that gives a conceptual handle to the clinician to refer to actions and to his or her monitoring of the effects of the role and presence of the therapist in relation to the family system. The very fact of assembling the family system or parts of it in the office of the therapist is a primary perturbation. The system can never be quite the same again because the members have brought the system and its internal problems into the office of someone who is perceived as an influence external to the system. As the family enters therapy as the result of experiencing difficulty and pain, the boundaries, coalitions, and secrets seem more vulnerable to discovery than they are at other times. The system often appears to be balanced tenuously between open inquiry and self-protection. This tenuous, ambivalent stance is a major reason why we as family therapists can never underestimate the power that we have when we are invited to become engaged with a family system.

Perturbation involves many levels of activity and influence, ranging from side-taking (Zuk, 1976) to "coaching" (Bowen, 1978) to "tickling the defenses" (Ackerman, 1958). Family therapists must not only monitor constantly what is transpiring with the family in general but also must pay attention to their influence on the family and the expected/predictable interventions and perturbations may range from subtly complimenting a husband on the color of his tie or holding an infant child to the dramatic actions of a Carl Whitaker who playfully "wrestles" an adolescent boy to the floor when he tries to leave the therapy session (Napier & Whitaker, 1978).

Beginning family therapists often have great difficulty in understanding and operationalizing the clinical role of perturbation. Feeling somewhat overwhelmed with five family members in their office, such therapists may play a relatively passive role and become "sucked into" the system on the system's terms. Thus they become what we have called the "invisible therapist" who is surrounded by the dysfunctional patterns of the family system and is unable to exercise therapeutic control. (Parenthetically, we should note here that some seasoned family therapists may have the ability to use a ploy and to feign "weakness" in such a manner as to be able to enter certain systems that probably could not be entered in any other fashion. However, such ability is comparatively rare even among highly experienced therapists and certainly is not to be expected in a beginning family therapist.)

Gradually the beginning therapist must learn how to place himself or herself in relation to the system so that he or she becomes a target to which the system must react and accommodate. The behaviors of the therapist in taking a role so as to achieve perturbation may at times be dramatic. Much more often, however, the therapist's behaviors in achieving a good degree of perturbation with the system are likely to be subtle and perhaps understated, rather than flashy and openly confrontational. Again, the efforts at perturbation on the part of the therapist may be neither dramatic nor subtle so much as they are primarily confusing to the system. The key issue, of course, is not the manner in which the perturbation role is taken but the fact that it is effective in achieving the aim of disrupting what is transpiring in a dysfunctional system so that therapeutic work can be done with the family system and its members and appropriate and helpful change can be set into motion.

The First Meeting with the Family

Having made the decision during the initial telephone contacts with the family regarding who or what parts of the system to invite to the initial session and having secured their presence, the next concern for the beginning therapist is to determine what to do and what to look for in the first meeting with the family. We shall address these issues here in terms of the total family and conjoint family sessions. The reader should be aware, of course, that concerns will vary considerably according to whether a first interview is being held with a couple for marital problems, with a parental subsystem because of problems with an identified child, or a complete nuclear family system. Again, our discussions in the remainder of this chapter through the termination of treatment in family therapy pertains to meeting with the entire nuclear family system in conjoint family sessions.

Engagement

The axial components of engagement, which involve separateness–connectedness and observation–action, are useful in illustrating the desirable patterns of a family therapist's initial meeting and engagement with a family system. While we are reluctant to quantify these two axes, we do so here in order to illustrate that a relative balance is desirable in an initial interview. Figure 7-4 provides such an illustration.

The proportions illustrated in the figure indicate very simply the amount of time and energy the therapist may wish to devote to the various

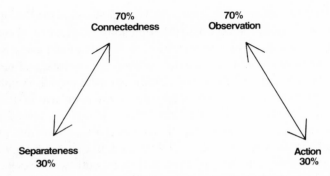

Figure 7-4. Engagement variables during the *initial* family interview.

role in the initial session. It often is assumed that in the beginning interviews the therapist should spend 90–100% of his or her effort in becoming
connected with the family system. In reality, when that occurs, the session
is left without structure and direction and the family may leave the
interview questioning the actual power and authority of the therapist.
While being available to the family and connecting with it is a matter of
high priority, we estimate that at least 30% of the therapist's effort should
be directed toward maintaining some separateness in order to be able to
define and maintain professional goals and boundaries.

    With regard to the observation–activity axis, we have estimated that a
similar balance of at least 30% activity and mild perturbation is necessary
in order to facilitate one's fulfilling of the priority role of observation–
learning and responding to the family's immediate problem or crisis.
Beginning therapists often become trapped too far in one direction or the
other, for example, spending 90–100% of the time asking questions, taking
notes, collecting history, or 90–100% of the time doing tasks, making
assignments, correcting perceptions in order to resolve the presenting
problems. Therapists should keep those suggested balances in mind regarding their own therapeutic style and functioning as we proceed to "walk
through" the first session and discuss issues of process and structure
defined earlier. Once again, keep in mind that a workable balance between
the two axes should be maintained and that the therapist should not get
trapped near either end of the line of either axis. There is nothing sacred
about the particular percentages that we have given, the major issue is
balance.

There is no easy way to address the use of oneself as a therapist to engage a family system. In large measure, for a beginning therapist in particular, this is a matter of supervision and the experience of the therapist under supervision. However, the manner in which the therapist interacts with the system will be facilitated by considering and responding to the issues covered in the following sections.

Structure

With regard to the structure of the initial session, the therapist will, of course, observe immediately who is present, how they feel about being there, and the meaning of the absence of persons who were expected to be present. Observation of the structure is facilitated by following the general rule of permitting family members to seat themselves according to their own choices. This is based on the assumption that the therapist does not reserve a certain seat for himself or herself and has individual movable seats in the office. The required room for the patterns and style of the family system to emerge is not present if family members are forced to sit in cramped love seats or sofas or in large overstuffed chairs that are difficult to move. Such furnishings in an office limit the flexibility to move the seating arrangements and restructure the system.

After some experiences, the therapist can begin to predict how some incoming families will seat themselves. For example, a family system that has a parentified child typically will sit with that child located within the spousal boundaries, if not actually between the father and the mother (see Figure 7-5). The system with a scapegoated child generally will sit with the

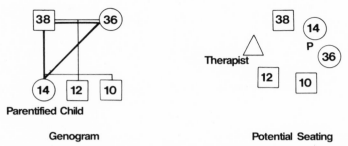

Genogram   Potential Seating

Figure 7-5. Genogram and potential seating arrangement of the therapist and family with a parentified child.

parents next to one another and the scapegoated youngster somewhat removed in distance (see Figure 7-6). In both of these examples, siblings typically sit near the parent with whom they have most comfortable alliance. The therapist should think about these illustrations and to attempt to relate the prediction to the theoretical materials given earlier.

Part of engaging the family involves letting them be comfortable with regard to their established needs for closeness and distance. Premature intrusion or strong perturbation of the system by the therapist produces expectable but unnecessary resistances.

Where does the therapist sit? The therapist may decide to sit in a vacant chair where it is located or move it to a more comfortable but strategic position. As a general rule, the therapist wishes to be seated next to the most powerful individual or subsystem of the family. Particularly in the beginning sessions, the therapist does not wish to be seated directly across from the family's major source of power because such an arrangement tends to create a geographical milieu of opposition and confrontation. In order to address that person, it is necessary to speak across everyone else rather than to speak as a friend would to someone in an adjacent seat. Being seated next to the source of power also gives a therapist access for physical gestures such as touching the person's arm to make a point or to get their attention or resting an arm on the back of their chair in order to communicate an alliance. Gentle and indirect actions generally give the therapist more power with most families than direct assertiveness.

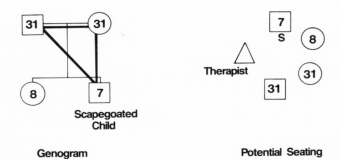

Genogram   Potential Seating

Figure 7-6. Genogram and potential seating arrangement of the therapist and family with a scapegoated child.

For a brief exercise, examine Figure 7-5 and imagine that the mother in the genogram is the most powerful force in the system and has the children aligned with her, while the father occupies a somewhat distant position. Where would the therapist sit? The natural place would be the vacancy between the father and the 12-year-old son. Since neither of those individuals seems to have much power in the system, a better choice would be to ask the 10-year-old son to change places with the therapist, who can do so either without explanation or by saying that he or she can see or hear the family better from there.

Now look at Figure 7-7. The therapist has moved from the edge of the system to the center. This move represents a planned perturbation that gives the therapist some indication of how flexible the boundaries of the system are and how readily the system accommodates to his or her presence. (In our own training settings, we simulate family situations, not through verbal role play, but by dealing with the structural location and role of members of the system. This can also be accomplished by letting the therapist move from one location to another and then reporting and comparing his or her perceptions of the location within the system regarding comfort, threat, and control issues with the perceptions of other members in the system.)

From such early interaction as that involved in the seating activity the therapist can begin to develop an image and "feel" regarding the respective subsystems and their members—how they connect, their relationships, and the quality of their boundaries. In the above examples, the reader will have tested the relative strength of the mother–10-year-old son alliance by the resistances manifested by the boy in relation to being moved and how he acted following the shift in seating. If the 14-year-old girl were assessed as

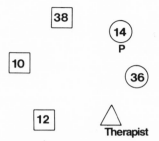

Figure 7-7. Repositioning the therapist within the system.

being parentified, the therapist certainly would not tamper with her place between the parents too early in the treatment. Not only would she resist being pulled out of her protective role but also such a move would threaten to expose the vulnerability in the spousal subsystem prematurely.

Process

Process issues in the initial session involve becoming aware immediately of the emotional climate of the system, that is, distance, fear, anger, superficial humor, or intellectualization. As part of the assessment of the family process, the therapist attempts to be sensitive to the presenting problem. Several important directions that we would offer to the beginning therapist at this time are:

• Ask them to help you understand what is happening and how long it has been occurring.

• Ask for clarifications and interpret what the issues represent for the system.

• Stay in control.

• Do not get swept away with the drama of the symptoms.

• Gradually move on to broaden issues around the presenting problem to include other influences on the family, for example, career, school, living environment, and others that are immediately available from current data.

• Observe the family's communication patterns, both the verbal and the nonverbal. Who speaks when and for whom? How do they address and look at one another? Is there physical touching? If so, what kind?

Making such observations and answering the questions we have posed will help the clinician to assess the relative power both for individual members and for the subsystems.

Additional directions for the clinician would include:

• Form some early impressions about the balance, distance, and intimacy among the members of the system and characterize the system along a continuum of enmeshing–disengaging.

• Decide how you wish to conclude the session.

• Define for the family your need to get to know them.

• Do not get trapped into premature assignments, prescriptions, and tasks.

• Remember that the system can survive with some continuing stress and anxiety. Hence, the quality of your early engagement is more important than what you do for them in the first session.

• Decide who you wish to see for the second session and work out, if possible, a regular and consistent appointment time for future sessions.

Following the initial appointment:

• Take a reflective inventory of your engagement with the system, its responses and accommodation to your presence.

• Can you anticipate resistances?

• Do you feel confident that the family members will keep the next appointment?

• Draw a genogram with the data that you have.

• Begin to hypothesize regarding roles, power, and intergenerational issues.

• Project where you may have been trapped by the system and try to determine the areas that you need to move toward in the next session.

The Second Meeting with the Family

If the clients cancel or simply do not keep their second appointment, or certain members of the family do not come or the family is quite late, it is likely that the initial session triggered opposition. The therapist may have been unsuccessful in engaging the family and may have moved too quickly into sensitive areas or inadvertently given the appearance of aligning prematurely or inappropriately with one component of the system.

With regard to appointments, the beginning therapist should learn to deal with cancellation calls directly and never accept them through a secretary, telephone answering service, or answering machine. Clients should be told in the first session that if they wish to change or cancel an appointment, they should talk directly with the therapist. This gives the therapist the opportunity to have direct access to clients and to problems that can be managed better prior to a missed or cancelled appointment rather than several days or a week or more later. Also, such an approach gives the family direct access to the therapist.

Engagement

The engagement variables for the second session should, in our judgment, balance approximately as illustrated in Figure 7-8. This figure represents a continuing high level of connectedness and considerably more activity

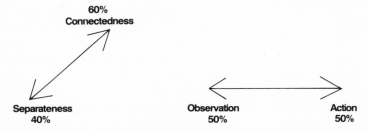

Figure 7-8. Engagement variables during the *second* family interview.

than in the first meeting with a family. If the therapist was reasonably successful in engaging the family in the first interview, it is possible to proceed with the exploration of initial clinical hypotheses as well as to generate and explore new hypotheses.

Structure

In the second session, the therapist needs to identify structurally the central triangles of the system. This can be done by identifying repetitive patterns of interaction, communication, and physical seating. Directions that we suggest to the beginning therapist include the following:

• Try to predict how certain members will handle certain issues or family themes.

• Observe how the individuals' movements lack self-determination and seem to flow either with a larger systemic process or in reaction to another member of the system, for example, a scapegoat.

• Push on the system and look for it to rebalance around the central triangle.

• As you continue in interaction with the system, broaden your inquiry to include the roles of grandparents and other family of origin material.

• Form a clear opinion about the relative internal and external boundaries of the family system.

Process

By the second session, the therapist should be attuned to the system's process. One should be aware of explicit parentified or scapegoated roles in the family. The following questions and directions for the therapist are important:

• Does the quality of the system's interactive process feel more centripetal or centrifugal?

• Have you identified the level of collusion and the patterns of complementarity in the spousal subsystem?

• What is the level of individuation of members in this nuclear system, as well as the level of individuation of the parents from their own respective families of origin?

• Do you sense implicit–explicit pulls from intergenerational loyalties?

• Broaden further the issues surrounding the presenting problem in order to include developmental patterns in the family and other crises that may have occurred earlier.

Perturbing the System

As therapy proceeds, the therapist should begin to interrupt the circularity that reinforces the dysfunctional patterns of the family system. For example, from our preceding illustration, one might interrupt the parentified child's efforts to speak for other family members or to protect the spousal subsystem. More indirectly, the therapist might dramatize the 14-year-old child's role with her siblings, for example, raising issues of playing with them and how it was to be a little girl. The therapist would be cautiously testing the rigidity by which the central triangle is connected. If the actions appear to be pushing the child into too vulnerable a position and role, one redirects efforts to the parents and tries to pull them away from the triangle by connecting them with the other two children.

Usually by the end of the second session, the therapist will be able to perturb the central triangle enough to cause some early accommodations and to secure data that will facilitate the formation of goals for the ensuing sessions. We wish to be clear that the issues we are suggesting here simply provide a guide for the use of the beginning therapist in gaining some "handles" on engaging the system. The hard work of moving in and out of a system and the attendant successes and failures accompanying such efforts should become evident in one's supervised clinical experience.

It should be noted that as therapists gain confidence in their skills and resources, much of what we have sketched here can be accomplished with some families in the initial session. However, it also should be remembered that some families are difficult to engage even for the seasoned family therapist. When a family proves too difficult to engage, it is important to consider restructuring the therapy and moving efforts either from the resistive subsystem to the entire nuclear family system or from the resistive nuclear system to a subsystem that may have some promise of being less resistive. Therapists need to be careful about proceeding to other concerns until they are comfortable with the level of engagement that has been achieved with the family. If there has been difficulty in achieving engagement, it is important with regard to future treatment to understand why the achievement of engagement was difficult.

Napier (1976) offers a succinct summary of the meaning of engagement: "The therapist works—perhaps for only one interview, but often for two or three—for that point when he senses a kind of subjective relief. The relief is a signal that the family has decided to be 'in therapy.' While other issues quickly become active, one phase of the struggle is at an end" (p. 10).

CHANGING THE SYSTEM

The engagement phase of family therapy involves intervention and accommodation in addition to observation. On occasion a system will make dramatic changes during this early phase of treatment, perhaps requiring only the protection of the therapy structure and the gentle prodding of the therapist in order to move in new directions. Unfortunately, most family systems with dysfunctions that are long-standing will not make such rapid movement and, in fact, will resist giving up much if any control at all to the therapist during the engagement phase. Change, when it occurs, does not necessarily take place in a simple fashion.

At the conclusion of the initial engagement phase, therapy moves into what is often referred to in psychotherapy literature as the "middle phase" of treatment. Sometimes such terminology as "beginning," "middle,' and "ending phase" of therapy is used as a reflection of the therapist's justifiable need not only to place his or her work along some logical continuum but also to have a gauge of clinical progress. Such terminology is not appropriate for family therapy if it connotes a predictable and linear movement from a starting point through a middle phase to an ending (termination). What goes on between the start of family therapy and the ending proceeds in anything but a linear fashion. There are many starts, stutters, sidewise moves, and backward slides between the chronological beginnings and endings of family therapy.

Family therapy is composed of circular, reciprocal, and recursive components. There may be repetitions of patterns occurring not only within the general and broad framework of therapy but also within the boundaries of each therapy session. There are initial entry and engagement problems when therapist and family system come into contact. With the renewal of contact at each session, there are reentry and reconnecting issues that must be addressed implicitly and perhaps explicitly. The process is not a simple one such as would be characterized by the ebb and flow of an ocean. Rather, it is more like the movements of the tides combined with the shifting thrusts of strong winds that create different valances in both predictable and predictably unpredictable ways. Within such a framework, there is some linearity both in terms of time and the activities and tasks that the therapist undertakes with the family and in terms of the reciprocal reactions of family to therapist and therapist to family.

It is possible to define a middle phase, somewhat artificially demarcated, between the beginning of the therapist–family contact and the ending or termination of that contact and working relationship. Similarly, there is in miniature a beginning, middle, and ending process operating in each therapeutic session, providing adequate contact and engagement is secured to permit some degree of interaction and working between the beginning and the closing of the session.

Gauges that would measure progress in family therapy are elusive. We see change in family therapy as more of a spiraling effect of concentric circles than as a linear progression. The spiral does not move up or down, but just around in larger and broadening circles that represent the system's accommodation to new experiences/data from therapy and its resultant rebalancing before further accommodation can occur. We have attempted to illustrate this concept graphically in Figure 7-9. Point A represents the system's dysfunctional state prior to the onset of treatment. Point B represents the first contact on the telephone with the therapist, and Point C depicts the first session. This conveys the sense that accommodation has already begun with the advent of the early contacts. Once the system has allowed entry of the therapist as a positive feedback loop, it can never to back to where it once was. It is much like the saying that once you have made love to someone, you cannot go back to a place of not having made love. If the family does not continue in therapy it can, of course, reject the brief intrusion of the therapist. To continue in therapy, however, implies

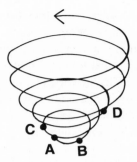

Figure 7-9. The spiraling effect of systemic change.

the continued process of accommodation. The system's first step into therapy is an opportunity to move it from a morphostatic phase (maintenance of constancy) to a morphogenic phase of potential change.

Any discussion of change in family therapy brings up the concept of homeostasis. We do not believe that homeostasis warrants the negative valuation that it has received in some recent family therapy literature. Homeostasis represents a balanced state that need not be regressive in nature. Our understanding and interpretation of homeostasis is similar to Ackerman's (1966) principle of "homeodynamics." This principle, according to Ackerman, "functions not merely to restore a pre-existing equilibrium; it also makes room for accommodation to new experience, for learning, change, and growth" (p. 69). We have defined the nonregressive balanced state on the spiral in Figure 7-9 as homeostatic renewal (Point D) in order to imply that the system had made enough adjustments to stabilize itself at a functional level. This level may resemble the functioning level prior to the onset of whatever change or crisis brought the family to therapy, but it reached that place by utilizing the feedback process of therapy.

The discussion in the family therapy literature differentiating first- and second-order change has been conceptually useful to the field. However, in terms of practical therapeutic change, the discussion seems to have unnecessarily dichotomized therapy into an either/or format. We are not convinced that many family systems actually would make dramatic "leaps of faith" from first- to second-order change (see Hoffman's [1981] discussion of the runaway system). In fact, we agree with the Duhls' (1981) observation that dramatic shifts that are often observed when systems are confronted/confused by a metaphorical intervention may be merely like a plastic that will return to its original shape when placed under pressure from certain amounts and kinds of heat and stress.

Change is hard work for the family and the therapist. While some movement on the spiral may come in spurts, overall it is based on developmental phenonema and a gradual process of accommodation.

Homeostatic Renewal

With many family systems that enter therapy, the goal of assisting them to reach a level of rebalanced functioning is reasonable and appropriate. This often can be accomplished through minor internal adjustments, the correction of relationship misperceptions, or by redefining intergenerational boundaries. In such instances, the family is able to restabilize itself subsequent to the events of crisis or stress that brought it into therapy. Some of the literature would describe this as first-order change. We have termed this "homeostatic renewal." It is premised on the function of therapy as a positive feedback loop involving a morphogenic condition in the system. This simply means that the system is able to incorporate new data in order to produce change. Many systems may never need to move along the spiral beyond the point of homeostatic renewal and some may not have the resources to move beyond this stage or point. Some systems achieve a rebalancing following a period of high stress and tension and then return to a morphostatic condition. At that time, their participation in therapy ceases, although they may return later if a future condition creates further imbalance.

Therapeutically evolving a condition of homeostatic renewal by no means implies short-term intervention, even through achieving such a condition does not involve major structural changes in the family system. From the viewpoint of the therapist, the balance of engagement components during the phase of therapy in which homeostatic renewal is being sought or accomplished begins to shift back to more of an equal division of separation and connectedness that reflects the therapist's movement in and out of the system. Similarly, the amount of activity surpasses that of observation (see Figure 7-10).

Here the therapist moves into the system in order to test the climate for change, to learn about and identify the system's sensitive areas, and to become aware of the rigidity of its coalitions. The therapist then moves

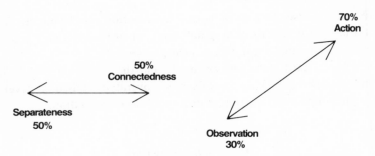

Figure 7-10. Engagement variables during the homeostatic renewal phase of therapy.

back out of the system in order to begin to push it in certain directions, sometimes taking the role of problem solver. In the case of a 6-year-old school phobic child, problem solving may involve helping the mother to become more emotionally attached to her spouse and committed in her marriage (through continuing marital therapy), moving her back closer to her family of origin by repairing intergenerational splits or conflicts, encouraging more family activity to rebalance her role and involvement with an older child, or helping her to form a broader social network or to move into a career in order to faciliate the emotional release of the 6-year-old child (see Figure 7-11). Often the mother in such a situation has felt lonely or depressed and has subtly held on to the child by keeping her or him home from school. Therapy becomes difficult work here because it includes not only dealing with the mother's needs but also moving her in one or all of the directions indicated above. In addition, the reciprocal aspects of the child's reinforcement for being at home and the issues behind the husband's lack of availability must be recognized and worked through. This means that even if the therapist achieves some movement with the mother, the child may not give up his or her special role and its accompanying attention, and the father may not move back into the marriage very easily.

Study the genograms in Figure 7-11, noticing in particular the patterns of rebalancing the system that are used. "A" characterizes the isolated role of the mother, which has created an imbalance resulting in excessive clinging to the 6-year-old boy, which in turn has produced school refusal symptoms. "B" illustrates how working therapeutically on several fronts (we have identified at least five, i.e., marriage, intergenera-

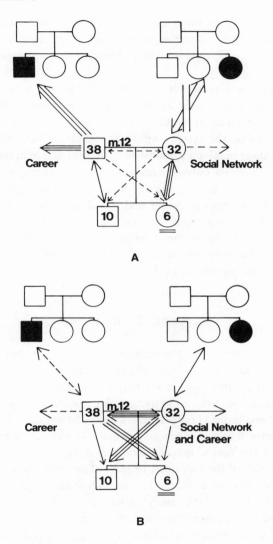

Figure 7-11. (A) Relative emotional ties and loyalties in a system with a school phobic child. (B) Multiple directions of potential therapeutic rebalancing of emotional ties and intergenerational loyalties.

tional, family group or other son, social network, and career), makes it possible to diffuse the immediacy and power of the crisis with the 6-year-old boy and to mobilize resources throughout a three-generational network.

In the illustration just given, if change occurred in only one of the five areas named, pressure on the mother–child relationship would be relieved and the system most likely would rebalance. If change occurred in three or more of the areas, the system would be venturing beyond homeostatic renewal to a stage in which some basic structural and process shifts would take place. If change occurred in only one area, for example, in the area of social networks and career, the therapist should be able to anticipate future adjustment crises as career and social network changes pulled the wife even farther away from the marriage until specific symptoms appeared in the husband or the marriage itself. Such disruption perhaps would prompt the system to be available for additional major restructuring or to face the possibility of dissolution.

Second-Order Reshaping

We do not at this time have the data or resources to predict which family systems may be available for second-order change. Some systems dealing only with recent transitional crises may never move beyond homeostatic renewal, while some chronically dysfunctional systems may move quickly to new structural levels. This discrepancy may be explained in part by the system's relative levels of stress or intensity as well as by timing factors such as when the family enters therapy and, in some instances, by the idiosyncratic role of the therapist. In spite of an inability to predict which family system may be available for second-order change, the therapist must always be aware of the family's potential for change as best he or she can determine it and learn ways to perturb the system in order to test its potential for major reshaping, where such change appears desirable.

When the therapist is working and intervening for the purpose of facilitating major change, the engagement variables of separateness–connectedness remain about the same. Activity level, however, should increase to approximately 90% (on the activity–observation axis) (see Figure 7-12). The therapist's activity increases sharply both in the form of perturbations and direct restructuring or process (metaphorical) interventions. The system that has reached a morphogenic place usually has

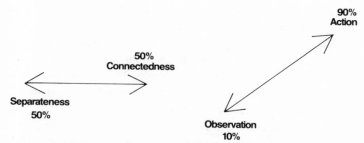

Figure 7-12. Engagement variables in the process of systemic change.

achieved good engagement with the therapist and has become somewhat open to new accommodations. This allows the therapist to assume greater risk by engaging in more activity. However, with the greater risk, the equal balance of separateness–connectedness is crucial in order to avoid either being pulled into the system by seduction or being unduly and prematurely threatening to the system.

In the case of a parentified 14-year-old child presenting symptoms of mild depression and social withdrawal (see Figure 7-13A), some early homeostatic renewal was obtained in the first 6 hours of family therapy.

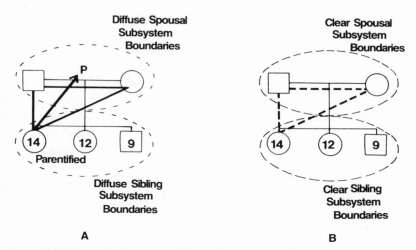

Figure 7-13. (A) Diffuse subsystem boundaries in a family with a parentified child. (B) Therapeutic restructuring to achieve clear subsystem boundaries.

This was achieved by a process of carefully realigning the adolescent with her younger siblings in selected areas such as shared family activities, shopping with a 12-year-old sister, and joining a social group at school.

The therapist had perturbed the system, perhaps prematurely, by challenging the central triangle and asking the 14-year-old, who was seated between her mother and father, to come over and sit next to him. The young female was very reluctant to move and did not do so until given tentative approval for the action by her father. The parents became uneasy and, as a result, cancelled the next scheduled appointment. This action, along with additional family data, clearly indicated the tenuousness and vulnerability of the marriage and demonstrated why the oldest daughter had been parentified for nearly 12 years. The desirable strategy would have been in the direction indicated previously, which did relieve the pressure on the daughter to some degree without pulling her totally out of the triangle and further threatening the parents.

As the family system became rebalanced, the parents became more comfortable in therapy and revealed for the first time their own disappointments with their marriage. This provided an appropriate time to shift the focus of the therapy to the spousal subsystem. The couple agreed to conjoint appointments which continued for approximately 14 sessions over a 3-month period. Early intimacy and bonding problems were worked through and family of origin loyalties for both adults were reduced markedly. As the marriage began to strengthen rather dramatically, the parents reported an increasing amount of pressure for attention and intrusive behavior on the part of the 14-year-old daughter. This was a predictable reaction to being asked to give up her attachment to the central triangle and her powerful role as parentified child.

At this juncture, the therapist made a good strategic decision by deciding not to shift back to the nuclear system in therapy but to see the sibling subsystem first. This action avoided the necessity and risk of dealing directly with the central triangle and gave the therapist some time to build alliances among the siblings. As expected, the 14-year-old was surprised at the resentment felt by her younger sister and brother because of the excessive attention she had been receiving from their parents. This awareness and sharing among the children opened up some new areas of closeness for the siblings. After two sibling sessions, the therapist moved back to the nuclear family system for 4 more hours of therapy. There the patterns and even the seating arrangement of the early sessions were reenacted on prompting from the therapist. This time, the 14-year-old was asked if she would like to get out from being stuck between her parents. She happily agreed and symbolically moved her chair next to her siblings. This shift was worked through effectively and new boundaries were clearly drawn around the spousal and sibling subsystems. The case was terminated after a follow-up session 1 month later (see Figure 7-13B).

Structural and Strategic Issues

In order to conclude the discussion of therapeutic change, it is important to identify issues of competing family therapy treatment orientations that tend to confuse the beginning family therapist.

There has been a considerable amount of attention in the family therapy literature regarding "integrating" different family therapy orientations and techniques. Much of the discussion has focused on the structural and strategic schools and the relative difficulty that a therapist experiences in trying to incorporate both approaches into a consistent therapeutic style and approach. As we noted earlier, it is easier to integrate two reasonably compatible approaches such as the structural and the strategic than it is to mesh together other very different orientations.

As we also indicated earlier, the family therapy field is moving away from reliance on single-theory approaches and is beginning to evolve a broader epistemological foundation for understanding systemically not only family process but also other aspects of human behavior. It is our opinion that to focus efforts simply on "integrating" divergent theoretical orientations into a single "family therapy approach" is a conceptually meaningless task.

While various orientations (e.g., psychodynamic, strategic, communication, experiential, structural, intergenerational, behavioral) may be grouped on the basis of sharing certain similarities, we need to compare only psychodynamic, strategic, and behavioral in order to recognize that each begins at a very different conceptual starting point. If integration means simply the reshaping of the differing orientations so that they "fit together" or taking the "best" of each of them and putting them together in an effort to make them one, then the effect is likely to be watered-down theory in which the differential strengths and contributions of each are diminished.

"Integration," in our understanding of the term, means putting together those generic theoretical and conceptual issues that emerge as a result of serious attempts to discover the common components in various approaches to working therapeutically with family systems. What are the common processes, problems, and mechanisms of change that evolve as we scrutinize different ways of looking at systems and family problems? The result of trying to identify generic mechanisms of change both through clinical observation and empirical research may be the discovery of richer, more refined theoretical concepts, practical understandings, and modes of intervention that effect and influence change than would result from searching for the contributions of a single theoretical orientation and approach to family therapy. Techniques for intervention should not be pulled from the context or setting in which they were evolved and developed and used without reference to such contexts.

We believe that by beginning from a generic systemic position and recognizing the structural and process components of all family systems, the need to integrate by borrowing from various orientations and formulating an applied technique becomes unnecessary and not very helpful. If therapists genuinely understand systems and can recognize how they function, then they are free to move into therapy with many different treatment strategies. Once again, the strategies should fit the needs of the family system and not merely the therapist's own biases or limited education and training. It is our experience that the beginning family therapist will benefit more from learning to think systemically than by borrowing from a "bag of tricks" or being trained in a single orientation. As students build a foundation of systemic epistemology and begin to move into clinical practice, they can then learn how the applied skills drawn from differing orientations can be used in ways that are consistent with assessment data and appropriate clinical strategies.

It is our experience also that—using "structural" in a generic sense— the beginning family therapist can benefit at this point from a structural orientation to family systems and systems intervention. A structural orientation is easily taught and is conducive to a clear descriptive understanding of the complexity of systems thinking. The perspective of structure that we have described should provide students with a conceptual understanding that can be used effectively when approaching a family, so that they are not overwhelmed by the system's complexity. For conceptual purposes, every beginning clinician should read Minuchin's *Families and Family Therapy* (1974) and test out their skills in recognizing and assessing the relationship between family subsystems. They do not have to follow Minuchin's particular therapeutic efforts in order to appreciate and use the clear concepts for understanding family structure that he provided.

Strategic techniques, on the other hand, are more difficult to teach than structural concepts. Their knowledgeable and effective use relies to a significant degree on the therapist already being in touch with and able to use very well his or her personal resources and skills. To permit a beginning family therapist to move into a system without the development of assessment skills or without assessing the system and to begin to perform strategic maneuvers with a supervisor watching is naïve and irresponsible.

As a beginning therapist becomes more comfortable working with and in a system, perturbing it, and anticipating its responses, then he or she can begin to use strategic interventions as part of an early perturbation. Unfortunately for the beginning therapist, most strategic acts of the kind demonstrated and written about by the masters of strategic work can be successful only if performed boldly. Thus, one needs to be prepared to intervene intrepidly and ready to deal with the consequences of success, as well as with the possibility of looking foolish and sacrificing control if the strong maneuver fails.

The experienced therapist can move back and forth between structural work and strategic work at different stages of treatment. Flexible and variable clinical work was used, for example, in the case of a referred delinquent adolescent. Fairly early in the therapeutic contact the focus of therapy was shifted to the marital subsystem because the marital partners indicated that they were considering divorce. It became apparent that both partners not only were structurally linked to their respective families of origin but also had been caught in an impasse of mutual ambivalence about the marriage for 5 years. As one partner would pull away from commitment to marriage and threaten divorce, the other reciprocally would defend the relationship. Both were careful not to go beyond an imaginary line that would end the marriage. Feeling that the system was stuck in an endless tangle and morass, the therapist made a bold move of announcing at the end of the fifth session that perhaps it was going to be too painful to work out any change and that it might be time to "bury" the relationship, concluding, "Sometimes it is less painful to grieve and walk away than to struggle to make changes." This dramatically separated the therapist from the marital subsystem and opened an unexpected commentary (meta-communication) on the future of the relationship, rather than permitting the struggle to continue at an interactional level. The issues were dramatized further by the use of a funeral metaphor and talk about "letting go." The partners were shocked and recoiled, pulling back emotionally and physically. The wife began to cry. For the first time, the husband moved over and put his arm around her. To further confuse the rigidity of their quasi distance, the therapist added a disqualifying remark, "Sometimes getting closer is also a way of letting go."

This strategic perturbation of a rigid interaction pattern effectively moved the marital partners off center and opened up an exploration of years of painful distance between them, lack of support, and sexual withdrawal and inactivity. The couple came back to the next session holding hands, reporting their first sexual intercourse experience in 18 months and describing some preliminary moves that they had made to gain some privacy within their relationship system. The remainder of the marital therapy conducted with them cleared out unresolved past issues and restructured both their subsystem within their nuclear family and their family of origin loyalties. The adolescent who was originally the identified patient soon settled down, his improvement in school coming almost immediately after the threat of divorce passed.

This case vignette illustrates our belief that strategic interventions may be valuable in moving a system or subsystem to new levels of potential for growth. Strategic interventions can result in lasting second-order change when they are thoughtfully and effectively intertwined with the many other structural and strategic approaches available to the informed therapist. They are never an end in and of themselves.

THE TERMINATION PROCESS

Progress in family therapy moves in a circular direction. The potential for reaching new goals depends on the growth that has occurred previously. If one understands systems to be open and changing, it is hard to define the conclusion of family therapy simply in terms of accomplished goals, for the goals themselves may change over the course of the therapy. Therefore, termination must be determined on the basis of assessment decisions that the family has reached a place on the spiral (see Figure 7-9) where it can remain open to continued growth without the need for further therapy or that it has reached a homeostatic balance sufficient to maintain its functioning and survival at this point in its development.

With this in mind, termination should always be open-ended and include an anticipation with the family of new issues, such as developmental transitions, losses in the family of origin, or role shifts in the system. Termination in family therapy may be planned or unplanned. The initiative to terminate may be taken by the therapist, by the family, or by the two parties entering into a mutual agreement that the therapy should be stopped.

Families sometimes decide to stop treatment on their own initiative, even though the therapist does not consider such a course of action desirable. This would be termed an "unplanned termination" from the perspective of the clinician. The family may not have attained the outcome goals of better and more effective functioning desired by the clinician, for example, and may not have attained even the intermediate goals the therapist considered essential for further growth. When this occurs, the clinician has the option of trying to dissuade the family from stopping or of accepting the family's decision in a way that will leave the door open for future contacts.

Ideally, one may wish to negotiate a planned termination with the family in the hope that termination can be accomplished in a way that will provide for continued positive change on the part of the family. Perhaps this is what Zuk (1975) meant when he wrote about the therapist working to take the decision to terminate out of the hands of the family. He also used a simile that compared intervening in the life of a family to dipping into the waters of a moving stream—sometimes the course of that stream can be influenced by the intervention.

Among the reasons that the therapist may wish to bring therapy to a close at a particular time would be the conclusion that planned goals had been achieved, that conversely therapy is not working or that continuing it is not worth the time and effort of family or therapist. This means that although desired goals have not been reached, the family has moved to a point that it functions better than it did previously and that it will not benefit significantly from additional therapy at this time, or that the family is manifesting behavioral indications that its motivation is not sufficient to sustain a continuing therapeutic endeavor. In the latter instance, the therapist needs to explore with the family their original reasons for seeking help, where things are at the present time, and the family's motives for wishing to continue or end the treatment. Depending on the outcome of this exploration, the therapist may either encourage the family to continue or may work to make the termination as much of a nonfailure and positive experience as possible. Follow-up may be discussed with the family as part of the termination process.

As we have indicated, change in family systems never reaches a linear end point. The life of the system continues to interact within itself and with its surrounding environment, always facing the challenge of accommodating to new influences and potential change. Thus, the termination process must be accomplished with care and openness.

In reality, many family cases go through several levels of termination. A case that presents itself for marital conflict may proceed often to involve serious conjoint sessions with the spouses until some clear reshaping of boundaries and new levels of bonding are begun. There the "exclusive" therapeutic relationship with the spouses may "terminate" as the therapist begins to work with the children and to integrate them into conjoint sessions for the entire system. When the parent–child issues have improved and the system has become reasonably well settled down, the frequency of therapy may slow down. The family may then be seen conjointly perhaps once every other week for three sessions or so in order to provide support and reinforcement for the changes. Then the conjoint family sessions may be "terminated" with sessions scheduled for the spouses on a monthly basis for perhaps 2 months. The therapist has supported the viability of the family's changes and yet continued in a nurturing and available role, as problems or crises might arise. It has been our experience that termination in such a manner facilitates the system's further growth and even allows the family to continue to test new behaviors and to take additional risks, knowing that the therapist is available if needed.

CHAPTER EIGHT

Marital Therapy

The marital pair in the nuclear family link together three generations: themselves, their children, and their own parents. Much of the change required to alter the lives of children—to free them of being either parentified or scapegoated—comes about through effecting changes in the marital subsystem and relationships between the parents. Similarly, much of the work of facilitating positive change in the lives of the marital partners often comes from helping them to resolve issues of differentiation from their own parents and families of origin. Therefore, clinical work with the marital subsystem often is central to systemic transgenerational family therapy.

Treatment of the marital subsystem may be entered into through one of several doors. That is, marital therapy may be asked for directly or may come about as a result of an original request for some kind of therapeutic assistance. One or both of the marital partners may seek assistance for marriage and family relationship difficulties, asking for "marriage counseling" or simply for "help." Marital therapy also may become the treatment of choice after one of the partners either has been in individual treatment or has asked for individual psychotherapy. Similarly, marital therapy may become the focus of treatment that began with a total family issue or with a child as the original identified client.

Marital therapy is intended to treat both the marital partners and the marriage, that is, the transactional system in which the partners are involved. Since the marital subsystem is central to the overall family system, we shall identify its special needs and treatment approaches in this chapter. Although the partners function differently in some ways here than in the total family system, where they fulfill parental roles (Paul, 1967), this subsystem continues to relate reciprocally with the other subsystems and the intergenerational network of the family.

269

Some therapists have given extensive lists of indications and contraindications for the use of marital therapy. For example, it has been suggested that the partners should be treated together when the presenting symptoms relate almost entirely to the marriage and when both mates are committed to the marriage (Grunebaum & Christ, 1976). Otherwise, the partners presumably would be given individual psychotherapy or, in some cases, group therapy. Other clinicians have decided that marital therapy has no genuine contraindications other than the inability of the therapist to prevent destructive behavior on the part of one member of the marital pair toward the other in the therapy sessions (Sager, 1966b). In this situation, working with the marital subsystem, in our judgment, not only may help to contain the symptomatology but also may provide a better glimpse of etiological factors than other modes of treatment. Marital therapy also may be a treatment of choice for a variety of diagnosed conditions with individuals such as reactive depression, anxiety reaction, certain personality disorders, and a number of other conditions.

Our own approach is very much in line with the broad stance taken by Willi (1984). That is, in deciding to use marital therapy, one takes into consideration the couple and their relationship, along with their marital situation and problems; the limitations and potential of the modality of treatment; and the therapist's own preferences, attitudes toward marital difficulties, and competence to perform marital therapy. In addition to these criteria, it is crucial, of course, to determine the reciprocal relationship between the marital subsystem and the structure and process of the broader family system vis-à-vis the presenting symptom or problem.

Our stated preference in treating marital complaints is to have both spouses participate in the therapy. It is risky to assume that changes that one partner can make in therapy can correct marital dysfunctions and successfully rebalance the dysfunctional relationship. In addition, it is likely that the absent spouse will sabotage therapeutic change that would be seen as threatening the "homeostasis" of the marital relationship. However, it often is the case that only one individual is available or motivated for therapy. This may not only reflect the marital dissonance but may also imply that separation and divorce are pending, in many instances.

As noted in Chapter 7, the therapist should always be aware that individual treatment may have negative effects on the person's marriage— it may dislodge the marital collusion and shift the complementarity between spouses—and should be cautious to advise them that change, including growth, experienced in therapy by an individual may exacerbate the present dysfunction and place the marriage in further jeopardy. If it is at all possible, the therapist should attempt to have the other spouse attend at least one session in order to establish a preliminary acquaintance and rudimentary relationship of trust with him or her.

When we do agree to treat a spouse individually, we do so from a systemic orientation that identifies and anticipates reciprocal changes throughout the system. The therapist needs to help the client to understand the impact of both the system on the spouse and the spouse's role and function in the system. This often involves exploring with him or her a paradigm of change, which goes as follows: If you change your behaviors, then others in the system react to accomodate the new behavior, and you must respond to them in order to effect a change in the system. Change is aborted and the system remains the same if you start to change and others react in ways that say "Don't change" and you drop your new behaviors and resume the old behavior patterns.

Marital therapy consists of several different forms of interviewing. The concurrent and collaborative forms of treatment used in the decades up to the 1960s are less commonly employed today and, indeed, are now rather rare. Essentially, they represent a carryover of individual orientations, a presystemic approach to assessing and treating marital difficulties in which intrapsychic problems were considered to be the source of difficulty and a transference relationship with a therapist was deemed to be the chief vehicle for treatment.

Conjoint marital therapy probably is the most widely used approach today, although it often is combined with family sessions or occasional individual sessions at both the initial assessment and ongoing treatment stages. This chapter is concerned primarily with illustrating conjoint marital therapy and its uses in flexible patterns of interviewing.

Couples group therapy in which three to five couples are seen together constitutes the approach of choice for some therapists. Framo (1980), for example, who relies heavily on such an approach, tells couples that they can reach any therapeutic goals that could be reached otherwise by participating in couples group therapy. He combines the group work with family of origin sessions in which an individual is seen with his or her parents and siblings but without the spouse being present.

Marital therapy methods have been characterized as fitting into two basic categories: growth-oriented techniques that focus on the conflict, including individual problems and difficulties; and problem-oriented, systems, and communications techniques (Willi, 1984). Our general approach may include elements of both approaches at times or follow basically one or the other of them, according to what we find in the assessment work that we do with the couple.

MARITAL ASSESSMENT

Assessment, as we have described the concept, involves not only an evaluation of problems and dysfunctions but also of strengths and adaptive and coping capabilities and successes. Assessment continues through the course of therapy. At the time of the initial assessment, there frequently is a tension between assessment and intervention. Although it is important to obtain a firm grasp of the problems being presented and to understand the nature and meaning of the symptomatology exhibited, it is equally vital in our judgment to recognize that establishing the beginning of a working relationship with the clients and making early interventions into the systems also may be crucial to the process of helping the couple.

The notion of abstinence from certain behaviors and the avoidance of taking important life steps while in therapy that has been promulgated by many psychoanalysts and psychoanalytically oriented psychotherapists simply is not realistic for couples and families. A couple or family seldom can wait several weeks after making initial contact while a diagnostician gathers data, makes a diagnostic determination, and prepares a treatment plan, as we have seen clients be asked to do in some clinical settings.

Assessment and intervention/treatment go hand in hand in our approach. Treatment proceeds by phases. Consequently, it is difficult, if not impossible, to establish the kinds of treatment plans with couples and families that many clinicians have been taught to establish for individual therapy. Sager and colleagues (1983) have demonstrated some of the better possibilities for the use of treatment plans with families in their work on remarried families.

Assessment typically differs according to the door through which the partners initially pass on their way to meeting with the clinician. When they first ask for help with the marriage, the assessment begins at a different point and with a different focus than when their initial contact is made in relation to a symptomatic child. When the initial contact is made for marital help, at least one of the partners has delineated certain marital difficulties that he or she considers troublesome. Those problems may or may not be the major sources of difficulties affecting the partners, but at least the focus of the therapeutic endeavor has been placed on the marriage. As a colleague has so aptly put it, "When one marital partner says that there is a marital problem, there is a marital problem." The major issue that we are pointing to here is that the problems may be self-defined by the clients as requiring marital therapy or the marital problems may be uncovered in the course of other therapeutic assessment–intervention and defined by the therapist and the couple as difficulties requiring marital therapy.

Rather than assuming facilely that marital problems are a reflection only of systems dysfunction or of individual pathology, we find it more accurate and appropriate to assume that marital problems typically are an amalgam from several processes. Individual pathology may be a result of marital/family dysfunction and may clear up following amelioration of difficulties in those systems. Conversely, assessment may disclose that one of the partners is sufficiently symptomatic to require the major focus of attention both at the beginning and throughout the course of therapy. In some extreme cases, such as those in which one partner has a manic–depressive disorder, marital therapy may be used in conjunction with other forms of therapy (Greene, Lee, & Lustig, 1975).

Where the presenting problems of one spouse are major and overriding, attention may need to be given to those difficulties before work is begun explicitly on the marital relationship. In one of the author's cases, for example, marital therapy was used as the treatment of choice when the presenting problem was a paranoid psychotic episode experienced by one spouse. The person was treated in the context of home and family rather than being hospitalized, the mate serving to reinforce reality and to provide support for several weeks until the acute phase of the episode had passed. Subsequently, the focus shifted primarily to the marital interaction with some attention being devoted to the lingering paranoid ideation and ideas of reference. In other presenting individual disorders such as borderline symptomatology, it may be desirable to focus on the nuclear family system rather than on the marriage because of the intensity and splitting present in the marital relationship (Everett, Halperin, Volgy, & Wissler, in press).

There are cases, of course, in which there is no presenting individual pathology. The marital problems result primarily from lack of maturity, ignorance, or situational factors culminating in a marked degree of friction and discord in response to the stress.

As systemically oriented therapists, we would not agree with the traditional approach that considers it necessary to establish a psychological diagnosis for each partner in the marriage (e.g., Smith & Grunebaum, 1976). One partner may be manifesting symptomatology that would warrant the use of a diagnostic label from a standard nomenclature. The spouse, who is a connecting and reciprocal part of the marital subsystem, sometimes does not require a label, but may receive it because of a priori considerations such as the bias of a therapist that calls for the location of pathology in individuals.

The focus of assessment involves the marital system. To call the marriage a "third personality" as some leading marital therapists have done is to go too far. There is present a marital system that is a core subsystem of the nuclear family. Difficulties in the marital subsystem as such may be viewed as stemming from an interactional imbalance or from a diminishing of emotional satisfactions for the partners. Therapy would consist in such an instance not of individual psychotherapy but of interventions aimed at restoration of balance in the system (Christ, 1976).

Because the marital subsystem is central to the three-generational family system, we find it important to gain a rudimentary understanding of the marital subsystem and the partners as well as of how transgenerational family functioning affects what is going on in the marriage and with the individuals. Just as it is not always easy or even possible to determine the degrees of commitment to the marriage or motivation for change early in contacts with clients, so also it is not easy or possible to ascertain at the very beginning how the transgenerational issues affect what is occurring currently in the lives of those with whom the therapist is trying to work.

Effective assessment must deal with both the marital/interactive subsystems and the individual/personal subsystems. As Framo (1980) has pointed out, the relationship between the intrapsychic world and the interpersonal world provides the greatest understanding and therapeutic leverage available to us. By this he means "how internalized family conflicts from past family relationships are being lived through the spouse and children in the present" (p. 58).

The therapist, in other words, needs to spend some time exploring the background of each of the partners. Such exploration is concerned not only with the past, with the childhood and developmental experiences of the man or woman who is being interviewed, but also with the current, active, and live relationships with family members, and, still farther, into the "carried-over" issues from the past that are affecting present relationships with his or her family of origin.

Out of such exploration may come an awareness that the therapist is concerned not primarily with how one related to his or her mother or father but with the *models of relationships* that existed in his or her family of origin. Those models of relationships pertained to interactions between his or her parents and, perhaps, between the grandparents or in other marriages that the person was exposed to over a prolonged period of time while growing up.

The concept of models of relationships can be used descriptively with clients. Once the concept has been presented to them in simple terms, they can grasp how they may have picked up ideas of what is desirable and normative through exposure to patterns of attitudes and behavior during the course of growing up. Similarly, many people can comprehend the possibility that they may have made some definite, conscious decisions to avoid certain things that they witnessed in their parents' marriage and patterns of relationships while growing up and still have retained an unconscious adherence to other parts of the patterns. For example, a therapist points out to a client that what they are experiencing and manifesting is similar to what happens sometimes in dealing with children, that is, "Do you ever find yourself growling at your kids or scolding them in the same tone of voice, with the same inflections perhaps, that you disliked in your father or mother?" It is not uncommon to have a client nod in agreement and then to begin talking about other manifestations of the same phenomenon.

Focusing on such developments as a normal part of living, as something that happens with most people rather than as something odd or strange or pathological, enables many people to open themselves up to the possibility that such behavior occurs with them. Equally important, it helps to prepare them for learning about themselves and how they function in marital and family relationships. It also helps to elucidate how transgenerational relationships affect their functioning. In other words, when the focus is placed on the models of relationships that existed in a client's family of origin, the spotlight is taken off the individual and the stigma of being viewed as pathological is removed. Instead, the clients are helped to look at the patterns and relationships with which they formerly lived and at those with which they currently live. In one set of concepts and language, clients are helped to become learners about things that have been of interest to them since childhood. The therapist helps them to keep the present marital and family relationships in mind, rather than getting bogged down or lost in exploring the past or the intrapsychic functioning of one partner as if their partner were living in a vacuum.

Assessment must be made, in other words, of both the individual and the marital subsystems, as well as of the relationship to the multigenerational family processes that can be discerned operating in them. The focus will vary according to the needs of the individuals and the needs of the system and the particular phase of assessment–treatment with which one is involved. Treatment, of course, must be done in context. It is not limited to the individual, but includes that part of his or her systems that it is deemed most necessary or desirable to include in order to bring about change most effectively.

The Initial Interview

Here we shall describe and illustrate one way of approaching therapy with couples who have specifically requested marital help. The actual procedures used will vary from one situation to another, depending on the assessment and needs of the situation and couple. For example, in some instances, the partners would not be seen separately when the original assessment work was done. On other occasions, one of the partners might be seen alone initially and then a request made to see the mate. There are pragmatic considerations involved in each of the variations that we would make from the procedural model that is described below.

What we are describing here in terms of form or procedure is what we would recommend for most marital cases for beginning clinicians or those with limited experience in working with marital couples. Increased experience allows for greater flexibility in interviewing and treatment procedures and modalities. We are aware that much of what we are writing pertains primarily to social classes from the working or blue-collar class upward in the social scale. It would not apply very effectively to lower-class clientele or others who may require a more focused and directive approach (e.g., see Rutledge & Gass, 1967).

With a typical case, when a telephone request is made for marital help, some brief information is obtained in order to determine the suitability of the request for marital treatment. "Can you tell me a bit about your situation?" is a common request made of prospective clients at that point. According to what is gained from this query, other questions may be asked, including whether either of the spouses is currently receiving psychotherapy, whether the mate is willing to come in for marital help, and others. Information also is provided the prospective clients regarding office location, fees, length of appointment (which may be limited to the usual 45- to 50-minute time slot or scheduled with opportunity for a longer initial meeting if the more flexible time period is available), and, in response to any pertinent questions raised by the potential client about procedures, information may be given concerning therapist qualifications and related matters.

When the clients come to the first interview, the opening gambit typically is a simple and stereotyped one. After getting them seated and perhaps after a pleasantry or two, the therapist may say something along the line of "I know what you sketched out for me on the telephone, but let's start off as if I know nothing at all about you. What brings you in?" (If only one of the partners has talked on the telephone, the therapist may repeat what was written down during that conversation and ask for confirmation from the partner who called regarding the accuracy of what is being said in the session, e.g., "Is that about it?")

The question "What brings you in?" is, at the same time, a broad and a specific query. It is a kind of focused "projective" question aimed at both partners. The concern is with both what they answer and how they respond. Do they agree? Are they there for the same reasons, at least insofar as they verbalize their reasons for being present? What are those reasons: to change their spouse, dump their spouse on a therapist and leave the marriage, find out what their difficulties are, get marital therapy, get divorce therapy, or what? A variety of responses typically come from the partners in terms of both content and mode of responding.

How the partners answer generally helps the therapist to begin forming a view of how they relate and interact. Individuals are different when witnessed in relation to and in interaction with their spouse than when they are seen alone. A seemingly sensible, reasonable, and mature man or woman who is otherwise a social or vocational success may become irrational, unreasonable, and immature in attitudes and behaviors when involved in interaction with his or her spouse. Although we shall not go into detail here to explain why this difference occurs, we shall point out that there are explanatory materials available to account for the question of why the nature of intimate relationships is different from other human relationships (Dicks, 1967; Fairbairn, 1952; Framo, 1970).

The intent in the first session is to get the best picture possible of what the partners have brought in and what the therapist and couple may be able to accomplish together. Was it a crisis or a chronic set of problems and difficulties that brought them to the appointment? Whose idea was it to come to therapy? What do they desire from the therapist? How do they interact? How committed to each other and to doing anything constructive about whatever problems that may be present are they? How willing and able are they to change? What is the prognosis for them and for the marriage? The last question may not be answered as quickly or easily as some of the others. The therapist may not be able to answer it even tentatively at the point of the initial assessment. Particularly in instances in which ambivalence is high and commitment unclear, a prognostic statement may be formulated only after therapy has been attempted for some weeks or even months. A more pressing question, perhaps, at the outset is that of what needs to be done with them and for them before they leave the first interview.

Some therapists have emphasized the significance of the first few minutes of contact with clients in beginning to establish hope in them and to launch a working alliance between clients and therapist (e.g., Greene, 1970). Harry Stack Sullivan (1954) stressed the importance of having a client leave each interview with a sense of having derived some benefit from the experience. Both points of view are correct, although initial errors in dealing with a couple should not automatically prove to be fatal. One can get off to a slow start on occasion and recoup before the end of the interview, particularly if the errors or omissions are clearly recognized by the therapist and the errors corrected or the behaviors altered.

Anxiety and discomfort should be expected among persons seeking professional help. There is no good reason why even highly sophisticated individuals and couples should not be apprehensive when appearing for an appointment to discuss their difficulties with a therapist who quite often is a stranger whom they have not seen prior to the appointment. As we have indicated, the scheduling of the interview itself serves as a quasi perturbation of the marital subsystem. Hence, they may not only be anxious about revealing their vulnerabilities to a therapist and to their spouse but they may also be frustrated, angry, discouraged, or frightened about the future or experiencing combinations of those feelings. Ambivalence involving a fluctuation between the wish to be dependent and to rely on a professional and a reluctance to do so is to be expected with many persons.

The emotional–motivational picture may be quite complex. Traditional psychodynamic psychotherapy has emphasized the resistances that the client manifests to treatment. Some marital and family therapists recently have stressed that dealing with resistance is not done effectively when an adversarial approach—one in which the client is viewed as being deliberately or pathologically obtuse—is used between therapist and clients (Wile, 1981). Others have pointed to concerns about change and changing as a source of anxiety for clients and thus a basis for resistive behavior on their part (e.g., Napier, 1976, as noted in Chapter 7).

Some therapists emphasize the transference aspects of the client–therapist relationship even when conjoint marital interviewing is being used (e.g., Willi, 1984). Our point of view is that most couples presenting themselves for marital therapy can be worked with effectively without extensive exploration of transference reactions of the clients to the therapist. As Sager (1976) has pointed out, such phenomena can be handled more directly by focusing on the marital relationship rather than on the couples' relationship with the therapist. Avoidance of the deliberate fostering of regression in the clients is a significant factor in the maintenance of a therapeutic relationship that remains appropriately focused on the marital subsystem, the family, and the clients. As noted in an earlier chapter, family therapy emphasizes dealing with the life situations of persons as directly as possible, rather than featuring the imposition of a therapist as a screen on which conflicts can be projected and then analyzed.

The therapist's major task is to help the clients "settle down" so that he or she can be useful to them and the therapeutic process can be helpful to them. This task certainly includes careful attention to the feelings and behaviors of clients, the therapist's own feelings and behaviors, and the ways in which the context of the treatment facilitate or hamper progress toward therapeutic goals. At all times during the assessment–treatment, it is important to try to monitor not only the content of the sessions but also the process factors. That is, it is necessary to keep in mind and in view how the clients are responding and how the therapeutic relationship and endeavor are proceeding so that the therapist can make alterations as needed in order to continue dealing effectively and sensitively with the clients.

Our basic stance is that therapists need to maintain a balance among assessment, alliance formation, and intervention that is appropriate for the particular couple and situation. With regard to the assessment versus intervention question in the first interview, the therapist should do enough assessment to know what he or she is dealing with in order to respond intelligently. On the other hand, there are cases in which a couple require immediate intervention. The problems are too acute and too pressing for them to accommodate themselves to an extended assessment process. That is, there may not be time for the clinician to hold several interviews and make leisurely decisions before attempting to intervene and to institute significant change processes.

Mr. and Mrs. Teacher (see Figure 8-1) provide an example of that

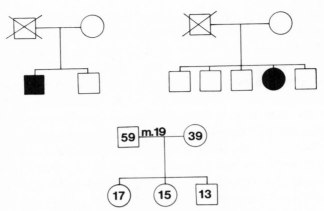

Figure 8-1. The Teacher family genogram.

kind of case. They were in a crisis of large proportions riding on top of a chronic history of discord. Immediate interventions were called for because of the crisis and the anxiety of the couple. Intervention involved repeated interruptions of their destructive interactions. In spite of the games of "uproar" and other seemingly nonsensical behaviors that they manifested, some patterns appeared to be discernible. Some quick impressions that held up later were that the husband tended to be dominant and the wife submissive, that they were tightly bound together not only by their religious values and cultural background but also by their interlocking and complementary sets of personal needs. Their major difficulties appeared to come on those increasingly frequent occasions when the wife refused to play the submissive role that she had taken on originally when she had married her husband, a professor several years her senior. The therapist thought that they were treatable, that he could work with them, but that intervention was necessary without delay or they would not be back for a second appointment.

Firmness in interrupting the destructive behaviors seemed to be the major ingredient in the therapist's joining of the marital subsystem, in establishing the beginnings of a relationship of trust and a working alliance with them. No formal history was taken, but important elements in the history of each of them were filled in as therapy moved along. The focus for the first several sessions and for most of the hour in all sessions was on the here and now, although relations with their respective families of origin were explored briefly at relevant points. Such brief exploration provided an adequate picture of the family systems and transgenerational processes. The therapist worked hard to help them *hear* what the other was saying, as well as to enable them to acknowledge their own hurts and the hurtfulness of their words and behaviors. This involved a considerable amount of time spent dealing with their disagreements, particularly in emphasizing implicitly and explicitly the possibilities for problem solving that could be found in their dealings with one another. When the initial endeavor to provide an atmosphere and climate in which dialogue and growth could occur appeared to have settled down to a marked degree, the therapy shifted to the exploration of individual issues and respective family of origin data for each of them in the presence of the other. This became something of a modeling process in which both had opportunities to witness treatment of their spouse that was very different from the ways that they typically dealt with him or her and the correspondingly different ways that their spouse acted in return. In this fashion, sufficient progress was made to encourage them to try new ways of relating and behaving. While some may wish to call this a pretreatment stage, it demonstrates how observational activity and engagement activity can be balanced in a case. Some lasting changes emerged from the early interventions and paved the way for additional progress with the couple.

The approach that we are recommending here for the beginning therapist is one in which the partners are first seen together and then separately for at least one session each, unless there are overriding issues such as those illustrated in the Teacher case. If there is time for an extended assessment period at the occasion for the first appointment, the clinician initially may see them conjointly, then split them for short individual sessions, and then bring them back together before closing the first session. Some clinicians would prefer to see each spouse individually for a full session the week following the initial conjoint session. Others would not see the spouses separately at all.

Whether one decides to split the first session as described depends on more than time allotment. It also depends on such factors as the clinician's impressions that the partners may be able to open up and reveal their concerns more freely and openly in the absence of the spouse, that there may be something or some things that they cannot discuss in the presence of their mate. Mrs. Farmer, for example, sat silently in the opening minutes of the first appointment. Her husband did almost all of the talking. Her body postures and nonverbal language bore mute testimony to the fact that she was constrained and inhibited by her mate, rather than simply being a passive individual. Sensing that she would be different when seen alone, as individuals frequently are, the therapist interrupted the session after 10–15 minutes and indicated that he wished to see them separately. With Mrs. Farmer alone the therapist started by asking, "Is there anything that we haven't talked about that you would . . ." Interrupting, she spewed out in staccato bursts her fears of her husband's violent and erratic behaviors, the details of one public outburst that had resulted in his arrest, the salient factors in his bisexuality, and the certainty of her intention to divorce him. When Mr. Farmer was seen alone, he also opened up with his concerns. When the conjoint meeting was resumed, it was possible to move rather directly and quickly into an examination of the salient issues. (See Figure 8-2, the genogam of the Farmer family.)

There are pros and cons regarding seeing individuals separately during the initial assessment phase or at any other time during the treatment, as opposed to using only conjoint interviews. For example, while it is true that a considerable amount of learning about each other can take place when history is gathered for each partner in the presence of the other, it also is true that important pieces of history may be omitted from conjoint sessions, particularly if such information relates to sexual histories, extramarital relationships, and other matters that may be embarrassing, guilt producing, or conflictual to the marital relationship. Not seeing the partners separately does entail some risk of missing such materials. On the other side, some clinicians conclude that the gains from individual sessions

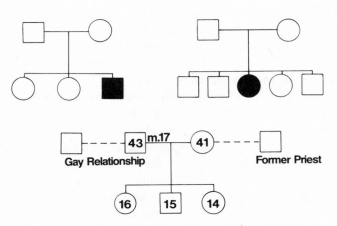

Figure 8-2. The Farmer family genogram.

are not worth the possibilities of creating loyalty and confidentiality conflicts on the part of the therapist and raising suspicion on the part of the absent spouse (Framo, 1980). A thoughtful statement on the individual interview as a treatment technique in conjoint therapy has been provided by Berman (1982). As we shall discuss later in the chapter, it is our experience that early individual sessions may effectively establish rapport for the therapist with each spouse and thereby bypass the spousal collusion and give each partner the opportunity to be himself or herself with the therapist.

Dimensions of the Marital Relationship

Where there is difficulty in determining what is going on with a couple, it may be helpful to move away from their self-directed and often global explanations of their problems. Instead, the clinician concentrates more explicitly on the various dimensions of the marriage. What follows is a description of one useful way of proceeding, using a framework adapted from Berman and Lief's (1975) work:

Boundaries of the Marital Subsystem. Exploring the boundaries involves helping the couple to focus on their relationship and on who is to be included within the boundaries of the relationship. This approach has three interrelated factors in it.

1. *Inclusion.* Who is to be included in the boundaries of the relationship and, hence, who is to be included in their work on the marriage? This approach is aimed at helping the couple to focus on dealing with the marriage and marital interaction. It becomes clear that for the immediate purposes of exploration and work in therapy, the focus is not on the job, the in-laws, the children, or other things, but on the marriage and how the partners deal with one another. (As it becomes appropriate to do so, the focus is widened in the therapeutic sessions.)

2. *Extrusion.* This involves exploration and discussion of what is being extruded from the marriage. Discussing who and what are to be included in the marriage relationship brings about in a normal progression of discussion the question of which problems are extruded from the relationship and assigned to the children. This, often, is how the therapist begins to learn about parentification of children, for example, as well as about other ways in which a couple are not dealing appropriately with marital issues.

3. *Intrusion.* Similarly, discussion of inclusion tends to bring about a consideration of intrusion. What persons, events, or other things are intruding into the marriage and in what ways?

Asking the couple to take a normative positon in the discussion is helpful in exposing their expectations rapidly. That is, asking them to take a stand and to spell out who/what is to be included in the marriage helps to bring into the open their expectations and the issues that currently are causing disagreement or agreement, conflict or cooperation. Also, asking such questions as what needs to be put out, fended off, or brought back into the relationship gives some rough indication as to issues that may be problematic in therapy. How the partners deal with such questions also provides some indication of the next dimension of the marriage that we wish to mention.

Power Dimension. What is the nature of the power relationship between the husband and wife? As we shall note subsequently, we are very concerned with how it has changed over time. Have there been recent alterations in the dominance–submission patterns, for example? Changes in the individual life cycles and in the family life cycle also frequently result in problems in the marriage; for example, increased striving for autonomy by the wife may bring about negative reactions on the part of the husband, as illustrated in the Teacher case and as we have witnessed so frequently in general with the recent rise in consciousness of women.

Intimacy–Closeness. Difficulties in tolerating and responding to needs and wishes of others for closeness or lack of closeness frequently form the major issues underlying a considerable amount of family and marital discord. For example, extrusion of the issue onto a child who will "cut up" so that a sufficient uproar is created to keep the husband and wife apart is seen just as definitely as the familiar dynamic of child misbehavior for the purpose of bringing parents together that is so often cited by family therapists. Not infrequently, the extrusive patterns turn out to be a basic factor that is underneath or behind a fairly wide range and number of disruptive marital and family behaviors. Until such dynamics are identified and appropriate interventions made, the partners are likely to keep shifting from one set of disruptive, sometimes argumentative actions to another. Hence, it is important to identify the intimacy–closeness issues early in the assessment process.

Marital Problems

There is no available taxonomy of marital problems. Most of the early research in that area (e.g., Goodrich, 1968) has not been pursued in a systematic fashion by researchers and the few efforts made to classify marital difficulties have been the work of clinicians.

Framo (1980) described four sources of marital discord—discrepancy between conscious and unconscious demands, relationship between the intrapsychic and the transactional, secret agendas of marital partners, and family problems repeating themselves from one generation to the next— and made a preliminary classification of marital problems. Martin (1976) delineated four pathological marriage patterns—the "love sick" wife and the "cold sick" husband ("hysterical" wife and "obsessional" husband), and "In-Search-of-a-Mother" marriage ("hysterical" husband and "obsessional" wife), the "Double-Parasite" marriage (hysterical–hysterical or dependent–dependent), and the paranoid marriage (including the *folie à deux*, paranoid, and conjugal paranoid patterns)—all of which involve significant amounts of interlocking pathology.

Two psychoanalytically oriented marital constructs have been set forth by Giovacchini (1958). The first is a "character object" relationship in which the partners have made a tenuous reciprocal relationship. They share an elemental intrapsychic bond and share defensive traits or symptoms. In those senses, there is a homogamous marriage. The second is a "symptom object" relationship in which the partners do not have a deep form of attachment and are characterologically heterogamous. Different forms of treatment have been recommended for the two types—individual therapy for the homogamous and conjoint or group psychotherapy for the heterogamous—by Moss and Lee (1976).

From the work of the family therapists at Palo Alto came some early attempts at classifying marital relationships. Haley (1963a) described a complementary marital relationship as one that occurs when the spouses exchange different kinds of behavior. For example, one partner gives and the other receives. He also described a symmetrical relationship as occurring when the partners exchange the same behaviors, as when both partners receive. He saw a marriage as being limited in its functioning capabilities to the extent that the marital partners were unable to form either a complementary or a symmetrical relationship.

Don Jackson (Lederer & Jackson, 1968) also attempted to construct a kind of classification based on exchanges of behavior between marital partners that resulted in a "more or less workable" relationship. By "workable" was meant a marriage that was maintained without great personal loss or damage to the mental or physical health of either spouse. To the two basic modes of relationship described by Haley, Jackson added a third, the parallel mode of relationship. Marriages were then described by Jackson as Stable–Satisfactory, Unstable–Satisfactory, Unstable–Unsatisfactory, and Stable–Unsatisfactory. Each of these had two subtypes, the Stable–Satisfactory having the Heavenly Twins and the Collaborative Geniuses, the Unstable–Satisfactory the Spare-Time Battlers and the Pawnbrokers, the Unstable–Unsatisfactory the Weary Wranglers and the Psychosomatic Avoiders, and the Stable–Unsatisfactory the Gruesome Twosome and the Paranoid Predators.

Rather than attempting to construct a taxonomy of marital problems, we choose to focus on some broader and more practically related issues such as why persons come to therapy and the difficulties that they are having in relating. That is not to say that we are not concerned with describing problems, but that we do not think it possible at this stage to arrange them into a systematic classificatory scheme. Over the years, we have evolved a number of concepts that are useful in making a broad assessment of how a marital relationship is functioning. These "rule-of-thumb" concepts can be used both by clinicians and by couples. They are listed and discussed in the following section.

Components of the Marital Relationship

Five concepts have proven to be useful in working with clients, partly because they refer to important areas of marital interaction and partly because they conceptualize issues in everyday language that is easily understood. The concepts are: "commitment," "caring," "communication," "conflict and compromise," and "volunteering." We shall define them briefly at this point and discuss them at various places in the remainder of this chapter. "Commitment" refers to the degree of attachment and intent to stay involved with the spouse and/or the marriage. "Caring" has to do with the kind and amount of cherishing, love, and similar feelings that one has toward the spouse. "Communication" refers to the kind, quality, and range of communication that exists between the marital partners. "Conflict and compromise" relates to how the partners are able to deal with differences, including their ability to compromise over genuine differences in order to make the relationship remain functional. "Volunteering" refers to behaviors taken by a spouse on behalf of the other partner freely and without expectation of immediate benefit, simply because one wishes to do something that is helpful or pleasing to the partner. We shall discuss two of the concepts in some detail here and return to the others later.

Commitment. A significant area of clinical assessment with the marital subsystem is the degree of emotional and intentional commitment in the relationship. What kind and level of commitment to the other do the partners have? What commitment to being married? Do they intend to remain in the marriage? Is there enough commitment to give the therapist something to work with, to provide a basis for marital therapy?

As a heuristic device, it is useful to think in terms of persons being either preambivalent, ambivalent, or postambivalent in their commitment to the marriage (see Figure 8-3). The first of these, the preambivalent stage, is found with individuals who have not seriously struggled with the question of getting out of the marriage. Their earlier positive feelings about the marriage have not been sufficiently disturbed to cause them to give serious consideration to ending the relationship. Hence, they assume that it will continue. With some persons, this stance takes the form of a genuine defense of denial. They are, in other words, positively committed and have not significantly questioned the relationship, even though there have been adjustment problems.

Ambivalent individuals look toward the mate and the marriage with a mixture of positive and negative feelings, often genuinely love–hate mixtures, and move back and forth between the two extremes.

The postambivalent stage is found among those who have seriously questioned whether they wish to remain in the marriage and have resolved their feelings one way or the other. Those who are postambivalent-positive have decided on staying. Those who are postambivalent-negative have decided to leave the marriage, a fact that they may or may not have communicated to their spouse. In some instances, if they have attempted to convey their decision, the mate may not have been willing or able to receive the message.

Some typical patterns with regard to commitment include the following:

• Mr. and Mrs. Donald: She was preambivalent and unaware of his ambivalence, which was shading toward postambivalence.

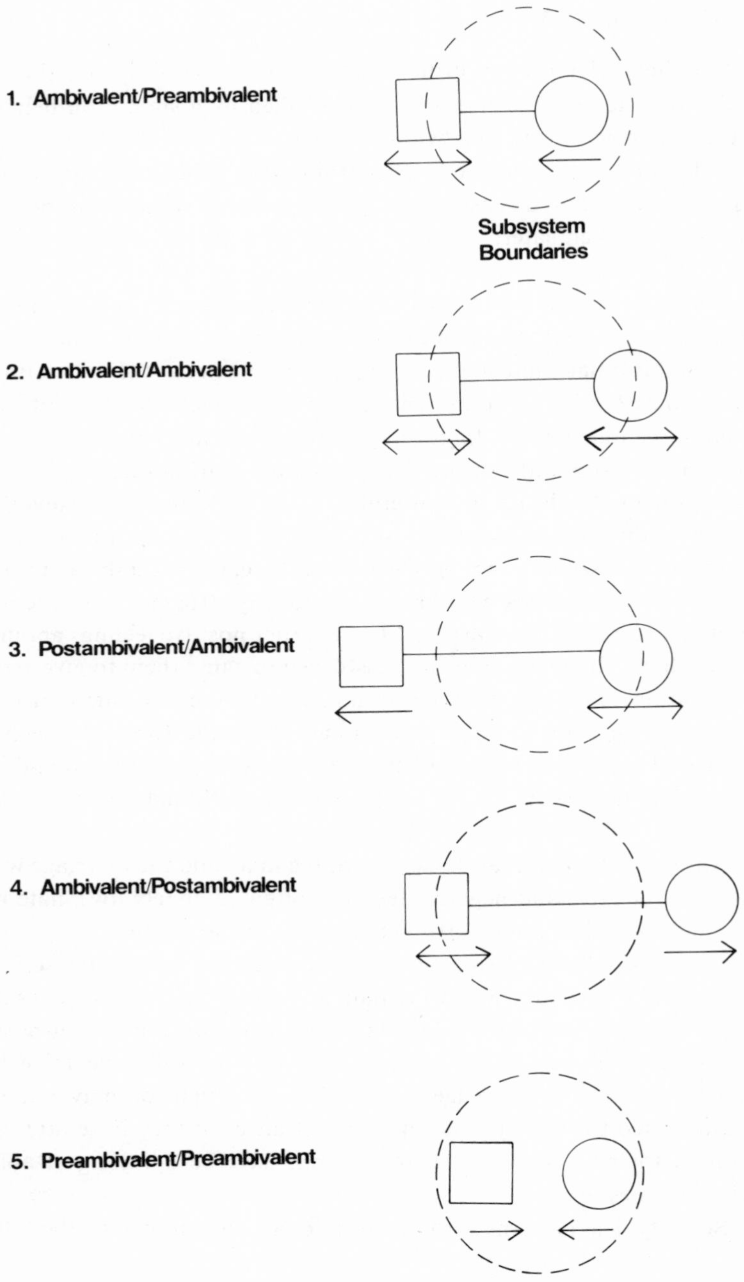

1. Ambivalent/Preambivalent

Subsystem
Boundaries

2. Ambivalent/Ambivalent

3. Postambivalent/Ambivalent

4. Ambivalent/Postambivalent

5. Preambivalent/Preambivalent

Figure 8-3. Patterns of spousal preambivalance, ambivalence, and postambivalence.

• Mr. and Mrs. Samson: Both were ambivalent. Six months of hard work in marital therapy could not get them off dead center. Four years later, she called to indicate that she had finally been able to make the break with her husband, had divorced him, worked out a new relationship with her daughter, and was doing well personally and in the career that she had entered during the time that the couple had been in treatment.

• Mr. and Mrs. Harold: He was essentially postambivalent but not totally to that stage. She was somewhere between preambivalent and ambivalent, being pulled toward ambivalence by his wishes to get out of the marriage.

• Mr. and Mrs. Charles: She was postambivalent-negative. He was ambivalent, tending toward denial of that fact and attempting to be preambivalent. Individual divorce counseling/therapy was recommended for each of them, along with attention to completing the emotional detachment on his part.

• Mr. and Mrs. Daniels: Both were preambivalent and planned to stay in the marriage, but wished to make some changes. This was the basis for conjoint work with an essentially normal couple who manifested no obvious symptomatology other than garden variety adjustment problems.

How does the clinician find out where the partners are with regard to their commitment to being married and with regard to their willingness to work on their marriage and to change personally? The following suggestions are offered:

1. Explore with them their feelings and assess their motivation as well as possible from both what they say and what they do. (This involves assessing the object relations capacities of each partner, for example, the emotional bases on which they need the other person and the level of maturity in their object choice, including their ability to give emotionally to their mate.)

2. Ask them individually where they stand, feed back to them the therapist's impressions of where they seem to be at the present in their commitment and where they seem to be heading, and subsequently secure their reactions to those impressions.

3. Ask them together in some instances about their commitments. There are contraindications to this approach, such as the obvious inability of one partner to accept an ambivalent or postambivalent statement by the other, and the therapist's need to gain some time for the strengthening of the dependent partner or for more complete and extensive examination of the stance of the partner who is considering leaving the relationship.

4. Share one's impressions with the partners together in some cases and get their reactions to the impressions and analysis of them and their situation. This can include as much straightforward explanation of an assessment on the matter of commitment as the marital partners seem able to absorb. (The issue of "secrets" will be discussed subsequently.)

5. Observe what the partners do after an initial assessment has been made and the therapist has given whatever observations–recommendations regarding their needs and therapy that it has been possible to share with them. (Other actions include practical steps that may be indicated and/or recommended to them regarding children, seeking legal advice and help, and other practical matters.)

6. Push on the emotional boundaries of their relationship by raising in a casual and yet sensitive manner issues that would challenge or threaten the protective collusion; for example, "Have you seriously considered or talked about separation?" Observe how they respond to such questions and pushing.

In some instances, a firm determination of how committed they are to being married or to marital and personal change cannot be made until after the partners have begun marital therapy and have attempted to deal with their problems and to begin changing.

Caring. This is another significant component of the assessment. How much does each partner care about the other? This question can be asked in either conjoint or individual sessions. It generally is a better question to ask than whether they love their spouse. "Care" or "caring" is used here rather than "love" because it is a less colored term and does not carry the idea that often accompanies ideology about love that "I don't love him or her any longer and, hence, there's no reason to stay married." In marriages of relatively short duration, this kind of thinking emerges at the time in which the initial idealization of the mate has given way before the onslaught of reality testing in close, everyday living. Many beginning family therapists become trapped with issues of whether the couple are "in love" or not. We tell our students that while we believe in love, it is neither a sufficient nor an acceptable clinical assessment criterion.

Are the partners capable of dealing with each other on a mutual, reciprocal basis? What degree of mutuality exists between them? Do they value their mate primarily as someone who can gratify their wishes and serve their needs? Or do they value the spouse for himself or herself alone, apart from their own needs or desires? Do they see the partner as a service station? In object relations terms, are they functioning primarily at some point in the need-gratification stage in which "the need is primary and the other person exists only to serve it?" (Blanck & Blanck, 1967, p. 70). At the need-gratification level, one partner can be exchanged for another fairly easily if the partner does not gratify or fulfill one's needs. Or are they at the level of object constancy or object love, so that they see the partner as a loved object? That is, they value the mate for himself or herself, whether or not he or she is fulfilling a particular need or desire at a given time?

Both levels of object relations represent part of the ego functioning and development of the individual persons. There are various degrees to be found in both the need-gratification and the object constancy/object love levels. One partner may be at a more mature level than the other, that is, may be more able to share and to consider the mate's wishes and needs as well as his or her own. The difference may be a significant factor in the prognosis for the individual and for the marriage.

The major point that we are making here is that caring, the ability to care, to temporarily lay aside one's own wishes, is related to the level of object relations development attained by the individuals in the marriage, and that the degree and kind of caring existing in the partners has major implications for the future of the therapy and the marriage. Such caring can be observed in nearly all of the partners' interactions and attitudes involving the other, from their division of roles to their sexual relationship.

Therapists cannot create caring, although they can help one or both of the partners to clear away some of the barriers to caring for their mate.

Complementarity. Both in commitment and in caring one of the major factors in the creation of discord is the amount of discrepancy between the positions or expectations of the partners. A number of clinicians (e.g., Kubie, 1956; Martin, 1976; Sager, 1976) have emphasized the problems arising from differences between the conscious and attainable expectations and the unconscious, unattainable expectations of marital partners. Sager (1976) in particular has affirmed the importance of expectations and what he has called the "contract" between marital partners in the creation of marital discord. He points out that expectations exist at three levels when men and women marry: conscious and verbalized expectations, conscious but not verbalized expectations, and expectations that are beyond the awareness of the individual. Sager also has noted that people who are marrying feel that they have the equivalent of a contract with the spouse that they will meet his or her expectations. Martin (1976) similarly has indicated that marital disharmony results when one of the mates fails to honor the "contract" either because of inability or lack of willingness to do so.

Marriages sometimes hold together with minimal discord and minimal caring because the expectations regarding what each of the partners is to do personally for the other are low. This can be found in marital relationships in which there is permissive extramarital involvement and marital stability at the same time. The amount of "fit" between the expectations of the partners in any one or more of several areas such as affection, power distribution, leadership, and others is a major factor in the degree of satisfaction and, often, of stability in the relationship. Discord following marriage frequently comes from differential growth rates. This has been called "the most common toxic process in marital disharmony" (Martin, 1976, p. 63).

It is exceedingly important for the therapist to learn something about the complementarity of the spouses, that is, how they are matched, how well they fit together, and where changes have taken place in their mating. If they are mismated, were they mismated at the beginning, or did it occur later? If they consider themselves mismated currently, how does each of them feel that this is the case? The therapist's own assessment of how well the partners were matched and where the difficulties lie may differ from that of the clients, but that becomes a matter for future consideration in therapy. Clients act on the basis of their perceptions, feelings, and reactions to events and processes in their relationship, not on the basis of the therapist's perceptions and analyses.

The major question, of course, for the therapist and the couple is not necessarily how the process of developmental mismating has come to pass—"schismogenesis," as Bateson (1972) termed such processes—but whether or not a workable balance can be reestablished between the marital partners. We regard the issue of whether a new balance or a new "complementarity" can be established as one of the major problems with which the therapist must begin grappling at the onset of marital therapy.

A considerable amount of useful information can be obtained from most couples in a short time by posing a few simple questions. If they have not already provided some descriptions of how things have developed and changed in talking about their problems, the therapist may focus there in the initial interview. "Tell me about yourselves. I wonder if things have always been this way. How did you meet? What attracted you to the other person? How did your dating go? How did you decide to get married? How did things go when you were first married?"

Each partner is asked to respond from his or her own point of view, if they do not do so automatically. The therapist looks for the areas of agreement, for the areas of difference in perception, motivation, and understanding, and for any assessment clues that may be available with regard to the nature of personal and marital strengths and dfficulties. Some individuals have never thought consciously about what attracted them to their future spouse and find this an intriguing question. It often makes for a smooth transition into talking about expectations.

Responses to the cluster of questions posed above vary widely, as one would expect. Some couples disclose that there were significant problems from the beginning of their relationship; for example, "We fought like cats and dogs from the start." Others demonstrate amazement that particular feelings were felt by the other spouse, "I didn't know that you felt like that. I always thought that you . . ." Still others indicate that the relationship started off well, only to encounter difficulties later. Sometimes this can be traced to certain events, most of which pertain to disappointments because the mate failed to live up to certain expectations and, in effect, broke the "contract" in Sager's (1976) terms.

From even a brief discussion with the partners, one may be able to gain two important pieces of information for the assessment. Some understanding of the degree of chronicity of the problems can be obtained. That is, the therapist can gain a picture of how long the partners perceive that they have had difficulty, whether the difficulties are chronic or of an acute, crisis nature. Also, a range of material may be forthcoming on how the partners have attempted to deal with their problems, the degree of difference or similarity in their feelings about the relationship, including something of their optimism or pessimism about its history and future, and, in general, some rudimentary grasp of the motivations of the partners. Both sets of information have obvious prognostic implications.

There are some obvious and predictable points where things have changed in the marriage. Included among them are what have been termed "serial impasses" such as the honeymoon, the first pregnancy, subsequent pregnancies and births, and the "10-year syndrome" (Warkentin & Whitaker, 1967). The latter, according to Warkentin and Whitaker, stems from an exhaustion of the "bilateral transference" on which the marriage was originally formed, resulting in the partners "falling out of love." Briefly put, if the original attachments based on needs carried over from growing up have been attenuated by the passage of time and not replaced by more appropriate and current attachments, crises are created after a period of several years.

Confidentiality and Secrets

At this point we wish to return to a set of issues that received some attention earlier in our discussion, the matter of confidentiality and secrets.

What is the therapist to do with material that one partner reveals that presumably is unknown to the other partner? Some therapists avoid such dilemmas by dealing with the partners only in conjoint sessions or by stating at the outset that there are no secrets, that whatever is communicated by either spouse belongs in the therapeutic arena to be shared with all three parties, husband, wife, and therapist.

Our approach is more involved: Each case has to be handled on its own merits and decisions have to be made in terms of the best judgment of the therapist. An ongoing extramarital affair is different, for example, from a 1-night stand of several years ago. Among the pertinent questions are the following: As best the therapist can determine, what is to be gained by exposure of the secret, by the sharing of it with the other partner? Does the second partner "really" already know or strongly suspect the secret? Does the second partner manifest a desire to know or not to know the secret? Does hearing the secret compromise the therapist and pull him or her into an ongoing conspiracy with the partner who has revealed the secret? Such questions are not easily answered or handled.

One approach that is successful for some therapists is to offer a conditional confidentiality to each spouse. This means saying to them that the therapist will not report issues or information gained in individual sessions (or via the telephone) to the second spouse in conjoint sessions. However, if an issue emerges that would directly inhibit or jeopardize the therapy process, the therapist and the reporting spouse must deal with it together and achieve some resolution. In the case of an extramarital affair, for example, the resolution may include agreement by the involved spouse to suspend the affair while the marital therapy proceeds. If the secret is a family of origin matter that is not known by the second spouse, resolution may involve an agreement to report the secret in a conjoint meeting so that it can be addressed by both partners with the therapist.

Keeping individual sessions confidential in this way can be precarious but often the early data that are obtained under such a framework can outweigh the therapist's concern by providing for a much more rapid elucidation of issues than would otherwise be possible. An example would be a postambivalent-negative wife who is involved in a serious extramarital relationship but cannot move to end the marriage because of concerns for her children. Processing such data in the second hour of therapy can save the therapist from struggling for perhaps weeks with the couple in treatment and not being certain why there are difficulties with commitment and movement.

The therapist is not in a position to keep confidential all information given by clients individually. Increasingly, therapists are being held accountable and liable if they do not warn a potential victim of threats made by their clients. Similarly, legal and ethical constraints require that therapists report to appropriate authorities knowledge of such illegal activities as homicide and, in some cases, child abuse or spouse abuse.

Seeing the partners separately has its pros and cons. In addition to the positive gains that it offers, individual interviewing may cause some suspicion on the part of individuals who are extremely frightened and anxious and who manifest tendencies to be untrusting in the situation.

ENGAGEMENT: THE EARLY PHASE OF THERAPY

At the conclusion of the initial assessment process, after the partners have been seen separately, they are seen together for stocktaking, recommendations, and decisions about where to go next with their difficulties. An experienced therapist may do both the initial assessment and what we call the recommendations/decision portion during the same session. We suggest that beginning therapists may need to spread out the process for a total of four interviews: an initial conjoint meeting, individual sessions with each of the partners, and another conjoint appointment, provided that the couple are not in a state of crisis that demands such immediate intervention that the more structured assessment approach is not feasible.

Recommendations

During the recommendations phase, several things are attempted. First, the therapist discusses with the clients his or her impressions of what they are presenting as their needs. This may take several forms and several degrees of disclosure. For example, the therapist may indicate, "Your relationship has been characterized by these periods of depressions for a long time." "You are correct, your communication does not seem to be very good. You don't convey to each other what you seem to mean." In many situations, the therapist reflects to the spouses impressions of how they seemed to fit together earlier during the period of mate selection and how the patterns of closeness and interaction have been altered over the course of their years together, for example, after the birth of children. Usually family of origin patterns will be reviewed, particularly for the purpose of pointing out differentiation issues such as the husband's enmeshment in his family of origin and patterns of disengagement in the wife's family of origin, or factors related to both spouses having been the oldest sibling in their family of origin. In such reflections, the therapist needs to balance the reflection of problem areas or deficits with the reflection of strengths and family resources, for example, they have been together for 18 years. Thus, the therapist attempts to lay a foundation that supports the feeling that although the partners are disappointed with the relationship, there are some resources and places to begin working on the problems. Such efforts should be based on the most accurate assessment and honest reflection that the therapist is able to make.

Second, the therapist shares with the couple his or her best professional judgment about what is needed in order to help them. This may or may not include a recommendation for marital therapy, or any therapy at all for that matter. In the latter instance, either the tasks have been accomplished through the assessment process or therapy is not usable by the partners at that time. Further marital assistance may not be feasible because the difficulties do not lie in the marital sphere or because there is no desire to change on the part of one or both of the mates. Sometimes, as illustrated in the Farmer case, there may be a need for therapy that is more concerned with individual problems and divorce adjustment than with marital adjustment.

The third task in a recommendations meeting is to try to clarify expectations and agreements regarding therapy if the partners are planning to seek further assistance from the therapist. The therapist and clients enter into an agreement that includes understanding about frequency of appointments, what is expected of the clients and therapist in the sessions, payment of fees if this differs from what was established initially, and the anticipated length of treatment. We call this understanding a treatment bargain or therapeutic agreement. It includes a proviso that reexamination of the bargain can be done at any time and that changes can be made as they are deemed necessary or desirable. The pattern of interviews, for example, can be altered in order to allow for some individual sessions if that is desired.

Clinicians vary in their use of an explicit therapeutic bargain with clients. Some therapists set time limits on the treatment at the outset, for example, agreeing that the therapy will be conducted for a particular period of time and that an assessment of the progress will be made at that juncture (Greene, 1970). Others spell out in detail the conditions for the conduct of the therapy that are agreed to by both clients and therapist. We vary in our practices on the use of an explicit or an implicit understanding with our clients, making the decision as to explicit agreements on an individual case basis. In many situations, the evolving life of the family system and its capacity for growth cannot be predicted adequately to allow the therapist to set goals for given changes to occur in 6 sessions or 15. However, if desired, progress in therapy can be examined every 6 weeks or so. On the far end of the spectrum from such planning are located therapists who simply ask clients at the end of each appointment whether they wish to return, for example, "What would you like to do about rescheduling?" Once again, practical considerations, including any need manifested by the clients for specific, detailed agreements, affect the actions of the therapist on the matter of treatment agreements.

Parenthetically, the establishment of a therapeutic bargain with clients is not the same thing as evolving a working alliance. A working alliance consists of a workable relationship of trust between the clients and the therapist. Establishing a clear therapeutic bargain may contribute to the evolving of a relationship of trust. Conversely, if the clients and the therapist are not able to establish a working alliance in which they trust each other and seek to work toward helping the clients, the therapeutic bargain is likely to be of limited value and duration.

Therapy Goals

Goals of treatment constitute a major concern in the recommendations phase. As with the therapeutic bargain or agreement on the conditions for treatment, the goals may be either explicit or implicit. The couple may have their own goals and the therapist may have his or her own goals, some of which may be explicit and some implicit on each side. Similarly, the goals may be limited or broad, concrete or general in scope. For example, Lewin (1948) noted more than 4 decades ago, that the general level of tension at which a person lives or a marriage functions strongly affects whether conflict occurs and emotional outbreak takes place. Among the outstanding causes for tension delineated by Lewin are the extent to which needs are being met, especially basic needs such as security or sex; the amount of space available for the free movement of the person; a lack of freedom to leave the situation; and the degree to which the goals of the partners contradict each other and their readiness to consider the spouse's point of view. Goals could include the general reduction of tension—which behaviorists would attempt to operationalize in terms of specific changes—as well as change in any one of the four causes Lewin named.

The goals of treatment often change as the therapeutic endeavor proceeds. What transpires at one point determines the possibilities for subsequent treatment efforts. If we are able to do this, then we reassess and see what is possible and desirable to attempt. Another way of viewing things is in terms of determining that a particular goal is desired and working on various ways of trying to reach that goal. If a couple should say, for example, "We wish to work it out, whatever it takes," then the therapy can be focused on the means of doing so that appear most promising.

A clinician may wish in accordance with professional ethics and social responsibility to provide the clients with as much "truth in packaging" as possible. That is, one endeavors to present and discuss recommendations and procedures in as honest and realistic a manner as possible. If it has not been done earlier, this is the stage at which the therapist may need to deal with the clients' feelings about working with him or her. A therapist may say something to the clients to the effect that "You also need to consider whether or not I am the kind of human being that you can work with, whether you feel that we can establish the kind of working relationship that will permit us to deal with the things that are bothering you." The couple may be urged to talk about any concerns they have along that line in the session or to do so outside of the therapist's office. The therapist also can offer to help them find another therapist, if there are any barriers to working with them, either from their personal, individual reactions or because of practical difficulties in scheduling appointments and so forth.

Following the recommendations session, the couple may be ready to go ahead with therapy or the partners may wish to think about what they wish to do. Sometimes, if there is doubt, question, or simply apprehension about going ahead, it is appropriate and wise to suggest that the couple go home, discuss the entire matter, and call back in a few days with their answer as to whether they wish to pursue therapy at this time. They also can be encouraged to raise any additional questions that arise as a result of their individual thinking and their consultation between themselves as a couple.

"Settling In" to Therapy

We recognize that treatment may not proceed with a distinct line between assessment and the early therapy stages. Our use of the concept of engagement refers to the entire process of assessment and beginning treatment. We have broken down the process here primarily for purposes of description. Treatment actually starts, as we hope we have made clear, with the first contact with the clients, usually in the form of a telephone call. From at least that point onward, and probably much earlier when the partners begin to consider getting help, what transpires is part of a process leading either toward entry into an ongoing therapy process or toward an abortive movement out of contact with the process. We call this the "settling in" phase of treatment.

Zuk (1969) suggests "that a major goal of treatment is achieved when the therapist obtains the commitment of the family to be treated on the therapist's terms. In my experience the settling of the terms of the commitment to be treated is a major determinant of outcome in family therapy, not simply a precondition of treatment as it characteristically has been considered in psychotherapy with an individual" (p. 544).

Some common issues begin to emerge in conjoint marital therapy during the "settling in" phase. These issues vary to some extent from case to case, of course, but a considerable amount of similarity is to be found in the early responses of couples in conjoint therapy. One of the first things couples generally do when they are seen in conjoint marital therapy is to seek to find the boundaries of permissible behavior. Some family therapists describe part of this process in terms of establishing the power relationship. We widen the concept a bit and refer to it as "finding the parameters." Getting into treatment often permits the mates to release anger and hostility that previously were held back or were partially restrained and seldom released fully. Having a third party present often may encourage the mates to engage in an emotional sparring match in the fashion of two boxers who feel each other out and then begin to throw punches, secure in the knowledge that a referee is present. Each may be seeking to get the referee to be a protector, advocate, or ally, but there generally is a more complex set of issues involved.

The therapist may be viewed at times as benign and at other times as unfeeling, depending on the particular salience that he or she has for the clients involved. Just as the therapist's presence may enable some couples to feel that they can release anger, so it also may make it possible for some other marital partners to probe out the possibilities of getting closer to each other emotionally and behaviorally. The anger that emerges may be a mixture of pent-up feelings and defense against anxiety and fear. Similarly, spouses often will move in the early sessions toward establishing a coalition with the therapist. Such efforts at establishing a coalition may range from simply behaving in a way that is intended to make the therapist "like" them to more overt manipulations aimed at getting the therapist to side with them against their mate.

Whatever the forms it takes, the clients' anxiety arises and protective mechanisms emerge against experiencing uncertainty and possible pain. What has often been described as resistance in therapy can be interpreted in many instances, as we have emphasized, as apprehension against proceeding into the unknown. The prospect of changing, even if the alteration is being accomplished in the company and presence of a benignly viewed therapist, can be unsettling for many persons.

Management of the exposure of feelings as the marital partners seek to find acceptable parameters in the sessions, as well as outside, is one of the early tasks of the therapist. As the partners begin their sparring or other behavioral and psychological probing, the therapist should attempt to adhere to a tight line between supporting appropriate exposure and encouraging adequate restraint. The couple should not be allowed to expose their feelings to the extent that they become unduly anxious and frightened over either the release of their own positive or negative feelings or the possible rejection or retaliation of their mate. At the same time, the therapist needs to facilitate their emergence from behind the bulwark of their defenses so that they can engage their spouse in sharing, communication, and problem solving as they are able to do so.

The task of supporting appropriate exposure and risking behavior while simultaneously encouraging restraint is an art, rather than a precise science. How well the therapist handles those matters depends to a significant degree on his or her ability to comprehend the nature of the marital subsystem and the personalities of the marital partners with whom he or she is working, rather than on observing others and picking up an abstract collection of strategies and techniques to use in whatever situations that come along. Much of the understanding and skill required for such work will be acquired in the beginning therapist's supervised clinical experience, although many years of experience are required in order to hone one's functioning to a high degree. Whatever the extent of one's experience, only an ongoing assessment of the meaning of the actions of the partners enables the therapist to deal intelligently with the behaviors. Early in treatment, for example, the couple may be moving too rapidly or too slowly. They may be "windmilling their punches" wildly on the one hand and "shadowboxing" and sparring cautiously on the other. Or, they may be shifting from one modality of interaction to another. Careful assessment is required in order to intervene appropriately.

During the initial appointments, the reluctant client may be able to hide behind his or her more overt defenses, throwing up a smokescreen of words and behaviors that befog the issues. Similarly, those sessions may give the client opportunity to vent his or her more pressing concerns. This may alleviate some anxiety and bring the client back to a state of relative quiesence. Once the anxiety has been lowered, there may be little or no desire to continue with therapy. That is, with some persons, once the immediate tension has been eased, there is not enough residual pain or overt conflict to push the client or clients toward continuing with therapy. Also, during the early stages, the interactions and exposure of feelings that occur may force them to face the possibility that feelings, reactions, and information that is too painful and threatening for them to deal with may emerge in subsequent sessions.

There is a significant change in many cases by the sixth to the tenth sessions. With the passage of time and with continued contact with the therapist and involvement in the therapeutic process, the clients begin to have some attachment to the therapist. A crisis occurs in that a decision point is reached. The most simple explanation is that the partners may begin to care about the therapeutic relationship and what it brings them, as well as to move back to the conflict that originally brought them in and the ensuing anxiety, so that they are faced with the question of really committing themselves to a process of change or stopping treatment.

Some couples do stop before the 10th to 15th session, particularly in those cases in which immediate problem-solving approaches and crisis intervention are the treatment of choice. Those who continue beyond the point that we have noted move into longer term treatment that may last for a year or 2, although the average time involved in marital cases is usually less than a year.

THE MIDDLE PHASE OF TREATMENT

We are using the concept of a middle phase of treatment in order to refer to that period in which the majority of change occurs in marital therapy.

Use of the concept does not imply a straight-line connection between beginning, middle, and ending of therapy in a way that would indicate that linear change is involved. We do not move from problem to "cure" and then terminate. Rather, the concept of a middle phase of treatment refers to a period of time in marital therapy.

Communication

During the early phase of treatment, therapists generally move beyond dealing so explicitly with the commitment and caring components of the marital relationship as they did during the assessment/engagement phase. Although those components remain part of the interest and concern of therapy, two more components—communication and conflict–compromise—move close to the center stage of the therapy. During the middle phase of treatment, and especially during the time that the therapist is seeking to repair, restore, or establish adequate communication between the partners, the therapist can use virtually everything that he or she has ever learned about the processes of human communication. The therapist can clarify, offer feedback, make observations, interpret not only the message that one partner is beaming to the other but also the intentions of the partners as one can understand them, serving as a mediator or go-between who persuades them as legitimately as possible of the benign intentions of the other, and generally removes the barriers and permits the flowing of the stream of as clear communication as possible.

There are some indications that one of the more helpful things that a therapist can do is to assist the couple to acquire the skills of marital communication. Thomas (1977), for example, has combined the study of marital communication and decision making by married couples and has devised step-by-step procedures for the assessment and modification of problems in both the communication and decision-making areas. There are self-help materials available, such as the 20 rules devised by Wahlroos (1974) and the popular work of Miller and associates (Miller, Wackman, Nunnally, & Saline, 1982).

As husband and wife begin to communicate more clearly, it may become more evident, as it frequently does, that communication is no panacea. They may begin to communicate clearly and find that as they understand the other, they disagree profoundly. Also, clearing up the communication may reveal the presence of deeper levels of wishes and needs that are discrepant and sometimes in very strong conflict. Occasionally our efforts to help the mates improve their communication get us into the area of conflict and compromise.

Conflict and Compromise

As the communication uncovers differences, the issue becomes that of how the partners deal with those revealed differences. Once the disagreements and differences come into the open, how do they deal with them? The differences may include not only their variant values and discordant ideologies but also their discrepant relationship wishes and needs. Sally may really wish to be largely dependent and Jim wishes her to be primarily independent of him and stand on her own two feet, whereas the "official" understanding previously had been that they would pursue their independent career paths. Similarly, George may wish to be primarily and essentially dependent on Mary, while she wishes him to be more independent.

The therapist's first task becomes that of observing and understanding how the clients respond to conflict and differences as those issues emerge. Does the appearance of conflict frighten the couple? Very often the answer is "Yes, it does." Hence, the immediate need may be to help them become more comfortable with the fact that differences do exist and will continue to do so in marital relationships, including their own. How therapists deal with such matters depends in large measure on their assessment of the situation and particularly on the understanding of how the clients have responded to differences and conflict throughout their life cycles, especially to conflict with persons intimately related to them.

There are several important facets to dealing with conflicts and obtaining the compromises necessary to secure accommodation or resolution. The first generally is the removal of major amounts of fear and anxiety in connection with the presence of differences per se. Another involves deciding how the particular problems that they are facing can be resolved, or if they can be resolved. Frequently, it is helpful to explore the problem or problems patiently and in some detail, setting forth the outlines of the differences as well as the areas held in common between husband and wife and examining how one or both of them may be able and willing to make changes in order to obtain a workable degree of agreement and possible harmony. Sometimes, the use of marital contracts or agreements, either explicit or implicit and either general or detailed in nature, may be used productively in dealing with differences. However, beginning therapists need to recognize that the premature use of contracting may not only lead to failure because of sabotage by one or both of the spouses but also it may inhibit crucial system and relationship growth.

During this stage, the treatment often seems to take three steps forward and one backward. The therapist may need to work doggedly and determinedly to help the spouses deal one by one with the issues that are raised. It often is not a question of reworking and resolving old problems and hurts, of doing repair, in other words, but also of helping the couple reach a level of functioning that opens the possibilities for growth, for making progress into new areas and new ways of relating. As we have indicated, it is necessary to deal with the new anxieties and new fears that may arise as questions of breaking new ground in the marital relationship are approached.

Mr. and Mrs. Roberts, for example, came to therapy following an attempted reconciliation after a separation. The initial treatment issue was to determine whether life could be breathed into a marriage that had been a polite friendship. Their shallow interaction and lack of depth communication had led to a situation in which they customarily acted largely on unverified assumptions about what the other thought, felt, and wanted. The passage of time and the beginning of the departure of their children from the home had worn down their rather shallow relationship and brought a "midlife crisis." To get them started talking and moving toward establishing a relationship of workable dependency and intimacy required a considerable amount of supportive work by the therapist. Breaking the patterns of years of parallel living in which they had essentially gone their own ways rather than engage in meaningful interaction raised anxiety that was initially hard for them to face and cope with, even though the therapist gave them a considerable amount of therapeutic support and help. Their needs called for patient "midwiving" efforts on the part of the therapist in order to make the relationship viable. (We shall return to the concept of "midwiving a relationship" in the following section.)

Once the therapist and clients get solidly into working on such issues as communication and conflict–compromise, therapy has moved into what we are calling the middle phase. This presumes that the therapist has been able to secure a sound working relationship or working alliance with the clients. During the middle phase, things typically go smoother in that the clients know what to expect, have moved past some of their earlier and more noxious anxiety, and are more likely to come to appointments ready to work productively than they were at the beginning. Nevertheless, in some cases the therapist may still be dealing with a situation that moves back and forth between eruptions of anger and misunderstanding on the part of the clients and the gaining of greater understanding and competence and the consolidation of therapeutic gains.

Sometimes, it may appear that the middle phase of treatment—in the sense of productive working—has been reached when, in fact, it has not been reached. For example, Mr. and Mrs. Jerry (see Figure 8-4) went through a series of hysterical scenes both in the therapist's office and in their life outside during the early period of attempted conjoint marital therapy. The therapist finally was able to get them past the point of exploding about things from the past that angered them and that were still unresolved when they came into therapy. By that time, the wife was ready to work on reestablishing their relationship and so, ostensibly, was the husband. Presumably, each of them was committed to working on the marriage and committed to the treatment process. However, every time that something was worked out, some concession made by the wife or some overture of affection or conciliation made by her, the husband would shift around so that they got no closer together than they had been previously. It soon emerged that he had not terminated his current extra-marital affair—as he had sworn he would do—and that he was doing a number of other things that were counterproductive to the development of a workable marriage. In brief, he was trying to hold on to a life pattern that was very disturbing to his wife and to maintain the marriage at the

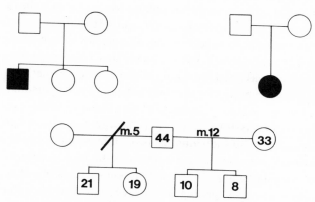

Figure 8-4. The Jerry family genogram.

same time. With a part of himself, he certainly did not wish to make the marriage work on her terms, which included fidelity, and wished her to know that he was having an affair. Evidently, he had been going along in a dual effort to see if he could work things out so that his wife would tolerate his extramarital liaisons and to buy himself time to get some of his considerable financial assets concealed in case there was a divorce. When his wife finally saw what he was really like—in contrast to the idealized version of him that she had maintained by means of defensive mechanisms of denial over the years—she moved ahead with divorce action, extricating herself from a relationship that had long been a mixed blessing for her. This case provides an example of a marital situation that required therapy efforts and the passage of time before it was possible to establish a firm prognosis.

By contrast, Mr. and Mrs. Samson's therapeutic work illustrates a middle phase in which both partners worked very hard. Once the initial rather tumultuous phase had been passed, the treatment settled into essentially one long impasse. The husband was able to make concessions and to do some giving, but the reward was continuing rigidity and some retaliation from his wife. She simply did not budge from her long-term stance of being highly defended against any change on his part. In other words, she behaved in ways that helped to prevent her husband from making lasting changes. This case was terminated because all three participants—therapist, husband, and wife—agreed that in spite of hard work, things were at an impasse and were not likely to change.

What happened in the first of these two cases was that the therapist and the couple got through the anxiety and parameter-establishing phases but were not able to work out the problems of dealing with the longer term and more serious issues after the couple had settled down in treatment. It was not possible to get a solid working alliance with the husband because his personality organization and character structure would not permit it. In the second case, as good a working alliance as the partners were capable of entering was achieved, but they did not possess the personal resources required to make necessary changes. The husband in the second case had slightly more capacity for change than the wife but not enough to either keep going and sustain individual changes that would force alteration in the relationship or to get himself out of the stagnant marriage.

While the middle phase of treatment tends to be somewhat smoother than the opening stages, getting into it does not guarantee that the outcome will be a successful resolution of the problems, either in terms of improvement in the marriage or cessation of the marriage. Treatment in the middle phase often is like a juggling act, several issues being worked on and kept in view at the same time. Some things are completed and put away. Others are put aside, or left up in the air temporarily like the juggler's objects, and returned to when it is possible and appropriate to go back to them.

The problem-oriented tasks implicit in the components of communication and conflict and compromise serve to support and direct the more subtle therapeutic process of systemic change in the relationship. The identification of these issues serves to pull out formerly unspoken concerns or disappointments as well as to stretch the relationship's typical method of managing those issues. Overall, this pushes spouses to begin to accommodate the functioning of their subsystem to new patterns and to begin to experience one another in a new and different manner. This is the focus of what we have termed "midwiving."

Midwiving the Relationship

The middle phase of marital therapy is when the therapist does most of the more subtle and sensitive "midwiving of the relationship" referred to earlier in this chapter. This is a descriptive term covering a variety of techniques, interventions, and other actions and stances taken by the therapist in order to help the marital partners do the following things:

1. discern what they are seeking in the marriage and in relation to their spouse;
2. resolve their ambivalances to a workable degree, if possible;
3. reduce their destructive interactions;
4. improve their communication;
5. face the fact that they have differences and effect viable compromises and accommodations, if possible;
6. establish a workable marital relationship in general or, if they decide and desire to move apart, to break the marriage and get out of the relationship in as nondestructive ways as are possible.

"Midwiving the relationship" is a more inclusive term than one referring only to techniques or strategies. It refers also to attitudes and a general atmosphere of warmth and support maintained by the therapist.

One does serve as a go-between as Zuk (1976) has indicated one can do in family therapy, remaining in control of the sessions. Being a manager and staying in control are essential to any form of therapy but particularly in any kind of systems therapy. Beyond this, however, we use the term "midwiving" to indicate that the therapist who performs the task of maintaining a growth-producing and reconciling and problem-solving atmosphere skillfully must deal intelligently and sensitively with the needs and personalities of both partners as well as with the marital subsystem.

Midwiving a relationship includes urging the spouses to take certain steps toward enhancing and deepening the relationship, once the therapist has determined that they have the ability to do so and, for the most part, wish to do so. This may include such direct interventions as asking one of the partners in a conjoint session how he or she feels about the other and then patiently and supportively leading that person to communicate his or her feelings to the spouse. For example, a client sometimes finally will tell the therapist that he or she loves the spouse. The therapist may respond, "Then, why don't you tell her (or him) right now how you feel?" Such simple-appearing techniques, used with appropriate timing, enable the spouse to reveal himself or herself and to risk being rejected or accepted by the partner in a relatively safe environment. Obviously, it is important for the therapist to be able to know when to be warm and accepting, when to be tender, and when to be bold.

Mr. and Mrs. George (see Figure 8-5), for example, were slowly reestablishing a relationship after an exceedingly bitter estrangement. In one session, the husband indicated that he had come in with the intention of asking his wife to accompany him to a significant sociopolitical event the following week, but was not extending the invitation because of something that she had done in the treatment hour. Having time to do so, the therapist decided to extend the hour and to see if it were possible to get them to go to the gathering together. It would be significant in many ways, including the fact that it would be a symbolic statement to many of their friends and acquaintances that they were reconciling after a publicly messy separation of several years duration. First, the therapist helped the husband to "get out of the corner" and to extend his invitation, while pointing out to Mrs. George what a gift and piece of volunteering behavior the invitation would be on the husband's part. Then it was necessary to deal with both of them on the meaning of their public appearance together. It was particularly important to point out to Mrs. George that she could survive some possible embarrassment and apprehensive feelings at the

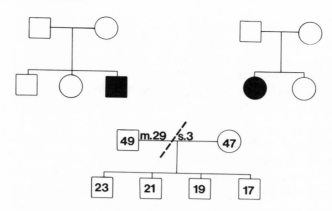

Figure 8-5. The George family genogram.

prospect of facing friends and acquaintances at the gathering. By this time in the session, the husband was helping the therapist to convince the wife that those present probably were not all that concerned with spending the evening gossiping about the Georges' reconciliation. Therapy then was focused on dealing with some of her fears about public gatherings, which she dated as coming out of her adolescence. The therapist finally said, "I'm going to do something that you know is very unusual for me to do, and that's to urge you to go. If it turns out badly, Mrs. George, you can come in next week and call me whatever you like, and I'll take it as my due." A little later, Mrs. George turned to her husband and said, "I'd be honored to go with you." The session ended there, and the couple embraced and left in a close, tender mood. They ended up going not to one but three sociopolitical gatherings in the next week. Subsequently, Mrs. George engaged in some very important giving and volunteering behavior, offering to help her husband with a major business problem, an action that made him feel deeply touched and appreciative.

Another aspect of midwiving a relationship consists of what we call a "Pollyanna" tactic. Others may refer to it as "accentuating the positive." Briefly, it means that the therapist helps the couple to recognize the positive thing or things that either or both of them have done, rather than to permit them to seize on and magnify their failures to do things perfectly. This is part of the therapist's efforts to try to help clients avoid self-defeating actions as much as possible and to recognize realistically what they have done that is successful. Instead of letting them consider their efforts a total failure because they did not succeed in doing whatever they attempted perfectly, the therapist points out to them as realistically as possible what they *have* succeeded in doing, and labels that endeavor successful effort. Sometimes, this refers primarily to the fact that they have *tried* to do something, that they have been willing and able to take an appropriate risk. Another designation for the "Pollyanna" tactic may be "reframing."

As indicated, midwiving also involves facilitating growth through the provision of a benign atmosphere and minimal interference. The therapist, on some occasions, primarily provides an understanding presence that enables and facilitates, instead of uncovering pathology or undoing old hurts. Mr. and Mrs. Daniel, for example, decided to keep coming in for assistance after they had worked through most of their worst marital tangles. They would come in every 3 to 4 or 5 weeks and talk as they seldom talked at home. They felt that the pattern of regularly scheduled appointments was necessary at that time in order to ensure that they continued to work at maintaining their improved communication and at obtaining greater flexibility and depth in their marriage. By the time that this way of dealing becomes the characteristic pattern of the sessions, the clients usually have reached the point that they can consider termination. The therapist has almost succeeded in reaching the treatment goal of putting himself or herself out of a job.

Problems of Intimacy

Problems of emotional closeness and intimacy often are at the root of many marital conflicts. As with many things, a given set of behaviors may stem from multiple backgrounds and may be interpreted and understood in several ways. The beginning therapist may not recognize the role of the issue of intimacy and closeness because it often is camouflaged by a broad array of external symptoms and complaints. For example, a man who gets into arguments with his children, "hassles" them, and so on when he comes in from work may be: (1) displacing anger and frustration that spill over from work; (2) consciously or unconsciously setting up a psychological "fence" around himself as he approaches home that shuts out not only the children but also his wife, as he behaviorally expresses his anxiety and/or hostility; (3) acting in accordance with a model of relationship behavior internalized when he was growing up (e.g., his father acted that way, or he thought that his father should have come home and "taken charge");

(4) acting in accordance with a cultural pattern in which "macho" male behavior is enhanced and held up as an ideal type of behavior; and (5) being influenced by combinations of the foregoing.

The immediate task for the therapist is that of focusing on the most likely path to follow in order to obtain clarification and moving the spotlight so that it shines on the question "What are the basic issues for the marriage and the family in the behavior?" Tactically, the therapist may start by offering understanding or seeking understanding of the man's job and by establishing a beachhead of sympathetic understanding with both the husband and the wife. Similarly, if that is the case, the therapist can move with the man to establish that he does not wish to maintain and continue a relationship with his children in which there is estrangement or angry, hostile behavior, and hurt feelings prevailing between himself and them. The therapist does this with the awareness that there may be other issues involved, for example, a need on the part of the wife to maintain a "fence" or a cloud of confusion between herself and her husband through the hostile and confused interaction with the children. That can be kept in mind by the therapist but not necessarily noted explicitly or mentioned to the clients. As conditions for change are created on the part of the husband, the therapist can begin to "pull the teeth" of the wife's resistance to change. This generally will involve doing some work with the family of origin issues that are carrying over into the marriage and contributing to the present problems. Frequently, exploring with the wife in a hypothetical way what it would call for or require from her if her husband changed his behavior opens the way for understanding and acknowledgement that getting close is not easy for the couple, and that they do have some *problems as a couple* in getting close.

Although the therapist could assess the state of the ego of each of the partners in an extended assessment approach, such tactics generally are not as productive as moving in to help them experience closeness to the degree that they are able to handle intimacy. The clinician does need to be able to assess the nature of the partners' anxiety about closeness, including the rigidity or permeability of their personal boundaries. For example, if there is strong anxiety about being swallowed up or about one's own solidity and separateness—as in schizophrenic or borderline personalities—the boundaries constructed by the person will be rigid, in an attempt to keep out what is perceived as external danger. The firmer a sense of self and the more internally secure about selfhood a person is, the more freely he or she may be to relate to others in an intimate manner and to allow the existence of permeability in relationship boundaries.

Kris's (1934) concept of regression in the service of the ego provides a mode of understanding that not only may help the clinician to work with the intimacy–relationship problems of couples but also may assist the marital partners themselves to become more comfortable with the idea of risking. The idea that one can temporarily regress, as in play or in sex, for example, and then move back to a position and stance of rational behavior and control is one that most individuals can comprehend. Regression is temporary and is allowed for purposes of pleasure and growth.

CLOSING PHASES OF TREATMENT

To illustrate the closing phases of treatment, we would like to refer to a case involving a combination of therapeutic modes. The husband was seen individually once a week at the beginning and subsequently every other week, and the partners were initially seen conjointly once a month and later were seen every other week. This case passed through most of the difficulties of the first phase of treatment mentioned earlier in the chapter and then settled into a middle phase that had its problems, its ups and downs. Several of the conjoint sessions were very tense hours, filled with recitations of arguments and confrontations in the everyday living of the couple, situations that were worked on and reworked in the treatment hours.

Mr. Chrysler was seen alone at first for several reasons. He had never communicated easily and had developed a number of patterns of relating and reacting that were causing him difficulty in interpersonal relationships. At the beginning, the therapist made the assessment that changes in Mr. Chrysler were the key to changes in the marriage. The man had the courage to accept the recommendations that were made about a combination of marital and individual therapy and committed himself rather wholeheartedly to treatment. It is unusual to have someone approach their problems with the problem-solving attitudes of Mr. Chrysler. Both the client and the therapist worked very hard in the individual sessions and all three participants put a considerable amount of effort into the conjoint sessions as well. In the husband's individual hours, examination was made of how he dealt with other persons and with various situations not only in his marriage but also in his work world. A large part of the time was spent in dealing with family of origin issues, most of which he would not have been able to deal with in the presence of his wife at that time.

By the final phase of the combined therapy, the clients had resolved several of the issues alluded to above and had acquired two things: success in coping with difficult situations and a reservoir of success experiences that gave them confidence in their ability to face and deal with problems together. They were basically individuals of solid integrity and, hence, as their hostilities and anxieties receded, it became increasingly easy for them to trust what they had accomplished together. Both were at the object love (object constancy) level of development, although he had regressed from it in some ways prior to entering treatment.

The decision to terminate with the Chryslers was reached in an ideal way: The therapist and the clients independently concluded that the time to stop was near. Mr Chrysler mentioned it first in his individual hour, noting that he did not feel that he had much more to work on. The therapist agreed that he was doing well and added that the marital interaction also seemed to be going well and that it seemed time to consider termination. As things worked out, the couple went on vacation and had a period of approximately 3 weeks away from therapy before they came in for the next conjoint appointment. At the termination time, the wife confided to the therapist in her husband's presence, "I've never seen as much change in a person as I've seen in Jim. He's a much happier person." The session involved some conjoint exploration of what had brought the couple in originally and where they were in their relationship at the present time.

Change had occurred that both partners could see and assess for themselves. The therapist and clients looked at the changes and the fact that the clients felt that the changes would be durable and lasting, as well as at some of the things that had contributed to the alterations. It was noted by the therapist that there had been a tapering-off process in that the clients had been entirely on their own for 3 weeks and had had opportunity to test their "new" relationship. The brief period of "swimming for themselves" had worked well. Given other considerations, it was enough of a trial period for the therapist and clients to conclude that they were ready to terminate without additional sessions.

Evaluating Preparedness for Termination

The several concepts that we discussed earlier—commitment, caring, communication, conflict–compromise, and volunteering—provide a kind of guide for both the therapist and the clients in assessing preparedness for ending therapy. These are used, of course, along with other criteria such as the amelioration or resolution of interactive problems and symptomatology. A brief depiction of the use of these concepts in two cases follows:

The Chrysler Case

With the Chryslers', *commitment* to the marriage and to therapy was strong and increased during the course of treatment, especially after things moved out of the first phase. Mrs. Chrysler in particular had been ready to leave the marriage at the beginning if things did not improve, but her preference had been to stay in the relationship. *Caring* for each other was strong and solid. It was necessary to work through the hurts and to get past the defensiveness of each partner, but the quality of feelings was benign underneath the exteriors that originally were alternately cold and stormy. One of the early things that was pointed out to the partners was that they were far from indifferent toward each other and that the relationship was troubled but still very much alive. Removing the barriers to the caring proceeded very well during therapy. (There was much more with regard to their mutual dependency and the object relations aspects of their relationship and dynamics, but this is enough for present purposes.) *Communication* was a major focus in the case. It was necessary to do a lot of interpretation and educational work with the husband in his individual sessions in order to help him function better in his work (a less threatening arena for him) and in his marriage. His increased ability to open up in his communication in his marriage—something that he tested out on the job and found worked well there—was the key to a lifting of Mrs. Chrysler's depression. It led to an opening of dialogue to discuss their differences in ways that led to accommodation and to more dialogue that, in turn, led to deeper understanding and appreciation of each other's feelings. With regard to *conflict and compromise*, most of the backlog of problems that they brought into therapy were worked out and a workable pattern for dealing with differences and conflicts in general was established. During the course of therapy, additional conflicts arose and were adequately resolved. They felt, as noted, confident enough about their ability to deal effectively with problems in the future. *Volunteering*, a major sign of a mature relationship, began to be a significant part of their relationship. In reality, they had resumed some of the volunteering behavior that had been present in their marriage before things had knotted up and become unsatisfactory. Volunteering, a kind of behavior that goes beyond the *quid pro quo* or "I'll do this if you'll do that" kind of interaction, means that the spouses act for at least a good part of the time in relatively nondefensive ways. The Chryslers did that; they were able to "stick out their neck" and risk being misunderstood, rejected, or unrewarded and to continue doing it until it once again became a part of their life pattern together.

The Samson Case

This case, referred to earlier in the chapter, was one that lasted approximately 6 months in therapy and remained at an impasse at the point of termination. Despite hard work by the therapist, nothing would move. Both partners saw lawyers during the course of therapy. Ostensibly, they did not go ahead with divorce because it would be financially quite difficult for them, disastrous and financially impossible according to Mrs. Samson. (She did call back 4 years later, indicating that she had finally taken the plunge, secured a divorce, and fared quite well emotionally, financially, and socially). Not only would the Samsons not move on to getting out of a marriage that was very unsatisfying but also they would not do anything to change it. How did they rank in terms of the concepts we are illustrating?

They were largely *committed* to being married rather than being committed to their mate. Even so, their commitment was primarily to staying as they were. Each wished to have the other change and neither felt that they had any changing to do themselves. However, they were locked into a collusive process in which they prevented the other from changing in significant ways or in maintaining a change. The processes of unconscious marital collusion to maintain the status quo were strongly operative. They were committed to the treatment process insofar as they were able to be, but this did not consist of the kind of commitment that was adequate to promote the necessary change.

Whatever *caring* may have been present in the past had largely disappeared many years earlier. The Samsons' ability to be hurtful in their interaction was diminished as a result of the therapy, but it was not replaced by genuine care and concern for the other partner. Unlike the Chrysler case, once the settling down task was accomplished in the first phase of treatment, there was no emergence of solid feelings of commitment and caring. Rather, the mates remained in self-protective stances and were unable to be concerned for the other. They were largely fixated at the need-satisfaction level of object relations. Efforts to work on significant family of origin issues were not successful. How permanent was the decrease in hurtful behaviors once therapy was terminated? There was some return, but the wife took the lead in stopping it by eventually moving to a position of indifference toward her husband and securing a divorce.

Communication was exceedingly difficult with the couple. They tended to engage in blaming, smokescreening, and getting bogged down in arguing about largely extraneous details, rather than focusing on the issues of the relationship and staying on target. By perseverance and active intervention, it was possible to secure clarity and agreement on some issues in therapy, but not enough to improve the interaction or the marriage significantly.

Conflict and compromise formed an area in which lasting positive results could not be achieved. The differences were too great, the needs and wishes too divergent and too strong, and the long years of hurtful actions too damaging to make it possible to resolve conflicts and obtain workable compromises and accommodation. They essentially played a series of "zero-sum" games in which a gain by one was seen as a personal loss by the other.

Volunteering behavior, for all practical purposes, was missing from the marriage. The Samsons' major defenses involved externalization and their difficulties were strongly characterological in nature, meaning that they did not experience internal pain or anxiety from their attitudes and behaviors. They did not regard what they themselves did as painful, but experienced the problems and pain as coming from their spouse.

The therapist's decision was to accept what appeared to be the inevitable, to point out to them that it seemed impossible to resolve the impasse, and that his best efforts did not seem to be helping them. The progress that had been made in stopping or modifying their destructive interaction was reviewed. Then a look was taken at where things were stuck and not changing. Admitting failure seemed to be the only honest course of action. The Samsons' marriage seemed to illustrate Don Jackson's concept of the Unstable–Unsatisfactory marriage, and seemed destined to stay that way at the time of termination.

Termination

Effective termination of marital therapy generally requires an adequate resolution of the problems that brought the marital partners into treatment as well as the attainment of a new balance in the relationship so that it produces adequate amounts of satisfaction for each of them. For much marital therapy it is necessary in our judgment to help the partners secure an adequate and appropriate connection between past and present in their lives and relationship. Similarly, it is vital that the interactive issues of being married to the other person be addressed. As Paul (1967) has put it, "Between the beginning and ending of therapy, each marital partner participates in the experience of becoming aware of the impact of the self on the other" (p. 187). Along with this awareness should come improved marital relations and enhanced abilities to function effectively in their concurrent stages of individual, marital, and family life cycles.

For extended marital treatment in which there has been long-term dependency on the therapist, effective termination probably does need to include explicit preparation of the couple for functioning without the therapist and the formal therapeutic process. Each partner has to be prepared to lose the therapist, as Paul (1967) has noted, and to engage in an appropriate mourning process. There are several possible patterns for ending the interviews when the treatment has been lengthy in nature. One is a "cold turkey" pattern in which sessions are stopped as of a given date which is acknowledged to be the final appointment time. There is agreement that the goals have been adequately met and that the couple can handle things on their own from that time forward. Another way to conclude is by "tapering off" the process by spreading out the time between appointments. They may be moved from once weekly to twice monthly to a once monthly or less frequent pattern of meeting. A third pattern or mode of ending is the "cold turkey with a scheduled checkup" pattern. In this one, therapy is stopped at a given time and a checkup is scheduled for some future date, typically 1 to 3 months later. During the interim, the couple are to see how well they can function on their own. At the checkup time, they come in for an assessment of how they are functioning and for a decision as to whether they wish to terminate completely at that point or to resume therapy. If treatment is resumed, it generally is opened up again for a short time in order to deal with an issue or issues not adequately resolved. Typically, the scheduled checkup appointment is cancelled by the couple because they do not feel that they need it. The last pattern we shall mention is the "will call if necessary" form of termination in which the partners depart with the understanding that they can call if things do not go as well as expected. This approach is not used very often and typically is instigated by couples that are not totally assured of their ability to function on their own, despite assurances from the therapist. Sometimes, it is used in conjunction with another pattern such as the "cold turkey" mode of termination.

In this chapter, we have described marital therapy as a process, doing so in a broad-brush fashion. We have referred to assessment and engagement phases and to a treatment process involving beginning, middle, and termination phases. Also, we have attempted to illustrate the process that we refer to as "midwiving a relationship" and to describe and illustrate some concepts that can be used by both the therapist and the clients.

By way of summary, the components of commitment, caring, communication, conflict–compromise, and volunteering may be used by the therapist in a threefold manner:

1. As part of the *assessment*: How much and what kind of commitment and caring are present? How does the communication function? How do the partners handle conflict and to what extent and in what ways are they able to compromise? To what extent and in what ways do they "volunteer" in their relationship?

2. As part of the *treatment*: How is commitment secured, caring manifested and fostered, communication enhanced, conflict handled and compromise achieved, and volunteering encouraged and implemented—or the reverse?

3. As part of the *termination* criteria: How is each of these components being or not being fulfilled in the relationship?

These concepts, once again, are to be used in conjunction with other assessment and treatment criteria and not as a replacement for them.

SPECIAL ISSUES IN MARITAL THERAPY

This section includes material that is primarily illustrative of some common and difficult kinds of cases and situations that present to the therapist.

Chronically Problem-Laden Marriages

Among the most difficult to understand and treat of the confusing and frustrating cases that come to the therapist is the chronically problem-laden marriage that lasts for many years in varying states of disharmony.

The partners seemingly cannot live together in peace and cannot sever their relationship. Such marriages have been described as "cat and dog" marriages (Dicks, 1967) and as conflict-habituated marriages (Cuber & Harroff, 1966). When the tensions in the relationship are elevated above tolerance levels for the partners, neurotic or psychotic reactions emerge that may be handled within the marital dyad (Stewart, Peters, Marsh, & Peters, 1975). Some of these cases tend to come to the attention of therapists and other professionals, but the mates do not necessarily make much progress in treatment.

The most helpful explanation that we have found of such relationships is contained in the work of Dicks (1967), who adapted Fairbairn's (1952, 1963) object relations theory to marital interaction. A useful summary of Dicks's concepts of splitting, projective identification, idealization, and collusion has been provided by Stewart and associates (1975). In Dicks's adaptation of the Fairbairnian object relations theory to marital interaction, he attempts to account for enduring but mutually provocative marriage relationships by viewing marriage as involving a latent transaction process between the spouses' hidden subidentities. In such relationships, the spouses invest each other with qualities derived from past psychological objects, particularly parents. Each spouse perceives the other as possessing some kind of shared internal object problem that fits with their own in a kind of complementarity. The mate is idealized in either negative or positive terms to fit the other's needs, as both partners hope unconsciously to obtain integration of their own personality by finding lost parts in their mate. Dicks describes mate selection as involving the recognition of a "fitness" in the other for mutual working through or repeating of unresolved conflicts or splits in each personality. At the same time, each mate senses a guarantee that the problem will not be worked through with that person. The resulting marital collusion, an unconscious agreement and patterns of interaction aimed at keepings things as they are, makes therapy exceedingly difficult and problematic with such cases. Those marriages continue because of the persons' real need for growth and integration, each partner representing part of the total personality that is found in the marriage, neither feeling that they can be a total personality on their own. A healthy marriage involves complementary growth in the direction of individual completeness and enhancement (Dicks, 1963, 1967). The reader is directed to Dicks's major work, *Marital Tensions* (1967) for a detailed explanation of his theory and for a large number of case illustrations. Willi (1982) has added some recent work on marital collusion.

Many of the chronically problem-laden marriages described by Dicks do not, as we have indicated, lend themselves to therapeutic progress to any significant degree. There are some indications from clinical observation that family of origin sessions may be much more efficacious than working on the cases from a transference perspective.

The Values: A Chronically Problem-Laden Marriage

In this section we shall summarize a conjoint interview and ensuing treatment in which marital collusion played a significant role and transgenerational issues were evident. The collusive process was not as virulent as some of the cases described by Dicks, but it nevertheless was effective in maintaining a long-term marriage with chronic problems.

Mr. and Mrs. Value (see Figure 8-6) had come into therapy after nearly a year with another therapist who had become ill and retired from practice. Mrs. Value agreed to 3 months of therapy as the maximum in which she would participate. The session described here was the sixth with the couple. Mr. Value started the appointment by relating an incident that had occurred earlier that day. He discussed it as an illustration of their ongoing interaction. Examination of the interaction and the use of some reality testing in the session elucidated several salient patterns in the marriage and their association to parental models of relationships from both families of origin.

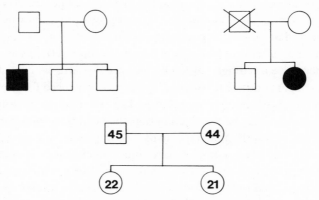

Figure 8-6. The Value family genogram.

The incident involved something at Mr. Value's work. His superior at the nonprofit foundation where he worked had charged another nonprofit organization for the use of a meeting room for a holiday event. Both Mr. Value and Mrs. Value were outraged at the superior's actions, feeling that charging another nonprofit group was against the policies of the board of directors of the foundation and that the superior had acted as if he were representing the policy of the board in making the charge. Understanding his wife to say that he ought to go directly to the board, Mr. Value felt put down, that he was not a success, and that he was considered a failure once again by his wife. Ordinarily the next step for him after feeling that way and thinking that it was unfair of her would be to get angry and to build a second layer of resentment and estrangement. This time, however, he brought the fresh event and his resultant feelings into the therapy session.

Surprised to learn that her husband felt as he did, Mrs. Value reported that she had said something essentially as follows, "If I were Jane Doe, I would go to the head of the board of directors and say, 'Thus and so' about this matter." She spelled out in brief detail what she would do in those circumstances as a means of correcting what both she and her husband considered wrong. She went on to say, however, "If I were not Jane Value, I would not know about it," meaning that she knew about what had happened because of her husband. Mr. Value agreed that those were the words that had been spoken earlier in the day.

During the exploration of the incident, it became evident that Mrs. Value had in fact given indications that she recognized the bind that it would put her husband in if she were to go directly to the chair of the board and that she was neither saying directly nor implying that her husband should go over his superior's head with the matter. As the therapist helped them to clarify what actually had transpired in the incident, Mr. Value pointed out that he still had difficulty in believing that his wife was not saying or implying that he should have done something. This led to a link with his relationship with his family of origin, specifically to a discussion of the fact that his mother had never been wrong and in particular felt that she had never told a lie. This connection led to some delineation of how his mother had externalized and, in turn, to some brief discussion of how this must have felt to him when he was growing up. It emerged that it was only after he had become an adult that he had really become aware of how his mother externalized and denied her responsibility for error or for anything being wrong. Again, the residual effect of living in relationship to such a pattern in a powerful parent was noted and reflected on briefly.

During the discussion, the clients moved over to mention some patterns that had prevailed in Mrs. Value's family of origin. Subsequently, Mr. Value pointed out that he felt his wife tried to put him down and to protect him as well, adding that Mrs. Value's mother had always protected her husband. Quickly, Mrs. Value exclaimed that her mother did so, but at her father's request. Later in the session, Mrs. Value said that she was glad that her (deceased) father was not around to know about the present behavior of the Value's oldest child, because "it would kill him." Mr. Value noted that she was again protecting her father. Mrs. Value was not able to deny that this was the case because it was evident from her explicit statement that she felt that her mother was handling the disappointment over the youngster very well.

A return was made to the theme of failure when Mr. Value mentioned his recent awareness that his athletic prowess—specifically his ability to keep pace with men 20 years his junior in racketball and volleyball—involved identification with his father's athletic successes. Athletics had been the only area in which his father had been successful in his life, according to Mr. Value. Portions of the tie between father and son were confirmed by Mrs. Value when she noted that currently her father-in-law was being stressed by a recent decrease in his physical abilities that would not permit him to maintain his former level of performance in tennis. An attempt was made to provide some relief for Mr. Value and to help him rationalize feeling good about his own athletic ability. The therapist pointed out that there were other reasons that one might feel elated at being able to perform better than younger persons than issues related to feelings about and relationship with one's father. These other reasons included, for example, "normal" competitive strivings and some zestful feelings about being able to perform despite one's middle-age status.

In the sixth session, Mr. Value's statement that he enjoyed being the underdog more than being at the top actually opened up the theme of success, which had been present as a theme in earlier appointments with the couple as well. Moving from relating his difficulties with success and enjoying it to his perceptions about his father's lack of success, the therapy returned to the success theme in the Values' marriage. Mr. Value complained that his wife did not and historically had not rejoiced in and appreciated his successes. She rejoined that she felt that she had to downplay her own successes—which she indicated that she actually enjoyed—because her husband responded to them in a manner that showed that he did not enjoy them. They were in agreement that he did not seem to get anything out of his own successes, even when he could admit that he had been successful in an endeavor.

It was possible to find the "protect husband" theme clearly appearing in the pattern in which Mrs. Value held back mention and enjoyment of what she had done that she felt was significant. As this occurred, it was also possible to point out to the couple how they had been "unconsciously colluding" to produce a pattern in which Mr. Value was protected from having to deal directly with feeling successful by feeling unsuccessful and by being helped to feel unsuccessful. His role in presenting himself in the marital relationship as unsuccessful and unable to acknowledge and enjoy his own successes was a largely unconscious but emerging-into-awareness pattern in which he virtually invited his wife to protect him by neither acknowledging nor appreciating her successes or his own.

By returning to an examination of the kind of process that was involved in the incident with which the hour was opened, it was possible to elucidate some of the mechanics of how the Values kept the collusive process operating. To the extent that Mrs. Value was ambiguous in her statements and communications to her husband about significant matters, it was possible for him to distort things very easily. Her need to protect him and her attempts to do so by ambiguity actually made her behaviors reminiscent for him of the behaviors that he had witnessed in his own parents' marriage. His invitations to her to protect him actually made his behaviors reminiscent for her of the behaviors that she had witnessed in her parents' marriage. The Values, in other words, had partially reproduced models of relationships witnessed in the marriages of their own parents. Mr. Value's mother had been "the right one." She evaded responsibility, "never" admitting responsibility. Mr. Value's father was "unsuccessful." By his wife's implicit definition and externalization of responsibility, he had taken on the role of being blamed and considered responsible for whatever went wrong in the work and family worlds in which he lived. He cooperated by accepting the externalizations. Compounding the difficulty was the fact that Mr. Value's grandfather, had been "super successful." In Mrs. Value's family, her mother was "the strong one." "She can take it." The mother had protected her husband because he had requested it, according to Mrs. Value. Her father had been "a good man." Mrs. Value identified with him in some ways and "practically worshipped him."

In the seventh session, an examination was undertaken of the context in which Mr. Value's father's failures had occurred in the Great Depression of 1929 and the early 1930s. The events were to some extent reframed and the failures redefined. Mr. Value emerged from that session noting that he had always accepted his father's own definition of his failure. The goal in that instance was to let the client see his father as being more successful than he had viewed him previously, thus beginning to open the door for Mr. Value to let himself consider being more successful without encountering transgenerational loyalty conflicts and fears. All of this was done with an awareness on the part of the therapist that Mr. Value was making a bid for his support.

In the Values' own marriage, Mr. Value felt responsible for whatever went wrong and felt that his wife always put him in that position, that she put him down continually. Mrs. Value was "strong" and "self-sufficient," and felt that her husband requested that she protect him. (In a sense she was correct, although she evaded responsibility in a manner somewhat reminiscent of how Mr. Value's mother had evaded responsibility for her attitudes and actions.) Mrs. Value felt scornful of her husband at times and expressed some deprecatory feelings, for example, about how he handled anxiety by "worrying out loud." By way of summary, she helped him in the need to be protected by being strong, by being scornful of his "weakness," and by being ambiguous. The latter permitted him to convert things into a relationship or situation similar to that in which he grew up, that is, one in which if there were anything wrong, it had to be the responsibility of husband, children, or anyone other than the wife/mother. As noted, Mr. Value contributed to the transactional picture by presenting himself as unsuccessful and blameworthy and by a tendency to convert ambiguous conditions into situations in which he felt that he was being blamed and considered inadequate. In brief, the Values not only reproduced some of the models of relationship seen in their parents' marriages but also manifested in a relatively mild fashion a complementarity of the kind discussed by Dicks (1963, 1967).

A brief summary of some of the major actions and dynamics of the session with the Values includes the following:

1. An initial examination of the incident that Mr. Value brought up at the outset as being indicative of the couple's ongoing interactions included some reality testing and clarification of what had transpired in the incident. Although the indications were that he had reacted somewhat inappropriately and had distorted the meanings of his wife's statements in

the incident, exploration led to a larger probing into their patterns of interaction, including some discussions of times in which there was evident ambiguity in her statements and communications to him.

2. An elucidation of their interaction included an outlining of the major features of their salient patterns, such as the "protect husband" and "avoid success" themes.

3. An examination of patterns in the parental marriages led to further understanding of how "models of relationship" from those marriages were being reproduced in their own marriage.

4. Some interpretation of the working of the unconscious collusive process by which the patterns were being manifested in their marital interaction was begun in the session.

5. Delineation of some ways in which the partners could begin to alter the patterns of transactions in their marriage was begun also. They included:

• Pointing out the role of increasing awareness of how they interacted as one first step toward securing some change.

• Emphasizing the important and practical value of reality testing, including some specific examples of how they could try to make observations and ask questions about what was happening or what was meant by the other partner without being accusatory or blaming, that is, as nondefensively as they could. Also, attention was given to helping them to learn how to respond more openly and less defensively when asked to do something by their mate.

• Emphasizing the value of attempting to be as clear as possible and as consistent as they could manage to be in their efforts to avoid ambiguity and distortion. This included some illustrations of clear communication, building on what had been done in earlier sessions.

• Emphasizing the value of continued efforts to understand what happened in their parental marriages and how those things were appearing in their own marriage, and emphasizing the importance of increasing their awareness and understanding of their families of origin, so that they could continue the process of differentiation of selves.

• Examining and beginning to interpret some of the transgenerational aspects of the relationships with one of their children, a situation in which Mrs. Value really brought the lineage and "nongenetic transmission" of family issues into explicit focus. This portion of the session served in large measure to confirm much that had gone on in the early part of the hour.

There were some things that were not handled as explicitly as they could have been in the session. One that was touched on slightly, for example, was the matter of family loyalty conflicts. Rather than being brought into the open and dealt with explicitly in this session, the issues inherent in making changes from patterns followed by parents were dealt with rather indirectly. This session should be viewed in the larger context of ongoing therapy. Several of the matters that stood out clearly here had emerged in a less clear form in earlier appointments. Although this couple made some progress, they did not remain in treatment long enough to deal adequately with some of the long-term difficulties in their relationship, stopping at the end of the 3 months established by the wife as the length of her participation prior to beginning with the therapist. Additional therapy would have included more family of origin work, including bringing the surviving parents into family of origin sessions.

The Sexual Relationship

We have not discussed the marital sexual relationship in this chapter. Sexual relating, including sexual satisfaction and sexual problems, may or may not be a significant part of a particular marital therapy case. While we do some exploring of the sexual relationship during the initial assessment period, we do not take formal sexual histories or focus on the sexual area unless it is problematic. Generally, the sexual relationship is a fairly valid barometer of the quality of relatedness and satisfaction for many married persons. However in contrast to some traditional views, over the years we have not found that couples who manifest a considerable amount of difficulty and discord in their relationship automatically encounter sexual problems. In fact, some do experience dissatisfaction and discord in other parts of their relationship and still indicate that they are quite satisfied with their sexual life. At the same time, sexual problems seldom appear to be a major source of difficulty without reflecting problems in other parts of the couples' life and relationship.

Although there are many good sources available on human sexuality and human sexual behavior, we regard Helen Singer Kaplan's two volumes, *The New Sex Therapy: Active Treatment of Sexual Dysfunction* (1974) and *Disorders of Sexual Desire and Other New Concepts and Techniques in Sex Therapy* (1979), as the best resources for the clinician who seeks well-researched information.

Sex therapy generally has been regarded as a specialized area and not part of marital therapy as such, and we agree with that orientation. We deal with sexual problems in marital therapy but primarily in terms of how they fit into the marital relationship and the general marital subsystem.

Rather than writing about sexual problems at length, therefore, we prefer to point the reader toward good sources of information and to issue the reminder that it is in the process of supervising trainees in the practice of marital therapy that we can best teach them how to understand how sexual problems affect marital therapy.

The material presented to this point has been concerned with intact marriages. The following chapter deals with what has become a significant feature of American life and life in the Western world in general, divorce and family reorganization. While there are no unusual therapeutic techniques that pertain solely to divorce situations and remarriage or stepfamily therapy, there is a large amount of information that the family therapist needs to master in order to work effectively with the sizable portion of the population that needs such help.

CHAPTER NINE

Marital Dissolution
and Systemic Reorganization

The life cycle in all family systems does not proceed without interruption from marriage until the death of both partners. On the contrary, by the late 1970s, the projections were that approximately half the couples marrying at that time would divorce. The first marriages that ended in divorce tended to do so after a relatively short time. Recently, the modal length of time between the first marriage and divorce has been 3 years. The average or median duration for all first marriages ending in divorce has been 7 years (Spanier & Glick, 1980). Most of the individuals who divorce do not "give up" on marriage, but remarry within a few years. Approximately one-third of those remarrying do so within 2 years of their divorce. The median period of time between the divorce and remarriage is approximately 3 years (Spanier & Glick, 1980). Eventually, four-fifths of all divorced persons remarry.

The frequency of divorce and remarriage creates significant changes in family organization, personal adjustment, and treatment issues. As we have reported elsewhere (Everett & Volgy, 1983), dissolution signifies the termination of the fundamental organization of the nuclear system. However, it initiates a new process of systemic reorganization and restructuring. While divorce causes dislocation in a family, it leads to a process of family reorganization. The marriage is dissolved by the divorce, but the marital partners only cease to be spouses when they divorce. They do not stop being parents. For better or worse, and whatever the form of custody adopted for minor children, they are linked together through their children for the remainder of their lives. Similarly, their parents remain grandparents—although the in-law ties dissolve, and the transgenerational ties remain a part of the life of all three generations, even though other persons are brought into the enlarged and more complex family constellation when remarriage occurs.

This form of family organization has been called variously "stepfamily" (from the Old English term *stoep*, meaning bereaved, cut off), "blended family," "reconstituted family," and "remarried family" (Sager *et al.*, 1983). We shall continue to use the term "stepfamily" because it lends itself well to various usages in connection with family reorganization.

Stepfamilies are no longer uncommon and cannot be regarded as an anomaly. Hence, they pose a new situation that did not exist a few short generations ago. Remarried family living has become a significant part of North American life in terms of the sheer number of persons involved. As far back as the beginning of the 1970s, an estimated half-million adults became stepparents annually and twice that number of children became stepchildren. By the year 1990, it is estimated that more than 7 million children, about 11% of all children under 18, will be living in stepfamily situations (Glick, 1980).

Stepfamilies have always been with us, but they were different in the past in that they typically were formed as a result of remarriage following the death of a spouse. A widower might marry a single woman and graft her onto his ongoing family. Or he might marry a widowed woman and the two of them would meld their truncated families into one unit as best they could. Subsequently, the man and his new wife might or might not have an additional child or children. Today's stepfamilies typically are formed following divorce. When remarriage occurs, there may be four living parents, as well as stepparents, who are involved in the life of the children, along with grandparents and other relatives who might not have been living in past generations (see Figure 9-1). Both the fact that stepfamilies typically are formed today following divorce, rather than after the death of one of the spouses, and the increase in the number and proportion of such families in the society face us with a new and unprecedented situation in family life.

The prevalence of the new family organizational forms may make necessary therapeutic intervention at various transitional points and adjustment periods. For those individuals who do divorce and remarry, the typical stages involve Dating/Courtship, Marriage, Discord and Separation, Divorce, Single Living (for the children and the noncustodial parent) or Single-Parent Living, Resocialization, Dating/Courtship, Remarriage. Not all of the help needed by divorcing persons and their children need be therapy. A variety of sound educational and supportive resources may be

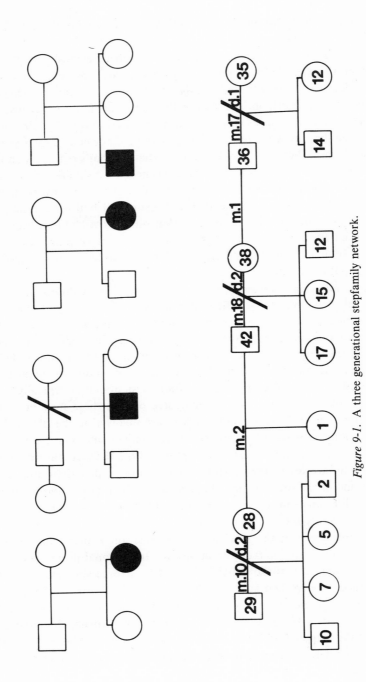

Figure 9-1. A three generational stepfamily network.

used to meet the transitional and adjustment needs either instead of or in addition to family therapy (Messinger, 1976; Messinger, Walker, & Freeman, 1978; Nichols, 1977a; Walker & Messinger, 1979).

DIVORCE

Marital dissolution is a complex process. While the emotional experiences of each family contain idiosyncratic patterns, there are broad issues that characterize the systemic process.

It is our belief that most divorcing persons never expected to get a divorce when they got married. Although it is true that some persons do enter marriage today expressing the attitude, "We can always get a divorce, if it doesn't work out," it seems unlikely that many, or any, of them actually expect the marriage to end in divorce. Even those who are fearful that they cannot succeed at making a particular relationship work or cannot succeed at anything still give the impression that with another part of themselves they do not expect to have the marriage fail.

The ending of the marriage may or may not produce positive outcomes for the divorcing partners. For some individuals, divorce will bring a "new freedom" (Fisher, 1974). Some may turn it into a "creative divorce" (Krantzler, 1974) and a growth experience. Others will find it neither creative, growth producing, nor a desirable form of freedom.

Since the pioneering research of Goode (1956), there have been indications that the time of physical separation is one of the hardest periods that individuals face in the divorce process. Not only does the departure of one of the partners from the home create a situation in which a loss is experienced and a kind of vacuum created, but it also symbolically becomes, for some persons, the time at which the "real divorce" occurs. Probably most separating and divorcing persons go through a period in which they miss the absent spouse. The departure of the other creates a vacuum in living and some degree of discomfort, even in cases in which the departed one was an irritant. Coping with the absence is one of the many adjustment problems that need to be addressed by the separating and divorcing individuals. Such coping is not necessarily easy, even when one experiences some relief at not having to deal with the departed spouse or exspouse on a daily basis.

Divorce is a time of pain and difficulty for the adults and children going through the experience. Many years ago, we conceptualized the process as involving loss and causing the same kinds of grief reactions as other losses of significant love objects (Nichols, 1977a). The subsequent years of clinical practice have continued to confirm the reality of the disruption both to the system and to its members. By contrast, we feel that much of the popular literature does a major disservice to both the children and the adults who are involved by emphasizing the positive aspects and ignoring the pain and the sense of loss that inevitably and invariably appear in the process of ending a marriage and restructuring a family.

A number of theories or models of stages have been offered to explain the process of divorce. An anthropologist, Bohannan (1970), evolved the first model in his "six stations of divorce." He distinguished among the overlapping experiences of emotional divorce (which is concerned with the deteriorating marriage), legal divorce (originally based on grounds but now largely granted on no-fault bases), economic divorce (concerned with money and property), coparental divorce (concerned with custody and related matters pertaining to children), community divorce (concerned with changes in friends and social setting), and psychic divorce (concerned with regaining individual autonomy). Subsequently, a seven-stage model was described by a clinician. Kessler's (1975) approach dealt with the issues from a more personal, individual level than did the work of Bohannan as she placed the stages on a continuum from disillusionment, erosion, detachment, physical separation, mourning, second adolescence, and so on through to hard work, the final stage.

Weiss (1975), a sociologist, described the divorce process as consisting of transition and recovery. Based on his research with both divorced and widowed persons, Weiss attempted to make some estimates of the time between the marital separation and the period in which they were fully themselves again. The period of transition was thought to end within the first year following the separation, often as early as 8 months or so after the break. The period of recovery involves the establishment of a coherent pattern of life that does not include the disorganization, depression, and unmanageable stress that prevailed earlier in the process. While the individual is on the way to recovery during this second phase, his or her functioning can be disrupted and integration fractured by strong new stress such as severe disappointments, losses, or defeats. Weiss estimated that this stage ends 2 to 4 years after the separation when the person has established a strong and stable new identity.

Kaslow (1981), who also has provided a summary of divorce and "divorce therapy," has devised a diaclectic model in which she differentiates among feelings, behaviors, and the requisite tasks to be accomplished during the various stages. Her model includes a predivorce deliberation period; a during-divorce litigation period; and a postdivorce reequilibration period. Each of these periods has two phases within it, each with its own set of feelings and requisite actions and tasks. This model appears to combine a description of what occurs and, to some degree, normative statements in the task area.

Although some of the authors describing stages of divorce have given attention to the needs and adjustments of children in other places, their models have focused essentially on the feelings and adjustments of the divorcing adults. Kaslow (1981) does offer some suggested therapeutic approaches for children's needs.

At least one attempt has been made to place divorce within a family life cycle framework. Carter and McGoldrick (1980) have developed a model that would outline the divorce process as a form of dislocation of the family life cycle that would require special steps in order for the family to restabilize and proceed developmentally. They divide the divorce process into four phases: the decision to divorce, planning the breakup of the system, separation, and the divorce. Each of those phases requires a prerequisite attitude necessary to the emotional process of transition, such as a willingness to continue a cooperative coparental relationship at the time of separation, and from one to three developmental issues for each stage. The developmental issue for the decision to divorce stage, for example, is the acceptance of one's part in the failure of the marriage.

Two observations need to be made about that model. First, it is useful if not interpreted rigidly, as if the stages occur invariably in the order described, and if it is recognized that the model has certain normative features about it. In reality, the decision to divorce may be made unilaterally by one partner and the separation may follow that decision. In another situation, a trial separation may be attempted and then a decision to divorce reached. Again, in another instance, a divorce action may be filed and the couple remain together until the divorce is granted, the details of breaking up the system being left to the last minute and in some cases essentially determined by the attorneys and the court. Persons often do not possess the requisite attitudes for successful emotional or practical transition. Second, the model refers solely to the adults who are divorcing and does not address the needs and developmental issues of children whose parents are separating and divorcing.

Clinically, as we have described previously, when individuals or couples present themselves for help in either continuing or ending their marriage, they often can be found to be preambivalent, ambivalent, or postambivalent about ending the relationship. The term "preambivalent" is used to refer to individuals who have never seriously considered the possibility of ending the marriage. "Postambivalent" refers to those persons who have decided that they wish to end the relationship and who give no indication that they would be seriously interested in reversing their position. (The postambivalent-positive individuals mentioned earlier would not be concerned with divorce.)

Putting things in another way, when couples present to a therapist, the following patterns are to be found:

1. *Both partners wish to continue the marriage.* Under this rubric there may be several variations:

   a. Both spouses wish to continue and the marriage is in relatively good condition. The spouses' emotional development and relationship patterns are basically functional. Of course, such couples rarely require therapeutic help.

   b. Both partners wish to continue and the marriage is in relatively poor condition. The balance or complementarity in the relationship has shifted and perhaps one spouse has grown significantly or the other spouse has been clinically depressed.

   c. Other combinations of the foregoing also may be seen.

2. *One partner wishes to continue the marriage and the other does not.* In this pattern, there may be concealment of the true intent on the part of one or both of the partners. For example, one spouse may have become emotionally invested in an external relationship or perhaps a spouse has simply "outgrown" the relationship and gradually withdrawn emotional attachment over the years. Discovering and elucidating the intent of the partners becomes the early task of the therapist in this situation.

3. *One partner wishes to continue the marriage and the other does not know whether he or she wishes to continue it.* There may be ambivalence on the part of the undecided partner or simply a fear of the unknown that would cause the undecided spouse to oppose ending the marriage to some degree while not being sufficiently committed to it to wish to be involved in a viable relationship with his or her spouse.

4. *Both partners are undecided about whether or not they wish to end or continue the marriage.* Ambivalence is the hallmark of many individu-

als coming in for marital therapy. "Ambivalence" as used here refers to combinations of love and hate toward the spouse, with first one emotion and then the other predominating, resulting in a lack of consistency with regard to feelings about continuation or dissolution of the relationship. The most difficult of all the patterns for the therapist is one in which one or both of the partners does not wish to stay in the marriage but does not wish to get out of it either.

5. *Various combinations of these patterns appear in changing forms,* one partner being undecided at one point and definite with regard to intention at another, both partners being definite at one time and undecided later, and others not knowing where they are at a given time, simply knowing that they are confused.

Our clinical experience has been that often once a decision has been made that the marriage is going to be ended, one or both of the partners may see no need for additional therapeutic help. The recent addition of divorce mediation to the field does cause some couples to seek help in dividing property and working on custody decisions, but we have witnessed little indication that there has been any significant change in the tendency of divorcing persons to shun therapeutic assistance aimed at helping them to comprehend what is happening and why it is happening.

Divorce may be one thing for the adults going through the process and quite another for the children of those divorcing adults. Most of the "positive emphasis" material on divorce focuses on the effects on adults and ignores what happens to the children. If it is true that one of the marital partners often may feel that he or she has no power to affect what is occurring, it is doubly true that the children are powerless to change what is happening when their parents sever their marital relationship. They can protest, particularly through their depressive or disruptive and even delinquent behaviors, but the divorce is an adult action. The symptomatology and problematic behavior manifested by children both during the predivorce period and subsequently may cover a wide range of behaviors, attitudes, and feelings. For the school age child and adolescent, school problems including school phobias, declining grades and school performance, listlessness and lack of interest, combativeness, and other changes in behavior and attitudes may present his or her conscious or unconscious protest.

Our clinical observations are that a considerable amount of preventive work can be done with children during the time that the breakup is occurring, either with one parent or with both parents. Our preference is for the involvement of both parents in a cooperative endeavor to help the children understand what is happening and to give them support. There are good, well-written materials available that deal with the kinds of questions that children typically raise, such as: Is it my fault? Do my parents love me any longer? Am I going to lose both parents? (Gardner, 1970). Many parents are willing to take the time and expend the effort to try to comprehend what their children may be wondering and experiencing. Many also, despite their estrangement from their spouse and even strong dislike or hatred, can be aided and persuaded to cooperate with the spouse in telling the children what they are doing in divorcing, why they are divorcing, and that the children are still loved and will be assured of a continued relationship with both parents.

Childrens' reactions must be considered in terms of the broader context in which they occur. Youngsters whose parents divorce must face and cope as best they can—with or without concerned and intelligent parental support—not only with changes in their family of origin but also with change and disruption in their lives over an extended period of time. The disruption and reorganization of the family system typically moves through one or more separations and then to the legal divorce. This is followed by family reorganization, typically into single-parent living and then eventually into remarriage on the part of one or both parents and the constituting of a new stepfamily system.

Careful study of the available materials on divorce and children, including both empirical research and clinical observations, shows that the major sources of distress for them are the losses that they suffer during the divorce and afterward, and the conflict between their parents and its impact on them (W. C. Nichols, 1984). The major losses typically include the loss of the father from the home; changes in their socioeconomic position; the absence of familiar supports; possible change in home, neighborhood, and school; and possible erosion of faith and trust in parents and other significant adults. Conflict between the parents not only may damage a child's self-esteem but also, particularly if it is prolonged, may have severe negative effects on the youngster's ability to cope and adjust to the changes that are occurring in his or her life. All of these are affected by the age and individual developmental stage of the youngster (W. C. Nichols, 1984).

Whether the child of marital discord and divorce requires personal psychotherapeutic assistance depends on a number of factors. Assessment of his or her problems and strengths and the need for treatment should include specific attention to developmental level, experience with the parents' separation and divorce and the response to those events, the available network of support, and symptomatic and problematic behavior (Kelly & Wallerstein, 1977). Our preference for psychotherapeutic assistance for the child is for family therapy that involves all of the relevant family members in the restructured family, interspersed with individual interviews with the child as indicated, rather than simply "child therapy" (W. C. Nichols, 1984). The focus of such treatment should be on the resolution of loss and the working through of grief, as well as the cessation or amelioration of parental conflict. Treatment efforts also should be conducted with an appropriate amount of attention given to the developmental stage and needs of the child.

An important assessment or diagnostic factor in all cases is the question of whether the behaviors manifested by the child are due to the fact that he or she is a child of marital discord/divorce or whether the behaviors result from the fact that the youngster is struggling with the tasks and difficulties accompanying his or her given stage of development as a human being.

Whether we are referring to children or adults, the statements made in Chapter 5 with regard to grief reactions and mourning processes apply in the case of marital breakup and divorce. The resolution of the losses is in fact one of the major tasks faced by adults and children as they move out of the divorce phase and especially as they attempt to enter new marriages and new family forms. Both adults and children have to grapple with damaged self-esteem, the loss of status, and the emotional loss of a partner in the case of an adult and, typically, in the case of children, some degree of loss with regard to the nonresident parent.

The status loss generally is different for men and women. Women, especially those who have been reared in traditional ways, have tended to have much more at stake in being married than men. The male's social identity and much of his personal identity have tended to be based primarily on his vocational role. The woman's social and personal identities have tended to be based traditionally on her wife/mother role. Unfortunately, in our judgment, she has lived vicariously too often, in the reflected light of her husband's status and identity, hers being contingent primarily on his. Although there is change occurring with the rise of feminism and new economic and social opportunities for women, the traditional picture has not faded from the scene.

Male-female reactions to the loss of status generally vary in some broad ways, according to clinical observations. The loss of the married status for the male may not make that much practical difference to him, because he still has his identity from his vocational role. The female may feel quite helpless and exposed to a world in which she is not accustomed to coping alone. Support groups provide a much-needed service here for many women, particularly in the early stages when they are feeling quite cast adrift. To the extent that she has been accustomed to being "the wife of" her husband and to being identified as the wife of somebody, she finds that she is missing her identification, as well as not possessing some of the coping mechanisms needed for everyday living as an autonomous person. Who is she now? Her former husband is still John Brown, salesman.

Emotional reactions of men and women may be similar and dissimilar. Both need to mourn appropriately, even when they are convinced on objective grounds that ending the marriage was the best step to take. Mourning appropriately may be more difficult for men than for women, particularly if they have been socialized to hold back and deny their feelings and to negate their dependency needs. Only recently have we begun to recognize that the man who leaves his home may find himself feeling adrift, alone and lonely, and sometimes considerably more anxious and depressed than stereotypes of males would imply.

Both men and women also require assistance in many cases in learning about the resources that are available in the community for adjusting to divorce, learning new behaviors, and adapting to new roles. In cases in which there is a long waiting period, some of this assistance is needed during the period before the divorce is final. For those who do not get started on adaptation to postmarital life in such an anticipatory fashion, help may be needed after the divorce in locating community resources that will assist in the life transition that they are undergoing.

There appears to be little or no doubt that marital disruption in the form of separation/divorce is a stressful event (Bloom, White, & Asher, 1979). Whether this kind of event will continue to be a stressor of top magnitude as social attitudes regarding divorce become more permissive is not clear. At the present, however, the emotional impact of marital disruption and separation from one's spouse continues to be a major source of pain. The "separation distress" described by Parkes (1973) may be caused primarily by the loss of attachment to the other person. Attachment may be present in strong terms long after the erosion of love (Weiss, 1975). "Separation distress" includes the focus of attention on the image of the lost figure, feelings of guilt for having caused the loss, and an "alarm reaction" composed of such feelings as fear or panic, restlessness, and extreme alertness to the possibilities of the return of the lost person, accompanied by sleeping and eating disorders (Weiss, 1975).

Although the point of physical separation, in which one spouse leaves the household, has long been identified by researchers and clinicians alike as one of the more painful times in the divorcing process, some recent research evidence suggests that establishing a new lifestyle may be more difficult for the divorcing person than adjusting to the breakup of the marriage. There is a two-way reciprocal connection between adjustment to a new lifestyle and adjustment to the separation. That is, adjustment to the separation tends to affect one's establishment of a new lifestyle, and establishment of a new lifestyle tends to help in resolving one's difficulties in dealing with marital dissolution. Those who are unable to form new relationships may continue to feel bitterness toward the former spouse or regret having separated/divorced (Spanier & Casto, 1979).

The adversarial nature of the legal process of divorce adds further dimensions to the stress of pain of separation and marital dissolution. Veteran family therapists and family mediators know that once a couple have entered the legal system, the level of anger and resentment often is heightened and former relationship conflicts and disappointments are exacerbated. All of this occurs typically at the time the spouses are trying to cope with their own sense of personal loss and struggling to manage the needs of their children.

The days of lengthy predivorce adversarial struggles with attorneys to establish "grounds" for divorce are coming to an end with the adoption of no-fault divorce legislation in many states. However, in the absence of the struggle over grounds, the adversarial battle has moved to issues of property and particularly child custody. It is common for the children to become pawns in an often bitter contest over property and assets or in a continuation of resentment from earlier relationship disappointments. These struggles often do not end with the divorce action. Custodial parents may withhold or deny visitation while noncustodial parents may withhold support payments or, in extreme cases, resort to "child snatching." It also is more common now for fathers, previously denied custodial standing in traditional courts, to reopen litigation for the purpose of seeking joint or sole custody. While in most cases this probably reflects a father's genuine desire to assume additional responsibility for his children, it may in some instances veil anger and reaction triggered by the remarriage of his former wife or other things that upset him. Similarly, litigation regarding the children may be taken up by others throughout the family network. We have reported elsewhere the high frequency of involvement of grandparents in custody litigation either directly or behind the scenes (Everett & Volgy, 1983).

Family Therapy Issues

We have intentionally not discussed "divorce therapy." It is our opinion that no such "field" or "technique" actually exists, nor is there a body of literature underlying such a practice or training settings that produce "divorce therapists." Rather, the term has been used primarily in a descriptive sense to refer to psychotherapy provided for divorcing and divorced persons or, perhaps more often, as a term to market "specialized" services to the public. We believe that it is the responsibility of the family therapist to be knowledgeable about what transpires with persons in all aspects of a family system and to work with them. This, of course, includes marital dissolution and the postdivorce systemic reorganization. Thus, our focus here is on extending the previously identified resources of family therapy to the stage of family reorganization.

The family therapist working with divorcing spouses must have extensive knowledge of the foregoing theoretical and developmental issues and must also be knowledgeable concerning the legal aspects of the divorce process within the jurisdiction in which he or she practices. Family therapists who work with spouses in marital therapy at a predivorce stage may have the opportunity to follow such couples through the emotional and legal divorce process. When couples who have been working in marital therapy and have made the decision to divorce agree to continue in therapy, the therapist has an exceptional opportunity as well as responsibility to provide continued support for the clients. At the time of the decision to divorce—which typically occurs prior to involvement with attorneys—the family therapist can assist the spouses in anticipating and working through critical issues of how to tell the children, what to do to protect each spouse's integrity and access to the children, the handling of separate residences, geographical and school district issues, optional patterns of custody and visitation that would be in the best interests of both the children and the parents, and matters of support, division of property, and assets.

Therapists must be very clear about the therapeutic boundaries both for themselves and for the couple and differentiate the therapeutic role from the role and responsibilities of the attorney. Unfortunately, many therapists are not knowledgeable about legal proceedings and thus tend to avoid or ignore those issues and to dump their clients into the legal system. Family therapists should always have available several legal colleagues (just as one would have medical consultants) who specialize in family law and who are supportive of spouses' ability to work out self-determined agreements with regard to custody and property. Many such attorneys are eager to work with capable therapists.

The family therapist who is involved at this early stage often can assist the couple in working through leftover or latent marital disappointments and resentments. These issues would not only inhibit a couple's potential for working out a dissolution agreement but could potentially disrupt their postdivorce parental adjustment and responsibilities for years following the divorce. In addition, the family therapist and the spouses can examine parental issues throughout the broader family network, such as problems with jealous or intrusive grandparents.

Following the actual divorce, the family therapist may at times work with the former spouses individually in order to assist them with their personal adjustment and resocialization, at times with each parent and the children together in order to deal with issues of restructuring the parent–child sybsystem, and at times with the former spouses together or both parents and the children together on managing matters of sharing custody or visitation as well as on ongoing concerns of communication and interaction.

At this stage, the family therapist also can begin to utilize effectively community resources such as divorce adjustment groups or single-parent groups. Obviously, most divorce cases cannot be followed smoothly throughout the entire divorce sequence. Some cases arrive for treatment after one spouse has already retained an attorney or filed legal documents. Others may arrive in the midst of bitter litigation when a child begins to display symptoms of depression or runs away from home. One of our graduate students encountered what apeared to be a typical marital case. Upon sitting down for the first interview with the couple, he was startled when the husband immediately announced that he planned to marry another woman, that there was nothing to work on in the marital relationship, and that he simply wished his wife to have a therapist before he left. The wife was even more surprised than the beginning therapist. Before the therapist could speak, the husband gave his wife his attorney's business card and left the office. In such cases, the clinical role and goals of the family therapist remain the same as those mentioned above, although they become more difficult the farther into litigation a couple has proceeded or the less access the therapist has to the broader family system.

How does a person know that he or she has recovered from the experience of separation/divorce? Weiss (1975) suggests from his research that two developments indicate that recovery has been achieved. One is the reestablishment of a stable and coherent identity by the individual. The other, which occurs simultaneously, is the reestablishment of a stable life pattern. By this, he means a pattern of organizing relationships with others in ways that are adequately self-sustaining, even if they are not entirely satisfactory. This process, in Weiss's judgment, takes from 2 to 4 years after the separation.

POSTDIVORCE: SINGLE-PARENT LIVING

For divorcing couples with children, the typical pattern following the separation and divorce is for the children to reside with the mother. Despite the fact that larger numbers of fathers have been obtaining custody and more parents are seeking joint or shared custody, the proportion continues at nine out of ten children retaining their primary residence with the mother. The stage of single-parent living involves the split and reorganization of the nuclear parent–child subsystem into two new systemic units, each headed by one of the parents. The process of reorganization carries many stresses and pitfalls.

Among the pitfalls and stresses are the following. Children who are living with the custodial parent often may blame that parent for the absence of the other parent from the home. In other instances, the child or children and the custodial parent, in the midst of their reactions to their losses, may form closer attachments than are healthy either for the adults or their offspring. Occasionally, the emotional needs of each parent and the children may become so great that a child is parentified, functioning as a surrogate adult and major source of support for the parent. This kind of attachment obviously retards the child's personal development as well as his or her eventual departure from home, in addition to inhibiting effective systemic reorganization. Such attachment also causes such a child to interfere dramatically when a parent begins to date socially because of the child's fear of losing this role with the parent and being replaced by the parent's new friend.

The children's own struggles for structure and security may evoke problematic behavior. For example, they may begin to play one parent off against the other, exploiting parental uncertainty and parental guilt feelings, or using other forms of "emotional blackmail." Simultaneously, it is a period in which the child may be experiencing delayed mourning reactions that surface in various behavioral forms. There are some indications that portions of children's reactions to separation/divorce may tend to emerge in the second year following separation or marital breakup. Our best understanding of this phenomenon is that it evidently is related to the actions and adjustments of both parents and the reorganization of the system. During the early months and through much of the first year following separation, the parents are likely to be involved significantly in their own processes of mourning. It is as if a parent has to be able to accomplish a good portion of his or her own grief work before the children are "given permission" to proceed with their mourning processes.

Children in many and perhaps most postdivorce situations live in what Ahrons (1979) has called a "binuclear family." By this, she refers to the fact that the residence patterns resemble barbells in that they tend to live in a house on one end and an apartment on the other, the residences being connected by an automobile.

The parents themselves are likely to experience difficulty, whether they have custody and live with the child or have less frequent contact through visitation. Common problems encountered by mothers who have the physical custody and charge of their children following divorce include feelings of depression and being overwhelmed by the magnitude of their task and the role that they have been called on to fill (Brandwein, Brown, & Fox, 1974). The exclusion of the noncustodial father from the family system has been found to produce numerous negative effects for fathers, including increased stress regarding role loss (Rosenthal & Keshet, 1978), increased dissatisfaction over the relationship with their children (Ahrons, 1979), and increased depression (Greif, 1979).

Clinicians may easily overlook the pain experienced by noncustodial parents. It is true that some parents use their children as pawns in struggles to gain an advantage or leverage for economic settlements, child support payments, and the like, or in an effort to maintain contact with their former spouse. However, it is increasingly clear that many fathers wish to remain active and responsible parents in the lives of their children, and many are willing to struggle through lengthy litigation in order to secure equal access to the children. There is growing evidence that single-parent fathers manifest a willingness to handle the tasks of parenthood (Orthner, Brown, & Ferguson, 1976), although some may demonstrate a genuine naïveté regarding normal child development (Mendes, 1976).

Living as a noncustodial single parent also has its stresses and difficulties, although they may differ some from the problems of custodial parents. Even casual observation discloses that the noncustodial parent frequently experiences loneliness and feels left out of the important features and experiences of the lives of the children. Those parents, typically fathers, who live in a different locality and see their children only on an occasional weekend have an even more difficult time than those who live nearby and have a residence where their children can visit for extended periods. Both in-town and out-of-town noncustodial parents quickly discover that there are limits to the number of trips to fast-food establishments, visits to zoos, and related recreation-centered activities that they can engage in satisfactorily with their children. Not only the expense entailed, but also the awkwardness and limited satisfactions available from such pursuits soon act to curtail such parent–child involvement. If there is continuing friction with the former spouse, it appears even more likely that after a year or so, those noncustodial parents are likely to join the ranks of divorced adults who begin to diminish their contact with their children. Some withdraw completely, particularly if they begin to become emotionally involved with another adult and to find alternate sources of emotional gratification.

The role that joint custody may play in moderating or ameliorating parent versus parent and parent–child friction in the postdivorce period is still under observation. In part the answers are related to the question of what is meant by the term "joint custody." It may be used to refer to shared decision making on the part of the divorced adults with the children residing primarily with one parent and visiting the other or it may refer to a pattern in which not only decision making but also residency is split into various proportions between the parents (Ahrons, 1980, 1981; Axelrod & Everett, 1983; Folberg & Graham, 1979). Ahrons's (1979) research on postdivorce adjustment has indicated that formerly married persons can cooperate for the benefit of the children more effectively and widely than has been assumed.

Family Therapy Issues

Presenting problems from single-parent family systems typically involve: (1) the individual postdivorce adjustments of the respective parents and the children; (2) the continued reorganization of the single parent–child subsystem within the new nuclear unit; (3) the rebalancing of attachments and loyalties within each single-parent family of origin and social network; and (4) the continuing interaction between the binuclear units (Ahrons, 1979), whether they be in the form of custodial–noncustodial or joint custodial. (Figure 9-2 depicts these issues.)

Individuals and families often will present themselves here with problems that reflect either depressive reactions of the former spouses, parent–child conflicts, or depressive or acting-out responses by the children. Many families will display all of these presenting areas. The family therapist must be careful to assess the reciprocal threads connecting the problem areas and not become preoccupied simply with an individual's complaint or a child's acting-out.

The single-parent system generally should be seen in therapy as a unit not only in order to gain access to the reorganization issues of the system

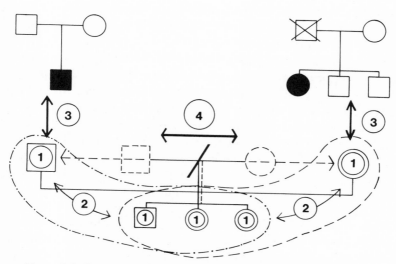

Figure 9-2. Reorganization of the nuclear parent-child subsystem.

but also in order to allow the members an opportunity to be open and to interact about their loss and confusion. Frequently the therapist will find triangular patterns from the former nuclear system that have been broken abruptly, leaving members' roles confused and members perhaps embittered. For example, a 14-year-old daughter, formerly triangulated with the parents and parentified in the nuclear system, may not only carry the guilt of being "unsuccessful in keeping Mom and Dad together," but may also become depressively withdrawn in the absence of her parentified role or turn dramatically to her peers for closeness and identity.

Eventually new roles and triangular patterns emerge within the single-parent system replacing those that formerly prevailed. A single parent may parentify a child into a pseudoadult role to diffuse the adult's loneliness as well as to have someone to oversee and manage both the household and the other children while the parent works or engages in social activities. Such patterns create both rivalry and stress within the sibling subsystem and deprive the newly parentified child of normal social and peer contacts.

Similarly, the frustration and anger of a parent toward the former spouse and the difficulty of single-parent living may become directed toward a child—who was perhaps the favorite of the former spouse—who then performs a scapegoat function for the system. From the sibling subsystem, children may begin to display failure in school or other problem behaviors in efforts either to bring the parents back together or to gain attention and nurturance from a depressive and preoccupied parent. All of these issues are best dealt with in conjoint family sessions rather than in individual psychotherapy.

Following the divorce and the formation of the single-parent system, there is a tendency for the external boundaries of the new system to swing to the extremes of closed or diffused. These are reactive patterns that may occur quickly in a systemic effort to provide protection and rebalance for the system. The boundaries may become closed tightly in order to avoid painful contact not only with the former spouse but also with family and social network members. The result is an isolated family system that is deprived of external support and intervention. The alternative pattern opens the boundaries widely to allow anyone who is willing to enter, thus attempting to diffuse the pain. Typically the single parent may reestablish his or her former role within the family of origin and may even relocate geographically so as to be near the family, or allow their parents or siblings to intrude in the single-parent system as substitute caretakers of both themselves and their children.

In most systems, these reactive boundary adjustments mark a transitional period and gradually return to a pattern consistent with systems needs prior to the divorce. However, many of the families presenting themselves for therapy may have rigidified the early boundary reactions and become helpless and ineffective in reorganizing the system. Where the family of origin members are prominently involved in the single-parent system's reorganization, the family therapist should have access to such members. Therapy with the three-generational network often is effective.

The issues between the former spouses and their respective single-parent systems will vary according to the pattern of custody. Where one parent is the sole custodian of the children, there is a clear imbalance of power. This may be used manipulatively by the parent with the power or reacted to by the parent without power. Here children frequently are caught in a power struggle that may be primarily an expression of past marital disappointments and resentments.

In joint custody patterns, presumably the parents have agreed to work cooperatively by sharing major decision making and responsibilities for the children. While the residential patterns of joint custody vary considerably, if both parents continue to reside in the same community, the children spend nearly equivalent amounts of time in each parent's household. This necessitates greater and more continual involvement between the two single-parent systems, and thus the potential for conflict, particularly with regard to presenting styles and parent–child attachment patterns. Generally, where children are identified as the presenting problem in joint custody systems, it is best to involve both parents in the therapy. If the parents are unwilling to meet conjointly, it is useful to meet with each single parent–child subsystem alternately, relying on the continuity of the children in both sessions to effect systemic change.

Regardless of the custody patterns, interactive problems between the two nuclear systems may reflect continuing coalitions or triangulation patterns from the nuclear system that formerly existed. For example, a parentified child from the former system may become pulled by either parent not only into a coalition against the other parent but also into fulfilling the adult's needs for closeness and nurturance. Similarly, intergenerational coalitions such as those between a mother and her mother may continue and pull the children into a coalition against the father. All of these patterns require careful assessment by the family therapist of the systemic dynamics both from the former nuclear system and of the evolving new single-parent system.

REMARRIAGE

The majority of divorced parents will remarry. For most of the divorced and for many widowed persons, with the exception of women in their 50s and older, being single again after once being married is a transitory state.

Some observers have estimated that the optimum time for remarriage is some 3 to 5 years after the initial separation (Hunt & Hunt, 1977; Sager *et al.*, 1983). Their assessment is that such a period of time permits one to recover from narcissistic injuries, complete the emotional divorce from the former mate, and achieve other tasks that permit one to live again in a marriage (Sager *et al.*, 1983). In Weiss's (1975) terms, the spouses are themselves again some 2 to 4 years after the separation.

Remarriage, even structurally, is a complex matter. Where only the adults are considered, there are eight patterns possible. Where there has been a divorce on the part of one of the partners, there are five possible patterns. These include marriage between a divorced male and a single female, a divorced male and a widowed female, a divorced male and a divorced female, a divorced female and a single male, and a divorced female and a widowed male. The other three patterns when only the adults are considered are marriage between a widowed male and a single female, between a widowed male and a widowed female, and a single male and a widowed female.

The remarriage picture becomes even more complicated when children are considered. The husband may or may not have children from his former marriage. The wife may or may not have children from her former marriage. Taken together, they may or may not have children from former marriages and may or may not have children from this marriage, in several permutations.

Sager and associates (1983) have calculated that there are 24 possible patterns of remarried couples when gender, previous marital status of each partner, and the presence of custodial and/or noncustodial children are considered. They also note, as we have here, that if the question of how the former marriage ended—by death or divorce—and whether there are children from the former marriage are included, the possible patterns of remarriage and stepfamily living increase even more.

A systemic approach to the stepfamily formed as a result of the remarriage of the couple would view that unit not only as a system in its own right but also as a subsystem of what Sager and associates (1983) call the "remarried family suprasystem." The larger network resulting from the divorce and remarriage includes not only the remarried couple but others such as the other biological parent of the child, grandparents, other relatives, and the child, who is the link between the stepfamily unit and the larger system.

As with the original nuclear family, however, it is the marriage of the remarrying adults that launches the process of family reorganization and restructuring out of the divorce–single-living stages.

Adults who are remarrying commonly encounter three sets of problems affecting their relationship that are not present in a first marriage. Significant resolution of those problems is essential to the attainment of a strong and viable union between remarried spouses and the formation of a cohesive remarital unit.

First, the spouses need to deal with latent conflict or concerns resulting from residues from the former marriage of either or both of them. There are likely to be some "ghosts from the past," regardless of whether the former spouse is living or dead. These may take the form of idealization of a deceased spouse and former marriage. If the former spouse is still alive there may be unresolved feelings of anger or hatred. The present spouse may be fearful that some attraction still exists between the formerly married persons. Also, there may be expectations that the present spouse will behave as the former spouse did and that some patterns followed in the first marriage may be repeated.

A spouse may work through feelings of bereavement and grief and still be uncomfortable with the idea of being married. A fear of failure or of being rejected and left again sometimes crops up in remarriages. Also, disillusionment with marriage, with risking oneself, with making oneself vulnerable to commitment and hurt, may last long after grief work connected with the loss of the former spouse as a person has been completed.

Discomfort may result from an attitude on the part of former in-laws that the remarried persons is an interloper, one who has no business replacing a former son-in-law or daughter-in-law whom they liked. One's new spouse also may be uncomfortable with the fact that friendly relations are maintained with one's former in-laws.

Whatever the form and quantity of such residues, they may pose major adaptive tasks for the remarrying adult.

Second, the presence of children frequently makes a remarriage different from a first marriage. At least one of the adults tends to have children and thus to be involved in a parent–child relationship that predates his or her relationship with the new spouse. This does not give the newly married persons private time to adjust to one another, as may be possible in a first marriage, which can last for several years without children entering the picture. One of the more obvious difficulties that may be presented by the preexisting parent–child relationship is the hindrance it may provide to the establishment of appropriate generational boundaries in the stepfamily.

Among the problems that may affect not only remarriage but also the total functioning of the stepfamily is the presence of unresolved grief feelings on the part of children over the loss of the parent and the change in the family structure. A case that presents originally with the temper tantrums of an 8-year-old, for example, may turn out to involve at the core of the difficulties an inability on the part of the child to share his parent with a new spouse. Another case that presents similarly may soon reveal that a salient difficulty is the inability of the new spouse to share the mate with his or her children. Whatever the age of the children, from the very young to the adult years, their presence is a significant factor in the adjustment of the remarried couple.

Property and money, including in some instances issues pertaining to inheritance and estate matters, provide the third set of problems that generally are not present at the beginning of a first marriage. It is not uncommon for a remarried couple to have to deal with the man's money/property, and perhaps debts and the woman's property and perhaps debts. In addition, they will have to deal with their own financial needs and money management and often with child-support payments by the husband to a former spouse. What tends to make this different from a first marriage is the greater amount of financial resources involved, as well as the fact that a third and perhaps a fourth person—one or more former spouses and children—have some stake in the resources. Children, for example, may object to a remarriage because of a fear of losing out on a portion of their inheritance or because of fears that their children will be economically harmed by the remarriage.

The presence of debts and financial obligations to a former spouse or one's children tends to place not only an economic but also an emotional strain on many remarriages. Money/property issues may be indicative of real problems for the marriage. They also may be a barometer of anxiety and level of trust. Do I sign over my equity in the house and make it part of the common marital property? I have more savings than he or she does. What do we do about that? Many professionals dealing with remarriage recommend the use of a premarital agreement in which such issues are handled in a contractual fashion.

Adults often are surprised at how much emotional uncertainty they experience when they enter into a remarriage. Clinicians frequently find them to be unprepared for the specific problems and strains that they face as they enter into remarriage. According to research in Canada (Messinger, 1976), children have been found to be the major source of difficulty, closely followed by financial problems. Time does help with the resolution of much of the anxiety and uncertainty found on the part of some remarrying persons. This seems to happen primarily as the result of slowly forming a relationship of trust with the new spouse.

Family Therapy Issues

As we have indicated, remarriage carries many more complex issues than first marriages. However, patterns of mate selection and complementarity remain central. Remarried couples presenting with marital complaints show a complex interplay of marital dynamics carried over from the first marriage and latent–reactive issues that will have influenced each spouse's needs in the new mate-selection process. This means that the mate-selection process for remarriage in some cases may reflect the same features that were found in the first marriage, as was the case of a 35-year-old woman who had been married to five alcoholic husbands. Patterns of complementarity in the remarried relationship often replicate those in first marriages, in other words, and thus heighten discouragement and resentment among a remarried spouse when, after a couple of years, the identical conflictual patterns experienced in the first marriage appear in the remarriage.

In addition, the remarried couple must struggle with overcoming continuing attachments with former spouses. These are often expressed through resentments displaced onto the new marital partner. Beyond the leftover emotional issues, however, are the very real continuing contacts with former spouses with regard to visitation of the children and parenting responsibilities. These not only create continuing stress for the remarried couple but also may intrude into their bonding efforts through anger and jealousy.

Similarly, the presence of children from one or both spouses' former marriage often precludes a "honeymoon period" of privacy and intimacy that would allow for the formation of an effectively defined and bounded marital subsystem.

Clinicians should recognize also that the event of remarriage often triggers dramatic responses through the broader system network. It effectively ends fantasies the other former spouse may have secretly held about "getting back together." This often provokes resentment and harrassment of the remarried couple by the former spouse. This reactivity may spread dramatically into a reopening of litigation for custody with allegations that demean the new spouse as unfit to be involved with the children. The therapist should not be surprised when family of origin members intrusively criticize their adult child for remarrying so soon, for they are often afraid that a new spouse may interfere with their access to the grandchildren. Similarly, former in-laws may encourage and/or financially fund a legal battle on behalf of their adult child for custody in reaction to the emergence of a stepparent into the system with their grandchildren.

The presenting problems associated with remarriage are rarely isolated within the new spousal subsystem. The family therapist must carefully examine both present and historical dynamics that may be linked through the broad intergenerational network.

We would add a note here that not all persons entering a remarriage experience such difficulties or carry over old patterns of mate selection. Some individuals do learn from their early and youthful mistakes and make better choices the second time around.

STEPFAMILY LIVING

In addition to those potentially difficult issues identified in relation to remarriage, the stepfamily system displays features that are not found in an original nuclear family unit. An understanding of those unique and unusual features is vital to working with such systems and their members in an effective way.

Among the more salient of the features that may cause problems for stepfamilies is the lack of clear definition that prevails. It is difficult to determine what constitutes the system, who should be included in the concept of family, and what members should be called or how they should be classified. We have already mentioned the fact that there is disagreement about what the family should be called, for example, stepfamily, blended family, reconstituted family, or remarried family. This lack of definition extends to kinship definitions and terms. What are the parents-in-law of a newly married person in relation to his or her children? Who are the former parents-in-law in relation to the divorced spouse after he or she has married someone else? What is a stepparent?

A closely related and somewhat overlapping issue is found in the absence of models and norms for stepfamily participants. What are the guides for being a stepparent? What kinds of responsibilities does a stepparent owe a stepchild? What is the role of the stepparent? What do stepchildren owe their stepparent? Also, there is an absence of the strong incest taboo that prevails in the original nuclear family and in the extended biological family. We shall return to these and related questions.

Another feature that is peculiar to stepfamily organization is the unusual form that power and authority assume. The power and authority are divided among various adults, typically being split between the biological parents and the stepparents. The boundaries of the family unit or subsystems within which the children reside may not be firm and fixed so that power and authority do not flow across them from the outside. The nonresident parent, for example, has effects on what transpires within that residential unit. Generally, the former spouse shares in both parental authority and economic decisions regarding the children, particularly if he or she is providing economic support for the children. A custodial mother, for example, may not be completely free to make decisions about summer camp, school attendance at a private school, dental work, or other matters, because her former spouse either must be consulted or may manipulate the payment of child support. Similarly, a child may be permitted to do some things when visiting with the nonresidential parent that he or she is not allowed to do at home, thus creating struggles between the child and the residential parent when the youngster returns home.

Interventions with stepfamilies may involve some educational work. It is often necessary to identify difficulties that are stemming from unclear and unrealistic expectations. Lacking clear-cut definitions and clearly applicable norms and models, members of stepfamily systems often attempt to apply the same kinds of expectations and behaviors to stepfamily living that they learned from either their earlier nuclear system or from their family of origin.

Some of the educational information that is useful to stepfamilies follows.

1. A stepparent is someone who has married a parent. It is not the

same as being the biological parent of a child. There are no guidelines for being a stepparent. Stepparents do not have rights or privileges in relation to their stepchild as natural parents have to their children. The legal relationship that exists is between the two remarried adults. Even being a stepparent for several years gives no one rights for custody and so forth.

2. A stepparent and a stepchild owe courtesy and respect to one another. That is the extent of their obligations. Neither owes the other love. If love develops in the course of interacting and maintaining a relationship, that is fortunate for the participants, but it should not be expected to emerge spontaneously and is not required in order to make a success of stepfamily living.

3. Two significant myths that need to be debunked are those of instant love and the wicked stepmother (Visher & Visher, 1979). As implied above, a stepparent has not failed if he or she does not experience instant affection for stepchildren or elicit instant love from the youngsters. The wicked stepmother myth probably stems from two sources. The first is from folklore and literature devolving from double standard, or sexist, attitudes which devalued women and blamed them for problems in family relationships. The second comes from the fact that, in the past, stepfamilies were formed following the death of a parent and that stepmothers frequently had their new spouse's children residing with them.

4. Stepparents may perform a variety of roles, but there is no one right or wrong pattern. Therapists should encourage stepparents to explore the possible roles open to them. Three models for the stepmother proposed by Draughon (1975) are "primary mother," "other mother," and "friend," for example. These roles can be generalized to both parents. Generally, we recommend that stepparents not try to substitute or compete with the biological parent, unless the biological parent is clearly psychologically and physically unavailable for the children. The major issues in the various forms of stepparent relationships that have been gleaned from research have been summarized by Visher and Visher (1979).

5. The nuclear family from which the participants in stepfamilies emerge does not provide guidelines or models that are workable for stepfamilies. A considerable amount of confusion, frustration, conflict, and disappointment may result from the efforts of stepfamily members to apply what they have learned in their "basic training" in their family of origin or in their first-marriage nuclear family to stepfamily situations.

The stepfamily at this juncture needs to understand not only that theirs is a different family form than the nuclear family but also that it is a new form that requires the development of new models of expectations and behaviors among its members. (A comprehensive and helpful listing of differences between the two kinds of family systems in terms of structure, purpose, tasks, nature of the bonding, factors influencing the children, and forces that impinge on the system itself has been provided by Sager and associates [1983].)

Entering into a therapeutic problem-solving relationship with the stepfamily system opens the way for careful exploration and clarification of various kinds of unresolved feelings including grief, anger, loss, hope, and others. It also helps the family to focus on the fact that there are a variety of ways in which stepfamilies can be organized rather than the patterns learned in nuclear families. Providing illustrations and examples of how stepfamilies may be different from nuclear families, including calling attention to the various patterns of remarriage and resultant relationship patterns mentioned earlier in this chapter, often proves useful in family therapy.

As implied, this kind of work with confused stepfamilies seems to be most effective when conducted in an atmosphere of sympathetic understanding and with an explicit acknowledgement of the complexity of the situation from the perspectives of individual members, that is, recognition of the fact that they are involved in multiple life cycle changes and development in their individual, marital, and family life cycles in a complicated pattern of process and change. Acknowledging the stress involved in comprehending and dealing with multiple change situations, as well as recognizing the loyalty conflicts faced by various members, helps members settle down and begin to function more cooperatively and effectively.

Family Therapy Issues

Because of the complexity of the stepfamily, it is necessary for the family therapist to begin work with a careful assessment of the nature of the organization of the stepfamily system, including both subsystems and suprasystem (the system of extended family and context of other systems in which the stepfamily functions and with which it articulates). Such assessment starts even at the telephone level, where some preliminary decisions are made about who is to be included in the assessment and treatment. In an original nuclear family, it is relatively simple to determine who is to be included in the therapy sessions. One usually includes the father, mother, dependent children, and anyone else living in the home, and, often, the grandparents in a multigenerational approach. Drawing the lines with stepfamilies is more complicated. With families in which the children are living in a binuclear situation, it is sometimes helpful to bring in all four adults, or three adults if one of the parents has not remarried, and, again, perhaps the grandparents. Decisions have to be made early about the potential assets and liabilities of trying to involve various groupings and individuals who compose the extended or suprafamily system in the assessment and treatment.

Organizationally, the stepfamily itself tends in some ways to resemble Aponte's (1976) urban poor family in that both are likely to be underorganized. This is particularly true in the early stages of stepfamily organization. Aponte dealt with family structure in terms of boundary, alignment, and force.

It is important to ask, "Who is to be included? What are the real boundaries of the family?" At the very outset, it may be necessary to spend some time getting the situation settled down sufficiently to determine who is to be included inside its boundaries. In strong contrast to the optimism that often goes with entry into a first marriage, there often is confusion, lack of confidence, and questioning about the second family. One has to keep in mind the fact that stepfamily members themselves may be quite uncertain as to who is in the family at a particular time.

The boundaries are not only permeable (Messinger, 1976), but they also may change suddenly. Members may move in and out of the family system with varying degrees of frequency. The shifting of boundaries may occur several years after a stepfamily has been formed and the boundaries ostensibly established. This can happen, for example, when a child abruptly leaves one parent and moves in with the other, beginning to reside permanently in the stepfamily where he or she previously has been a weekend or vacation guest. Part of the immediate therapeutic task that accompanies integrating the youngster into the ongoing daily living routines of the family consists of examining whether there is any need for mourning on the part of any of the participants, whether there are significant loyalty conflicts on the child's part, and whether there are unrealistic expectations for "instant love" on the part of a stepparent or the child (Nichols, 1980).

Common boundary disputes that arise include disagreements over the custody rights or privileges of custodial and noncustodial parents. The grandparents may be involved where there is change from past family holiday patterns and observance of rituals. When there is little contact between the various adults involved in situations and little clarity or agreement, the children have many opportunities to manipulate one system against the other (Visher & Visher, 1979).

Common complaints also arise from the fact that the children move back and forth between households that may have very different sets of standards and expectations. One household may embody strict behavioral expectations and the other may be much less restrictive and more permissive. One of the early therapeutic tasks may be that of helping the child to recognize the differences and to realize that one has to learn how to cope and adapt in the face of diverse expectations in different settings. At the same time, there may be a need to help the formerly married persons diminish their continuing emotional ties and struggles with each other for the sake of the child or to help a stepparent clarify his or her role so that the boundary issues become more clear.

Family boundaries also may be assessed in terms of rules that determine the limits of the family system. What are the rules concerning how each of the formerly married persons deals with and relates to his or her children? How clear are they? How adequate are the rules? Are they flexible and adaptable enough to fit changing developments and needs? Both an independent relationship between each parent and each child and a viable relationship of cooperation between the formerly married persons is required if a successful transition is to be made through divorce and into a workable stepfamily situation (Ahrons, 1980).

Carter and McGoldrick (1980) have identified four areas of boundary difficulty that have to be negotiated in the stepfamily. These, as adapted here, can be recalled through a mnemonic or memory device of M-A-S-T. Membership: Who are the "real" members of the family? Authority: Who is in charge of decisions, discipline, money, and so forth? Space: Where does one really belong and what space is theirs? Time: Who gives how much to whom?

"Alignment," as used by Aponte (1976), refers to the ways in which one member of the family may be united with or opposed to another with regard to conducting family operations. We are using the term here primarily to refer to the structuring of generational boundaries. One very important task in many families, for example, is the rebuilding of generational boundaries that have been weakened during the period subsequent to divorce and prior to remarriage. During that time, a child, as we have noted, may have become parentified into a surrogate spouse role. The remarriage of the parent can be used as the beginning of the liberation of the child who has been in a spousal role (confidant, companion to the single parent) or in a parental role (in relation to another child). However, it may be seen as a threat and potential loss for the youngster. Even after he or she has been replaced by the parent's new spouse following the parental remarriage, there may be a need and opportunity to help the young person become a child again and to function at an age-appropriate level with the siblings.

Parent–child alignments in the stepfamily also may need to be strengthened. The biological parent and the child can be united around the task of taking responsibility for the child's behavior. Reinforcing the authority and disciplinary ties between them may prevent stepparent and stepchild conflict. Clashes arising from resentment on the part of the youngster at being disciplined by a stepparent and role confusion on the part of the stepparent can be avoided and tensions diminished in this kind of situation by strengthening parent–child alignments. The uncertainty of stepparents, stemming largely from the lack of norms for stepfamilies, as well as from their frequent fears about security in either the marriage or the stepfamily, contribute significantly to alignment problems.

The alignment in a family may be too tight, excessively rigid, or too loose. In an underorganized family, it is not clear who can be depended on to carry out what tasks or responsibilities. The important issue not only for children but also for adults in stepfamilies in this regard frequently is, "Who can be counted on to help with family-related tasks or functions?" If it is true that a significant number of things may "fall between the cracks" in nuclear families, it is even more likely to be the case with stepfamilies. One biological parent, for example, may assume that a certain task is the responsibility of the other parent with whom he or she has limited communication and who simply may not be in a position to handle the task. The alignments in a family system, as is the case with boundaries, shift over time as different circumstances arise and there is a need to fulfill different tasks.

"Force," the third ingredient in this approach to organization, refers to the distribution of power in the family system. Power may be assigned in a system on the basis of position or role. It also may be assumed by an individual. In an underorganized family, the force or power is not distributed in an orderly way (Aponte, 1976).

Difficulties may arise from various sources. Some members may not use the power assigned to their position. Other members may inappropriately assume power and use it in ways that disrupt the family system. For example, in a stepfamily situation in which a widowed man and his teenage daughter joined a divorced woman and her younger daughter, the father abdicated the authority/disciplinary position almost entirely. Into the vacuum created by the father's failure to use his assigned power, his adolescent daughter moved to assume and exercise power considerably out of proportion to her age and developmental level. Although he was the legitimate possessor of power, the daughter was the user. The result was an ongoing conflict between his daughter and her stepmother. In another family composed of two parents who had brought their children together in one residence in an effort to create a genuinely blended family, the wife was both the possessor and the user of power. She used not only power that was assigned to her because of her position as an adult and parent but also assumed additional power in the face of her husband's failure to use the power assigned to his position. This resulted in the kind of skewed system sometimes observed in original nuclear families.

It is helpful at the point of initial assessment, as well as subsequently, to observe not only the location of the power but also the movers of the power in the stepfamily. The term "mover" refers to persons who do not possess significant power on their own but who are able to get those who do to use the force in particular ways. For instance, in one stepfamily, the biological father was the possessor of the power and his second wife, who lived with him and his children, was the mover. She created a number of crises and carried her efforts too far and lost her ability to influence his use of power when she insisted that he put the children out of the home.

The distribution of power and the use of force varies as time passes in the life cycle and as certain activities are undertaken (Aponte, 1976). For example, the parent's power and use of force typically diminish and the children's increase as the children grow older. The dependency of the child on the adult decreases and his or her own independence appropriately increases with age.

One clinical example may help to tie together our use of "boundary," "alignment," and "force." The original assessment of the Jones family (see Figure 9-3) disclosed that a major problem centered around the efforts to integrate Mr. Jones into an ongoing family unit with his new wife and her three adolescent daughters. The alignment between Mrs. Jones and her daughters was so well established and powerful that Mr. Jones was excluded from effective participation in the stepfamily. When the marital partners were apart from the adolescents, their relationship worked well. During the year that the new marriage had existed, there had been conflict and explo-

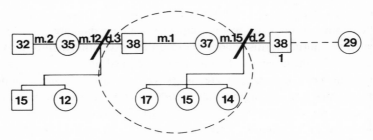

Figure 9-3. The Jones family genogram.

sions whenever Mr. Jones attempted to exert a parental type of influence or force that he did not possess. The therapeutic intervention involved changing boundaries, alignments, and the use of force. Roles were clarified. The mother was given primary responsibility for guidance and discipline. The excessively strong ties between the mother and her daughters that had developed during the single-parent living stage gradually diffused and the marital bonds and spousal subsystem simultaneously strengthened as the partners were aided to become more dependent on each other for companionship and assistance with decision making. Also, Mr. Jones was aided in coping with problems of sexual attraction and defenses against his impulses so that he could relate to the adolescent females more comfortably. As this occurred and his position was made more secure in the marriage and the stepfamily, he was able to decrease his tendencies to try to exert force inflexibly. Over a period of time as the subsystems in the stepfamily were clearly differentiated and the generational boundaries clearly and adequately established, it became possible for the teenagers to move back into appropriate places in their developmental cycles and to begin moving toward adulthood in a timely and orderly fashion.

Achieving stepfamily reorganization is seen as the goal of family therapy by the Vishers (1979). Certainly this is true in the early stages of stepfamily formation. There are some indications that the initial reorganization period, the time needed for stepfamilies to become integrated and to begin functioning as a family unit, lasts approximately 2 years, sometimes longer. The establishment of good marital bonding and freedom of movement for children between two different living situations typically are key elements in the achievement of stepfamily reorganization (Visher & Visher, 1979). If the relationship between the two new marital partners is strong and can overcome efforts by children and others to weaken the alliance, the stepfamily is likely to function adequately. Both clinical observation and research, as we have noted, indicate that the cohesiveness of the couple in the family is a very important dimension in emotionally healthy families (Lewis, Beavers, Gossett, & Phillips, 1976). Clinically, one seeks to determine the strength of the marital relationship, how it is affected by others and especially by the children, and the length of time the new partners have had to secure bonding and integration.

Stepfamilies that have existed for 10 or more years are well past the reorganization stage, but still may be coping with "ghost" issues. Assessment and intervention strategies for use with stepfamilies can be evolved from the developmental model described in Chapter 6 with regard to the particular life cycle stage of the family system and its members.

There are different issues between the stepfamily in the process of formation, sometimes called the "reconstituting stepfamily," and the step-family that has moved past the reforming or reconstituting stage. The developmental phases of the family in the process of formation have been described as recovering from loss and entering the new relationship, concep-tualization and planning of the new marriage, and reconstitution of the family (Ransom, Schlesinger, & Derdeyn, 1979). To date, developmental tasks for stepfamilies have not been set for stages that go much beyond the formation period. Sager and associates (1983) have provided some excellent material on adolescents in stepfamilies that are related to developmental task schema for stepfamilies.

As a stepfamily evolves over time and begins to become something of an established unit, there may be shifts in the attitudes and allegiances of the new family that require particular attention. For example, in one new family involving a wife/mother, her 8-year-old daughter from a previous marriage, and the husband/stepfather, things began to change after approximately 2 years. The child's biological father had remarried and had an 11-year-old stepdaughter who had served as a kind of sibling for the younger child. Things went reasonably well in the binuclear arrangement until the biologi-cal father, a substance abuser, created a wild physical scene in which he fought his second wife and virtually wrecked the house during a weekend in which the 8-year-old was present. As a result, the child's mother decided to allow only daytime visits in the future, but to forbid overnight visits, some-thing that was within her scope of power under the custody arrangements. In response, the biological father cut off contact with his daughter. The mother worked in what appeared to be an appropriate manner to help the child recognize that the father was a seriously disturbed individual. Even though she wished to maintain contact with her stepsister, the child began to diminish her investment in the biological father and his family as she began to realize that the man had become very disturbed emotionally and that he did not love her. The stepfather, a warm and caring person, began to function as a genuine father and father figure for the child. The binuclear situation withered and the stepfamily in which she resided became essentially the family of the 8-year-old. This does not appear to be an unusual outcome of binuclear family living after a period of years.

Many stepfamilies eventually begin to function much after the fashion of nuclear families. Treatment in such cases primarily is concerned with the same kinds of issues that arise in nuclear families. Mr. and Mrs. Smith asked for help with their children some 3 years after forming a stepfamily. Each had two children from a former marriage. Mr. Smith's children had come to live with him and his new wife when their mother had been killed in an accident a few weeks after the remarriage. Mrs. Smith's children spent 1 or 2 weeks a year with their biological father. Otherwise, the six persons in the Smith family functioned essentially as a nuclear family. An assessment of the situation with Mr. and Mrs. Smith disclosed that their concerns about their children were basically normal childrearing concerns related to a variety of common problems such as hours, limits, and so on that fitted with the developmental stages that the children had reached. It was apparent that the more pressing concerns of the Smiths pertained to their marital relationship. Marital therapy became the treatment of choice. The presenting problems about the children were handled by the couple without the necessity of the children attending therapy sessions. The Smith family was notable in that it had worked through the early developmental issues of mourning and establishment of relationships so that the youngsters had been permitted to get back on their appropriate individual life cycle paths. The boundaries were clear and the subsystems adequately separated and delineated.

Failure to resolve early tasks may create problems later or contribute to perennial difficulties in remarriage and stepfamily living. After nearly 20 years of marriage, Mr. and Mrs. Williams still had not succeeded in obtaining stepfamily organization that would have enabled them to function without large amounts of friction. As a widower with three young children, Mr. Williams had remarried a single woman some 13 years younger than himself. During the early days, she struggled with her mother-in-law over control of the children, trying to take over the mothering role that the older woman had assumed during her son's days as a widower. The young woman's continuing conflicts with her stepchildren were a textbook example of "instant love" and "wicked stepmother" problems. The harder she tried to be a good mother to the three children, to make up to them for their losses, the more they resisted, and the more she became labeled a bad stepmother throughout the extended family system. When the Williams sought professional help, it was for the purpose of resolving marital problems. Working first with conflict over continuing relations with Mr. Williams' by then grown children, the therapist spent some time in clarifying current and original expectations on the part of both partners as to stepmother–stepchildren relations. A considerable amount of support and interpretation resulted in the diminishing of bewilderment and hurt on Mrs. Williams's part and resentments on the part of both partners. Understanding how things had gone off the track in the early days and had continued because of unclear and incompatible expectations aided them to lower tensions. As this occurred, it was possible to move on to deal with other more specifically marital issues including temperamental differences between the mates. Mrs. Williams also was able to alter her current dealings and relationships with her stepchildren so that tensions there were lowered as well. They probably will never be close to her, but a workable degree of amiable relating was obtained.

In summary, assessment and intervention with the stepfamily system is concerned with the current organization and functioning of the various individuals in the system, with the remarriage, with the family system itself, and with the system as part of a larger intergenerational network. What are the strengths of the stepfamily and its members? What are the strengths of the remarriage? What are the problems of the individuals, of the remarriage, and of the stepfamily?

Although it is axiomatic in a family therapy orientation that issues are examined and understood in terms of their systemic context, that point needs to be doubly emphasized where stepfamily assessment and treatment are concerned. Working with stepfamilies seems to stir the clinician's emotional reactivity more readily than almost any other therapeutic challenge. Not only the emotional reactions but also the clinician's lack of knowledge about and experience with stepfamilies contributes to his or her difficulty in comprehending what is being presented. Even veteran clinicians can become confused by the behavior of stepfamily members.

Sager and associates (1983) have noted that the intensity of responses that they found, particularly among children who were reacting to parental separation and remarriage, often led them to regard stepfamily members as being very disturbed. When reexamined more carefully, the behaviors were seen as appropriate responses to disturbing and chaotic stepfamily situations. They found that more than four-fifths of the children in their clinical population were involved in a dysfunctional relationship with parents or stepparents. Not all required treatment. Many of those children and adults could be helped through educational channels.

CHAPTER TEN

Professional Development

Throughout this work, we have alluded to our belief that the education and training of a family therapist involves more than the acquisition of theoretical knowledge and applied skills. We have suggested that of equal importance are the personhood of the therapist and the standards and milieu that the profession offers. This chapter deals with the family therapist as a professional and with the professional practice of family therapy. In the first section, we shall attempt to sketch briefly some of the major features of the professional field as it exists today, primarily in the United States and Canada but with some attention to other parts of the world. These features have been grouped somewhat arbitrarily under the headings of education, accreditation, credentialing, and professional organizations.

Entry into the profession is the focus of the second section. The process of socialization into the profession, with its components of identity and identification with the profession, and the nature and role of supervision in the socialization and entry processes are tied together in that section. A number of issues are addressed under the heading of professional practice in the third section. Those include an examination of the work setting of the family therapist, reimbursement for services, the use of research, ethics and ethical behavior, and the general career development of the therapist. The final portion of the chapter consists of a look forward, including questions about the future of this professional field as it continues to struggle to solidify its place among the major approaches to dealing with human behavior.

Before moving into the issues to be discussed in the major sections of the chapter, however, we shall deal with some background materials on professions and professionalization. First, we shall look at general issues in professionalization and then at specific applications to family therapy.

PROFESSIONALIZATION

The sociological study of occupations and professions has provided a theoretical framework from which we can understand the phenomenon of emerging professions—"professionalization," and the process by which new members are inducted into the culture and society of the profession— "professional socialization." The early literature was concerned with defining the essential characteristics of the professions in contrast to other occupations (Carr-Saunders & Wilson, 1933; Flexner, 1915; Greenwood, 1953). Historically, as the industrialization of Western society unfolded, the concept of professionalization evolved as a means of describing the phenomenon of many new and general occupations seeking to acquire the social status of the traditional professions of medicine and law (Wilensky, 1964). An industrializing society is a professionalizing society (Goode, 1960). As we noted in the first chapter, the increasing complexity of industrial and urban living rendered ineffective and irrelevant many traditional approaches to dealing with human behavior as the context of marital and family living changed, thus contributing to the rise of professional marriage and family counseling/therapy.

Studies of professionalism attempted to differentiate the evolving professions from other occupations in different ways. Goode (1960) identified ten requisites for the professionalization of an occupation including self-regulation, autonomy, and ethics. Friedson (1971) found exclusive knowledge in an area and an imperialistic belief in favored rights to practice to be essential to the achievement of professional status by an occupation. Earlier, Carr-Saunders and Wilson (1933) had emphasized "the existence of specialized intellectual techniques, acquired as the result of prolonged training" (pp. 284–285) as underlying professionalism and contributing to its particular features. The classic description was provided by Greenwood (1953), who called it a career or a "calling." He suggested that a profession was never a means to an end but an end itself and that professional services were performed primarily for psychic satisfaction and secondarily for monetary compensation. Distinguishing attributes of a profession, as identified by Greenwood, were (1) systematic theory from which applied skills evolve, (2) professional authority arising from extensive knowledge, (3) community sanctions of power and privilege, (4) a regulative code of ethics, and (5) a professional culture with its values, norms, and symbols.

In recent years, traditional conceptions of what constitutes professionalization of an occupation have been undergoing drastic changes in the United States and much of the rest of the world. Those changes, which we shall address momentarily, make the task of achieving recognition for family therapy practitioners much more difficult today than it would have been in the past. Again, the hallmarks of a profession in the past were considered to be commitment to a service ideal, educational attainment (including specialized education and training beyond the provinces of the layperson), organization, autonomy, and similar attributes. Using those criteria, family therapy has long since arrived at the status of a profession in the United States. A body of knowledge requiring specialized education and training for its mastery, a formal organization, a code of ethics, journals, a newspaper for the field, accreditation of its graduate educational programs, and in some places, even legislative recognition have been obtained.

The major issue facing a new profession today is not that of showing that it manifests the attributes traditionally associated with professionalization but that of organizing and influencing the political and social systems of the society in order to obtain professional status. This new perspective is termed the "power approach" (Ritzer, 1971), which pertains to the ability of an occupation to secure and retain certain rights, privileges, and obligations from other societal groups. Practically speaking, this involves "recognition," the fact of being known to the public, other professional groups, legislators and other public officials, third-party payers, and business and industry; and "legitimization," which refers to being accepted as a legitimate profession in the mental health field. A profession can, for example, be clearly recognized by others but not be considered a legitimate member of the mental health field or considered a useful and valuable provider of services by business and industry.

By our definition, a "qualified family therapist" is an individual who has been substantively *educated* in the body of knowledge deemed essential for the understanding and practice of family therapy and adequately *trained* through supervised experience in the application of that knowledge and the use of appropriate techniques. The "practice of family therapy" (or marital and family therapy) means the diagnosis and treatment of nervous and mental disorders, whether cognitive, affective, or behavioral, within the context of family systems. "Family therapy" involves the professional application of psychotherapeutic and family systems theories and techniques to the delivery of services to individuals, marital pairs, and families for the purpose of treating such diagnosed nervous and mental disorders. "Marital and family counseling" is that specialized part of family therapy that focuses on marital adjustment, preparation for marriage, and parent–child and other family relationships in which there is no diagnosed nervous or mental disorder (Clark & Nichols, 1984).

There are several other terms and concepts that laypersons and professional persons alike do not understand and, consequently, frequently misuse. This understandably contributes to a considerable amount of confusion. Among the salient terms for our present discussion are "education," "training," "accreditation," "credential or credentialing," "licensure," and "certification." As used here, the terms are defined as follows:

"Education" refers to graduate-level coursework in family therapy and the accompanying substantive materials on which the foundation is based. "Training" consists of clinical training, the development of skills, and the accrual of experience in the practice of family therapy under appropriate supervision. These two terms refer to the preparation of individuals.

"Accreditation" refers to the approval of educational programs or postdegree training programs by the determination on the part of an impartial outside agency that such programs have met specified standards. This concept, of course, deals with programs and not with individuals.

A "credential" is a statement or attestation that an individual has the right to be regarded with confidence by others, that he or she possesses qualifications that give the public and other professionals reason in this instance to trust in his or her preparation to perform as a family therapist and the belief that this will be done in a responsible and ethical manner. Credentials may be provided by private organizations and may be referred to as voluntary in that they generally have no legal standing whereas those established by law are statutory.

Laws regulating family therapists and family therapy practice may be of two broad types: licensing or certification. "Certification" restricts the use of a title. That is, no one except an individual who meets the qualifications established by law may use the restricted title, "certified marital and family therapist" or "certified psychologist." "Licensure" laws, on the other hand, restrict function as well as title. An individual may not engage in the practice of family therapy, for example, as it is defined in the law unless he or she meets the requirements set forth in the law and obtains a license permitting such practice. Licensure laws also restrict title and are more restrictive than certification laws (Nichols, 1974).

Education

The major route to practice in the evolving field of family therapy in the early days in the United States was through an apprenticeship under a supervisor of clinical work. There were postdegree training programs open to individuals who had been education previously in one of the established disciplines. (This is the route open to individuals in many other countries of the world today.) As early as the 1950s, there were a few graduate programs that offered a substantive curriculum, for example, Columbia University Teachers College, Florida State University, Purdue University, and the University of Southern California, as well as in the Marriage Council of Philadelphia program, which became part of a degree-granting program at the University of Pennsylvania. Some academic content courses were required also as part of the Merrill–Palmer Institute's post-doctoral training program. For the most part, however, training through an apprenticeship route was essentially the path followed by entrants into the field until recently.

Today, a significant body of essential and functional knowledge has accumulated that cannot be mastered through an apprenticeship route. The qualified family therapists of today, in our judgment, are individuals who have not only been immersed in the substantive materials of family study, family theory, and family therapy, but who also have been educated and trained so that they have the ability and tools to use new research–theory materials as they appear in the literature of the field, adding them to what is already known and making alterations in their approach to treatment where necessary. The basic education and training in family therapy as well as in the substantive area of family studies lays a foundation from which new findings may be evaluated.

Insofar as the preparation of the therapist is concerned, the historical movement in the field has been a shift from an early emphasis on the provision of service to training and finally to education (Nichols, 1979b). In the early days of family therapy, the focus was on meeting the needs of the clients, getting the job done as best it could be done, often on the basis of commonsense and trial-and-error efforts. Training or retraining of individuals who had already secured a graduate or professional degree generally came next. The clearest illustration of the development from the service orientation through apprenticeship training in informal settings and post-degree institutes to the acquisition of basic education in university graduate programs is found in a study of standards for training and education issued by the American Association of Marriage Counselors (AAMC)–

American Association of Marriage and Family Counselors (AAMFC)–
American Association for Marriage and Family Therapy (AAMFT) over
the years. These were: marriage counselors (1949), centers for marriage
counseling (1953), training centers in postgraduate professional marriage
counseling (1958), graduate education in marriage counseling (1959), related doctoral programs with a major in marriage counseling (1962),
training centers in marriage and family counseling (1971), and graduate
degree programs in marriage and family counseling (1974), as well as in
the accreditation manuals issued since 1973 by the AAMFT's Commission
on Accreditation for Marriage and Family Therapy Education (formerly
the Committee on Accreditation). The changes through 1974 have been
examined in detail by Nichols (1977b).

A predictable change from specialization at a postdegree level to
specialization at the graduate degree level can be traced as the field
evolved. As the emphasis on fundamental knowledge in marital and family
development, dynamics, interaction, and therapy occurred in the curriculum, there was a corresponding decrease in emphasis on family law,
genetics, medicine, and religion in the preparation of the therapist. The
result has been the evolution of a more precise and distinctive curriculum,
rather than the older general education and specialized curriculum approach.

By the mid-1970s, a basic educational curriculum for professional
education in family therapy had evolved. Originally accepted by the
AAMFT's Committee on Accreditation as the standard for graduate
programs, it was, by 1981, accepted in essence by the AAMFT as the basis
for attainment of clinical membership in that organization. The basic
curriculum or "core curriculum" consists of six distinct but interrelated
areas of study. The basic substantive materials and the supervised clinical
practica that form an introduction to the field require at least 2 calendar
years to complete in a masters degree program (Everett, 1979) and longer,
of course, in a doctoral program (Nichols, 1979a). The basic curriculum
includes:

Human Development. Studies in human development, personality
theory, human sexuality, and behavior pathology/psychopathology go
under this heading. Normal growth and development and adnormal manifestations are given the major emphasis in this group of courses and
applied work.

Marital and Family Studies. This concentration includes family development, family systems and the various family subsystems: marital,

parent–child, sibling, and individual, along with other materials from the general family studies area.

Marital and Family Therapy. Treatment orientations and theories are the focus here, for example, systems, object relations (psychodynamic), behavioral, communications, structural, and others.

Research. Research design, methodology, statistics, and research specifically in marital and family studies and therapy are required in this part of the core curriculum. For masters degree students, an orientation is intended so that graduates can be informed consumers of research findings. For doctoral degree students, the intent is to provide the skills for the graduates to perform research in family therapy. Such training and education and training must go beyond traditional methods courses in research so as to be focused specifically on the methods and topics of family therapy (Sprenkle & Piercy, 1984).

Professional Studies. A solid grounding in ethical concepts and an orientation to marriage, family, and divorce law and to statutory and case law affecting the delivery of services is the intent for this part of the curriculum.

Supervised Clinical Practice. A minimum of 1 year of supervised clinical practice within the framework of the graduate program, including at least 15 hours per week in a clinical setting with approximately 8–10 of those hours spent in direct clinical contact with individuals, couples, and families has been accepted as the standard. The AAMFT standard calls for 2 additional calendar years of clinical work under supervision following completion of the graduate degree as a minimum before beginning to work independently.

Entry into the field today in the United States tends to be through either one of two routes, through the traditional pattern of education in older, established professions where family therapy is added on as an area of specialization or through primary education in family therapy at the graduate/professional level. That is, a practitioner may be a psychologist, psychiatrist, social worker, psychiatric nurse, or physician who "does" family therapy as part of his or her work or one whose sole professional education is in family therapy and whose sole professional identification is that of family therapist. Our concern is not with where an individual starts graduate/professional education, but with whether he or she ends up with an adequate grounding in the substantive knowledge and orientation that is required in order to perform responsible family therapy.

For individuals from the older professions to receive education and training that enables them to be appropriately prepared to perform as a family therapist requires some significant changes in traditional orientations. The traditional emphases in several established health care professions can be depicted briefly as follows:

Profession/occupation	Focus	Orientation of education
Psychiatry	Individual	Medical
Psychology, clinical	Individual	Assessment, psychotherapy
Social work	Variable	Casework, psychotherapy
Nursing, psychiatric	Individual	Medical

Family therapy training is being added to the traditional education of some students in medicine, psychology, and social work. For part of that group, the experience leads to deep involvement in family therapy, whereas for others the experience simply provides the ability to use certain family therapy techniques. As Bloch and Weiss (1981) have pointed out: "The fact that some professionals merely add family therapy as a modality to their treatment armamentarium, whereas others become specialists, parallels experience in other professions. Specialist interest leads to specialization and ultimately to professionalization" (p. 139).

A brief and illustrative look at some of the developments in some of those professions is in order at this point. A study of family therapy training in doctoral programs in clinical psychology by Cooper, Rampage, and Soucy (1981), for example, showed that only 10% of the faculty members nationwide identified themselves primarily as family therapists in orientation. A third of the responding programs (102 of the total 131 doctoral degree programs in clinical psychology responded) had no family-oriented faculty members and a fifth had no family therapy programs at all. Interships nationwide noted that clinical psychologists came least prepared in family therapy for their intership experiences. Nevertheless, the American Psychological Association formed a division of family psychology in 1984 and a significant number of clinical psychologists indicate in directories that they provide marital and family therapy. Presumably, a considerable amount of the training in family therapy is secured at the postdegree level and some psychologists enter the field with little or no education and training specifically in family and family therapy. Although the future is difficult to predict, there do not appear to be any signs that interest among psychologists in family therapy is lagging and there are some indications that it is increasing.

Family therapy training in general psychiatry residency programs has increased markedly in the last decade and questions about family therapy are now being included on psychiatry board examinations (Sugarman, 1984). A survey undertaken by Sugarman (1981) showed that the vast majority of psychiatric residencies in the study provided some family therapy training, although the amount varied from none to 1000 hours with an average of 300 hours over the course of the residency. Sugarman also found that slightly more than half of the 51 training directors who replied (out of a total of 80 surveyed) viewed family therapy as a conceptual viewpoint, rather than merely as a technique of treatment. He also discovered a widespread belief that the different epistemology of family therapy is difficult to synthesize with the individual orientation traditionally used in psychiatry, although program representatives indicated that they had made the conceptual synthesis satisfactorily. Sugarman (1984) tackled the problems of integrating family therapy training into such psychiatry residency programs in his later paper, making recommendations for dialogue within departments, making the training and practice complementary to the philosophy of the total psychiatry department, tying family therapy into a comprehensive psychiatry program, and making family therapy training the "right size," meaning not too small and not too large too soon. He concluded that family therapy training in general psychiatry residency programs is continuing to evolve and that complex issues such as economic and political factors and territorial struggles between disciplines may slow down the integration at times.

Family practice physicians in both the United States and Canada also are involved in family therapy training in many of the existing family practice residency programs. Canadian residents in Montreal, Toronto, Guelph, Kitchener, Winnipeg, Calgary, and elsewhere in Canada are being required to develop some skill in family counseling, sexual counseling, and supportive care (Guldner, 1982). The picture is somewhat different and more varied in the more than 300 family practice residency programs in the United States. Generally, it seems to have been difficult to teach family systems theory to family physicians and to blend family systems theory with the discipline of family medicine (McDaniel & Amos, 1983). Portions of the difficulty have been associated with larger controversies within medicine about the nature of family practice itself (Schwenck, 1984). The new model of practice has been applied to several psychosocial problems such as substance abuse, depression, child discipline problems, and compliance with medication regimens (Doherty & Baird, 1983). One limited study of the results of using a voluntary family therapy training approach in a family practice residency program (Soman & Soman, 1983) obtained results as follows: "While residents did not develop expertise as family therapists, we feel that they were better able to make informed, constructive referrals and to be sensitive to family issues" (p. 76). This limited set of expectations appears to be more fitting in conceptualizing an appropriate role for family physicians than would be the expectation that they become primarily family therapists.

Bloch's (1981) introduction to a series of articles on family therapy training is interesting:

> It seems to me that their implications are clear: that training in family therapy at a sophisticated level is now to be a regular part of the future training of psychiatrists (possibly all physicians), psychologists, social workers, and psychiatric nurses and that, in addition, as a second distinctive career line, there is a new profession of family therapist, with its own entry point and academic pathway. My view is that society will support both lines of career development into the future as far as one can reasonably hope to see. (p. 131)

Accreditation

How does one determine whether a graduate program offers acceptable education and training in family therapy? There are many ways, but one of the more basic and reliable would be a demonstration that a given program met specified objective standards as judged by an outside group or organization. That is essentially what transpires through the process of accreditation. That is, the gaining of accredited status from a recognized accrediting body means that a graduate program has met the criteria for approval set forth in accepted and published standards. Other graduate programs that are not accredited may be equally strong or better, but there has been no impartial investigation and judgment to that effect. The content that has been offered in an accredited program not only has been shaped according to substantive guidelines but also has been presented in accordance with standards requiring a logical sequencing of courses and practical experiences. Faculty and supervisors must meet certain standards, as must the facilities in which the education and training occur.

Accreditation in general in the United States is of two types, general and specialized. The regional accrediting bodies such as the North Central Association of Colleges and Secondary Schools provide general accreditation for a university as a whole. Specialized accreditation covers a particular area or program; for example, social work programs are accredited by the Council on Social Work Education. A specialized body will accredit a chemistry program, and so on. Once again, accreditation has to do with institutions and programs, not with individuals. It is related to but separate from the standards for the practice of family therapy that guide individuals.

The relationship of accreditation to licensure often is misunderstood. State licensure in a field provides the public with minimum protection by screening out individuals who do not meet the criteria stated in law and by licensing those who meet the technical qualifications of the law. The state is limited in its ability to identify programs that meet minimum requirements for quality if there is no accreditation. Some few states may attempt to provide their own accreditation standards and agencies, for example, through a state department of education, but states generally rely on accrediting bodies that have national standing and are recognized by some national organization as a standard setter for the field. Ideally, licensing and accreditation work together to provide for quality education and training (through accreditation) and public protection of consumers of services (through licensure).

Specialized accreditation in the field of family therapy has a long background and a short history. The AAMC began a kind of accreditation work more than 30 years ago, initially on an intramural basis in conjunction with the preparation of individuals for membership in the organization. That is, the AAMC/AAMFC approved educational and training programs as a means of identifying places where preparation for practice and organizational membership were occurring. This pattern was followed until 1974, when the shift was made to independent accreditation in which there was no direct tie between programmatic accreditation and individual certification for practice or organizational membership (Nichols, 1979b). The then AAMFC board of directors was persuaded to turn its committee on training and standards into a committee on accreditation and to seek the recognition of the U. S. Department of Education (then in the Department of Health, Education, and Welfare) as an accrediting body for marriage and family counseling (the terminology still in use by the organization at that time).

The first manual on accreditation (Nichols, 1975a) was published in 1975, and an initial petition to the U. S. Office of Education was made in 1976. In denying the initial petition, the governmental committee took the unusual action of naming a special committee of experts from education, psychology, and family sociology to investigate the question of whether a separate field of education did exist or whether, as staff analysts had questioned, marital and family therapy was merely "an amalgam of psychology, social work, and pastoral counseling." Following the hearings and submission of a large amount of documentary evidence from established graduate degree programs, the special committee took the unequivocal stand that there was a separate and distinct field of study and recommended recognition of the AAMFC Committee on Accreditation as the accrediting body for the field in 1978. The historic action by the U.S. Office of Education marked the first recognition by an important outside agency of the fact that the separate and distinct academic and clinical discipline and field of education existed. Stated in another way, the meaning of the governmental recognition was that "it validated that the field has a separate body of theory and technique for which a distinct training process is appropriate" (Bloch & Weiss, 1981, pp. 145–146).

Later in 1978, the AAMFT renamed the committee the Commission on Accreditation for Marriage and Family Therapy Education. The committee/commission, already a quasi-autonomous organization that was financed by the AAMFT but that functioned independently of the policies and control of that body, formed an Advisory Committee on Education, Standards, and Training, composed of outstanding leaders from the field and took other steps to make its work representative of the field as a whole. The recognition of the commission was continued by the U.S. Office of Education in 1980 and again in 1984.

What graduating from an accredited program means for an individual depends in part on where he or she lives and intends to work. Judging from our experience as educators/trainers and from a continued monitoring of position advertisements, graduation from an accredited program seems to be increasingly required or listed as desirable by employers. Both the acquisition of credentials and the obtaining of jobs seem to be enhanced by graduation from an accredited program, because accreditation provides an acceptable attestation of quality by an independent standard-setting entity.

Credentialing

By way of review, we have indicated that credentials may be statutory (licensing/certification) and nonstatutory (voluntary certification, organizational, and other), and that credentials have varying amounts of value and recognition attached to them.

The route taken to obtaining credentials in the family therapy field contains both emotional and practical implications for the entrant. The emotional issue for many persons coming into family therapy from one of the older professions—medicine, nursing, psychology, or social work, for example—is whether the person regards himself or herself primarily as a psychiatrist, psychologist, nurse, or social worker who "does" family therapy or explicitly as a family therapist who is doubly credentialed. The practical issue is whether the individual decides to retain the dual identity or, again, to stick with the older and safer designation as a member of one of the more established professions (Framo, 1975; Haley, 1975). Individuals from one of the older professions who take up an identity primarily as a family therapist often experience either conflict with or condescension from their more traditional colleagues. The temptation can be very strong to stay close to the original profession and not to become too different from more traditional peers. Pressures can become quite intense when conflicts arise between professions, making it difficult to maintain a dual identity.

Those entering the field of family therapy directly from a background of education and training only in family therapy, however, face a much more difficult experience and task in establishing themselves than individuals who carry a dual identity. Our examination with aspiring graduate students of the question of whether they are prepared to be "bastards" is not merely an exercise in dramatization or perversity. Persons seeking to establish themselves solely as family therapists at this stage in history need to be prepared for struggles to be recognized. They *may be better prepared* to function as family therapists than they would be if they had come through a graduate or professional program in another field—that is, as graduates in family therapy, they may know more and be better prepared substantively and clinically than their colleagues from the more traditional disciplines—*but* their efforts to gain recognition probably will be more difficult and painful than those efforts coming from members of the more established professions. Psychology, for example, went through similar struggles a few decades ago. Social work's history is replete with chronicles of struggles for recognition.

Entry into the professional world through one of the older professions gives one easier access, more ready acceptance, and a preexisting credential that can be claimed by meeting the criteria for that field. The recognition gained as a member of the more established profession often makes it possible for an individual to function without recognition or credentialing as a family therapist and without going through the arduous task of mastering the substantive materials of family study. Individuals who are credentialed in one of those fields also may be in a position to secure third-party reimbursement for their services. That is, as members of that profession, they may be positioned so as to be reimbursed by third party payers for whatever kind of psychotherapy that they perform—whether they are doing individual psychotherapy or family therapy—because they are members of a profession that is recognized for reimbursement. Our point here is not that pleas should be made for reimbursement for family therapy or family therapists, but that those persons entering the field through one of the older professions may have recognition for what they do whether or not they are educated and trained adequately and appropriately to perform the services. On the other hand, individuals coming into the family therapy field through the route of actual preparation for what they are doing may not be recognized and rewarded without a struggle, and sometimes not even then, insofar as parity with other professions is concerned.

Securing recognition for one's education, training, and ability to deliver needed services in an adequate and appropriate way does not come easily or rapidly. Legitimacy—the recognition by all pertinent parties that family therapy is a legitimate profession in the mental health field and that family therapists are legitimate health care providers—will come even more slowly than general recognition that family therapists exist. The meaning of most credentials, including a license, is that the holder possesses certain qualifications and meets certain standards with regard to education and training. They do not denote that an individual possesses a given level of competence.

Legal regulation of the field in the United States has been in effect for nearly a quarter century. California passed a marriage, family, and child counselor bill in 1963 that covered both the use of the title and the practice of "marriage, family, and child counseling." That weak law has been amended many times but was still receiving criticism from family therapy leaders at the time of this writing. Other states providing regulation in one form or another of marital and family counseling/therapy are Michigan (1966), New Jersey (1968), Nevada (1973), Utah (1973), Georgia (1976 and 1984), North Carolina (1979), Florida (1982), Connecticut (1983), South Carolina (1985), and Tennessee (1985). The regulations range from licensure with full title and practice protection and restriction to North Carolina's pure title-protection law, which does not restrain anyone from practicing but does prevent them from advertising themselves as a "certified marital and family therapist" unless they are state certified. Georgia's original law was removed from the books through a "sunset" action but a new law was passed in 1984. The Michigan and Utah laws and boards both survived sunset review in the early 1980s, both evidently coming out of the review process in stronger positions than they had previously occupied.

Professional Organizations: United States and Canada

Two major organizations are to be found in the family therapy field in the United States and Canada, the AAMFT and the American Family Therapy Association (AFTA). There is a certain amount of overlap between the membership of the two groups, although the AAMFT is large (approximately 14,000 members at the time of writing) and has no plans to limit its growth, whereas AFTA has consciously determined to hold its membership in the hundreds.

The larger organization, as noted earlier, was founded in 1942 as the American Association of Marriage Counselors and remained small until membership requirements were changed in the late 1960s and membership expansion became an official policy. The name was changed to the American Association of Marriage and Family Counselors in 1970 and to the American Association for Marriage and Family Therapy in 1979. Members are grouped into divisions in most of the states and Canadian provinces. A person joins at the national level and is automatically made a member of a geographically constituted division. The association holds an annual meeting and at times in the past sponsored special conferences and regional meetings. Since 1980, it has left the field of special and regional meetings to its divisions. It publishes the *Journal of Marital and Family Therapy* and the *Family Therapy News*.

The AAMFT has an active student organization and has tied itself strongly to the development of graduate education and strong clinical supervision. Not only does it provide the financial support for the Commission on Accreditation for Marriage and Family Therapy Education, but it also now has a quasi-autonomous Commission on Supervision, which identifies and certifies Approved Supervisors. The organization has recognized and encouraged the development of supervisors for more than 2 decades, and created the category of Approved Supervisor in 1971. The recent move to a commission approach, rather than a committee pattern, also included widening the mechanisms for obtaining approval to ensure that the entire field of family therapy and not merely the organization's needs would be served in the process of finding, recognizing, training, and certifying supervisors.

The AFTA was officially founded in 1979, after some of the founding members had been meeting as an interim board and guiding group for more than a year. Following a considerable amount of internal discussion and ferment about the role of the organization and formation of a liaison committee to explore issues of common concern with the AAMFT in 1981, a complementary relationship was worked out between the two organizations. AFTA decided to remain a small organization composed of experienced and senior researchers and teachers of family therapy and not to involve itself in issues of credentialing, accreditation, and the like. AFTA publishes a newsletter for its members and holds an annual meeting. Both AFTA and AAMFT are now headquartered in Washington, D.C.

Professional Organizations: Outside North America

Family therapy education and organizational life grew rapidly on the international scene during the 1970s in particular and have shown no signs of letting up in the 1980s. What follows is intended to serve as an illustrative rather than as a complete description of such developments. We doubt that it would be possible to provide an exhaustive listing of organizations and facilities, because such a list would be suffering from some degree of obsolescence by the time it was published, given the ferment and growth of family therapy in the world today.

Much, if not most, of the development started at the local level in the countries where family therapy has flowered outside of North America. Family therapy in Australia, as reported by Stagoll (1981), "has evolved through the usual stages." Drawing on an account by the editor of the *Australian Journal of Family Therapy* (founded 1979), he describes the picture "Down Under" as follows:

The first stage was in the 1950s and 1960s, with isolated and sometimes ridiculed pioneers. In the early and mid 1970s the second stage emerged when the early pioneers were joined by therapists returning from overseas training. . . . From 1979–80 a third stage is identifiable with the linking up of the various pockets of family therapy activity via a journal, a national conference, and the formation of state associations. (p. D)

South America's development has been uneven. "Although family therapy has been a growing movement in Brazil for some years, there is no association to connect its practitioners nor a journal to spread and link their knowledge and findings" (DeMello, 1982). By contrast, the Center for Family and Marital Therapy in Buenos Aires, Argentina, often has been regarded as a pioneer center for South America. The Argentine Association for Family Therapy was founded in 1978. By 1982 it had a membership of 300 and published the *Argentine Journal of Family Therapy*. Chile's development has been somewhat slower. The first family institute in that country, the Institutio de Terapia de Santiago, was founded in 1983.

South Africa saw the development of local institutes by the late 1960s. By the early 1970s, the South African Family Therapy Institute, the equivalent of a professional organization in other countries, had been organized and had 10 members. By 1981 it had grown to 600 members.

There were important developments in Italy and Switzerland in 1967 and 1968. The Institute for Marriage and Family in Zurich opened in the former year, as did the Institute of Family Studies in Milan where Mara Selvini-Palazzoli and associates decided to adopt a pure systems orientation after being impressed with the Palo Alto group's ideas. Selvini-Palazzoli's group developed its own version of a systems approach, now called "systemic" in Europe. The Milan Associates later became the name by which Selvini-Palazzoli and colleagues were known. Maurizio Andolfi's Institute of Family Studies in Rome was founded in 1968. By 1975, the Italian Society for Family Therapy was strong enough to conduct its first international family therapy conference, which was followed by another in 1978.

The first family therapy journal in Europe, *Fokus pa Familien*, appeared in Norway in 1973 as a quarterly publication. Under the sponsorship of the Church Counselling Central Organization and a private psychiatric clinic, it flourished. By 1980 the journal had approximately 1,800 subscribers in the Scandinavian countries. Norway had several training programs by 1980.

Family therapy boomed in Germany by the mid-1970s. Following a period of study in the United States, Helm Stierlin established the Heidelberg Institute as part of the university there in 1974. A half-dozen years later, there were six or so training centers in operation and a journal, *Familien dynamik*, coedited by Stierlin.

The Iberian Peninsula probably can count its significant beginnings in family therapy organization from 1977. That was the year that the Portuguese Society for Family Therapy was founded by eight mental health technicians. Simultaneously, the first private center for family therapy was started. The first national meeting of Spanish family therapists occurred in Zaragoza in 1981. It represented an initial attempt to coordinate a variety of different independent family therapy efforts in Spain.

1977 also saw the beginning of national organization in Israel. The Israel Association for Marital and Family Therapy was organized that year during the Second International Congress of Family Therapy. The Israeli organization has a national board of directors and regional branches. By 1982 it had 300 members.

Although family therapy was late in coming to the United Kingdom according to Howells (1978), it has developed rather strongly. The Association for Family Therapy was formed in 1975 and had 1,000 members in the United Kingdom by 1982 and 1,600 by 1984. The Institute of Family Therapy was founded in London in 1977. A Family Institute at Cardiff had originated in 1971. The *Journal of Family Therapy* was inaugurated in 1979. The national organization holds a major annual conference and has several regional branches and groups that meet throughout the year in different parts of Great Britain.

Among the other organizations formed recently was the Dutch Association for Relations and Family Therapy, which was founded in 1983. There had been interest in family therapy in the Netherlands since 1963, but no national organization was established until 2 decades after the initial birth of interest in this approach to dealing with human problems and difficulties.

A year earlier, 1982, the inaugural conference of another North American organization was held. Canadian professionals formed the Canadian Association for the Treatment and Study of the Family.

ENTRY INTO THE PROFESSION

The focus in this section is on how individuals enter into the profession of family therapy. This is not the same as how one begins to "do" family therapy. Rather, it involves how individuals secure an identity as a family therapist, how they learn to think and act like a professional in the field. We are aware, as we have indicated, that many practitioners have entered the field as an outgrowth of practicing first in another field and moving gradually into family therapy. Similarly, we also are well aware that an increasing number of persons are coming into the field in the United States directly through basic graduate and professional education and training in family therapy. There are differences in the socialization processes attached to those two routes. We are concerned primarily with the socialization process in the latter instance, that is, with those entering through the route of basic education and training as family therapists.

Professional Socialization

The educational experiences provided by the profession generally are expected to be responsible for the dual functions of transmitting a theoretical base of knowledge and applied skills and inculcating the values and norms of that particular profession's culture. Socialization for a profession involves more than the acquisition of substantive knowledge and the attainment of practice skills. It also entails securing the integration of attitudes and beliefs regarding the place of the profession in the society and one's role within that profession. Professional socialization, broadly speaking, is the process by which one learns the necessary norms, values, and roles to become a functional member of a particular occupational group and culture. It is a kind of initiation into a new role and culture (Hughes, 1956).

Occupational socialization is different from the socialization experiences of children being inducted into the society and culture in which they live. As Pavalko (1971) has noted, the comparative socialization experiences of children and adults can be contrasted in two ways. First, children acquire norms and roles where none existed previously, whereas adults must learn new roles and norms and unlearn others. Second, adult socialization, in contrast to that of the child, is essentially voluntary.

At this stage in the development of the field of family therapy, very little is known about the motivations that attract students to graduate and professional education and training in the field. We think that both the role of the family therapist in the society—still quite ambiguous in many respects—and the prior experiences or lack of experiences of the aspiring students with professional family therapists help to make the socialization process more difficult for all concerned than the work of socializing individuals into more established professions and occupational groups. Military schools and medical schools, by contrast, certainly attract students who have had opportunities to observe and often to interact with and to relate to practitioners of those respective occupations. Similarly, most aspiring dentists have had considerable contact with one or more dentists, and some psychology and social work students have had the opportunity to observe or form impressions about those occupational groups.

We do not know what kinds of experiences students entering family therapy graduate programs have had with professional practitioners in the field. Most probably have not had the opportunity to observe family therapists at work. Few seem to have been involved in family therapy personally with their family of origin. Our supposition is that this lack of experience and opportunity to observe and interact with members of the profession makes the task of forming an image of what family therapy is like and what a family therapist does much more difficult than if extensive contact and observation had been possible. The image that they have is likely to be more vague and ill defined in comparison to those preformed ideas arising out of contact with or opportunity to observe members of other professions even if only in their functioning as citizens in the community.

We recognize that altering the image that beginning students have of the field from a romanticized view to a more realistic one is a problem for any faculty educating and training occupational groups. This is true at an undergraduate nursing level, where a highly glamorized view of "helping people" in a Florence Nightingale fashion has to be replaced with a more realistic view and at a law school level, where students seeking certainty and possessing distorted ideas of helping to make justice prevail have to revise their outlooks to allow for uncertainty, the existence of large areas of gray, and an awareness that justice may not even be distinguishable at times, much less clearly accomplished. Educators in family therapy graduate programs and their students may not have so much unlearning to contend with as those in other programs, but they do have the problem of forming views and images in the face of deficiencies in experience and prior solid and accurate conceptualizations concerning the profession. The paucity of experience and shortage of models may help to account for the rather widespread tendency of students and other newcomers to the field to glamorize certain highly visible spokespersons and practitioners.

During the process of professional socialization, the student/trainee specifically acquires a professional identity, commitment to the field, and a sense of career. Part of the process of socialization consists of identification with the elements of the occupation itself and part with identification with persons. Bucher and Stelling (1977) have studied the process of becoming professional, identifying in doing so five dimensions of the concept of professional identity: a definition of the nature of the field—its boundaries, basic tools and methods, and the problems with which it is concerned; beliefs about the mission of the profession—the larger social values that it serves; the appropriate conditions for performing the work of the field; the appropriate relationship among practitioners and clients, colleagues, and workers in other fields; and where the field fits within the larger society. A considerable amount of emphasis has been placed on identification with teachers and supervisors for those being educated and trained in clinical occupations (Everett, 1980a). The part played by identification with the "heroes" in the field and by *esprit de corps*—a feeling of identification with peers in the field during both the education/training and the subsequent phases of practicing—is difficult to assess precisely, but appears to be important for producing and maintaining a sense of identification with the field for many persons.

The research of Bucher and Stelling (1977), as they studied the professional socialization process involving trainees in four medical programs, was interesting in that it showed the process of identification taking several diverse forms. Charismatic models were found to be too high, too far above the trainees to draw anything other than attempts to approximate what the individual represented. Trainees, in other words, could not see themselves being like the charismatic models. Bucher and Stelling found that the trainees constructed their own ideal models and put together a composite of what they would like to see themselves become as professionals. It seems likely that this was the case both because the trainees were going into well-established fields and because there were a sizable number of teachers and supervisors from whom they were able to pick and choose in putting together their ideal models. Within programs, they found that role playing, or doing the work of a professional in a field; the use of role models; the use of peer groups in training; and other factors contributed to the outcome of the professional socialization process.

Career, the second component that we listed for professional identity, has been defined as "a succession of related jobs, arranged in a hierarchy of prestige, through which persons move in an orderly (more or less predictable) sequence" (Wilensky, 1961, p. 523). For students entering the field through graduate education in family therapy, there is available a fairly predictable sequence. First, they are students and trainees. Second, they enter the field as new graduates who must work under supervision for a specified period of time in order to obtain a credential that either attests that they are considered capable of practicing on their own through recognition by a professional organization (the AAMFT) or by state licensure/certification. Third, they move into a status in which they are recognized as independent professionals who can work on their own without supervision, establishing relationships with their colleagues within and outside the field in which they are accepted as peers. Up to this point, it would seem that the model envisioned by many students/trainees for step three has been that of private practice. What we refer to here when we speak of independent practice is the recognition that the practitioners can function on their own, either in an agency or institutional setting or in independent, private practice. The question is not whether an individual is ready for a salaried position or for functioning on a fee-for-service basis in private practice, but whether or not that person has reached the stage of making clinical decisions without the necessity of being supervised. The stage of independent practice does not have to do with compensation but with decision making and the assumption of responsibility for work and action. Beyond the third step are other stages such as those of teaching and training, of preparing other persons for functioning in the field. Entering into a research role within the field would appear to be taking a parallel path.

Commitment to the field, to the profession, is a complex phenomenon. Not only does it involve an internal disposition of positive feelings toward the field and the work involved but also toward other persons who are doing the same work (Coser & Rockoff, 1971). Kanter (1968) has referred to "continuance commitment"—the commitment to continuing membership and participation in the occupational group and social system—and to "cohesion commitment"—the formation and continuation of affective ties and attachments with colleagues and social relationships in the professional group. Involvement in the field following completion of one's education and training generally is necessary in order to nourish and maintain the sense of commitment and thus to continue one of the major elements of identification with the profession.

Medical education has been recognized as the prototype of professional socialization. Friedson (1970) has suggested that medical education is the single most important factor in determining professional practice through its process of socializing one to become a physician. The intensity of the medical socialization experience has been described by Hughes (1956) as follows: "One might say that the learning of the medical role consists of a separation, almost an alienation, of the student from the lay medical world; a passing through the mirror so that one looks out on the world from behind it, and sees things as in mirror writing" (p. 14). We are not suggesting that such alienation is desirable for family therapy students—it may not be that desirable for medical students and physicians—but simply are pointing out that an emphasis on learning what is essential to one's profession is an important part of forming one's professional identity.

There is no direct parallel between education/training and socialization into family therapy and similar processes in another profession. Probably the clearest analogies are to be drawn from studies on the field of psychotherapy. Henry, Sims, and Spray (1971, 1973) have traced the process by which individuals from the broad fields of medicine, psychology, and social work direct themselves into the specialties of psychiatry, psychoanalysis, clinical psychology, and psychiatric social work, and by which some individuals from each of those routes move into the "fifth profession" of psychotherapy. They found that the social backgrounds and cultural origins of those entering into what they termed the "fifth profession" were highly similar. As indicated earlier, we are not all that well-informed about the motivations, and the backgrounds, of individuals entering family therapy as a profession so that we can make broad generalizations. However, we suspect that the conflicts of those entering the new profession of family therapy—whether from one of the more established professions or from direct entry at the graduate level—are greater than those of individuals who retain a basic identity in one of the older professions and begin to practice primarily as a psychotherapist. Psychotherapy, in general, can be described as a "profession" only if quote marks are put around the term. It is an activity, one that we think should be engaged in only by professional persons, but psychotherapy itself is not a profession based on a solid body of substantive knowledge in the sense that psychology or family therapy rest on such foundations. The situation does parallel that faced by family therapists, in that individuals becoming psychotherapists do face conflict and identity problems, but, in our estimation, at a lower level of intensity than family therapists.

Supervision: Orientations, Emphases, and Issues

Supervision, as an aspect of clinical education and professional socialization, performs the vital function of linking for the student the acquisition of theoretical knowledge with the learning of clinical skills. The kind of supervision that the student/trainee receives is, understandably enough, related to the theoretical orientation of the supervisor(s). Emphases tend to vary considerably. We shall describe two broad and different approaches and the particular emphases accompanying each one, acknowledging as we do that we run the risk of oversimplifying the picture.

Historically, clinical supervision in psychotherapy arose in connection with the training of individual psychotherapists and was especially influenced by the training of psychoanalysts and psychodynamically oriented therapists. Modifications of what can be termed the "classical psychodynamic" approach most recently described by Ekstein and Wallerstein (1972) have come into the family therapy supervision field (Everett, 1980a, 1980b).

Individual dynamics are the focus in psychodynamically oriented supervision. The focus is on individual dynamics in the client, in the supervisee, and in the supervisory relationship. The task of the student is to be able to perform individual diagnosis and to gain understanding of the ways in which the intrapsychic conflicts of the individuals may be projected onto the marriage and acted out in marriage and family relationships. The intrapsychic conflicts are seen as coming from problems rooted in the individual's past. In supervision, psychodynamically oriented supervisors have the task of recognizing and managing intrapsychic conflicts or resistances in the student (and perhaps in themselves) that interfere with the supervisory process or the treatment of clients. This does not mean that the supervisor serves as a therapist for the supervisee. Psychotherapy for a trainee may be recommended by the supervisor (Everett, 1979) or provided by the program in a coordinated but separate manner (Nichols, 1968). The student's personal growth and development, including abilities to employ clinical skills, are carefully monitored in supervision.

Supervision in a psychodynamic approach usually is given to individuals, although small-group supervision sometimes is provided. As noted earlier, observation of the student at work through a one-way mirror had long been used in individual psychotherapy training and was brought over into family therapy training. Examination and analysis of the student's extensive intake materials, continuing process notes, and audio recording were the staples of what we have termed "retrospective supervision." By retrospective supervision we refer to supervision performed after a session with clients has been completed, rather than during an ongoing appointment with an individual, couple, or family. Although supervisors may observe a session in progress, they do not interfere with the ongoing treatment, but deal with issues later in the supervisory hour. The use of mechanical aids in supervision was considered more appropriate by those dynamically oriented supervisors who viewed supervision as primarily a learning experience in which the focus was essentially on the client/patient. Others, who saw it as more of an interactional task between supervisor and supervisee, were more likely to attend more closely to the content of the supervisory hour and of the therapeutic hour in some instances and to use the supervisory hour content as "prime data" for understanding and comprehension.

The other approach in the traditional tripartite perception of dynamic supervision into process-centered, patient-centered, and therapist-centered, allows for a developmental approach to supervising students. A two-stage process involving initially the use of a preceptorship role for students, followed by an apprenticeship stage for the more experienced trainee, has been described by Ard (1973). Nichols (1975b) described the use of close, intensive supervision with beginning students, which gradually moved to a form of consultative relationship in which the trainee took the major responsibility for bringing issues to the supervisor.

The focus on the student as the major concern and the use of a developmental approach to supervision in which the form depends on the background, experience, and skill of the trainee also is a model used by some systemically oriented supervisors.

What we are describing here as a systemic approach to supervision has some quite different emphases from the individual approach of psychodynamic orientations. Under the general heading of a systemic family approach we are including supervision from a general systemic orientation, from a structural, and from an existential or experiential viewpoint. All of these have in common the focus on family dynamics and process rather than individual dynamics and process. The focus may be more specifically on such things as communication patterns in the family or on the reorganization of dysfunctional relationships and interaction. The task of the therapist is to learn how to enter, join, or otherwise work with a family system in order to recognize and manage the dysfunctional components for the purpose of effecting change, while simultaneously maintaining a therapeutic position as a helper. Supervisors who have been intensely concerned with how the student manages to perform those tasks have tended to use three broad approaches, video recordings, "live" supervision, and cotherapy. The use of cotherapy, in which the supervisor serves as one of the therapists, has been advocated by Whitaker (Keith & Whitaker; 1977; Napier & Whitaker, 1978).

So-called "live supervision" in which the supervisor observes the trainee's work with a family from behind a one-way mirror and intervenes in the ongoing process has a variety of forms. Sometimes not only the supervisor but also other trainees watch the student's work and offer either observations, suggestions, or directions. Such input may come about in one or more ways, for example, calling the student out of the room, entering the room and joining in as a cotherapist, taking over the treatment and requesting that the student observe, or using a telephone to call the student during the session. The preceived values of live supervision have been rather widely discussed and various approaches described and illustrated (Birchler, 1975; Haley, 1976; Kempster & Savitsky, 1967; Montalvo, 1973). These include the ability of the supervisor to gain direct observation and make direct interventions, instead of having to wait and discuss issues in a later supervisory session as would be the case with retrospective supervision. The maintenance of therapeutic control by the supervisor also has been described as a value of live supervision. Other advantages have been described, such as the ability to quickly correct or to avoid misperceptions because of the presence and involvement of the supervisor and the opportunity to comprehend nonverbal behavior in particular. (The latter task can also be accomplished through the use of video recordings that can be viewed in retrospective supervision.) One other perceived advantage is the opportunity for the supervisor to deal with both the student and the family and not simply with the student.

Criticisms of live supervision and particularly of its misuse have been voiced by some observers such as Russell (1976). Specifically, he has pointed to the interference posed by supervisors who intervene too actively and excessively in the sessions, thus providing problems for both the trainee and the family. Russell has been specifically disapproving of the use of the "bug in the ear" technique, indicating that it provides distraction and interference for the student. Additional criticisms have been made by Nichols (1975b), who has named the unnecessary production of anxiety for the trainee, the creation of unnecessary dependence on the part of the student on supervisory intervention and control, the potential stunting of professional growth and development on the part of the student, and interference with the therapeutic process so that the service needs of the case (i.e., the concerns that the family get "good treatment") take precedence over the educational and training needs of the developing young professional. It is possible to get quick movement on the part of trainees with live supervision and extensive supervisory involvement, but the literature of the field dealing with live supervision has not to this point paid much attention to the long-term effects of such teaching and training methods on the career development of students.

This is not to imply that family therapists are not concerned with the growth and personal development of students. Many are, and require that students participate in therapy as an adjunctive experience in their training (Kaslow, 1977). The focus, however, is not on individual psychotherapy, as has been the case in traditional psychotherapy training, but on family or marital therapy for the trainees (Framo, 1975; Guldner, 1978). The immediate tie with the treatment being provided is the need for the student to be sufficiently individuated and differentiated from his or her family of origin to be able to work effectively with other families. Therapeutic work with the therapist's own family of origin has become, as noted earlier, a very important part of the family therapy field. One approach has the student being "coached" (Bowen, 1978) on how to return to the family of origin and to deal with unresolved issues with parents and siblings, as is done by some family therapists with clients. Another approach, as noted, calls for bringing in the parents and other members of the family of origin for therapy sessions with the student.

The supervisor is in a very powerful role, particularly in those cases in which one individual performs most of the supervision. This holds true whether the supervisor is functioning in a university setting as part of a graduate program or in a private practice setting. The power comes in part from the dependency relationship between supervisor and supervisee in which the students rely on a more seasoned and veteran member of the profession to guide them into performing at a more effective and knowledgeable level and in part from the dependency relationship element in which the supervisor serves as a gatekeeper who has some power over the aspirant's attainment of credentials and entry to the field.

The best model of supervision in our judgment is one in which the supervisor functions as a professional person who is ethically concerned with the needs of clients and with the needs of the learner and who balances those needs in an appropriate way so that the student's development and learning are enhanced and adequate treatment is provided. Not only does the supervisor keep in mind who is supposed to be the therapist—the trainee and not the supervisor—but also the supervisor should retain a commitment to the provision of therapy based on the best theoretical knowledge that can be mastered by the trainee. Both supervisor and supervisee strive to continually update the knowledge on which treatment is based. We make it as clear as we can to our students that we expect them to identify with and follow the principles enunciated here as they develop their own skills and styles of performing therapy. We do not expect or desire them to follow slavishly our ways of treating families but to follow similar principles while doing therapy ethically, knowledgeably, and responsibly in their own manner.

One last note on the relationship between the education of students and their clinical training: The integration of theory and practice in the process of professional socialization is intended to facilitate the growth of students toward becoming competent clinicians. This can only be done effectively if there is an appropriate sequencing of coursework leading into the clinical practicum experience. Personality theory, psychopathology, and family studies should come early in the educational program, followed by clinically related courses on marital and family therapy theories, and courses in professional development. When possible, such background and foundational materials must be mastered in an orderly sequence prior to involvement in clinical work. Experiences in which we have served as consultants— one graduate program experiencing ineffective clinical work by students and frustration among supervisors was found to permit the taking of courses in psychopathology and personality theory at any time in the clinical year, and another did not require a course in marital therapy until 6 months after students began supervised practicum work—demonstrate some of the problems in taking students into clinical work without building a proper foundation of substantive knowledge (Everett, 1980a, 1980b).

Career Development

Professional preparation or preparation for functioning as a professional should be undertaken and conducted with a career development perspective in mind. That is, the educational and training experiences of the person entering the field of family therapy should be tailored to both the particular stage of development of the student/trainee and to the future needs and goals of that individual. This emphasis is not only consistent with our earlier position regarding tailoring of treatment to the needs of the family as opposed to fitting the family to the therapeutic approach of the clinician but is also consistent with our observation as clinicians and clinical educators that the preparation and maturing of family therapists is a lengthy and multistaged process. To bring a clinician in the field to the point that he or she is functioning as a mature, first-rate clinician or even one working at the top of his or her professional skill level requires many years of experience and development following the completion of graduate work and professional training.

A career development perspective embodies the idea that a professional person moves along a path that has various stages. While the stages may not be as well demarcated for the family therapy field as they are for some others that have been in existence longer, three stages are emerging as fairly definitive: the first is education/training within the context of graduate school; the second is a period of postdegree experience under supervision; and the third is independent practice. There may be other stages formed in the future, including those of researcher and teacher.

At the present, we also can point to stages in the learning of family therapy, such as the processes that students typically go through in learning approaches in graduate school, getting out of school and beginning to challenge some of what they have learned, going into a process of reexamination of their knowledge, and repeating the process over again, perhaps several times, during the course of their professional career. A significant part of this process involves casting aside their early modeling after others and identifying with the work of others and replacing that modeling with treatment approaches, orientations, and techniques that are more compatible with their own life experiences, belief systems, and personality. The process of integrating theory and practice that began earlier proceeds in more complex and enduring ways as their career unfolds.

PROFESSIONAL PRACTICE

What are the major issues facing therapists once they complete graduate or professional education in family therapy? For the individual receiving education and retraining in order to move from another discipline into family therapy, the issues would be essentially the same. The matters that we will discuss in this section are the work setting for the family therapist's practice, reimbursement for services, the use of research, ethical concerns, and continued professional development. Our focus here is primarily on the United States, although part of what we have to say applies to other settings as well.

Work Setting

Where will family therapists work and practice their profession, delivering services to clientele? To date, the demands for such services have been sufficiently high to make it possible for the field to absorb sizable numbers of individuals into the private practice area under a fee-for-service delivery system. Depending on the location, a therapist may have to be licensed/certified by the state before launching into independent practice. Generally, that requires working for a period ranging from 2 to 5 years under supervision acceptable to the licensing body. In our judgment, if the young professional—young either in age or in years in the field—wishes to proceed in a way that typically is regarded as the most appropriate and responsible fashion, he or she will work under the supervision of an experienced family therapist for at least 2 years before "hanging out a shingle" as an independent practitioner of family therapy, whether or not such supervised experience is required by law.

The field of private practice on a fee-for-service basis may or may not continue to be a viable possibility on a large scale for those whose sole identity is that of family therapist. Not only the number of practitioners entering the field from graduate programs in family therapy—still comparatively small but growing—but also the volume of individuals from other professions who enter the field with or without education/training in family therapy and with or without licensure/certification in those jurisdictions providing for legal regulation of the field, as well as several other factors such as a changing reimbursement picture, may make the outlook less bright for future graduates who wish to be solo practitioners.

There are locales in the United States in which the provision of supervision to individuals wishing to become credentialed as family therapists has become a major part of some established practitioners' practice and income. An apprenticeship pattern has been followed in which the established practitioner has served not only as a supervisor but also in many instances as a gatekeeper. Such a pyramiding system cannot be expected to continue indefinitely. Not only the growth of graduate programs but also recent changes in the supervisory picture can be expected to make significant alterations in the apprenticeship model. Among these is the continued proliferation of graduate programs in family therapy, which is occurring even in a period of academic cutbacks and university limitation of programs.

The field at this time is still able to absorb doctoral graduates into private practice and educational settings. Many of the graduate programs and postdegree training institutes still have difficulties at times in finding doctoral level family therapists to fill teaching and supervisory positions. A small but evidently growing number of university positions also call for individuals who can perform research specifically in family therapy. The new developments in family therapy require researchers who can perform their work specifically in family therapy, and not merely in the family studies area or in the area of psychotherapy in general, and whose research in this area is comparable in caliber to that in other fields (Gurman, 1983; Sprenkle & Piercy, 1984).

As graduate programs have arisen and have turned out increasing numbers of graduates in family therapy, larger numbers of those graduates inevitably have sought positions in various kinds of clinics and agencies. This has been particularly true for masters degree graduates. Some have held clinical placements in community agencies and have continued to work in the agency following graduation, the progression from student/ trainee to employee/staff member being a natural one. Others have sought employment wherever they could find it and have ended up in clinic and agency positions either by choice or by default.

Several issues face graduates who move into agency and clinical settings. The problems set forth graphically by Framo (1975) and Haley (1975) when family therapy was added to community mental health centers and the "horror stories" told by others of their experiences in the 1960s when they began to practice family therapy—ostracism and pressures of various kinds—in institutional settings probably are not occurring in the same ways today because family therapy has become more accepted. However, entering a mental health agency on the same level as other practitioners and staff members often is not possible for family therapists. The position descriptions and requirements typically are written with practitioners and graduates of the older professions such as psychology and social work in mind. Social work agencies can use family therapists with masters degrees and meet the accreditation criteria for social work and child welfare agencies. However, family therapists may be compensated at a lower level than staff members with masters degrees in social work. Another group with whom family therapists often have to compete for positions on mental health clinic staffs are "substance abuse counselors," who have been added to traditional agencies, mental health centers, and to free-standing substance-abuse clinics. Alcoholism was identified as a major health and industrial problem in the 1950s and other forms of chemical dependency and abuse came to the fore as a major problem in the 1960s. Sometimes, family therapists have to be hired under another title such as psychologist or counselor in order to gain a staff position and to practice family therapy. However, due both to the demand for family therapy related services from the public and the wider acceptance of family therapy by mental health programs, the climate is clearly improving with regard to the hiring of family therapists and the designation of family therapy positions in mental health settings.

The situation for family therapists in free-standing family institutes is not much better than in private practice, agencies, mental health clinics and social work settings. There are still problems of being recognized, credentialed, and regarded as legitimate, as well as being compensated in such settings. Individuals from the older and more established professions who work in family institutes do not face the same problems or confront them to the same degree as those family therapists who do not have another professional credential.

The field faces several interrelated tasks with regard to providing positions for family therapists in a variety of work settings. Currently, some of these tasks are being pursued by professionals and by professional organizations. They include securing the inclusion of a definition and description of the family therapist in the U. S. Department of Labor's *Dictionary of Occupational Titles,* an authoritative source in the federal and state occupational worlds. Also, legislation and guidelines need to be secured that would make it possible for family therapists to secure positions in community mental health centers and in military and veterans' programs and facilities, that is, for them to fill such positions as family therapists and to provide family therapy services. In addition, legislation and personnel system requirements at the state level in the United States (and the provincial level in Canada) need to be examined and changes made that would make it possible for family therapists to work as family therapists in hospitals, medical centers, substance-abuse clinics, university clinics, juvenile and family court settings, and health maintenance organizations, as well as to be included in such new health delivery services as preferred provider organizations.

At this stage it is not possible to predict how long independent practice will be a viable option for professionals from any one of the mental health fields. Several factors are involved, including the shifting patterns of reimbursement from fee-for-service to capitation, prospective reimbursement, and other patterns intended to place a cap on spiraling health care costs; and the industrialization of the health care field through the assumption of care and delivery of service through large corporate structures.

Reimbursement

Reimbursement for services of family therapists in the private fee-for-service sector has been primarily through payment for the services by clients. There has been little direct third-party payment for family therapy as such. Some family therapy service has been paid for by third-party payers under the general heading of psychotherapy, with payment being made for the services of professionals who hold credentials and vendorship status as psychiatric physicians, psychologists, or perhaps social workers.

Family therapists have been reimbursed directly under the Civilian Health and Medical Program Uniformed Services (CHAMPUS) for treatment of dependents of military personnel, provided certain conditions pertaining to peer review and physician referral and supervision are met. A few privately insured groups and organizations providing employee assistance services have designated the directory of clinical members of the AAMFT as a source from which the names of reimbursable clinicians may be drawn. That is, they have decided to use that directory as a guide for determining which providers will be eligible, much as other third-party payers use the *National Register of Health Service Providers in Psychology* (Council for . . . , 1983) as a guide. Such determinations are voluntary.

Freedom-of-choice legislation at the state level that would permit users to select family therapists as providers who could be reimbursed when such services were insured and reimbursable has been very rare. Given the general concern over containment of health care costs at the present time, it seems that freedom-of-choice legislation or any other steps that could be viewed by legislators as potentially increasing costs or even not decreasing costs could face rough sledding. Florida's 1983 passage of such legislation was a rarity.

In general, reimbursement appears to be headed in the direction of payment by the consumer. One potential benefit of not being dependent on third-party payers is that those providers who have established fee levels affordable to consumers on a direct pay basis and who have maintained reputations for helpful service may not be ruined if third-party payment passes from the scene. If, however, the industrialization of the health care field proceeds to the extent that salaried individuals who are otherwise protected by large-scale organizations are competing against independent practitioners—including psychologists and social workers—the disadvantages of the independent provider will be very great.

Use of Research

The family therapist's acquaintance with research methodology and research findings begun during graduate education days is only the beginning of the use of research in an informed professional career. As noted earlier, doctoral students are trained to perform research as well as to be consumers of research. Masters level students should be equipped to function as intelligent consumers of research findings throughout the course of their professional careers.

Research recently has experienced a resurgence to a position of prime importance in the family therapy field. Wynne (1983), in accepting the first family therapy research award of the AAMFT, declared that research had again become an intrinsic component of the family therapy field following a period in the 1960s and 1970s when research and therapy had become separate spheres. He called particular attention to outcome research: "Family and marital therapists have been almost abruptly convinced, especially by Alan Gurman (Gurman & Kniskern, 1978, 1981), that such research is possible and also yields respectable, encouraging results in comparison to other approaches" (p. 115). Confirmation of Wynne's statements about the welcome research is receiving from family therapists may be found in several developments. The AAMFT's Research Institute, founded in 1980, was by 1983 the largest of the institutes at the annual meeting of the organization and was spawning ongoing research efforts in family therapy.

Research on the family is best represented by the theory construction and research methodology workshops of the National Council on Family Relations, (NCFR). Since 1982, an annual working conference on the assessment of family therapy has been held at the annual meeting of the NCFR, jointly sponsored by the AAMFT research committee. Family research and family therapy research findings and discussions also are found within the conferences of other organizations, for example, the American Orthopsychiatric Association. AFTA encourages the sharing of research and clinical findings at its meetings as do sections of the American Psychological Association. The major outlets for the publication of family therapy research in the United States and Canada are the *Journal of Marital and Family Therapy* and *Family Process*. For family studies and general family research reports the *Journal of Marriage and the Family* is the major outlet. A number of other journals and listings of abstracts also are available.

For the practitioner, there are several reasons why an ongoing acquaintance with empirical research findings is important. As Gurman (1983) and others (Gurman & Kniskern, 1978a, 1981; Pinsof, 1981) have suggested, practicing clinicians need to know about the multitudes of factors that influence therapeutic outcomes not only for their applied value, that is, for general guidance in clinical decision-making and treatment planning, but also in order to understand the mechanisms of change that are common to different treatment methods and the factors that have meaning within individual methods. Also, clinicians need to keep abreast of empirical research trends and findings in order to be able to maintain dialogue with and provide information to professionals in other fields, consumers, and public policymakers such as governmental officials and lawmakers and insurance company executives who make decisions about reimbursement. There are important practical reasons, in other words, for being able to understand research findings in order to inform and persuade others regarding various aspects of the efficacy and effectiveness of family therapy. Through the ongoing integration of research findings a practitioner's theoretical knowledge, clinical practice, and professional/political relations may be strengthened and modified.

Clinicians also need to be aware of major controversies in the field of research, just as they need to be aware of struggles in the area of clinical method and emphasis. Issues concerning the meaning and implications of the "new epistemologies" need to be known and understood by the clinician (Gurman, 1983).

Ethics

Historically, professions have attempted to hold their members to conformity to ethical principles that govern their relationship and dealings with clients, colleagues, and the general public. Codes of ethics generally have no legal standing, except in instances in which a state has written into law a provision that licensed/certified individuals shall be held accountable to a particular code of ethics or ethical principles or has established the same provision under administrative rules promulgated by the regulatory body. Typically, however, codes of ethics apply only to members of the particular professional organization that established them. The major sanction or most severe penalty that an organization can bring against its members for violation of ethical principles and codes is expulsion from the organization. A governmental regulatory body that holds individuals accountable to an ethical code may find violations the basis for suspension or revocation of their license to pratice or certificate of registration.

In the United States, professional organizations no longer have any effective control over advertising by their members. Rulings by the Federal Trade Commission (FTC) have treated most restrictions against advertising by members of a profession a "restraint of trade." FTC rulings have been held up in legal tests sufficiently to establish that professionals may advertise many things that were considered improper and unethical by professional organizations in the past, for example, fees, including special prices for a given procedure. The most general guideline appears to be whether an advertisement is accurate or, conversely, whether it is not "false and misleading." The FTC does not appear to have been concerned with such questions as whether an advertisement or presentation to the public is in poor taste. Many professionals seem to be slowly learning that there are no legal or ethical violations involved when a colleague purchases a flamboyant or gaudy advertisement in the print or electronic media.

Ethical codes are changing instruments, just as the laws of a society change with the passage of time and with alterations in the social and cultural orders. Ethical principles are more broad than the code and, hence, are subject to lesser degrees of change.

The AAMFT's *Ethical Principles for Family Therapists* (1982) contains eight major ethical principles. The principles are:

1. *Responsibility to Clients. Family therapists are dedicated to advancing the welfare of families and individuals, including respecting the rights of those persons seeking their assistance, and making reasonable efforts to ensure that their services are used appropriately.*

The subprinciples for this area include antidiscriminatory provisions on the basis of race, sex, religion, or national origin; prohibitions against sexual intimacy with clients; and other provisions for the protection of clients.

2. *Competence. Family therapists are dedicated to maintaining high*

standards of competence, recognizing appropriate limitations to their competence and services and using consultation with other professionals.

This principle involves requirements that family therapists seek help for themselves for personal problems or conflicts that are likely to impair their work performance, as well as requirements that appropriate consultation be sought on problems with clients that are outside the recognized boundaries of their competence.

3. *Integrity. Family therapists are honest in dealing with clients, students, trainees, colleagues, and the public, seeking to eliminate incompetence or dishonesty from the work or representations of family therapists.*

This principle in its application is concerned with honesty in advertising and other representations, prohibitions against using professional relationships for improper purposes, prohibitions against using sexual harassment in working relationships, and related matters.

4. *Confidentiality. Family therapists respect both the law and the rights of clients and safeguard client confidences as required by law.*

Confidentiality is one of the more misunderstood concepts and areas with which professionals deal in their practice. Frequently, it is confused with privilege, which is the right of a client to entrust certain information to a professional person with the assurance that that information will remain with that professional person and not be communicated to others, except under specified circumstances and conditions. The privilege belongs to the client and not to the professional. Case law, starting with the Tarasoff case in California, has begun to make the matter of "duty to warn" an exceedingly important concern for all mental health professionals. That is, mental health professionals have been held accountable for warning individuals who have been named as potential targets of violence by the professional's clients. There are other social limits on the privilege, such as the social and legal responsibilities imposed by case and statutory law.

There are particular problems with confidentiality and privilege when the therapeutic modality involves marriage and family situations. The Michigan law of 1966 regulating "marriage counselors" contains an essentially ironclad provision of confidentiality, prohibiting the clinician from revealing the contents of sessions, except when he or she needs to do so in self-defense in legal actions. The intent of the passage was to protect the marital counseling situation from being used in divorce and other litigation between the spouses, that is, to make it safe for both partners to deal with their difficulties in a clinical setting. More recent legislation proposed by the AAMFT in its legislative manuals and documents has included the proviso that the privilege be waived if both spouses or all adult members in marital and family therapy agree to the waiver. This seems much more realistic in view of the case law developments subsequent to the 1966 Michigan legislation.

Family violence, particularly child abuse and child abuse reporting laws, is also making the confidentiality issue more complex than it was formerly. The legal requirement that professionals report known or suspected cases of child or spouse abuse brings one social value—physical safety—into confrontation with another—the privilege of making confidential statements to a professional—and rather clearly places the physical safety value on top. This puts therapists in a position where they can no longer say facilely to clients, "Whatever you tell me will be held in strictest confidence, and will not be revealed to anyone else."

5. *Professional Responsibility. Family therapists respect the rights and responsibilities of professional colleagues and, as employees of organizations, remain accountable as individuals to the ethical principles of their profession.*

This principle includes such matters as fairness and accuracy in publication and assigning publication credits, and holds the individual professional responsible for his or her actions as employees. That is, therapists cannot pass on the responsibility for unethical and unfair practices to their employer, but remain personally accountable for actions in which they are participants.

6. *Professional Development. Family therapists seek to continue their professional development and strive to make pertinent knowledge available to clients, students, trainees, colleagues, and the public.*

This principle pertains to the responsibility of the professional person to continue both informal and formal learning experiences in order to remain abreast of new developments in family therapy knowledge and practice. The same principle holds with regard to responsibility for helping to encourage and enhance the professional growth and development of those individuals for whom they accept responsibility as supervisors.

7. *Research Responsibility. Family therapists recognize that, while research is essential to the advancement of knowledge, all investigations must be conducted with full respect for the rights and dignity of participants and with full concern for their welfare.*

Essentially, this principle is concerned with the responsibility of conducting research in an ethical manner that protects participants.

8. *Social Responsibility. Family therapists acknowledge a responsibility to participate in activities that contribute to a better community and society, including devoting a portion of their professional activity to services for which there is little or no financial return.*

This principle involves the acceptance of responsibility for social concerns including not only the provision of services at low cost or no cost in some instances but also involvement in seeking laws and regulations that are in the public interest as they seek legislation concerning family therapy and family matters.

Career Development

Entry into the field is, as we have indicated, only the beginning of a career that generally is expected to last for decades for most professionals. Not only should a therapist expect to improve clinical skills but also the knowledge on which such skills are based.

A major issue facing professionals, once they have completed their basic education and training and secured their credentials is the kind of role and participation that they take in the professional field, as well as in society as a whole. Does the professional simply maintain his or her practice, research, teaching, or combinations of those activities and pursuits and engage in whatever professional growth and personal enhancement activities that he or she desires to follow on an individual basis? Is the maintainence and development of the profession and the profession's contribution to society left to others? Or does the developing professional take some responsibility for the maintenance and development of the profession and for the profession's contributions to the betterment of society?

If the developing professional decides to do something other than to nurture and nourish his or her own personal development, what kind of role and what kind of activities within the professional field and within society shall he or she take?

These and other questions are personal in nature and yet profoundly practical for the profession, the society, and the individual professional. The same arguments against living in society with only one's own interests and pursuits as a guide can be made with regard to functioning as a professional with only one's own interests and pursuits as a guide, and contrasted in each case with functioning as a citizen in the larger collectivity. Additionally, if a person makes a claim to being a professional, he or she is making a claim to have something significant to offer to the society and, historically, has claimed special privileges in the society. Not even the changes that have occurred with regard to the place of professions in society have reduced the role of the profession's and the professional's responsibility for striving to be competent, ethical, and actively involved in fostering social betterment.

THE FUTURE

We do not know what lies ahead for the field of family therapy. There are indications of trends scattered throughout this book. Without trying to name or discuss all of them, we shall simply indicate here that there are many signs that by the 1980s the field had entered a period of integration and consolidation. Research has become much more important than it was through the 1960s and 1970s. Educational programs at both the masters and doctoral level continue to develop. Legislation regulating family therapy and providing greater consumer protection and guidance continues to advance slowly. There has been a tremendous amount of ferment with regard to epistemology. The number of individuals gaining relevant credentials based on substantive education in the family field along with supervised clinical experience continues to grow at a significant rate.

What effects the current health care ferment and changes will have in both the short run and the long run cannot be predicted. In our estimation, family therapy will continue to be around, although the modes of delivery may be altered drastically within the next few years. We also may face a period of short-term dislocations in which health maintainence organizations, preferred provider organizations, and other cost-cutting efforts and the industrialization of mental health service delivery will seriously affect family therapy as well as general psychotherapy and other health services. Following such dislocations, we may experience a partial return to traditional service delivery patterns. Nobody knows precisely what will happen.

Whatever the picture in the future, the more adequately educated and trained and the more flexible and adaptive the clinician, the better chance he or she has to change in ways that permit the provision of appropriate services to clients.

The individual who functions with a career development perspective in mind, staying abreast of developments within and outside the profession, is the person who is likely to survive and thrive as a professional family therapist.

References

Ackerman, N. W. (1937). The family as a social and emotional unit. *Bulletin of the Kansas Mental Hygiene Society, 12* (2). (Reprinted in 1938 as The unity of the family. *Archives of Pediatrics, 55,* 51–61.)

Ackerman, N. W. (1954). The diagnosis of neurotic marital interaction. *Social Casework, 35,* 139–149.

Ackerman, N. W. (1956). Psychoanalytic principles in a mental health clinic for the preschool child and his family. *Psychiatry, 19,* 63–76.

Ackerman, N. W. (1958). *The psychodynamics of family life.* New York: Basic Books.

Ackerman, N. W. (1964). Prejudicial scapegoating and neutralizing forces in the family group. *International Journal of Social Psychiatry, 2,* 90–94. (Reprinted in Bloch, D. A., & Simon, R. [Eds.] [1982]. *The strength of family therapy: Selected papers of Nathan W. Ackerman* [pp. 195–200]. New York: Brunner/Mazel.)

Ackerman, N. W. (1966). *Treating the troubled family.* New York: Basic Books.

Ahrons, C. R. (1979). The binuclear family: Two households, one family. *Alternative Lifestyles, 2,* 499–515.

Ahrons, C. R. (1980). Redefining the divorced family: A conceptual framework for post-divorce family system reorganization. *Social Work, 25,* 437–441.

Ahrons, C. R. (1981). The continuing coparental relationship between divorced spouses. *American Journal of Orthopsychiatry, 51,* 418–428.

Allen, F. H. (1948). The Philadelphia Child Guidance Clinic. In L. G. Lowery (Ed.), *Orthopsychiatry, 1923–1948* (pp. 394–413). New York: American Orthopsychiatric Association.

Allport, G. W. (1961). *Pattern and growth in personality.* New York: Holt, Rinehart & Winston.

American Association for Marriage and Family Therapy. (1982). *Ethical principles for family therapists.* Upland, CA: Author.

American Association for Marriage and Family Therapy. (1984). *Family therapy glossary.* Washington, DC: Author.

American Journal of Public Health. (1935). Should marriage counseling become an American public health service function? *25,* 354–356. (Editorial)

American Psychiatric Association. (1980). *Diagnostic and statistical manual of mental disorders* (3rd ed., DSM-III). Washington, DC: Author.

Anderson, C. M., & Stewart, S. (1983). *Mastering resistance: A practical guide to family therapy.* New York: Guilford Press.

Aponte, H. A. (1976). Underorganization in the poor family. In P. J. Guerin (Ed.), *Family therapy: Theory and practice* (pp. 432–448). New York: Gardner Press.

Ard, B. A. (1973). Providing clinical supervision for marriage counseling: A model for supervisor and supervisee. *Family Coordinator, 22*, 91–97.

Ard, B. A., & Ard, C. C. (Eds.). (1969). *Handbook of marriage counseling*. Palo Alto, CA: Science & Behavior Books.

Ashby, W. R. (1952). *Design for a brain*. New York: Wiley.

Axelrod, P. D., & Everett, C. A. (1983). Joint custody. In A. M. Haralamdie (Ed.), *Handling child custody cases* (pp. 50–62). Colorado Springs, CO: Shephard's/McGraw-Hill (Family Law Series).

Ballard, R. G., & Mudd, E. H. (1957). Some theoretical and practical problems in evaluating effectiveness of counseling. *Social Casework, 38*, 533–538.

Bank, S. P., & Kahn, M. D. (1982). *The sibling bond*. New York: Basic Books.

Barnhill, L. R., & Longo, D. (1980). Fixation and regression in the family life cycle. In J. G. Howells (Ed.), *Advances in family psychiatry* (Vol. II, pp. 51–64). New York: International Universities Press.

Bateson, G. (1972). *Steps toward an ecology of mind*. New York: Ballantine Books.

Bateson, G. (1980). *Mind and nature*. New York: Bantam Books.

Bateson, G., Jackson, D. D., Haley, J., & Weakland, J. (1956). Toward a theory of schizophrenia. *Behavioral Science, 1*, 251–264.

Bateson, G., Jackson, D. D., Haley, J., & Weakland, J. (1963). A note on the double-bind—1962. *Family Process, 2*, 154–161.

Beaglehole, E. (1958). *Social change in the south pacific*. New York: Macmillan.

Beavers, W. R. (1976). A theoretical basis for family evaluation. In J. Lewis, W. R. Beavers, J. Gossett, & V. Phillips (Eds.), *No single thread: Psychological health in family systems* (pp. 46–82). New York: Brunner/Mazel.

Beavers, W. R. (1977). *Psychotherapy and growth: A family systems perspective*. New York: Brunner/Mazel.

Beavers, W. R. (1981). A systems model of family for family therapists. *Journal of Marital and Family Therapy, 7*, 299–307.

Beavers, W. R. (1982). Healthy, midrange, and severely dysfunctional families. In F. Walsh (Ed.), *Normal family processes* (pp. 45–66). New York: Guilford Press.

Beavers, W. R., & Olson, D. H. (1983). Epilogue. *Family Process, 22*, 97–98.

Beavers, W. R., & Voeller, M. N. (1983). Family models: Comparing and contrasting the Olson circumplex model with the Beavers systems model. *Family Process, 22*, 85–97.

Beels, C., & Ferber, A. (1972). What family therapists do. In A. Ferber, M. Mendelsohn, & A. Napier (Eds.), *The book of family therapy* (pp. 168–209). New York: Science House.

Bell, J. E. (1961). *Family group therapy: A new method of treatment for older children, adolescents, and their parents*. Public Health Monographs No. 64. Washington, DC: U. S. Department of Health.

Bell, J. E. (1963). A theoretical position for family group therapy. *Family Process, 2*, 1–14.

Bell, J. E. (1975). *Family therapy*. New York: Jason Aronson.

Bell, J. E. (1978). Family context therapy: A model for family change. *Journal of Marriage and Family Counseling, 4*, 111–126.

Bell, J. E. (1983). Family group therapy. In B. B. Wolman & G. Stricker (Eds.), *Handbook of marital and family therapy* (pp. 231–245). New York: Plenum.

Berg, B., & Rosenblum, N. (1977). Fathers in family therapy: A survey of family therapists. *Journal of Marriage and Family Counseling, 3*(2), 85–91.

Bergler, E. (1948). *Divorce won't help*. New York: Hart.

Berman, E. M. (1982). The individual interview as a treatment technique in conjoint therapy. *American Journal of Family Therapy, 10,* 27–37.

Berman, E. M., & Lief, H. I. (1975). Marital therapy from a psychiatric perspective: An overview. *American Journal of Psychiatry, 132,* 583–592.

Berman, E. M., Lief, H. I., & Williams, A. M. (1981). A model of marital interaction. In G. P. Sholevar (Ed.), *The handbook of marriage and marital therapy* (pp. 3–34). New York: SP Medical and Scientific Books.

Bettelheim, B. (1943). Individual and mass behavior in extreme situations. *Journal of Abnormal and Social Psychology, 38,* 417–452.

Birchler, G. R. (1975). Live supervision and instant feedback in marriage and family therapy. *Journal of Marriage and Family Counseling, 1,* 331–342.

Bird, H. W., & Martin, P. A. (1956). Countertransference in the psychotherapy of marital partners. *Psychiatry, 16,* 353–360.

Bittermann, C. M. (1966). Character adjustment patterns of clients with compulsive character disorders: Implications for treatment. *Social Casework, 47,* 575–582.

Blanck, R., & Blanck, G. (1968). *Marriage and personal development.* New York: Columbia University Press.

Bloch, D. A. (Ed.). (1973). *Techniques of family psychotherapy.* New York: Grune & Stratton.

Bloch, D. A. (1981). Family therapy training: The institutional base. *Family Process, 20,* 131.

Bloch, D. A., & Simon, R. (Eds.). (1982). *The strength of family therapy: Selected papers of Nathan W. Ackerman.* New York: Brunner/Mazel.

Bloch, D. A., & Weiss, H. M. (1981). Training facilities in marital and family therapy. *Family Process, 20,* 133–146.

Bloom, B. L., White, S. W., & Asher, S. J. (1979). Marital disruption as a stressful life event. In G. Levinger & O. C. Moles (Eds.), *Divorce and separation* (pp. 184–200). New York: Basic Books.

Bohannan, P. (Ed.). (1970). *Divorce and after.* Garden City, NY: Doubleday.

Boszormenyi-Nagy, I., & Framo, J. L. (Eds.). (1965). *Intensive family therapy.* New York: Hoeber Division, Harper & Row.

Boszormenyi-Nagy, I., & Spark, G. H. (1973). *Invisible loyalties.* New York: Harper & Row.

Boszormenyi-Nagy, I., & Ulrich, D. N. (1981). Contextual family therapy. In A. S. Gurman & D. P. Kniskern (Eds.), *Handbook of family therapy* (pp. 159–186). New York: Brunner/Mazel.

Bowen, M. (1960). A family concept of schizophrenia. In D. D. Jackson (Ed.), *The etiology of schizophrenia* (pp. 346–372). New York: Basic Books.

Bowen, M. (1966). The use of family theory in clinical practice. *Comprehensive Psychiatry, 7,* 345–374.

Bowen, M. (1976). Family reactions to death. In P. J. Guerin (Ed.), *Family therapy: Theory and practice* (pp. 335–348). New York: Gardner Press.

Bowen, M. (1978). *Family therapy in clinical practice.* New York: Jason Aronson.

Bowlby, J. (1949). The study and reduction of group tensions in the family. *Human Relations, 2,* 123–128.

Bowlby, J. (1969). *Attachment and loss* (Vol. 1: *Attachment*). New York: Basic Books.

Bowlby, J. (1973). *Attachment and loss* (Vol. 2: *Separation: Anxiety and anger*). New York: Basic Books.

Bowlby, J. (1980). *Attachment and loss* (Vol. 3: *Loss: Sadness and depression*). New York: Basic Books.

Bowman, H. (1947). The teacher as counselor in marriage education. *Marrige and Family Living, 9,* 1–7.

Boyer, C. L. (1960). Group therapy with married couples. *Marriage and Family Living, 22,* 21–24.

Brandreth, A., & Pike, R. (1967). Assessment of marriage counseling in a small family agency. *Social Work, 12,* 34–39.

Brandwein, R., Brown, C., & Fox, E. (1974). The social structure of divorced mothers and their families. *Journal of Marriage and the Family, 36,* 498–514.

Brangwin, L. C. (1955). Marriage counseling—the viewpoint of the caseworker. *Social Casework, 36,* 155–162.

Broderick, C. B., & Schrader, S. S. (1981). The history of marriage and family therapy. In A. S. Gurman & D. P. Kniskern (Eds.), *Handbook of family therapy* (pp. 5–35). New York: Brunner/Mazel.

Bucher, R., & Stelling, J. G. (1977). *Becoming professional.* Beverly Hills, CA: Sage Publications.

Burgum, M. (1942). The father gets worse: A child guidance problem. *American Journal of Orthopsychiatry, 12,* 474–485.

Burton, G. (1962). Counseling with alcoholic husbands and their nonalcoholic wives. *Marriage and Family Living, 24,* 56–61.

Burton, G., & Young, D. (1961). Family crisis in group therapy. *Family Process, 1,* 211–223.

Campbell, A. (1975, May). The American way of mating: Marriage si, children only maybe. *Psychology Today,* pp. 37–43.

Capra, F. (1983). *The turning point.* New York: Bantam Books.

Carr-Saunders, A., & Wilson, P. (1933). *The professions.* Oxford: Clarendon Press.

Carter, E. A., & McGoldrick, M. (1980). The family life cycle and family therapy: An overview. In E. A. Carter & M. McGoldrick (Eds.), *The family life cycle: A framework for family therapy* (pp. 3–20). New York: Gardner Press.

Christ, J. (1976). Treatment of marital disorders. In H. Grunebaum & J. Christ (Eds.), *Contemporary marriage: Structure, dynamics and therapy* (pp. 371–399). Boston: Little, Brown.

Clark, T. E., & Nichols, W. C. (1984). *Marital and family therapy: A definition.* Unpublished manuscript.

Cohler, B. J., & Geyer, S. (1982). Psychological autonomy and interdependence within the family. In F. Walsh (Ed.), *Normal family processes* (pp. 196–228). New York: Guilford Press.

Concord, J. C. (1924). The matrimonial advice bureau. *The Family, 5,* 60–63.

Cooper, A., Rampage, C., & Soucy, G. (1981). Family therapy training in clinical psychology. *Family Process, 20,* 155–166.

Coser, R. L., & Rockoff, G. (1971). Women in the occupational world: Social disruption and conflict. *Social Problems 18,* 535–554.

Council for the National Register of Health Service Providers in Psychology. (1983). *National register of health service providers in psychology.* Washington, DC: Author.

Crist, J. R. (1955). An experiment in marriage counseling training. *Journal of Counseling Psychology, 2,* 35–38.

Crist, J. R. (1956). The use of literature in marriage counseling. *Journal of Counseling Psychology, 3,* 37–43.

Cuber, J. F. (1948). *Marriage counseling practice.* New York: Appleton-Century-Crofts.

Cuber, J. F. (1951). Editorial: Unsolved problems of the teacher–counselor in marriage education. *Marriage and Family Living, 13,* 127–128, 144.

Cuber, J. F., & Harroff, P. (1966). *Sex and the significant Americans.* Baltimore: Penguin Books.

Daniels, P., & Weingarten, K. (1982). *Sooner or later: The timing of parenthood in adult lives.* New York: W. W. Norton.

Dell, P. F. (1982). Beyond homeostasis: Toward a concept of coherence. *Family Process, 21,* 21–41.

DeMello, D. N. (1982, November). Report from Britain: Struggling to become established and approved. *International Network of Family Therapy Newsletter,* p. A.

de Shazer, S. (1983). diagnosing + researching + doing therapy. In B. Keeney (Ed.), *Diagnosis and assessment in family therapy* (pp. 125–132). Rockville, MD: Aspen Systems.

Dicks, H. V. (1963). Object relations and marital studies. *British Journal of Medical Psychology, 36,* 125–129.

Dicks, H. V. (1964). Concepts of marital diagnosis and therapy as developed at the Tavistock family psychiatric units, London, England. In. E. M. Nash, L. Jessner, & D. W. Abse (Eds.), *Marriage counseling in medical practice* (pp. 255–275). Chapel Hill, NC: University of North Carolina Press.

Dicks, H. V. (1967). *Marital tensions.* New York: Basic Books.

Doherty, W. J., & Baird, M. A. (1983). *Family therapy and family medicine: Toward the primary care of families.* New York: Guilford Press.

Draughon, M. (1975). Stepmother's model of identification in relation to mourning in the child. *Psychological Reports, 9*(1), 183–189.

Dreikurs, R. (1951). Family group therapy in the Chicago Child Guidance Center. *Mental Hygiene, 35,* 291–301.

Duhl, B. S., & Duhl, F. J. (1981). Integrative family therapy. In A. S. Gurman & D. P. Kniskern (Eds.), *Handbook of family therapy* (pp. 483–513). New York: Brunner/Mazel.

Duhl, F. J., & Duhl, B. S. (1979). "Structured spontaneity": The thoughtful art of integrative family therapy at BFI. *Journal of Marital and Family Therapy, 5,* 59–75.

Durand-Weaver, A. M. (1930). Marriage advice stations for married and engaged couples. *The Family, 11,* 85–87.

Duvall, E. M. (1971). *Family development* (4th ed.). Philadelphia: J. B. Lippincott.

Duvall, E. M., & Hill, R. (1948). *Report of the committee on the dynamics of family interaction.* Prepared for the National Conference on Family Life, Washington, DC, 1948.

Ehrenkranz, S. M. (1967a). A study of joint interviewing in the treatment of marital problems. part I. *Social Casework, 48,* 498–501.

Ehrenkranz, S. M. (1967b). A study of joint interviewing in the treatment of marital problems, part II. *Social Casework, 48,* 570–574.

Eisenstein, V. (Ed.). (1956). *Neurotic interaction in marriage.* New York: Basic Books.

Ekstein, R., & Wallerstein, R. (1972). *The teaching of psychotherapy* (2nd ed.). New York: International Universities Press.

Elkaim, M. (1981). Non-equilibrium, chance and change in family therapy. *Journal of Marital and Family Therapy, 7,* 291–297.

Ellis, A. (1956). A critical evaluation of marriage counseling. *Marriage and Family Living, 18,* 65–71.

Ellis, A. (1958). Neurotic interactions between marital partners. *Journal of Counseling Psychology, 5,* 24–28.

Ellis, B. G. (1964). Unconscious collusion in marital interaction. *Social Casework, 45,* 79–85.

Erickson, G. D., & Hogan, T. P. (Eds.). (1972). *Family therapy: An introduction to theory and technique.* Monterey, CA: Brooks/Cole.

Erikson, E. H. (1950). *Childhood and society.* New York: W. W. Norton.

Everett, C. A. (1976). Family assessment and intervention for early adolescent problems. *Journal of Marriage and Family Counseling, 2,* 155–165.

Everett, C. A. (1979). The masters degree in marriage and family therapy. *Journal of Marital and Family Therapy, 5,* 7–12.

Everett, C. A. (1980a). An analysis of AAMFT supervisors: Their identities, roles, and resources. *Journal of Marital and Family Therapy, 6,* 215–226.

Everett, C. A. (1980b). Supervision of marriage and family therapy. In A. Hess (Ed.), *Psychotherapy supervision* (pp. 367–380). New York: Wiley.

Everett, C. A., Halperin, S., Volgy, S., & Wissler, A. (in press). *Treating borderline families.* Orlando, FL: Grune & Stratton.

Everett, C. A., & Volgy, S. (1983). Family assessment in child custody disputes. *Journal of Marital and Family Therapy, 9,* 343–353.

Fairbairn, W. R. D. (1952). *Psycho-analytic studies of the personality.* New York: Basic Books.

Fairbairn, W. R. D. (1963). Synopsis of an object-relations theory of the personality. *International Journal of Psycho-Analysis, 44,* 224–225.

Farber, B. (1964). *Family organization and interaction.* San Francisco: Chandler.

Feldman, L. B. (1976). Goals of family therapy. *Journal of Marriage and Family Counseling, 2,* 103–113.

Feldman, L. B. (1979). Marital conflict and marital intimacy: An integrative psychodynamic–behavioral–systems approach. *Family Process, 18,* 69–78.

Fibush, E. W. (1957). The evaluation of marital interaction in the treatment of the partner. *Social Casework, 38,* 303–307.

Finck, G. (1962). Marriage counseling—A service in behalf of children. *Family Life Coordinator, 11,* 39–42.

Fisher, E. O. (1974). *Divorce: The new freedom.* New York: Harper & Row.

Fisher, L. (1977). On the classification of families. *Archives of General Psychiatry, 34.* (Reprinted in Howells, J. G. [Ed.]. [1979]. *Advances in general psychiatry* [Vol. I, pp. 27–52] New York: International Universities Press.)

Fisher, M. S. (1936, April–May). The development of marriage and family counseling in the United States. *Parents Magazine,* p. 8.

Flexner, A. (1915). Is social work a profession? *Proceedings of the National Conference of Charities and Corrections* (pp. 576–590).

Fogarty, T. F. (1975). *The family, emptiness and closeness.* New Rochelle, NY: The Center for Family Learning.

Fogarty, T. F. (1976a). Marital crisis. In P. J. Guerin (Ed.), *Family therapy: Theory and practice* (pp. 325–334). New York: Gardner Press.

Fogarty, T. F. (1976b). Systems concepts and the dimensions of self. In P. J. Guerin (Ed.), *Family therapy: Theory and practice* (pp. 144–153). New York: Gardner Press.

Folberg, H., & Graham, M. (1979, Spring). Joint custody of children following divorce. *University of California–Davis Law Review.* (Special Symposium on Children and the Law), *12* (2), 523–581.

Foley, V. (1974). *An introduction to family therapy.* New York: Grune & Stratton.

Foster, R. G. (1935). A device for premarital counselors and teachers of courses of marriage. *Journal of Home Economics, 27,* 575–576.

Foster, R. G. (1936a). Advising young people on marriage. *National Parent–Teacher, 30* (6), 28–31.

Foster, R. G. (1936b). Is marriage counseling a profession? *Journal of Social Hygiene, 22,* 125–139.

Foster, R. G. (1950). Marriage counseling in a psychiatric setting. *Marriage and Family Living, 12,* 41–43.

Framo, J. L. (1970). Symptoms from a family transactional viewpoint. In N. W. Ackerman (Ed.), Family therapy in transition. *International Psychiatric Clinics, 7* (4), 125–171.

Framo, J. L., (Ed.). (1972). *Family interaction: A dialogue between family researchers and family therapists.* New York: Springer.

Framo, J. L. (1973). Marriage therapy in a couples group. In D. A. Bloch (Ed.), *Techniques of family therapy* (pp. 87–97). New York: Grune & Stratton.

Framo, J. L. (1975). Personal reflections of a family therapist. *Journal of Marriage and Family Counseling, 1,* 15–28.

Framo, J. L. (1980). Marriage and marital therapy: Issues and initial interview techniques. In M. Andolfi & I. Zwerling (Eds.), *Dimensions of family therapy* (pp. 49–71). New York: Guilford Press.

Framo, J. L. (1982). *Explorations in family therapy: Selected papers of James L. Framo* New York: Springer.

Friedson, E. (1970). *Professional dominance: The social structure of medical care.* New York: Atherton.

Friedson, E. (1971). Professions and their occupational principle. In E. Friedson (Ed.), *The professions and their prospects* (pp. 19–38). Beverly Hills, CA: Sage Publications.

Fromm-Reichmann, F. (1948). Notes on the development of the treatment of schizophrenia by psychoanalytic psychotherapy. *Psychiatry, 11,* 263–274.

Gardner, R. A. (1970). *The boys and girls book about divorce.* New York: Bantam Books.

Garrigan, J. J., & Bambrick, A. F. (1975). Short-term family therapy with emotionally disturbed children. *Journal of Marriage and Family Counseling, 1,* 379–385.

Garrigan, J. J., & Bambrick, A. F. (1977a). Family therapy for disturbed children: Some experimental results in special education. *Journal of Marriage and Family Counseling, 3,* 83–93.

Garrigan, J. J., & Bambrick, A. F. (1977b). Introducing novice therapists to "go-between" techniques of family therapy. *Family Process, 16,* 237–246.

Garrigan, J. J., & Bambrick, A. F. (1979) New findings in research on the go-between process. *International Journal of Family Therapy, 1,* 76–85.

Gehrke, S., & Kirschenbaum, M. (1967). Survival patterns in family conjoint therapy. *Family Process, 6,* 67–80.

Gehrke, S., & Moxom, J. (1962). Diagnostic classification and treatment techniques in marriage counseling. *Family Process, 1,* 253–264.

Geist, J., & Gerber, N. M. (1960). Joint interviewing: A treatment technique with marital partners. *Social Casework, 41,* 76–83.

Gerard, M. W. (1948). Direct treatment of the child. In L. G. Lowery (Ed.), *Orthopsychiatry, 1923–1948* (pp. 494–523). New York: American Orthopsychiatric Association.

Giovacchini, P. (1958). Mutual adaptation in various object relationships. *International Journal of Psycho-Analysis, 34,* 1–8.

Giovacchini, P. (1976). Symbiosis and intimacy. *International Journal of Psychoanalysis, 5,* 413–436.

Glick, I. D., & Kessler, D. R. (1974). *Marital and family therapy.* New York: Grune & Stratton.

Glick, P. C. (1980). Remarriage: Some recent changes and variations. *Journal of Family Issues, 1,* 455–478.

Goldiamond, I. (1965). Self-control procedures in personal behavior problems. *Psychological Reports, 17,* 851–868.

Gomberg, M. R., & Levinson, F. T. (Eds.). (1951). *Diagnosis and process in family counseling.* New York: Family Service Association of America.

Goode, W. J. (1956). *After divorce.* New York: Free Press.

Goode, W. J. (1960). Encroachment, charlatanism, and emerging professions: Psychology, sociology, and medicine. *American Sociological Review, 25,* 902–914.

Goodrich, W. (1968). Toward a taxonomy of marriage. In J. Marmor (Ed.), *Contemporary psychoanalysis* (pp. 407–423). New York: Basic Books.

Gottlieb, A., & Pattison, E. M. (1966). Married couples group therapy. *Archives of General Psychiatry, 14,* 143–152.

Gray, W., & Rizzo, N. R. (1969). History and development of general system theory. In W. Gray, F. J. Duhl, & N. J. Rizzo (Eds.), *General systems theory and psychiatry* (pp. 7–31). Boston: Little, Brown.

Green, R. (1964). Collaborative and conjoint therapy combined. *Family Process, 3,* 90–98.

Green, R., & Framo, J. L. (Eds.). (1981). *Family therapy: Major contributions.* New York: International Universities Press.

Greene, B. L. (1960). Marital disharmony: Concurrent analyses of husband and wife by the same psychiatrist. *Disorders of the Nervous System, 21,* 73–78.

Greene, B. L. (Ed.). (1965). *The psychotherapies of marital disharmony.* New York: Free Press.

Greene, B. L. (1970). *A clinical approach to marital problems: Evaluation and management.* Springfield, IL: Charles C Thomas.

Greene, B. L., Broadhurst, B. P., & Lustig, N. (1965). Treatment of marital disharmony: The use of individual, concurrent, and conjoint sessions as a "combined treatment." In B. L. Greene (Ed.), *The psychotherapies of marital disharmony* (pp. 135–151). New York: Free Press.

Greene, B. L., Lee, R. R., & Lustig, N. (1975). Treatment of marital disharmony where one spouse has a primary affective disorder (manic–depressive illness): I. General overview—100 couples. *Journal of Marriage and Family Counseling, 1,* 39–50.

Greene, B. L. & Soloman, A. P. (1963). Marital disharmony: Concurrent psychoanalytic treatment of husband and wife by the same psychiatrist. *American Journal of Psychotherapy, 17,* 443–456.

Greenwood, E. (1953). The attributes of a profession. *Social Work, 2,* 45–55.

Greif, J. B. (1979). Fathers, children, and joint custody. *American Journal of Orthopsychiatry, 49,* 311–319.

Group for the Advancement of Psychiatry. (1970). *The field of family therapy* (GAP Report No. 78). New York: Author.

Groves, E. R. (1940). A decade of marriage counseling. *Annals of the American Academy of Political and Social Science, 212,* 72–80.

Groves, E. R. (1946). Professional training for family life educators. *Marriage and Family Living, 8,* 25–26.

Groves, E. R., & Blanchard, P. (1930). *Introduction to mental hygiene.* New York: Henry Holt.

Grunebaum, H., & Chasin, R. (1982). Thinking like a family therapist: A model for integrating the theories and methods of family therapy. *Journal of Marital and Family Therapy, 8,* 403–416.

Grunebaum, H., & Christ, J. (Eds.). (1976). *Contemporary marriage: Structure, dynamics, and therapy.* Boston: Little, Brown.

Grunebaum, H., Christ, J., & Neiberg, N. (1969). Diagnosis and treatment planning for couples. *International Journal of Group Psychotherapy, 19,* 185–202.

Guerin, P. J. (1976). Family therapy: The first twenty-five years. In P. J. Guerin (Ed.), *Family therapy: Theory and practice* (pp. 2–22). New York: Gardner Press.

Guldner, C. A. (1978). Family therapy for the trainee in family therapy. *Journal of Marriage and Family Counseling, 4,* 127–132.

Guldner, C. A. (1982, May). Training family practice physicians. *Family Therapy News,* p. 5.

Gullerud, E. N., & Harlan, V. L. (1962). Four-way interviewing in marital counseling. *Social Casework, 43,* 532–537.

Gurman, A. S. (1973). The effects and effectiveness of marital therapy: A review of outcome research. *Family Process, 12,* 145–170.

Gurman, A. S. (1978). Contemporary marital therapies: A critique and comparative analysis of psychoanalytic, behavioral, and systems theory approaches. In T. J. Paolino & B. S. McCrady (Eds.), *Marriage and marital therapy* (pp. 445–556). New York: Brunner/Mazel.

Gurman, A. S. (1980). Behavioral marriage therapy in the 1980s: The challenge of integration. *American Journal of Family Therapy, 8* (2), 86–96.

Gurman, A. S. (1981a). Creating a therapeutic alliance in marital therapy. *American Journal of Family Therapy, 8* (3), 84–87.

Gurman, A. S. (1981b) Integrative marital therapy: Toward the development of an interpersonal approach. In S. H. Budman (Ed.), *Forms of brief therapy* (pp. 415–457). New York: Guilford Press.

Gurman, A. S. (1983). Family therapy research and the "new epistemology." *Journal of Marital and Family Therapy, 9,* 227–234.

Gurman, A. S., & Kniskern, D. P. (1978a). Research on marital and family therapy: Progress, perspective, and prospect. In S. L. Garfield & A. E. Bergin (Eds.), *Handbooks of psychotherapy and behavior change: An empirical analysis* (2nd ed., pp. 817–901). New York: Wiley.

Gurman, A. S. & Kniskern, D. P. (1978b). Deterioration in marital and family therapy: Empiricial, clinical, and conceptual issues. *Family Process, 17,* 3–20.

Gurman, A. S., & Kniskern, D. P. (Eds.). (1981). *Handbook of family therapy.* New York: Brunner/Mazel.

Gurman, A. S., Kniskern, D. P., & Pinsof, W. N. (1985). Research on the process and outcome of family therapy. In S. L. Garfield & A. E. Bergin (Eds.), *Handbook of psychotherapy and behavior change* (3rd ed., pp. 525–623). New York: Wiley.

Haley, J. (1962). Whither family therapy? *Family Process, 1,* 69–100.

Haley, J. (1963a). Marriage therapy. *Archives of General Psychiatry, 8,* 213–234.

Haley, J. (1963b). Marriage therapy. In J. Haley (Ed.), *Strategies of psychotherapy.* New York: Grune & Stratton.

Haley, J. (1967). Toward a theory of pathological types. In G. H. Zuk & I. Boszormenyi-Nagy (Eds.), *Family therapy and disturbed families* (pp. 11–28), Palo Alto, CA: Science & Behavior Books.

Haley, J. (1971). Family therapy. *International Journal of Psychiatry, 9,* 233–242.

Haley, J. (1973a). Strategic therapy when a child is presented as the problem. *Journal of the American Academy of Child Psychiatry, 12,* 641–659.

Haley, J. (1973b). *Uncommon therapy: The psychiatric techniques of Milton H. Erickson.* New York: W. W. Norton.

Haley, J. (1975). Why a mental health clinic should avoid family therapy. *Journal of Marriage and Family Counseling, 1,* 1–13.

Haley, J. (1976). Problems of training therapists. In J. Haley (Ed.), *Problem-solving therapy* (pp. 169–194), San Francisco: Jossey-Bass.

Haley J. (1980). *Leaving home: The therapy of disturbed young people.* New York: McGraw-Hill.

Haley, J., & Hoffman, L. (Eds.). (1967). *Techniques of family therapy.* New York: Basic Books.

Hallowitz, D., Clement, R. G., & Cutter, A. V. (1957). The treatment process with both parents together. *American Journal of Orthopsychiatry, 27,* 587–607.

Hardcastle, D. R. (1977). A mother–child, multiple family counseling program: Procedures and results. *Family Process, 16,* 67–74.

Hareven, T. K. (1982). American families in transition: Historical perspectives on change. In F. Walsh (Ed.), *Normal family processes* (pp. 446–465). New York: Guilford Press.

Harper, R. A. (1953). Should marriage counseling become a full-fledged specialty? *Marriage and Family Living, 15,* 338–340.

Harper, R. A. (1958). Neurotic interaction among counselors. *Journal of Counseling Psychology, 5,* 33–38.

Harper, R. A. (1960). Marriage counseling as rational process-oriented psychotherapy. *Journal of Individual Psychology, 16,* 197–207.

Havighurst, R. J. (1953). *Human development and education.* New York: Longmans, Green.

Headley, L. (1977). *Adults and their parents in family therapy: A new direction in treatment.* New York: Plenum.

Healy, W., & Bronner, A. F. (1948). The child guidance clinic: Birth and growth of an idea. In L. G. Lowery (Ed.), *Orthopsychiatry, 1923–1948* (pp. 14–49). New York: American Orthopsychiatric Association.

Henry, W., Sims, J., & Spray, S. (1971). *The fifth profession.* San Francisco: Jossey-Bass.

Henry, W., Sims, J., & Spray, S. (1973). *Public and private lives of psychotherapists.* San Francisco: Jossey-Bass.

Hill, R. (1970). *Family developments in three generations.* Cambridge, MA: Schenkman.

Hill, R. (1971). Modern science theory and the family. *Social Science Information,* pp. 7–26. (Reprinted in Sussman, M. B. (Ed.), (1974) *Sourcebook in marriage and the family* (4th ed.) (pp. 302–313). Boston: Houghton Mifflin.)

Hill, R., & Hansen, D. A. (1960). The identification of conceptual frameworks utilized in family study. *Marrige and Family Living, 22,* 299–311.

Hobbs, D. F., & Cole, S. P. (1976). Transition to parenthood: A decade replication. *Journal of Marriage and the Family, 38,* 723–731.

Hoffman, L. (1975). Enmeshment and the too richly cross-joined system. *Family Process, 14,* 457–468.

Hoffman, L. (1981). *Foundations of family therapy.* New York: Basic Books.

Hogan, D. B. (1979). *The regulation of psychotherapists,* (Vol. II). Cambridge, MA: Ballinger.

Hollingshead, A. B. (1950). Cultural factors in the selection of marriage mates. *American Sociological Review, 15,* 619–627.

Howells, J. G. (1975). *Principles of family psychiatry.* New York: Brunner/Mazel.

Howells, J. G. (1978). Developments in family psychiatry in the United Kingdom. *Journal of Marriage and Family Counseling, 4,* 133–141.

Hughes, E. C. (1956). The making of a profession. *Human Organization, 14,* 14–25.

Huneeus, M. E. (1963). A dynamic approach to marital problems. *Social Casework, 44,* 142–148.

Hunt, M., & Hunt, B. (1977). *The divorce experience.* New York: McGraw-Hill.

Jackson, D. D. (1957). The question of family homeostasis. *Psychiatric Quarterly Supplement, 31* (1), 79–90.

Jackson, D. D. (1959). Family interaction, family homeostasis, and some implications for conjoint family psychotherapy. In J. H. Masserman (Ed.), *Individual and family dynamics.* New York: Grune & Stratton.

Jackson, D. D. (1961). Family therapy in the family of the schizophrenic. In H. Stein (Ed.), *Contemporary psychotherapies* (pp. 272–287). New York: Free Press.

Jackson, D. D. (Ed.). (1968). *Communication, family, and marriage* (Vol. I). Palo Alto, CA: Science & Behavior Books.

Jackson, D. D., & Satir, V. (1961). A review of psychiatric developments in family diagnosis and family therapy. In N. W. Ackerman, F. L. Beatman, & S. N. Sherman (Eds.), *Exploring the base for family therapy* (pp. 29–51). New York: Family Service Association of America.

Jackson, D. D., & Weakland, J. H. (1959). Schizophrenic symptoms and family interaction. *Archives of General Psychiatry, 1,* 618–621.

Jacobson, N. S., & Margolin, G. (1979). *Marital therapy.* New York; Brunner/Mazel.

Jacobson, N. S., & Martin, B. (1976). Behavioral marriage therapy: Current status. *Psychological Bulletin, 83,* 540–556.

Johnson, B. (1938). Laws relating to venereal disease and marriage. *Journal of Social Hygiene, 24,* 409–410.

Johnson, D. (1957, June 18). *Summary of the relation of specific courses in the marriage counseling training program curriculum to the goals of marriage counseling training.* Mimeograph, Menninger Foundation, Topeka, KS.

Jolesch, M. (1962). Casework treatment of young married couples. *Social Casework, 43,* 245–251.

Kanter, R. M. (1968). Commitment and social organization: A study of commitment mechanisms in utopian communities. *American Sociological Review* 33, 499–517.

Kaplan, H. S. (1974). *The new sex therapy.* New York: Brunner/Mazel.

Kaplan, H. S. (1979). *The new sex therapy,* (Vol. II: *Disorders of sexual desire*). New York: Brunner/Mazel.

Karpf, M. J. (1951a). Some guiding principles in marriage counseling. *Marriage and Family Living,* 13, 49–51, 55.

Karpf, M. J. (1951b). Comments on legal status of the marriage counselor: A psychologist's view. *Marriage and Family Living 13,* 118–119.

Karpf, M. J. (1951c). Marriage counseling and psychotherapy. *Marriage and Family Living, 13,* 169–178.

Karpman, B. (1948). Milestones in the advancement of the knowledge of the psychopathology of delinquency and crime. In L. G. Lowery (Ed.), *Orthopsychiatry, 1923–1948* (pp. 100–189), New York: American Orthopsychiatric Association.

Kaslow, F. W. (1977). Training of marital and family therapists. In F. W. Kaslow (Ed.), *Supervision, consultation, and staff training in the helping professions* (pp. 199–234). San Francisco: Jossey-Bass.

Kaslow, F. W. (1981). Divorce and divorce therapy. In A. S. Gurman & D. P. Kniskern (Eds.), *Handbook of family therapy* (pp. 662–696). New York: Brunner/Mazel.

Keith, D. V., & Whitaker, C. A. (1977). The divorce labyrinth. In P. Papp (Ed.), *Family therapy: Full length case studies* (pp. 117–131). New York: Gardner Press.

Keith, D. V., & Whitaker, C. A. (1983). Co-therapy with families. In B. B. Wolman & G.

Stricker (Eds.), *Handbook of marital and family therapy* (pp. 343–355). New York: Plenum.

Kelly, J. B., & Wallerstein, J. S. (1977). Brief intervention with children in divorcing families. *American Journal of Orthopsychiatry, 47,* 23–39.

Kempster, S., & Savitsky, E. (1967). Training family therapists through live supervision. In N. W. Ackerman, F. Beatman, & S. Sherman (Eds.), *Expanding theory and practice in family therapy.* (pp. 125–134). New York: Family Service Association of America.

Kerr, M. E. (1981). Family systems theory and therapy. In A. S. Gurman & D. P. Kniskern (Eds.), *Handbook of family therapy* (pp. 226–264). New York: Brunner/Mazel.

Kessler, S. (1975). *The American way of divorce.* Chicago: Nelson-Hall.

Kimber, J. A. M. (1959). The science and profession of psychology in the area of family relations and marriage counseling. *American Psychologist, 14,* 699–700.

Kimber, J. A. M. (1961). An introduction to the marriage counselor and his work. *Psychological Reports, 8,* 71–75.

Kimber, J. A. M. (1963). Marriage counselors and psychologists in the United States. *American Psychologist, 18,* 108–109.

Kimber, J. A. M. (1967). Psychologists and marriage counselors in the United States. *American Psychologist, 22,* 862–865.

Kluckhohn C., & Murray, H. A. (1956). Personality formation: The determinants. In C. Kluckhohn, H. A. Murray, & D. M. Schneider (Eds.), *Personality in nature, society, and culture* (2nd ed.) (pp. 53–67). New York: Knopf.

Kniskern, D. P. & Gurman, A. S. (1980). Clinical implications of recent research in family therapy. In L. R. Wolberg & M. L. Aronson (Eds.), *Group and family therapy, 1980* (pp. 217–223). New York: Brunner/Mazel.

Kopp, M. E. (1938). Marriage counseling in European countries. *Journal of Heredity, 29,* 153–160.

Korchin, S. K. (1976). *Modern clinical psychology.* New York: Basic Books.

Krantzler, M. (1974). *Creative divorce.* New York: Evans.

Kressel, K., & Slipp, S. (1975). Perceptions of marriage related to engagement in conjoint therapy. *Journal of Marriage and Family Counseling, 1,* 367–377.

Kris, E. (1934). *Psychoanalytic explorations in art.* New York: International Universities Press.

Kubie, L. S. (1956). Psychoanalysis and marriage. In V. Eisenstein (Ed.), *Neurotic interaction in marriage* (pp. 10–43). New York: Basic Books.

Kubler-Ross, E. (1969). *On death and dying.* New York: Macmillan.

L'Abate, L., & McHenry, S. (1983). *Handbook of marital interventions.* New York: Grune & Stratton.

L'Abate, L., & Thaxton, M. L. (1980). Popularity or influence? The use of citation index to identify leaders in family therapy. *Family Process, 19,* 327–339.

Laidlaw, R. W. (1950). The psychiatrist as marriage counselor. *American Journal of Psychiatry, 106,* 732–736.

Laidlaw, R. W. (1960a). The psychotherapy of marital problems. In J. H. Masserman & J. L. Moreno (Eds.), *Progress in psychotherapy* (Vol. V, pp. 140–147). New York: Grune & Stratton.

Laidlaw, R. W. (1960b). The use of the interpersonal system of diagnosis in marital counseling. *Journal of Counseling Psychology, 7,* 10–18.

Laidlaw, R. W. (1967). The constellation approach to marriage counseling. *American Journal of Psychoanalysis, 27,* 132–134.

Laing, R. D., & Esterson, A. (1964). *Sanity, madness, and the family.* Baltimore: Penguin Books.

Lantz, J. E. (1978). *Marital and family therapy: A transactional approach.* New York: Appleton-Century-Crofts.

Lawton, G. (1958). Neurotic interaction between counselor and counselee. *Journal of Counseling Psychology 5,* 28–33.

Lederer, W. J., & Jackson, D. D. (1968). *The mirages of marriage.* New York: W. W. Norton.

Lehrman, N. S. (1963). The joint interviews: An aid to psychotherapy and family stability. *American Journal of Psychotherapy, 17,* 83–94.

LeMasters, E. E. (1957). Parenthood as crisis. *Marriage and Family Living, 19,* 352–355.

Leslie, G. R. (1964a). Conjoint therapy in marriage counseling. *Journal of Marriage and the Family, 26,* 65–71.

Leslie, G. R. (1964b). The field of marriage counseling. In H. T. Christensen (Ed.), *Handbook of marriage and the family* (pp. 912–943). Chicago: Rand McNally.

Levine, D. L. (1953). Teacher–counselor: Role and qualifications. *Marriage and Family Living, 15,* 313–315.

Levine, M., & Levine, A. (1970). *A social history of helping services.* New York: Appleton-Century-Crofts.

Levinson, D. J., Darrow, C. M., Klein, E. B., Levinson, M. H., & McKee, B. (1974). The psychological development of men in early adulthood and the mid-life transition. In D. F. Ricks, A. Thomas, & M. Roff (Eds.), *Life history research in psychopathology* (pp. 243–258). Minneapolis: University of Minnesota Press.

Levinson, D. J., Darrow, C. N., Klein, E. B., Levinson, M. H., & McKee, B. (1978). *The seasons of a man's life.* New York: Alfred A. Knopf.

Levy, D. (1943). *Maternal overprotection.* New York: Columbia University Press.

Lewin, K. (1948). The background of conflict in marriage. In *Resolving marital conflict* (pp. 84–102). New York: Harper & Row.

Lewis, J., Beavers, W. R., Gossett, J. P., & Phillips, V. (1976). *No single thread.* New York: Brunner/Mazel.

Liberman, R. P. (1970). Behavioral approaches to family and couple therapy. *American Journal of Orthopsychiatry, 40,* 106–118.

Liddle, H. A. (1982). On the problem of eclecticism: A call for epistemological clarification and human-scale theories. *Family Process, 21,* 243–250.

Liddle, H. A. (1983). Diagnosis and assessment in family therapy: A comparative analysis of six schools of thought. In B. P. Keeney (Ed.), *Diagnosis and assessment in family theory* (pp. 1–33). Rockville, MD: Aspen Systems.

Lidz, R., & Lidz, T. (1949). The family environment of schizophrenic patients. *American Journal of Psychiatry, 106,* 322–345.

Lidz, T. (1980). The family and the development of the individual. In C. K. Hofling & J. M. Lewis (Eds.), *The family: Evaluation and treatment* (pp. 45–70). New York: Brunner/Mazel.

Lidz, T., Cornelison, A., Fleck, S., & Terry, D. (1957a). Intrafamilial environment of the schizophrenic patient: I. The father. *Psychiatry, 20,* 329–342.

Lidz, T., Cornelison, A., Fleck, S., & Terry, D. (1957b). Intrafamilial environment of the schizophrenic patient: II. Marital schism and marital skew. *American Journal of Psychiatry, 114,* 241–248.

Lidz, T., Cornelison, A., Terry, D., & Fleck, S. (1958). Intrafamilial environment of the schizophrenic patient: IV. The transmission of irrationality. *Archives of Neurology and Psychiatry, 79,* 305–316.

Lidz, T., Fleck, S., & Cornelison, A. R. (1965). *Schizophrenia and the family.* New York: International Universities Press.

Lief, H. I. (1980). Introduction to M. D. Schechter & H. I. Lief, Indications and contraindications for family and marital therapy: An illustrative case. In C. K. Hofling & J. M. Lewis (Eds.), *The family: Evaluation and treatment* (pp. 240–270). New York: Brunner/Mazel.

Lindemann, E. (1944). Symptomatology and management of acute grief. *American Journal of Psychiatry, 101,* 141–148.

Lorand, S. (1968). The role of the psychoanalyst in marital crisis. In S. Rosenbaum & I. Alger (Eds.), *The marriage relationship* (pp. 225–236). New York: Basic Books.

Lowery, L. G. (1948a). The birth of orthopsychiatry. In L. G. Lowery (Ed.), *Orthopsychiatry, 1923–1948* (pp. 190–208). New York: American Orthopsychiatric Association.

Lowery, L. G. (1948b). Orthopsychiatric treatment. In L. G. Lowery (Ed.), *Orthopsychiatry, 1923–1948* (pp. 524–549). New York: American Orthopsychiatric Association.

Luckey, E. G. (1963). Relationship of marriage counseling and family life education. *Personnel and Guidance Journal, 41,* 420–424.

Lurie, L. A. (1948). Residential homes in orthopsychiatry. In L. G. Lowery (Ed.), *Orthopsychiatry, 1923–1948* (pp. 484–493). New York: American Orthopsychiatric Association.

Mace, D. R. (1945). Marriage guidance in England. *Marriage and Family Living, 7,* 1–2, 5.

Mace, D. R. (1958). Marriage counseling in Britian today. *Marriage and Family Living, 20,* 379–383.

Madanes, C., & Haley, J. (1977). Dimensions of family therapy. *Journal of Nervous and Mental Disease, 165* (2), 88–98.

Mahler, M. (1979). *The selected papers of Margaret S. Mahler* (Vols. 1 & 2). New York: Jason Aronson.

Marion, B. V. (1951). Counseling in connection with marriage courses. *Marriage and Family Living, 13,* 129–130.

Marriage Council of Philadelphia. (1959). Unpublished materials.

Marsh, E. M. (1952). Unpublished paper reported in *Marriage and Family Living, 14,* 66–67.

Martin, P. A. (1976). *A marital therapy manual.* New York: Brunner/Mazel.

Martin, P. A., & Bird, H. W. (1953). An approach to the psychotherapy of marriage partners. *Psychiatry, 16,* 123–127.

McDaniel, S. H. & Amos, S. (1983). The risk of change: Teaching the family as the unit of medical care. *Family Systems Medicine, 1*(3), 25–30.

McDonald, G. (1975). Coalition formation in marital therapy triads. *Family Therapy, 2,* 141–148.

McFarlane, W. R. (1983). Multiple family therapy in schizophrenia. In W. R. McFarlane (Ed.), *Family therapy in schizophrenia* (pp. 141–172). New York: Guilford Press.

McGoldrick, M. (1980). The joining of family through marriage: The new couple. In E. A. Carter & M. McGoldrick (Eds.), *The family life cycle: A framework for family therapy* (pp. 93–119). New York: Gardner Press.

McGoldrick, M., Pearce, J. K., & Giordano, J. (Eds.) (1982). *Ethnicity and family therapy.* New York: Guilford Press.

Mendes, H. A. (1976). Single fathers. *Family Relations, 25,* 439–449.

Messinger, L. (1976). Remarriage between divorced people with children from previous marriages: A proposal for preparation for remarriage. *Journal of Marriage and Family Counseling, 2,* 193–200.

Messinger, L., Walker, K. N., & Freeman, S. (1978). Preparation for remarriage following divorce: The use of group techniques. *American Journal of Orthopsychiatry, 48,* 263–272.

Midelfort, C. F. (1982). Use of the family in the treatment of schizophrenic and psychopathic patients. *Journal of Marital and Family Therapy, 8,* 1–11.

Miller, J. G. (1969). Living systems: Basic concepts. In W. Gray, F. S. Duhl, & N. R. Rizzo (Eds.), *General systems theory and psychiatry* (pp. 51–133). Boston: Little, Brown.

Miller, J. G., & Miller, J. L. (1980). The family as a system. In C. K. Hofling & J. M. Lewis (Eds.), *The family: Evaluation and treatment* (pp. 141–184). New York: Brunner/Mazel.

Miller, S., Wackman, D., Nunnally, E., & Saline, C. (1982). *Straight talk.* New York: New American Library.

Minuchin, S. (1974). *Families and family therapy.* Cambridge, MA: Harvard University Press.

Minuchin, S., Montalvo, B., Guerney, B., Rosman, B., & Schumer, F. (1967). *Families of the slums.* New York: Basic Books.

Mishler, E., & Waxler, N. (1968). *Interaction in families.* New York: Wiley.

Mittelman, B. (1944). Complementary neurotic reactions in intimate relationships. *Psychoanalytic Quarterly, 13,* 479–491.

Mittelman, B. (1948). The concurrent analysis of married couples. *Psychoanalytic Quarterly, 17,* 182–197.

Montalvo, B. (1973). Aspects of live supervision. *Family Process, 12,* 343–359.

Morgan, M. I., Johannis, T. B., & Fowler, S. E. (1953). Family counseling: Toward an analysis and definition. *Marriage and Family Living, 15,* 119–121.

Moss, D. M., & Lee, R. R. (1976). Homogamous and heterogamous marriages. *International Journal of Psychoanalytic Psychotherapy, 5,* 395–412.

Moultrup, D. (1981). Towards an integrated model of family therapy. *Clinical Social Work Journal, 9,* 111–125.

Mowrer, H. R. (1940). The nature of family counseling. *Marriage and Family Living, 2,* 45.

Mudd, E. H. (1937). An analysis of one hundred consecutive cases in the Marriage Council of Philadelphia. *Mental Hygiene, 21,* 198–217.

Mudd, E. H. (1951). *The practice of marriage counseling.* New York: Association Press.

Mudd, E. H. (1955). Psychiatry and marital problems: Mental health implications. *Eugenics Quarterly, 2,* 110–117.

Mudd, E. H. (1967). *AAMC: The first 25 years, 1942–1967.* Pamphlet.

Mudd, E. H., & Lundien, A. (1940). A cooperative project in marriage counseling. *Journal of Human Fertility, 5,* 121–125.

Mudd, E. H., & Rose, E. K. (1940). Development of Marriage Counsel of Philadelphia as a community service, 1932–1940. *Living, 2,* 40–41.

Mudd, E. H., Stone, A., Karpf, M. J., & Nelson, J. F. (Eds.). (1958). *Marriage counseling: A casebook.* New York: Association Press.

Murstein, B. I. (1961). The complementary needs hypothesis in newlyweds and middle-aged married couples. *Journals of Abnormal and Social Psychology, 63,* 194–197.

Murstein, B. I. (1976). The stimulus–value–role theory of marital choice. In H. Grunebaum & J. Christ (Eds.), *Contemporary marriage: Structure, dynamics and theory* (pp. 165–186). Boston: Little, Brown.

Napier, A. Y. (1971). The marriage of families: Cross-generational complementarity. *Family Process, 10,* 373–395.

Napier, A. Y. (1976). Beginning struggles with families. *Journal of Marriage and Family Counseling, 2,* 3–12.

Napier, A. Y., & Whitaker, C. A. (1978). *The family crucible.* New York: Harper & Row.

Nash, E. M., Jessner, J., & Abse, D. W. (Eds.). (1964). *Marriage counseling in medical practice.* Chapel Hill, N.C: University of North Carolina Press.

Neill, J. R., & Kniskern, D. P. (Eds.). (1982). *From psyche to system: The evolving therapy of Carl Whitaker.* New York: Guilford Press.

Nelson, J. F. (1952). Current trends in marriage counseling. *Journal of Home Economics, 44,* 253–256.

Nichols, M. (1984). *Family therapy: Concepts and methods.* New York: Gardner Press.

Nichols, W. C. (1968). Personal therapy for marital therapists. *Family Coordinator, 17,* 83–88.

Nichols, W. C. (1973). The field of mariage counseling: A brief overview. *Family Coordinator, 22,* 3–13.

Nichols, W. C. (1974). *Marriage and family counseling: A legislative handbook.* Claremont, CA: American Association of Marriage and Family Counselors.

Nichols, W. C. (1975a). *Marriage and family counseling: A manual of accreditation.* Claremont, CA: American Association of Marriage and Family Counselors.

Nichols, W. C. (1975b). *Training and supervision* (Cassette Recording No. 123). Claremont, CA: American Association for Marriage and Family Therapy.

Nichols, W. C. (1977a). Divorce and remarriage education. *Journal of Divorce, 1,* 153–161.

Nichols, W. C. (1977b). *Marriage and family therapy: Some educational issues in context.* Unpublished paper.

Nichols, W. C. (1979a). Doctoral programs in marital and family therapy. *Journal of Marital and Family Therapy, 5,* 23–28.

Nichols, W. C. (1979b). Education of marriage and family therapists: Some trends and implications. *Journal of Marital and Family Therapy, 5,* 19–28.

Nichols, W. C. (1980). Stepfamilies: A growing family therapy challenge. In L. R. Wolberg & M. L. Aronson (Eds.), *Group and family therapy 1980* (pp. 335–344). New York: Brunner/Mazel.

Nichols, W. C. (1984). Therapeutic needs of children in family system reorganization. *Journal of Divorce, 7*(4), 23–44.

Nimkoff, M. F. (1931). Pioneering in family social work. *The Family, 11,* 276–281.

Nimkoff, M. F. (1934). A family guidance clinic. *Sociology and Social Research, 18,* 229–240.

Oates, W. E. (1955). *Anxiety in Christian experience.* Philadelphia: Westminster Press.

Oberndorf, C. P. (1934). Folie à deux. *International Journal of Psychoanalysis, 15,* 14–24.

Oberndorf, C. P. (1938). Psychoanalysis of married couples. *Psychoanalytic Review, 25,* 453–475.

O'Leary, K. D., & Turkewitz, H. (1978). The treatment of marriage and marriage disorders from a behavioral perspective. In T. J. Paolino & B. S. McCrady (Eds.), *Marriage and marital therapy* (pp. 240–297). New York: Brunner/Mazel.

Olson, D. H. L. (Ed.). (1976). *Treating relationships.* Lake Mills, IA: Graphic Publishing.

Olson, D. H., Russell, C., & Sprenkle, D. (1983). Circumplex model of marital and family systems: IV. Theoretical update. *Family Process, 22,* 69–83.

Olson, D. H., Sprenkle, D., & Russell, C. (1979). Circumplex model of marital and family systems: I. Cohesion and adaptability dimensions, family types, and clinical applications. *Family Process, 18,* 3–15.

Orthner, D. K., Brown, T., & Ferguson, D. (1976). Single-parent fatherhood: An emerging life style. *Family Relations, 25,* 429–437.

Paolino, T. J., & McCrady, B. S. (Eds.). (1978). *Marriage and marital therapy.* New York: Brunner/Mazel.

Papajohn, J., & Spiegel, J. (1975). *Transactions in families.* San Francisco: Jossey-Bass.

Parkes, C. M. (1973). *Bereavement.* New York: International Universities Press.

Parloff, M. B. (1961). The family in psychotherapy. *Archives of General Psychiatry, 4,* 445–451.

Parsons, T., & Bales, R. F. (1955). *The family, socialization and interaction process.* Glencoe, IL: Free Press.

Patterson, G. R. (1974). Retraining of aggressive boys by their parents: Review of recent literature and followup evaluation. *Canadian Psychiatric Association Journal, 19,* 142–161.

Patterson, G. R., & Reid, J. B. (1970). Reciprocity and coercion: Two facets of social systems. In C. Neuringer & J. L. White (Eds.), *Behavior modification in clinical psychology* (pp. 137–177). New York: Appleton-Century-Crofts.

Paul, N. L. (1967). The role of mourning and empathy in conjoint marital therapy. In G. H. Zuk & I. Boszormenyi-Nagy (Eds.), *Family therapy and disturbed families* (pp. 186–205). Palo Alto, CA: Science & Behavior Books.

Paul, N. L., & Paul, B. P. (1975). *A marital puzzle: Transgenerational analysis in marriage counseling.* New York: Norton.

Pavalko, R. (1971). *Sociology of occupations and professions.* Itasca, IL: F. E. Peacock.

Peck, E. (1971). *The baby trap.* New York: Bernard Geis.

Perelman, J. S. (1960). Problems encountered in group psychotherapy of married couples. *International Journal of Group Psychotherapy, 10,* 136–142.

Pincus, L., & Dare, C. (1978). *Secrets in the family.* New York: Pantheon Books.

Pinsof, W. M. (1981). Family therapy process research. In A. S. Gurman & D. P. Kniskern (Eds.), *Handbook of family therapy* (pp. 699–741). New York: Brunner/Mazel.

Pinsof, W. M. (1983). Integrative problem-centered therapy: Toward the synthesis of family and individual psychotherapies. *Journal of Marital and Family Therapy, 9,* 19–35.

Pollak, O. (1964). Issues in family diagnosis and family therapy. *Journal of Marriage and the Family, 26,* 279–294.

Ransom, J. W., Schlesinger, S., & Derdeyn, A. P. (1979). A stepfamily in formation. *American Journal of Orthopsychiatry, 49,* 36–43.

Rapoport, A. (1968). Foreword. In W. Buckley (Ed.), *Modern systems research for the behavioral scientist* (pp. xiii–xxii). Chicago: Aldine.

Reimers, J. A. (1941). Social case work and problems of family life. *Living, 3,* 63–66.

Reiss, D. (1980). Pathways to assessing the family: Some choice points and a sample route. In C. K. Hofling, & J. M. Lewis (Eds.), *The family: Evaluation and treatment* (pp. 86–121). New York: Brunner/Mazel.

Richter, H. E. (1967). *The family as patient.* New York: Farrar Straus Giroux.

Ritzer, G. (1971). Professionalism and the individual. In E. Friedson (Ed.), *The professions and their prospects* (pp. 59–74). Beverely Hills, CA: Sage Publications.

Rivesman, L. (1957). Casework treatment of severely disturbed marriage partners. *Social Casework, 38,* 238–245.

Robinson, L. R. (1979). Basic concepts in family therapy: A differential comparison with individual treatment. In J. G. Howells (Ed.), *Advances in family psychiatry* (Vol. I, pp. 428–435). New York: International Universities Press.

Rodgers, R. H. (1962). *Improvements in the construction and analysis of family life cycle categories.* Unpublished doctoral dissertation, University of Minnesota, Minneapolis, MN.

Rodgers, R. H. (1973). *Family interaction and transaction: A transactional approach.* Englewood Cliffs, NJ: Prentice-Hall.

Rollins, B. C., & Feldman, H. (1970). Marital satisfaction over the family life cycle. *Journal of Marriage and the Family, 32,* 20–28.

Rosenbaum, S., & Alger, I. (Eds.). (1968). *The marriage relationship.* New York: Basic Books.

Rosenthal, K. M., & Keshet, H. F. (1978). The impact of childcare responsibilities on part-time or single fathers. *Alternative Lifestyles, 1*, 465–491.

Rossi, A. S. (1968). Transition to parenthood. *Journal of Marriage and the Family, 30*, 26–39.

Russell, A. (1976). Contemporary concerns in family therapy. *Journal of Marriage and Family Counseling, 2*, 243–250.

Russell, C. (1979). Circumplex model of marital and family systems: II. Empirical evaluation with families. *Family Process, 18*, 29–44.

Russell, C., Olson, D. H., Sprenkle, D. H., & Atilano, R. B. (1983). From family symptoms to family system: Review of family therapy research. *American Journal of Family Therapy, 11*(3), 3–13.

Rutledge, A. L. (1960, April). *A further look at marital diagnosis.* Paper presented at the Midwestern Regional Meeting of the American Association of Marriage Counselors, Columbus, OH.

Rutledge, A. L., & Gass, G. Z. (1967). *Nineteen negro men.* San Francisco: Jossey-Bass.

Sager, C. J. (1966a). The development of marriage therapy: An historical review. *American Journal of Orthopsychiatry, 36*, 458–467.

Sager, C. J. (1966b). The treatment of married couples. In S. Arieti (Ed.), *American handbook of psychiatry* (Vol. 3, pp. 213–224). New York: Basic Books.

Sager, C. J. (1976). *Marriage contracts and couple therapy.* New York: Brunner/Mazel.

Sager, C. J., Brown, H. S., Crohn, H., Engel, T., Rodstein, E., & Walker, L. (1983). *Treating the remarried family.* New York: Brunner/Mazel.

Satir, V. (1964). *Conjoint family therapy.* Palo Alto, CA: Science & Behavior Books.

Saul, L. J., Laidlaw, R. W., Nelson, J. F., Ormsby, R., Stone, A., Eisenberg, S., Appel, K. E., & Mudd, E. H. (1953). Can one partner be successfully counseled without the other? *Marriage and Family Living, 15*, 59–64.

Scheflen, A. E. (1974). *How behavior means.* Garden City, NY: Anchor/Doubleday.

Schmidl, F. (1949). On contact with the second partner in marriage counseling. *Journal of Social Casework, 30*, 30–36.

Schultz, S. J. (1984). *Family systems therapy: An integration.* New York: Jason Aronson.

Schwenk, T. L. (1984). Care of the family for the benefit of the patient: Family therapy skills for the family physician. *Family Systems Medicine, 2*, 170–175.

Seagraves, R. T. (1982). *Marital therapy: A combined psychodynamic–behavioral approach.* New York: Plenum.

Segal, L., & Bavelas, J. B. (1983). Human systems and communication theory. In B. B. Wolman & G. Stricker (Eds.), *Handbook of family and marital therapy* (pp. 61–76). New York: Plenum.

Selvini-Palazzoli, M., Boscolo, L., Cecchin, G., & Prata, G. (1978). *Paradox and counter-paradox.* New York: Jason Aronson.

Shapiro, R., & Budman, S. (1973). Defection, termination, and continuation in family and individual therapy. *Family Process, 12*, 55–67.

Sheldon, S., Dupertius, G. W., & McDermott, E. (1954). *Atlas of men.* New York: Harper.

Sheldon, S., & Stevens, S. (1942). *The varieties of temperament.* New York: Harper.

Sheldon, S., Stevens, S., & Tucker, W. B. (1940). *The varieties of human physique.* New York: Harper.

Silverman, A., & Silverman, A. (1971). *The case against having children.* New York: David McKay.

Singer, M. T., & Wynne, L. C. (1963). Differentiating characteristics of parents of childhood schizophrenics, childhood neurotics, and young adult schizophrenics. *American Journal of Psychiatry, 120*, 234–243.

Singer, M. T., & Wynne, L. C. (1965a). Thought disorders and family relations of schizophrenics: III. Methodology using projective techniques. *Archives of General Psychiatry, 12*, 187–200.

Singer, M. T., & Wynne, L. C. (1965b). Thought disorders and family relations of schizophrenics: IV. Results and implications. *Archives of General Psychiatry, 12*, 201–212.

Skidmore, R. A., & Garrett, H. (1955). The joint interview in marriage counseling. *Marriage and Family Living, 17*, 349–354.

Skinner, B. F. (1953). *Science and human behavior.* New York: Macmillan.

Skynner, A. C. R. (1981). An open-systems, group analytic approach to family therapy. In A. S. Gurman & D. P. Kniskern (Eds.), *Handbook of family therapy* (pp. 39–84). New York: Brunner/Mazel.

Slipp, S., Ellis, S., & Kressel, K. (1974). Factors associated with remaining in or dropping out of conjoint family therapy. *Family Process, 13*, 413–426.

Sluzki, C. E. (1975). The coalitionary process in initiating family therapy. *Family Process, 14*, 67–77.

Smith, J. W., & Grunebaum, H. (1976). The therapeutic alliance in marital therapy. In H. Grunebaum & J. Christ (Eds.), *Contemporary marriage: Structure, dynamics, and therapy* (pp. 353–370). Boston: Little, Brown.

Smith, V. G., & Anderson, F. M. (1963). Conjoint interviews with marriage partners. *Marriage and Family Living, 25*, 184–188.

Smith, V. G., & Hepworth, D. H. (1967). Marriage counseling with one marital partner: Rationale and clinical implications. *Social Casework, 49*, 352–359.

Solomon, M. A. (1973). A developmental, conceptual premise for family therapy. *Family Process, 12*, 179–188.

Soman, R., & Soman, M. (1983). Resident evaluation of a voluntary family therapy program. *Family Systems Medicine, 1*(4), 72–77.

Spanier, G. B., & Casto, R. F. (1979). Adjustment to separation and divorce: A qualitative analysis. In G. Levinger & O. C. Moles (Eds.), *Divorce and separation* (pp. 201–227) New York: Basic Books.

Spanier, G. B., & Glick, P. C. (1980). Paths to remarriage. *Journal of Divorce, 3*, 283–298.

Speck, R., & Attneave, C. (1973). *Family networks.* New York: Pantheon.

Sperry, I. V. (1952). Cooperative research in family life. *Journal of Home Economics, 44*, 179–181.

Spiegel, J. (1957). The resolution of role conflicts in the family. *Psychiatry, 20*, 1–6.

Sprenkle, D., & Olson, D. H. (1978). Circumplex model of marital systems: IV. Empirical study of clinic and non-clinic couples. *Journal of Marriage and Family Counseling, 4*, 59–74.

Sprenkle, D., & Piercy, F. P. (1984). Research in family therapy: A graduate level course. *Journal of Marital and Family Therapy, 10*, 225–240.

Stagoll, B. (1981, November). Report from Australia: One up and two down. *International Family Therapy Network Newsletter,* p. D.

Stanton, M. D. (1975). Psychology and family therapy. *Professional Psychology, 6*, 45–49.

Stanton, M. D. (1981). Strategic approaches to family therapy. In A. S. Gurman & D. P. Kniskern (Eds.), *Handbook of family therapy* (pp. 361–402). New York: Brunner/Mazel.

Steinglass, P. (1978). The conceptualization of marriage from a systems theory perspective. In T. J. Paolino & B. S. McCrady (Eds.), *Marriage and marital therapy* (pp. 298–365). New York: Brunner/Mazel.

Stevenson, G. S. (1948). Child guidance and the national committee for mental hygiene. In

L. G. Lowery (Ed.), *Orthopsychiatry, 1923-1948* (pp. 50-82). New York: American Orthopsychiatric Association.

Stewart, R. H., Peters, T. C., Marsh, S., & Peters, M. J. (1975). An object-relations approach to psychotherapy with marital couples, families, and children. *Family Process, 14*, 161-178.

Stierlin, H. (1974). *Separating parents and adolescents.* New York: Quadrangle.

Stierlin, H. (1977). *Psychoanalysis and family therapy.* New York: Jason Aronson.

Stokes, W. R. (1951a). A marriage counseling case: The married virgin. *Marriage and Family Living, 13*, 29-34.

Stokes, W. R. (1951b). Legal status of the marriage counselor. *Marriage and Family Living, 13*, 113-115.

Stone, A. (1949). Marriage education and marriage counseling in the United States. *Marriage and Family Living, 11*, 38-40.

Strodtbeck, F. L. (1954). The family as a three-person group. *American Sociological Review, 19*, 23-29.

Strodtbeck, F. L. (1958). Family interaction, values, and achievement. In D. C. McClellan, A. L. Baldwin, A. Bronfenbrenner, & F. C. Strodtbeck (Eds.), *Talent and society* (pp. 135-194). Princeton, NJ: Prentice-Hall.

Stuart, R. B. (1969). Operant interpersonal treatment for marital discord. *Journal of Consulting and Clinical Psychology, 33*, 675-682.

Sugarman, S. (1981). Family therapy training in selected general psychiatry residency programs. *Family Process, 20*, 147-154.

Sugarman, S. (1984). Integrating family therapy training into psychiatry residency programs: Policy issues and alternatives. *Family Process, 23*, 23-32.

Sullivan, H. S. (1927). The onset of schizophrenia. *American Journal of Psychiatry, 7*, 105-134.

Sullivan, H. S. (1953). *The interpersonal theory of psychiatry.* New York: W. W. Norton.

Sullivan, H. S. (1954). *The psychiatric interview.* New York: W. W. Norton.

Talbot, H. (1937). Certification for marriage. *Journal of Social Hygiene, 23*, 87-89.

Teismann, M. W. (1980). Convening strategies in family therapy. *Family Process, 19*, 393-400.

Textor, M. R. (1983). An assessment of prominence in the family therapy field. *Journal of Marital and Family Therapy, 9*, 317-320.

Tharp, R. (1965). Marriage roles, child development, and family treatment. *American Journal of Orthopsychiatry, 35*, 531-538.

Tharp, R., & Otis, G. (1966). Toward a theory for therapeutic intervention in families. *Journal of Consulting Psychology, 30*, 426-434.

Thaxton, L., & L'Abate, L. (1982). The "second wave" and the second generation: Characteristics of new leaders in family therapy. *Family Process, 21*, 359-362.

Thibaut, J. W., & Kelley, H. H. (1959). *The social psychology of groups.* New York: Wiley.

Thomas, E. J. (1977). *Marital communication and decision making.* New York: Free Press.

Todd, T. C., & Stanton, M. D. (1983). Research on marital and family therapy: Answers, issues, and recommendations for the future. In B. B. Wolman & G. Stricker (Eds.), *Handbook of marital and family therapy*, (pp. 91-115). New York: Plenum.

Toman, W. (1976). *Family constellation* (3rd ed.). New York: Springer.

Troll, L. E. (1975). *Early and middle adulthood.* Monterey, CA: Brooks/Cole.

Tymchuk, A. J. (1979). *Parent and family therapy.* New York: SP Medical & Scientific Books.

Veevers, J. E. (1973). Voluntary childlessness: A neglected area of family study. *Family Coordinator, 22*, 199-205.

Veevers, J. E. (1974). Voluntary childlessness and social policy: An alternative view. *Family Coordinator, 23,* 397–406.

Veevers, J. E. (1975). The moral careers of voluntarily childless wives: Notes on the defense of a variant world view. *Family Coordinator, 24,* 473–487.

Vesper, S., & Spearman, F. W. (1966). Treatment of marital conflict resulting from severe personality disturbance. *Social Casework, 47,* 583–589.

Vincent, C. E. (1972). An open letter to the "caught generation." *Family Coordinator, 21,* 143–150.

Vincent, J. P. (Ed.). (1980). *Advances in family intervention, assessment, and theory.* Greenwich, CT: JAI Press.

Visher, E. B., & Visher, J. S. (1979). *Stepfamilies.* New York: Brunner/Mazel.

Vogel, E., & Bell, N. W. (1960). The emotionally disturbed child as a family scapegoat. In N. W. Bell & E. Vogel (Eds.), *The family* (pp. 382–397). Glencoe, IL: Free Press.

von Bertalanffy, L. (1968). *General system theory.* New York: Braziller.

Wahlroos, S. (1974). *Family communication.* New York: New American Library.

Walker, K. N., & Messinger, L. (1979). Remarriage after divorce: Dissolution and reconstruction of family boundaries. *Family Process, 18,* 193–212.

Ware, A. B. (1940). Family counseling through family case work. *The Family, 21,* 231–234.

Ware, A. B., & Goodwin, M. S. (1941). Family counseling through family casework. *Marriage and Family Living, 3,* 10.

Warkentin, J., & Whitaker, C. A. (1967). The secret agenda of the therapist doing couples therapy. In G. H. Zuk & I. Boszormenyi-Nagy (Eds.), *Family therapy and disturbed families* (pp. 239–243). Palo Alto, CA: Science & Behavior Books.

Watson, A. S. (1963). The conjoint psychotherapy of marital partners. *American Journal of Orthopsychiatry, 33,* 912–922.

Watzlawick, P., Beavin, J. H., & Jackson, D. D. (1967). *Pragmatics of human communication.* New York: W. W. Norton.

Weeks, G. R., & L'Abate, L. (1982). *Paradoxical psychotherapy.* New York: Brunner/Mazel.

Weiss, R. L. (1978). The conceptualization of marriage and marriage disorders from a behavioral perspective. In T. J. Paolino and B. S. McCrady (Eds.), *Marriage and marital therapy* (pp. 165–239). New York: Brunner/Mazel.

Weiss, R. L., Hops, H., & Patterson, G. R. (1973). A framework for conceptualizing marital conflict: A technology for altering it, some data for evaluating it. In L. A. Hamerlynck, L. C. Handy, & E. J. Mash (Eds.), *Behavior change: Methodology, concepts, and practice* (pp. 309–342). Champaign, IL: Research Press.

Weiss, R. S. (1975). *Marital separation.* New York: Basic Books.

Wells, R. A., Dilkes, R., & Trivelli, N. (1972). The results of family therapy: A critical review of the literature. *Family Process, 11,* 189–207.

Westley, W. A., & Epstein, N. B. (1960). Family structure and emotional health: A case study approach. *Marriage and Family Living, 22,* 25–27.

Westley, W. A., & Epstein, N. B. (1970). *The silent majority.* San Francisco: Jossey-Bass.

Whitaker, C. A. (1958). Psychotherapy with couples. *American Journal of Psychotherapy, 12,* 18–23.

Whitaker, C. A., & Miller, M. H. (1969). A re-evaluation of "psychiatric help" when divorce impends. *American Journal of Psychiatry, 126,* 57–64.

White, E. N. (1933). Experiments in family consultation centers. *Social Forces, 12,* 557–562.

Wile, D. B. (1981). *Couples therapy.* New York: Wiley.

Wilensky, H. L. (1961). Orderly careers and social participation: The impact of work history on social integration into the middle mass. *American Sociological Review, 26*, 521–539.

Wilensky, H. L. (1964). The professionalization of everyone? *American Journal of Sociology, 70*, 137–158.

Willi, J. (1982). *Couples in collusion.* New York: Jason Aronson.

Willi, J. (1984). *Dynamics of couples therapy.* New York: Jason Aronson.

Williamson, D. S. (1981). Personal authority via termination of the intergenerational hierarchical boundaries: A "new" stage in the family life cycle. *Journal of Marital and Family Therapy, 7*, 441–452.

Williamson, D. S. (1982). Personal authority via termination of the intergenerational hierarchical boundaries: Part II. The consultation process and the therapeutic process. *Journal of Marital and Family Therapy, 8*(2), 23–37.

Wills, T. A., Weiss, R. L., & Patterson, G. R. (1974). A behavioral analysis of the determinants of marital satisfaction. *Journal of Consulting and Clinical Psychology, 42*, 802–811.

Winch, R. F. (1958). *Mate selection.* New York: Harper & Row.

Winston, A. (1978). Understanding and treating schizophrenics: A review of some contributions of communication and family system theories. In M. M. Berger (Ed.), *Beyond the double bind* (pp. 31–37). New York: Brunner/Mazel.

Wolf, A. (1950). Psychoanalysis of groups. *American Journal of Psychotherapy, 4*, 27–28.

Wolpe, J. (1958). *Psychotherapy by reciprocal inhibition.* Stanford, CA: Stanford University Press.

World Health Organization. (1979). *The international classification of diseases* (9th rev.). *Clinical modification (ICD-9-CM)*, (Vol. 2). Ann Arbor, MI: WHO Commission on Professional and Hospital Activities.

Wortis, S. B. (1945). Counseling in the premarital interview. *Marriage and Family Living, 7*, 86.

Wynne, L. C. (1961). The study of intrafamial alignments and splits in exploratory family therapy. In N. W. Ackerman, F. L. Beatman, & S. Sanford (Eds.), *Exploring the base for family therapy* (pp. 95–116). New York: Family Service Association of America.

Wynne, L. C. (1981). Current concepts about schizophrenia and family relationships. *Journal of Nervous and Mental Disease, 169*, 82–89.

Wynne, L. C. (1983). Family research and family therapy: A reunion? *Journal of Marital and Family Therapy, 9*, 113–117.

Wynne L. C., Ryckoff, I. M., Day, J., & Hirsch, S. I. (1958). Pseudomutuality in the family relations of schizophrenics. *Psychiatry, 21*, 205–220.

Wynne, L. C., & Singer, M. T. (1963a). Thought disorder and family relations of schizophrenics: I. A research strategy. *Archives of General Psychiatry, 9*, 191–198.

Wynne, L. C., & Singer, M. T. (1963b). Thought disorder and family relations of schizophrenics: II. Classification of forms of thinking. *Archives of General Psychiatry, 9*, 199–206.

Zemon-Gass, G., & Nichols, W. C. (1981). *Changing marital developmental tasks: Continuing family therapy issues.* Unpublished paper.

Zuk, G. H. (1969). Triadic-based family therapy. *International Journal of Psychiatry, 8*, 539–548.

Zuk, G. H. (1975). *Process and practice in family therapy.* Haverford, PA: Psychiatry & Behavioral Science Books.

Zuk, G. H. (1976). Family therapy: Clinical hodgepodge or clinical science? *Journal of Marriage and Family Counseling, 2*, 299–303.

Zuk, G. H. (1981). *Family therapy: A triadic-based approach.* New York: Human Sciences Press.

Zuk, G. H., & Boszormenyi-Nagy, I. (Eds.). (1967). *Family therapy and disturbed families.* Palo Alto, CA: Science & Behavior Books.

Zuk, G. H. & Rubinstein, D. (1965). A review of concepts in the study and treatment of families of schizophrenics. In I. Boszormenyi-Nagy & J. L. Framo (Eds.), *Intensive family therapy* (pp. 1–31). New York: Hoeber Division, Harper & Row.

Index

THE GUILFORD FAMILY THERAPY SERIES
Alan S. Gurman, Editor